Kenya's War of Independence

Mau Mau and its Legacy of Resistance to Colonialism and Imperialism

1948-1990

By

Shiraz Durrani

VITA BOOKS

P.O Box 62501-00200
Nairobi. Kenya
http://vitabooks.co.uk
info.vitabkske@gmail.com; info@vitabooks.co.uk

Distributed Worldwide by:
African Books Collective
PO BOX 721
Oxford, OX1 9EN
orders@africanbookscollective.com
www.africanbookscollective.com
Copyright ©: Shiraz Durrani 2018

ISBN 978-9966-1890-1-1 (Paper)
ISBN 978-9966-1890-2-8 (eBook)

DEDICATION

To all those who lost their limbs, livelihoods and lives in the struggle for the liberation of Kenya.

To those who have continued the struggle to this day.

To the youth of Kenya, East Africa, and the world who are seeking solutions to ending exploitation, domination, oppression, inequality, and unjust distribution of resources of the planet.

May the future bring justice and liberation.May the future bring justice and liberation.

The picture shows armoured cars parading the streets of Nairobi during the general strike of 1950, when the Kenya Government used tear gas, baton charges, Auster "spotter" aircraft, R.A.F. planes, Bren-gun carriers, armoured cars and police in order to break the strike and destroy the East African Trade Union Congress.

Picture and caption from WFTU (1952).

ACKNOWLEDGEMENTS

Photos from Nazmi Durrani photo collection; WFTU (1952); Umoja; Kenya National Archives; Mwakenya; Africa Events, Kenya Committee for the Release of Political Prisoners; Khamis Ramdhani; Oswaggo; Rahim.

Saleh Mamon and the Kenya Land and Freedom Depository for permission to reproduce the Timeline; Various sources as listed in Appendices for texts.

Kimani Waweru for research support.

Cover Design by Heavyconcious Art Movement - pittzmaine@gmail.com

Design and Layout by Vincent Uba
Cell: +254724 592 309. www.vumacoolgraphics.com

ABBREVIATIONS & TERMINOLOGY

AWF	African Workers Federation (1947)
COTU	Central Organisation of Trade Union
DTM	December Twelve Movement
EAA	East African Association (1921) formerly: Young Kikuyu Association
EATUC	East African Trade Union Congress (1949)
Homeguards	Colonial Government created the Homeguards made up of loyalists to colonial government. By 1954, the numbered 25,000 and were issued with rifles and shotguns. Many used their power to abuse civilians, but the Colonial Government overlooked atrocities committed by Homeguards as they represented African opposition to Mau Mau. (Maxon and Ofcansky, 2000)
KAIF	Kenya Anti Imperialist Front
KASU	Kenya African Study Union (1944)
KAU	Kenya African Union (1946)
KCA	Kikuyu Central Association (1926); Proscribed in 1940; reactivated as KAU
KDC	Kenya Defence Council (1953)
KFL	Kenya Federation of Labour
KFLA	Kenya Land and Freedom Army
KKM	Kiama Kia Muingi
KP	Kenya Parliament (1954)
KPU	Kenya Peoples' Union (1966-69)
LTUK	Labour Trade Union of Kenya
LTUEA	Labour Trade Union of East Africa (1937)
MWAKENYA	Muungano wa Wazalendo wa Kukomboa Kenya (Union of Patriots for the Liberation of Kenya).
NFD	North Frontier District/Province
NPP	Northern Peoples' Party
ODK	Organisation for Democracy in Kenya (Sweden)

PALIAct	Progressive Library and Information Activists' Group (details at: http://vitabooks.co.uk/projects-for-change/paliact/
Passive Wing	The term often used to describe those who supported armed resistance led by Mau Mau. The preferred term in this book is "people's forces" which includes all those who were part of Mau Mau but did not engage in armed resistance, e.g. see the roles under the section "Women".
People's Forces	See "Passive Wing" above.
Settlers	Refers to Settlers from Britain and other European countries and from Southern Africa who settled in Kenya. The terms "White Settlers" and "European Settlers" are also used in this book.
SYL	Somali Youth League
TJRC	Truth, Justice and Reconciliation Commission
TUC	British Trades Union Congress
Uhuru	Independence
UKENYA	Umoja wa Kupagania Demokrasia na Umoja Kenya (Britain); Movement For Unity and democracy in Kenya (Britain)
UMOJA	United Movement for Democracy in Kenya
USA	United States of America (often incorrectly referred to as "America")
West Asia	Sometimes incorrectly referred to as "Middle East"
YKA	Young Kikuyu Association (1921). Changed to EAA

Note:

The author is aware that the correct Gĩkũyũ spelling for Kimathi and Kimathi wa Waciuri should be "Kĩmathi" and "Kĩmathi wa Waciũri," respectively and would have preferred to use these versions in recognition of the imperative of indigenous self-naming. However, since most search engines use the former spelling, this publication has opted to keep to it in the interest of accessibility.

CONTENTS:

Abbreviations & Terminology 5
Introduction   11
Foreword by Dr. Willy Mutunga 13

PART 1: INTRODUCING KENYA'S WAR OF INDEPENDENCE 17
Mau Mau and the Struggle for Land and Freedom 36
Historical Context: Imperialism and Resistance   39
Three Pillars of Resistance 43

Explosion Inevitable - Resistance Before Mau Mau 54
Resisting Colonial Violence 61
Resistance in Northern Kenya: The Somali Nationality 64
Contradictions Sharpen: Settlers & Homeguards Create Chaos 69
The Necessity For Armed Resistance 72
Terrorists or Freedom Fighters? 75
Illustrations 1: Colonial Violence 80

Trade Unions Light A Spark 82
Trade Unions and Mau Mau 82
Organising for Economic and Political Rights 88
Classes and Class Struggle 95
Enter Makhan Singh 102
Kenya's TUs in the Context of TU Struggles in Africa 108
Workers and Peasants Unite for Armed Resistance 110
Illustrations 2: Trade Unions 113

PART 2: MAU MAU, 1948-1960 115
Mau Mau, The Revolutionary Force 115
Preparations for Armed Struggle 115
The War Begins 120
The Establishment of Liberated Territories 122
The Birth of Kenya Defence Council (1953) 127

Kenya's War of Independence   7

The Kenya Parliament Takes Control - Kimathi is Prime Minister (1954) 133

Elements of Mau Mau Governance 137
Anti-Imperialist Ideology 137
Organisation 140
Strategy 142
Infrastructure 146
Politics of Information 150
Leadership 180

A Movement of All People 183
Women 188
The Kamba Nationality 193
The Maasai Nationality 196
South Asian Kenyans 200
Illustrations 3: Mau Mau 214

The Final Stage: Battles Lost, Battles Won 221
Forces of Repression 224
Primary Aim 228
Possible Shape of a Mau Mau Government 235
Reparation 237
Neo-colonialism, the Legacy of Colonialism 239
A Prison Without Walls 241
Sina Habari, Mwanangu: I have No News, My Child 246
A Brief Recap 248

PART 3: TRANSITION TO NEO-COLONIALISM 271
Independence but "Not Yet Uhuru" 277
December 12th - Poem by Nazmi Durrani 278
Opposition Continues 283
Worker Resistance 286
Peasant Resistance 291
Student Resistance 294

PART 4: UHURU, 1963: UNDERGROUND ORGANISED RESISTANCE 303

Underground Organised Resistance   303
December Twelve Movement   303
Mwakenya   309
Resistance goes Overseas: the Birth of Umoja   314
Kenya Committee For the Release of Political Prisoners   317
Illustrations 4: Underground & Overseas Resistance 322

Conclusion: Uhuru Bado   336

References & Bibliography   342

APPENDICES   361
A: Jeremy Corbyn: The Fight for Justice Continues   361
B: Selected Documents   365
   The Struggle For Kenya's Future (1972)   365
   Kimathi's Truce Offer (1953, An extract) 373
   The Kenya Terror (1953)   374
   The Land & Freedom Army Letter (4-4-1955)   378
C: Research Aid   381
   Saleh Mamon (2014): Kenya Resistance, Repression & Revolt: A Timeline   381
   Ladislav Venys (1970): Mau Mau, A Chronological Outline – A Selection   408
   Shiraz Durrani (1997): The Other Kenya: Underground and Literature   414
   Maina wa Kinyatti (1978): Foreword, Ndegwa's Mau Mau Bibliography   434
   South African History Online – Towards a People's History   436
   Marx, Karl and Frederich Engels (1850): Address to the Central Committee   437
   The Kenya Land & Freedom Depository 438

Index   440

Not Sitting Idly

As is the nature of all foreign occupations, the basic reason for all these invasions was economic exploitation of the local wealth and resources. But a free people who have been conducting and running their own affairs for centuries before the advent of foreigners couldn't be expected to sit idly by and witness their dignity and sovereignty being trampled - Umoja (1987a).

The Creators of Fragrance and Colour

The earth belongs to those
Who soak the soil with their sweat
Under the open skies;
Who, with the warmth of their blood,
Make fertile the earth
Whose touch
Makes the earth's silence to speak
Who seed the land and harvest the crop
But are left without even a loaf of bread.
The ones toughened by toil
Who never say no to work,
Are the creators of all this fragrance and colour.

- Ahmad Faraz

"Hungry man, reach for the book: it is a weapon" - Bertolt Brecht[1]

"Such a lot is won when even a single man gets to his feet and says No" — Bertolt Brecht, Galileo[2]

---

1 Available at: https://www.goodreads.com/author/quotes/26853.Bertolt_Brecht [Accessed: 16-10-17].

2 Available at: https://www.goodreads.com/author/quotes/26853.Bertolt_Brecht [Accessed: 16-10-17].

INTRODUCTION

This book brings together two strands of writing on aspects of Kenya's history. The first, dealing with Mau Mau, started as a short article published in 1984 for *Sauti ya Kamukunji*, a publication of the Student Union of the University of Nairobi. It then saw new life in the booklet, *Kimaathi, Mau Mau's First Prime Minister of Kenya* (Vita Books, 1986). This version continued circulating underground in Kenya and later formed the basis of a talk in London. A revised version was then published in the *Communist Review* Nos. 67-69 (2013). New sections have been added to it over the years.

The second strand, that dealing with resistance after Kenya's independence in 1963, is based on two papers: one, entitled: "Pambana" - The Legacy of Resistance in Kenya, 1963-68"[3] and "Voices of Resistance: Underground Publishing in Kenya, 1963-1990", an unpublished paper written in 1990 for Umoja in London.

I believe that this long journey that this book has taken reflects the need for material for general readership in Kenya on the anti-colonial and anti-imperialist struggles by people of Kenya. Thus, one of the aims of the book is to present this history from the perspective of the working-class and to make it available to people in Kenya – in particular the young people – and elsewhere. Most histories available through educational institutions, the mass media or other easily available sources reflect Kenya's history either from the perspective of colonialism or imperialism or from the perspective of the ruling elites after independence. This book makes no claims to such "neutrality" but is focused on looking at this history from the point of view of ordinary, working-class people trying to resist exploitation and oppression. It aims to make academic and other research more accessible to the general reader.

---

3 "Pambana" - The Legacy of Resistance in Kenya, 1963-68). Presentation at the Review of African Political Economy Conference, Liverpool, 1986. It was to have been included in the proposed publication, "Liberation Struggles in Africa. A Collection of Papers from ROAPE Conference, 1986".

The style of the book reflects the aim of making it an accessible version of a part of history that is not easily available to the readers in Kenya. Long quotes are provided from various sources so that the voices of those who were directly involved are allowed to narrate history, and by using these sources in this way, this is an attempt to highlight documents and records that may not be easily available for political or economic reasons to many in Kenya. It is hoped that using these resources in this way will encourage readers to seek them directly for themselves so that they can build a true picture of the history of Kenya. Some of these documents are already available in the newly established PALIAct Liberation Library in Nairobi, set up by PALIAct[4] with the support of Vita Books and Mau Mau Research Centre. It is expected that over time, more of the items listed in the References and Bibliography of this book will be deposited there.

---

[4] The Progressive African Librarian and Information Activists' Group (PALIAct). Further details on PALIAct available at: http://vitabooks.co.uk/projects-for-change/paliact/.

FOREWORD

Dr. Willy Mutunga, D.Jur,SC,EGH. Former Chief Justice/President, Supreme Court of Kenya

In writing Foreword to this patriotic and revolutionary book I can do no better than reproduce some excerpts from a Lecture I delivered at the British Institute of East Africa in Nairobi. I delivered the Lecture on February 18, 2017 on the 60th Anniversary of the hanging by the British of the Field Marshall Dedan Kimathi wa Waciuri. Dedan Kimathi was the leader of the Land and Freedom Movement and the Land and Freedom Army, both of the Mau Mau War of Independence, 1952-1957. The title of the Lecture is "Devolution: The Politics and Jurisprudence of Equitable Distribution of National Resources" which is available on the Website of the Institute.

...

I: Remembering Dedan Kimathi wa Waciuri

Sixty years today Dedan Kimathi was hanged at Kamiti Maximum Security Prison. In an ASA Conference in Washington DC last December Kenyan and foreign scholars participated in a panel on Dedan Kimathi and discussed his trial that took place sixty years ago. The panel was attended by Professors Ngugi wa Thiong'o and Micere Mugo who were among the panelists.

While serving as the 14th Chief Justice and 1st President of the Supreme Court of Kenya I was privileged to receive a file of court records of the Kimathi Trial, appeal, and the record of his execution from Professor Julie McArthur of University of Toronto. Professor McArthur has also kindly given us the Kimathi photographs displayed in this room. I was privileged also to hand over the copies of the file to Kimathi's widow, Mukami, and her family. I also handed over another copy of the file to the Mau Mau Veterans Association that is led by Shujaa Gitu wa Kahengeri.

Kimathi fought for the land that the British stole from Kenyans. His struggle was national. It has now become clear that the Mau Mau War of Independence was a multi-ethnic, multi-racial, and nationalist project. One cannot discuss the politics of devolution without discussing the politics of land in the counties. One cannot discuss the jurisprudence of devolution without addressing the colonial jurisprudence that our 2010 Constitution has sought to decolonize. As our politics and jurisprudence have to face up to the challenges of neoliberalism both have to confront the politics of national interest that is limited by neoliberal global forces.

Two clarion calls by Kimathi for the struggle for land and freedom remain relevant to our discussion today. Repeating a sentence in phrase of two sentences in the signature Spanish Civil War exhortation of the great Basque revolutionary from an earlier period, Dolores Ibarruri, he declared, "It is better to die on our feet than to live on our knees." The other sentence that Kimathi left out was; "They shall not pass." In one of his letters written in 1955 from his Nyandarua headquarters he stated that "only the revolutionary justice of the struggles of the poor can end poverty of the Kenyans." Clearly, neither Kimathi nor the British left Kenya. My Lecture today historicizes and problematizes some of the ongoing struggles that pertain to the implementation of devolution under the vision of the 2010 Constitution. Indeed, the title of one of Ngugi wa Thiong'o's think pieces Mau Mau is Coming Back: The Revolutionary Significance of 20 October 1952 in Kenya Today (Journal of African Marxists) now becomes one of the burning questions of our time.

The agitation for a heroic burial for Kimathi has been sporadically, but consistently, going on since independence. It has always been assumed that both the British and Kenyan governments know where his remains are in Kamiti Maximum Security Prison. None of the governments has been helpful in this endeavour. The Grand Coalition government headed by President Mwai Kibaki and Prime Minister Raila acceded to putting up of a statue of Kimathi at the junction of Mama Ngina Street and Kimathi Street in the central business district in Nairobi.

The struggle to give Kimathi a heroic burial continues. One of the locations for his burial has been identified at the Uhuru Park facing Jomo Kenyatta's Mausoleum. Traditional religionists, and Kenyan revolutionaries, continue to tell us that Kimathi's spirit in captivity continues to wail for freedom. His heroic burial would be a fitting tribute to the words and spirit of the Preamble to our 2010 Constitution We, the people of Kenya- HONOURING those who heroically struggled to bring freedom and justice to our land: We would be breathing into life the patriotic words of our Preamble if we dig up his remains and give him a heroic burial at the Freedom Corner of Uhuru Park, Nairobi.

I believe I have a reason why both the British and Kenyan governments (and their respective ruling classes) have not been useful in the six decades campaign for the search of Kimathi's remains and a national heroic burial for him. It must be the fear that his shrine will be a living and shining symbol of our land and freedom struggles, going forward. Such a struggle is anti-imperialism and also against its comprador agents in Kenya.

...

iv: Conclusion: the Politics of Humanity

In this discussion on the jurisprudence and politics of devolution around the devolution of political power and equitable national resources, we should pay attention to issues that are apparent, but rarely analyzed. These are what I have alluded to as the politics and jurisprudence of national interest and public participation. Both are drivers of making clear that elite projects at the centre and at the counties are subjected to the sovereignty of the will of all Kenyans. They also will reinforce the role of the judiciary as a fundamental institution in the issue. Through public participation in the implementation of decisions of the judiciary, the Judiciary will become a political actor as envisaged by the Constitution. State power will be devolved to the majority of the Kenyan people. Constitutional vision that all sovereign power belongs to the Kenyan people could become a reality, signaling our rebellion, reform, and revolutionary restructuring of national, regional, and global status quo.

I end where I began. I pose the question whether Mau Mau is coming back? I believe we can discern a trajectory of resistance since colonial period, through the neocolonial independent era, that continues into the neoliberal era. The economic, social, political, cultural, intellectual, and ideological contexts of course have been dialectical. The broad common denominator has been the search for a just and equitable planet in which resources are equitably shared among the citizens of the world. Socialism and social democracy as alternatives to neoliberalism may have collapsed (depending on the lack of consensus on what really collapsed), but the vision that capitalism (imperialism and neoliberalism)/globalization is a just and equitable system has never captured the imagination of the global citizens. Otherwise, the struggle would not have been continuous even after the system made concessions. New imagination of change by invoking the past revolutionary paradigms (based on ruthless criticism and building on lessons learnt) do exist since neoliberalism's financial meltdown of 2007-9, and which has not ended. I agree with Samir Amin and other revolutionary organic intellectuals that the new struggles against global status quo will revolve around solidarities of the citizens of the Global North and Global South. The World Social Forum (WSF) slogan, Another World is possible is the revolutionary optimism of our times.

Dr. Willy Mutunga

14th Chief Justice of Post-Independence Kenya & the First President of the Supreme Court of Kenya

Nairobi

November 2017

PART 1: INTRODUCING KENYA'S WAR OF INDEPENDENCE

Some studies on Mau Mau see history in almost watertight compartments with very few connections between different compartments and historical stages. This gives a warped view of history. In the context of Kenya, this approach sees Mau Mau in isolation from the history of resistance to colonialism by the people of Kenya from the earliest days of British - and before that, Portuguese - colonialism. Seen from this narrow perspective, Mau Mau appears on the scene out of the blue in a sudden realisation that colonialism had taken over the country and needed to be expelled by force.

In contrast to this common view, this book reports the historical resistance of the people of Kenya against colonialism and imperialism, during a long War of Independence and liberation with many different stages. These range from the peasant and nationality resistance in earlier period of British colonialism, to resistance by various nationality-based organisations, followed by resistance by country-wide organisations. This continuing process of resistance saw a qualitative change when organised working class, led by militant trade unions, added a new dimension to the struggle: that of national resistance by organised trade unions guided by anti-capitalist and anti-imperialist ideologies. There was a realisation that economic, political and social demands could only be met as part of the struggle against capitalism and imperialism, thereby combining the economic and political aspects of the war of independence. It was when workers' struggle and militant national political struggles came together that a new phase of the War of Independence began. This armed resistance movement, which came to be known as Mau Mau with its political and economic demands, was summarised as Land and Freedom.

It is interesting to note that the cry for "land and freedom" that defined Mau Mau was also the slogan used during the Russian Revolution, as documented in the posters in the State Central Museum of Russian Contemporary History. Some of these are reproduced below from Panfilova (2017) as they show the similarities of demands. The slogan "Land and Freedom" was a key demand in both the revolutions. The Russian one added "Only in battle will you obtain your rights!" – something that Mau Mau also took to heart in action.

"Armed men hold slogans reading: 'Land and Freedom!' and 'Only in battle will you obtain your rights!'" - Panfilova (2017).

Panfilova (2017) explains the poster:

This comes from the leftist publishing house Parus, founded before the revolution by writer Maxim Gorky. Their posters were often created by famous poets and artists such as Vladimir Mayakovsky and Alexei Radakov. The top image shows a soldier defending the bourgeoisie with the caption "This is who the soldier used to defend". The second, post-revolutionary, image features banners bearing the slogans, "Land and freedom!", "Democracy and the Republic!" and "Liberty!" The caption reads: "That's who he defends today".

It is difficult to decide whether such

18   *Kenya's War of Independence*

slogans influenced Mau Mau, but it is clear that the demands of both movements were reflected in the slogan, "Land and Freedom".

This new stage started roughly after the Second Imperialist World War, but this was reached as a result of learning from the experiences, the lessons and the suffering of the earlier struggles. The primary lesson was that peaceful means of opposing colonialism and imperialism would not lead to meaningful change and that armed resistance was necessary. Thus, Mau Mau's resistance is linked to these earlier struggles, just as, too are the struggles after independence. And so in the post-independence period, there started yet another phase of the war of liberation - the War of Economic Independence. This was again waged as political and economic resistance, but this time it was against the comprador regime installed by the departing colonial government as neo-colonialism tightened its grip on Kenya. British administration, Settlers and companies were replaced by US corporations and "advisers" aided by IMF and World Bank officials.

This resistance against neo-colonialism and imperialism continues over 50 years after independence. This book examines Mau Mau movement and one aspect of post-independence resistance — that undertaken by the December Twelve Movement and Mwakenya - as an indication that this resistance, like the ones against the colonialism, is likely to be long and difficult, perhaps bloody, if pro-people changes cannot be made peacefully.

What's in a Name?

Imperialism controls the concepts, the consciousness and terms people use to describe their ideas and experiences. If people lack the language to describe reality, they cannot understand the relevant links and connections attached to that reality, nor can they fully resist forces that are against their interest.

Imperialism agrees to call USA's struggle for independence as its War of Independence. Algeria's struggle against French colonialism is sometimes seen today as its War of Independence. But colonialism and imperialism decided that Kenya's struggle was *not* its war of independence. For example, the Guidance by the British Department of Education (Gt. Brit. Dept. Education, 2013) mentions only the American War of Independence and no similar mention is made of struggles against the British Empire by other colonies, including Kenya. It is interesting to note that none of the wars of independence against British colonialism in Africa or India are called by their real names. This is no accident, as colonialism deemed that giving these struggles their real name — wars of independence — which reflects the key message and meaning, the very essence of the fight would not only give legitimacy to these struggles but would also encourage other colonised and oppressed people to carry out their own wars of independence and liberation. They were thus referred to as emergencies (as in Kenya) or as dealing with communist insurgencies (as in Malaya-Malaysia). It is no wonder that the Mau Mau's struggle was not called Kenya's War of Independence as colonialism decided that it had nothing to do with independence, everything to do with primitive people going mad in a frenzy of violence. Barber (2004) provides the economic reason why the name "emergency" was preferred to the term "War" in the case of Malaya:

> A War or an Emergency? - It was a war but there was a curious reason why it was never called one. As the author John Gullick ... points out, 'It was a war - though out of regard for the London insurance market ... no one ever used the word'. This misnomer continued for twelve years, for the simple reason that insurance rates covered losses of stocks and equipment through riot and civil commotion in an emergency, but not in a civil war.

That colonialism and imperialism manipulate language to misrepresent history is, perhaps, understandable. The wonder is when the newly independent countries also continue to avoid the term "war of independence". It is, however, not just the wars themselves that were not given their appropriate name. The combatants were also given derogatory names to create an incorrect impression of their motives for fighting. The most common term used was "terrorists", indicating that the term is not a recent invention by US governments but that it was used and popularised by British - and other - colonial powers. Again, the Malayan (Malaysian) usage of terms for combatants by British colonialism is relevant. The guerrilla fighters there were initially referred to as bandits, but later called terrorists (Barber, 2004). The wars against "terrorists" by colonialism and imperialism are an important aspect of their need to deny people their liberation. India faced a similar fate when the British colonialism trivialised their First War of Independence (1857) by calling it the Sepoy Mutiny (Tharoor, 2016).

The term, "Kenya's War of Independence" restores Kenya's stolen history to its rightful place, stripped of previous colonial interpretations. Mau Mau and working class struggles followed generations of peasant, nationality and national resistance against colonialism. They learnt from previous experiences and marched ahead to anti-imperialist struggles in independent Kenya.

Imperialism replaced colonialism, African elites replaced White Settlers, neo-colonial government replaced colonial government. Resistance changed from War of Independence to War of Economic Independence, Worker and peasant resistance is evident once again. History is on the march. The struggle continues. What names and terms are used for this march of history are important for those resisting oppression. Language itself becomes a battleground. This book attempts to capture some of the highlights of this struggle.

Sinning Quietly

In January 2005, Gordon Brown, the then Chancellor of Exchequer, said that he wanted Britain to stop apologising for its colonial past (Brogan, 2005). Instead, the Chancellor called for the "great British values" - freedom, tolerance, civic duty - to be admired as some of our most successful exports. For Kenya, such "great British values" included mobile gallows to "pacify" Mau Mau activists and Kenyans struggling for their independence. The reality is that facts readily available even in 1950s have been intentionally ignored by successive British Governments. Three quotes from Newsinger (2006) show some of these facts which have been hidden by the British Establishment[5] "to erase all traces of the darker deeds of Britain's colonial enterprise" as Cobain (2016) puts it:

> One
>
> The defeat of the Mau Mau involved a degree of savagery that is

---
5 For a definition of the the term *Establishment* as used here, see Jones, O. (2015), especially pp.2-6.

quite unprecedented in British 20th century colonial wars. One really has to go back to the suppression of the Great Indian Rebellion of the 1850s to find a comparable episode. The reality was that in Kenya the flogging, torture, mutilation, rape and summary execution of suspects and prisoners were everyday occurrences.

Two

One should not mince one's words about this. Elements within the security forces in Kenya, particularly the police, used the methods of the Gestapo at their worst. This is no exaggeration or hyperbole, but a plain statement of fact.

Three

... the [colonial] Government [of Kenya] presided over what can only be described as a judicial massacre. Between the declaration of the emergency[in October 1952] and November 1954, 756 rebels were hanged ... By the end of the emergency [the number] had reached 1,090 ... A mobile gallows was specially built so that prisoners could be hanged in their home districts to provide an example.

That British politicians could so blatantly misrepresent history is a matter of concern, not only for the people of Kenya and other victims of British colonialism and imperialism, but for British people as well. It is worth comparing the British attitude to its colonial past with those of other European colonial powers. Huggler (2016) reports on recent German reaction:

> Germany is to recognise as genocide the massacre of 110,000 of the Herero and Nama people of Namibia by German troops between 1904 and 1908 in a landmark admission of historical guilt.
>
> A spokesman for Angela Merkel's government said Germany would formally apologise to Namibia.
>
> The systematic extermination of up to 100,000 Herero and some 10,000 of the Nama people by German colonial troops is widely regarded as the first genocide of the 20th century, and a precursor to

the Holocaust.

Tens of thousands of Herero and Nama were driven into the Namibian desert to die of starvation and dehydration.

Others were sent to concentration camps where they died of disease and abuse. Many victims were beheaded, and their skulls sent to Germany for scientific experiments.

Emmanuel Macron, the President of France, as a presidential candidate for the 2017 elections, condemned France's colonial past in Algeria, as *The Guardian* (2017) reported:

> On a visit to Algiers on Tuesday Macron said France's history in Algeria was a "crime against humanity". "It's really barbaric and is part of that past that we must face up to also by apologising to those who were hurt," he said…
>
> … but Macron refused to back down, and in a video statement sent to Reuters, he said: "We must find the courage to call things by their name," he said. "Are we condemned to forever live in the shadows of this traumatic experience for our two countries?"

And yet France's record as a colonial power is no better than Britain's. Louati (2017) provides some details:

> The revolution of 1948 which overthrew the monarchy and reinstated the republic, did not put an end to France's colonial enterprise - on the contrary … The current Fifth Republic was proclaimed with the 1958 constitution, in the midst of the bloody repression in Algeria and while France was still dreaming of keeping its grip on its colonies. But the end of colonialism brought no assessment of what had gone wrong and what lessons needed to be learned. Rather, the country entered into voluntary amnesia without addressing this poisonous legacy. Indeed, France's ruling elite under the leadership of Nicolas Sarkozy attempted in 2005 to pass a law requiring the school curriculum to 'recognise the positive role of the French presence overseas'. The relevant article was dropped after uproar from academics put an end

to the initiative.

The response of leaders in Algeria today contrasts sharply with that of the leaders of Kenya. While the latter remains silent or totally uncommitted about the attacks on Kenya by colonialism, the Algerian President Abdelaziz Bouteflika said "Paris should be held accountable for crimes during its rule" (Telesur, 2017) adding:

> My people are still demanding that their sufferings during the colonial era should be recognized by France. By remembering our tragic past due to the French invasion, we are actually exercising our duty to remember our ancestors, millions of whom fell in the field of resistance, hundreds of thousands of others were imprisoned or deported, while millions were dispossessed of their lands and possessions.

Telesur adds: "The president also stressed that celebrating Independence Day is 'exercising a duty to remember one and a half million of our sons who sacrificed their lives for the recovery of independence and national sovereignty'. Kenya has no prospect at present of such assessment of the War of Independence.

Such realism needs to come to British Government policy too, in order to ensure justice for its colonised people. But President Macron was quick to change his tune once he settled into Presidency, as Anyangwe (2017) shows:

> While still campaigning for the presidency, Macron called France's colonial history in Algeria "a crime against humanity". But this centrist politician quickly changed his mind when his rebuke of France's brutal past was met with criticism at home. In a speech in the south-eastern city of Toulon, Macron apologised for having hurt voters' feelings, and dumbed down his accusation to speak instead of the need for France to face its "complex past". But what about the feelings of the millions of Africans you casually slur, Monsieur Macron?

And yet this misrepresentation of history by imperialism is related not only to isolated incidents or events in just one country; the deliberate destruction and hiding of information affects all the colonies that came under British Empire. It is also important to understand the linkages between histories of Britain and its colonies and the impact that the "history theft" has had on both – the colonies and Britain. Cobain (2016) asks:

> How do we judge the final days of Empire when we now know they were accompanied by an extraordinarily ambitious act of history theft, one that spanned the globe, with countless colonial papers being incinerated or dumped at sea? This conflagration... was intended to erase all traces of the darker deeds of Britain's colonial enterprise. Thousands more files were spirited away from the colonies and hidden for decades in a high-security intelligence facility in the southeast of England.

Cobain (2016) then looks at the impact that this theft of history has had on Britain and its people:

> The British state... was attempting to protect the reputation of the British state of generations earlier, concealing and manipulating history – sculpting an official narrative – in a manner more associated with a dictatorship than with a mature and confident democracy.

The British society itself is then faced with a democratic deficiency as well as facing moral decay at the heart of the state. These have led to what can only be called crimes against humanity on a massive scale. The impact of this is still felt on the surviving victims and their descendants in the former Empire. Thousands lost their lives, lands, education, health and livelihood to colonial plunder. In order to gain a stronger foothold in their former colonies, imperialism rewarded those local people who sided with them with power, land and national resources including those stolen from people who fought for independence.

Then, as if to add insult to injury, the British Establishment sought to change the history of the colonies as well as their own history as a means of falsifying records to promote a misinterpretation of their histories. This affects people of the former colonies as well as people in Britain today. Even when such manipulation of historical facts has been exposed, the British state continues in its time-honoured practice of ignoring or denying facts by refusing to release even the few documents that had not been destroyed.

Mohsin (2016) examines the impact of such manipulation of historical facts on British students, and ultimately on the British public too, by quoting Dr Mukulika Banerjee, Director of the South Asia Centre and Associate Professor of Anthropology at the London School of Economics:

> ... students "arrive at university completely ignorant about the empire, that vital part of their history. When we talk of Syria today, they have no knowledge of Britain's role in the Middle East in the last century. When discussing burning political questions today, they have no historical context to draw on links with Britain's own past with those events. Similarly, they have no clue about the history of immigration. They don't understand why people of other ethnicities came to Britain in the first place. They haven't learned any of it at school. So, in their second year at university, when my students discover the extent of their ignorance, they are furious."

Mohsin (2016) hints at the possible ramification, intended or otherwise, of this historical amnesia:

> I don't know whether this amnesia is due to embarrassment or fear of reparations or, indeed, a sinister desire to keep the electorate ignorant and pliable.

When the British Establishment can so casually allow ignorance among people of their own country, it is no surprise that they would care even less about the impact of this theft of history on the people of former colonies. It is only in 2016 that the full and real extent of efforts by the British Establishment to hide its history has been revealed. It may have been assumed by some that such actions to hide and distort the colonial history were caused by an oversight, poor administration or mistakes by a few civil servants. But as Cobain (2016) reveals, these were a direct result of British Government policies which relied on "secrets and lies" to further its imperialist endeavours. The ramifications of this official approach were significant and serious for people of all the colonies.

The history of Mau Mau, examined in the next section of this book, cannot be fully understood if not seen in the overall context of British colonial policy and practices. If these colonial actions are excluded from history, it then becomes easy for those who support colonialist interpretations of history to claim that Mau Mau were primitive people who turned to violence for its own sake, rather than seeing their actions as part of Kenya's War of Independence and the people's struggle for liberation from colonialism and imperialism.

The ruling elites in Britain and Kenya share the need to project a distorted historical interpretation of the history of Kenya's national liberation movement as a way of maintaining control over people and resources. They thus influence national consciousness and terms of national dialogues to ensure that the facts revealed by Cobain and other historians are buried. People, then, in both countries remain in ignorance about the brutality of the colonial power, about resistance of the colonised people. It is important to understand fully that lack of awareness of the true situation on the part of people is not accidental, but has been officially sanctioned. Cobain (2016) examines the systemic use of acts of brutality against the people of Kenya:

> Throughout the conflict, those atrocities were always assiduously recorded by the authorities in Kenya and reported to the British public by a media that tended, very often, to take its lead from the Colonial Office. Any misconduct on the part of the British, in the prison camps and out in the forests, was hidden from view. As a consequence, British government ministers and officials had been able to maintain that any acts of brutality inflicted by the colonial authorities had been isolated and unauthorised, rather than systemic. It was a claim that took root and flourished, in the British national memory, and across much of the West.

And of course, this interpretation flourished in Kenya as well, under the watchful eyes of the post independence governments, thus consolidating this colonial perspective as the official history of Kenya, no matter that facts and evidence presented by many victims and some historians challenged this interpretation. Cobain (2016) continues the tragic story of the British Establishment's game of lies and secrecy:

> ... in May 2011...the Foreign Office finally admitted the truth: it was

holding a further 1,500 historical Kenyan files. The files had been concealed for years, held where no historian or lawyer or interested member of the public could find them...the files took up 200 feet at Hanslope Park.

He then goes on to examine the "reasons that they had remained hidden for so long":

> They [the files] detailed the way in which suspected insurgents had been beaten to death, burnt alive, raped, castrated... and kept in manacles for years. Even children had been killed.

And it gets worse for the British Establishment as Cobain (2016) reveals the connivance of senior British officials in crimes which would surely qualify as crimes against humanity:

> Among the most damning papers were a number of letters and memoranda written by the colony's Attorney General, Eric Griffith-Jones. At one point, Griffith-Jones describes the mistreatment of detained Mau Mau suspects as "distressingly reminiscent of conditions in Nazi Germany or Communist Russia. Despite this, in June 1957 he agreed to draft legislation that sanctioned a new regime of abuse known as the "dilution technique", as long as the beatings were carried out with care. "Vulnerable parts of the body should not be struck, particularly the spleen, liver or kidneys'" Griffith-Jones wrote. Anyone who protested would have "a foot placed on his throat and mud stuffed in his mouth ... in the last resort [he would be] knocked unconscious". While Griffith-Jones may not have been too concerned with the victims of this abuse, the papers showed him to care deeply about the future well-being of those who were to inflict it. "The psychological effects on those who administer violence are potentially dangerous; it is essential that they should remain collected, balanced and dispassionate."

When one compares the above torture with that inflicted today on political prisoners by USA in the presence of British officers, it becomes clear that the techniques go back in time to the practice under British colonialism. Nor can it be claimed that the highest ranks in the British Government were unaware of these crimes, as Cobain (2006) confirms:

> These proposed instructions [The "dilution technique"] were contained in a memo that Griffith-Jones sent to the colony's governor, Sir Evelyn Baring... "If we are going to sin", Griffith-Jones advised Baring, "we must sin quietly".

The matter did not end there. "Baring forwarded the memo to Alan Lennox-Boyd, Secretary of State for the Colonies with a covering letter which asserted that inflicting 'violent shock' was the only way of dealing with Mau Mau insurgents", records Cobain (2016).

British colonialism was meticulous in recording its activities in the colonies. And this included documenting murders and torture. Describing a case of Colonial torture, Cobain (2016) explains that the colonial documents "contained accounts of torture that colonial officials were writing and passing on to their superiors throughout the eight years of the insurgency":

> One [document] described how an African employee of Special Branch 'pushed pins into their (i.e. detainees') sides, buttocks, fingers and, on at least one occasion, the head, and ... pinched the sides of their bodies, penis and scrotum with pliers. He crushed the fingers of one detainee.'

However, Cobain (2016) explains that the British government was careful to ensure they met the "requirement that British officers and their African subalterns should escape prosecution for their acts". He gives one example:

> In January 1955, for example, [Governor of Kenya] Baring informed Lennox-Boyd [the Secretary of State for the Colonies] that eight European officers were facing accusations of a series of murders, beatings and shootings. They included: 'One District Officer, murder by beating up and roasting alive of one African.' All eight received an amnesty.

These are not the first recorded incidents of murder and torture that have come to light as there have been many such records in the public domain, particularly from the victims, their families and associates. However,

Cobain's revelations are based on colonial files, which had been deliberately hidden away. Many other files were destroyed by being thrown in the sea so it is difficult to know what further damming evidence they contained.

Cobain (2016) finally examines the overall picture revealed by the hidden files:

> With the disclosure of the Hanslope Park archive, the fiction that the abuses in Kenya had been isolated and unauthorised could no longer be maintained. The torture and murder had been systemic - choreographed, in fact, by colonial administrators and the colony's law officers - and ministers and officials in London had been fully aware of the details of the abuses for which they were responsible: abuses that the British public had repeatedly been assured, throughout the 1950s, were not happening.

But the colonial files revealed not only the murders and tortures that the British colonial authorities carried out in Kenya; they also revealed the extent of their efforts to hide information that documented these murders and tortures. Cobain (2016) again fills in the gaps in official reports:

> From the moment that the 'migrated archive' became available for public scrutiny at Kew in 2012, it was clear that it contained numerous other papers that testified to a worldwide purge of sensitive or damning documentation: there was correspondence that described the laborious burning of papers; there were telegrams from London giving precise instructions for methods of destruction; there were even 'destruction certificates', signed and witnessed by colonial officials to confirm that certain classes of documents had been incinerated.

Yet these revelations, damaging as they are, come as a surprise only to those influenced by imperialist spin and propaganda. Such actions, as also in the case of slavery, were in the very nature of the exploitative system of capitalism, colonialism and imperialism. This is emphasised by Corbyn (2013) who explains:

> Only a century ago at the height of Empire, Europe controlled two-thirds of the world's land. The Empires were for mercantile demands,

rivalry with others and for enormous wealth for a few... Settlement in Kenya continued and the 'White Highlands' resulted from the land rush and greed of the Europeans. Occupying land and developing a farming system that made them personally wealthy was part of the process, but also a social system separate from the huge African majority around them. Sustained by arms and arrogance, they thought these privileges would last forever.

The history of Kenya can be seen, at one level, as finance capital and corporations working with imperialist governments and local allies to put into power those they could easily manipulate to serve corporate and imperialist interests. In the pre-independence days, this was done by the use of violence. After independence, subtler, but equally devastating, means were used. Vltchek (2016) looks at the use of culture as a controlling mechanism:

> 'Culture' is used to re-educate and to indoctrinate mainly the children of the local elites. Funding and grants are put to work where threats and killing were applied before. How does it work? It is actually all quite simple: rebellious, socially-oriented and anti-imperialist local artists and thinkers are now shamelessly bought and corrupted. Their egos are played on with great skill. Trips abroad for 'young and talented artists' are arranged, funding dispersed, scholarships offered.
>
> Carrots are too tasty, most would say, 'irresistible'. Seals of approval from the Empire are ready to stamp those blank pages of the lives of still young, unrecognized but angry and sharp young artists and intellectuals from those poor, colonized countries. It is so easy to betray! It is so easy to bend.

And so imperialist attacks continue - as does resistance to imperialism. It is time that Gordon Brown and current leaders of British Government make public apologies to the people of Kenya - and make appropriate reparations, for these as well as earlier colonial crimes against the people of Kenya. The first step in the liberation of the country is the liberation of history and information on colonial and imperialist crimes against Kenyan people and on their resistance.

Colonial Violence

A systematic study is needed on the various methods used by colonialism to control and subdue colonised people. At one level these were brutal attacks on lives and properties of people. Some of the methods used have been well documented. Among these were the use of collective punishment of entire villages and towns for "crimes" supposedly committed by one or a few people from that area.

Systematic sexual violence is another method. Women as well as men have been victims of colonial brutality at a number of levels. Not only have peasant and working class women suffered along with men from the ravages that capitalism and imperialism brought to Kenya, they have also suffered sexual violence used by the colonial administration as a form of punishment. Just as collective punishment became a norm as a weapon of war, so did sexual violence, particularly against women. The British state sanctioned such brutal means of punishing people speaks volumes for the moral standing of those behind colonial and imperial adventures of the British Empire. But the violence was not a mindless, incidental matter. It was part of the process of subjugating people and as much a planned activity as was the use of guns to kill people. Violence was the show of power over lives of powerless people and was intended to show who was in control. Bufacchi (2017) comments on the effects of such violence:

> Violence makes the victims and survivors feel vulnerable, violated, degraded and inferior to the perpetrators of violence, morally and politically. Being the subject of arbitrary violence undermines a person's self-respect, self-esteem, and epistemic status. Violence captures the unequal relationship of power between perpetrators and victims or survivors, exposing the powerlessness of the latter... violence is first and foremost a social act, characterized by the desire to establish a social relation of violence in which what matters is that the victim realizes that the aggressor intends to harm them: in performing an act of violence "one is inflicting harm on the victim with the concomitant intention that the victim becomes aware of the damage and of its 'author'".

Colonial violence in Kenya included systematic sexual violence not only against women but men as well. That a so-called civilising mission by the British state sanctioned such brutal means of punishing people speaks volumes for the moral standing of the colonial and imperial adventures of the 20th Century.

Mau Mau Today

Mau Mau liberation movement was active in Kenya around the period 1948-1960. Its impact can be seen in Kenya even today as people look back to the unmet aims of an equal and just society that the Movement fought for. But it survives in yet another way as well, as shown when the Mau Mau veterans sought compensation from the British Government for the atrocities committed against them during the colonial period. The battle ground, for the moment, shifted to British courts. In October 2012, three Mau Mau veterans were given permission by the British high court to claim damages for "the grave abuses they suffered when imprisoned during the Mau Mau rebellion".

The court cases have created a new interest in the West in the movement, and indeed in the entire history of British Empire and colonialism. A number of new sources of information on the period have become available in recent years. There have been new research reports, books and, most important, colonial files of the period that have been released recently.[6] All these throw new light on the subject. Prominent books include Caroline Elkins' *Britain's Gulag, the Brutal End of Empire in Kenya* (2005) and David Anderson's *Histories of the Hanged, Britain's Dirty War in Kenya and the End of Empire* (2005).

Jeremy Corbin (2012) highlighted one of the reasons that Mau Mau remains

---

6 "The documents, believed to have been destroyed, were secretly sent back to the UK when former colonies became independent. They shed new light on how British officials ran overseas territories. This included Kenya where it is alleged thousands of people were killed, tortured or died of disease or starvation during the uprising - or Emergency - against the British colonial administration in the 1950s and early 1960s." - Leigh Day welcome release of Mau Mau documents. 18 April 2012. Available at: www.leighday.co.uk/News/2012/April-2012/Leigh-Day-welcome-release-of-Mau-Mau-documents. [Accessed: 11-02-17].

in the news:

> We are in an era of historical re-writing of the whole role of Empire and its alleged civilising qualities. Empires are set up for military power, for financial gains; the brutality of the exploitation, the theft of land and the imposition of unfair laws is the price paid by the victim. To achieve this exploitation the colonising Empire needs an ideology of racist superiority to justify it to its own population, and to enable its agents to carry out this process.

The same reasons, "military power and financial gains," drive USA and its allies, including Britain, to wage wars today against the people of Iraq, Afghanistan, Libya, Syria and possibly extended to North Korea and Iran if imperialism has its way. In this sense, the issues that arise as a result of the Mau Mau court cases have significance far beyond legal matter, as Riri (2012?) explains:

> History will judge this case, not on the basis of who had the more powerful military and weapons of mass destruction during this colonial war; but who, the British or the Kenyans, had the right and justice on their side.

But "justice in this case can never be entirely done", as Corbyn (2012) maintains:

> Compensation for what happened may be paid, an apology may be given but the lives lost, the villages burnt, the reign of terror the British imposed in a colonial era that was rapidly approaching its sunset will never be forgotten.

Thus, the need for justice for those who were active in the movement is in focus today. But justice for the war veterans cannot be achieved fully until there is justice for their *movement*: Mau Mau. But there has been no justice for Mau Mau for over 60 years. It suited colonialism to brand the movement as cruel and primitive and to hide its real aims, cynically dismissing the sacrifice of millions as misguided, thereby hoping to justify its brutal repression of the people of Kenya. The movement was condemned easily, as were its supporters, activists and sympathisers. But while individuals can go to courts to seek redress, movements cannot, and without that judicial option it is all the more important to examine the movement and see what it represented, and to explore the impact it had – and continues to have – today.

Speak[7]
Speak, for your lips are free;
Speak, your tongue is still yours,
Your upright body is yours -
Speak, your life is still yours.

Speak, this little time is plenty
Before the death of body and tongue:
Speak, for truth is still alive -
Speak, say whatever is to be said.

---

7 Poems by Faiz: Faiz Ahmad Faiz (2002) Tr. V. G. Kiernan. New Delhi: OUP.

Mau Mau and the Struggle for Land and Freedom

There has been much debate on the term Mau Mau, and about what it means and whether it is an appropriate way to describe the movement and its activities. The term "Kenya Land and Freedom Army" is preferable as it encapsulates the aim of the resistance movement succinctly while indicating that it was a national movement. It is not the intention here to explain or justify the use of one title or the other. But as "Mau Mau" is widely known and has developed its own connotation and social and political context of resistance to colonialism and imperialism, both in Kenya and internationally, it is used in this book. However, there are a number of "points of caution" that need to be addressed with regard to the naming of the movement either way.

The term Mau Mau refers to the organisation and its actions - political, social and military - as part of the struggle for national resistance and liberation in Kenya. The movement was anti-colonialist, anti-capitalist and anti-imperialist. It sought political independence, but also aimed for full economic liberation from all aspects of social oppression and economic exploitation. It did not fight to replace white masters for black ones under the false pretence of "independence". The term used to describe it, whether Mau Mau or the Kenya Land and Freedom Army, should not obscure this fact.

The imperialist interpretation of the movement considered the movement to comprise just one nationality - the Kikuyu. Evidence shows that this was not the case as activists from many other nationalities joined to fight during struggle. Including some South Asian communities which had often been used by colonialist and following the adoption of capitalism, with its policies of the "rich getting richer and the poor getting poorer", by the ruling classes. It would be an incorrect interpretation of history if the liberation movement is seen as the activity of just one nationality.

Almost every nationality in Kenya resisted colonialism from its earliest intrusion long before the Mau Mau phase, from the early years of British colonialism up to independence, and during the earlier period of Portuguese colonialism. The resistance was nationwide.

Another result of the "boxing-in" of the national liberation movement under an unclear label is that it is seen as a movement of only a section of the population, whereas Mau Mau was a people's movement. Equally, the victims of British colonial policies were the entire people of Kenya – in the sense of the long term economic, political and social consequences of the policies of British colonialism. . Making out that "only Mau Mau" were involved in the movement and were the only victims of colonial policies ignores the fact that varying proportions of the populations of towns and villages were active in the struggle. In the Central province, hundreds of thousands were put into concentration camps. In other parts of the country, small elite groups were groomed to become "leaders" by British colonialists and the rest of the working people were victimised in different ways. Such victims included men, women and children. An incorrect understanding of the struggle may not grasp the full implication of the actions of, or the impact on, the people as a whole. Many people's losses included lives, livelihoods, land, livestock, the deprivation of services such as education and opportunities for acquiring wealth and resources, not only for one but subsequent generations as well. This loss has not been compensated for. Of course, the British policy of divide and rule created a powerful Homeguard - comprador - force which was not involved in the struggle for liberation. Their actions have had a lasting negative impact on the people of Kenya.

An important aspect of the liberation struggle that is often misunderstood is that it was led by organised working class people brought together by a well-established trade union and working class ideology, organisations and activities. Many workers who had previously participated in peaceful strikes and activities had resorted to armed resistance as a necessity as there were no peaceful ways of dislodging colonialism from Kenya, particularly after the declaration of war - or, as the British Establishment called it, the Emergency. This class aspect of the liberation that shows workers and peasants as the backbone of the struggle, is misrepresented in imperialist interpretations by many Kenyans as well as other historians. They gloss over the fact that workers in towns and countrysides suffered as much as peasants whose land and cattle was forcefully taken, and that this was a contributory factor to the growth of the militant resistance. Mau Mau was thus a movement of workers and peasants from across the nation.

That leads to another question about the movement, who can qualify to be called Mau Mau? Was it the fighters in the forest alone? Or did others, such as the network of activists and organisers in towns and countryside who were active in other aspects of the struggle for liberation, play their part? How do we look at the workers who played an important part in organising Mau Mau cells around the country - those women and children who took food and other material to the fighters in the forest, the South Asian activists who helped set up Mau Mau factories and provided food and shelter to the fighters and protected their families, the lawyers, the doctors, the political activists from all nationalities who opposed colonialism and supported the armed resistance or joined people's forces of national liberation?

And who has the right to decide on such definitions? The reality is that many of those who were not involved in any aspect of the struggle, past and present, Kenyans and non-Kenyans, with power to re-interpret history, are often the ones who decide on these issues. And they come with the baggage of their class interests and positions of power and influence. Those who fought and sacrificed all, including their lives in many cases, are forced into silence by their lack of economic, political and social power.

Mau Mau had a clear perspective on this when the two wings were identified, the active fighters and the people's forces, which supported the movement in other ways. Each depended on the other and was part of the overall movement.

While these questions cannot be answered in the abstract by a few self-appointed interpreters of history, one approach would be to let those who were active in many different ways decide their own role in the movement. In this book, the term Mau Mau is used for the organised force that actively sought the overthrow of colonialism and imperialism by economic, political and military means. At one level, it included those who took up arms. At another, it includes thousands who supported the organisation by supplying information, arms, food and helped the armed struggle in various ways. It is the organisational aspect and activism within it that perhaps decided who was a Mau Mau. Gachihi (1986) mentions this aspect:

> The mistake has often been made of identifying the Mau Mau movement with only the group that actually took up arms to fight it out in the forest against the colonial authorities and their African

collaborators. ... the bulk of the membership of the Mau Mau which supplied and carried under hand activities for the movement pervaded every sector. Among the urban dwellers were to be found zealous Mau Mau followers comparable to the squatters in European farms. Supporters of the movement infiltrated right through the Police Force and even the notorious homeguards.

Aiyar (2015) raises this issue in the context of South Asians:

> Caught up in explicating arguments about tribalism, nationalism, and neocolonialism, Indian voices have similarly died a "second death" in historical scholarship and popular narratives. These voices included Indian journalists who fought with pens in Indian-owned newspapers; members of the Congress who fought through rhetoric at public meetings; Indian lawyers who fought with words in courts while defending detainees; and individual Indians, entangled in their houses and sawmills with forest fighters and the police, who joined the Mau Mau's passive wings as suppliers of provisions or protected their Kikuyu employees from the excesses of the colonial state.

While it can be accepted that such activists and actions need to be recognised as part of the liberation movement, there needs to be a word of caution that such arguments can be used by the Homeguards to implicate that they were hidden supporters of the struggle. However, it should not be too difficult to distinguish the genuine fighters for liberation from the opportunists whose only interest was personal gain.

Historical Context: Imperialism and Resistance

Colonialism and imperialism in Kenya cannot be seen outside their global context. Nor can resistance in Kenya be seen outside the context of resistance to imperialism around the world. They are indelibly linked, and they influence each other in ways that may not at first be obvious. Thus, in order to understand colonialism and imperialism in Kenya fully, one needs to understand them in their global, colonial context. Other cases of imperial destruction include the elimination of native populations in USA and Australia, the slavery of African people, the imposition of the state of

Israel on Palestine, the massacres in Malaysia and the recent attacks on the countries and people of West Asia (sometimes referred to as "Middle East"). Destruction and atrocities in India carried out by Britain are well documented by Tharoor (2016) and need to be studied to understand colonialism and imperialism better. British imperialism was directly or indirectly involved in all these destructive activities. But again, this needs to be seen within the overall context of European colonisation and imperialism. Germany, Belgium, France and earlier imperialist superpowers, Spain and Portugal, had all carried out massacres and looting of their own in their colonies, with Belgium having massacred over ten million people in the Congo.

History is sometimes seen in mutually exclusive time capsule with no links between the different periods, so links such as those between British atrocities over centuries, and the rise of people's resistance are ignored. Similarly, the disjointed events between different periods of history are not seen as links to Kenya's War of Independence. What is forgotten is that Mau Mau was part of a larger War of Independence with many aspects in which all nationalities were involved. It takes on a new perspective when seen in its dynamic reality and diverse manifestations.

Imperialism used similar tactics to control people and countries all over the world. This remained the same whether one looks at Kenya and Africa or Latin America or Asia. It is necessary to understand this common imperialist practice in order to get a correct picture of how and what imperialism was up to and to get a better global perspective of how imperialism managed to create a global system of exploitation.   Petras and Veltmeyer (2018) record the experience that was common globally:

> By this time the sun had set on the British Empire, and the diverse countries and peoples that had been colonized and subjected ... had begun to rebel and rise up against their masters, ... the guardians of the capitalist system and the imperial world order turned towards the notion of 'development' and the project of 'international cooperation' ... The aim of this project of international cooperation was twofold. One was to ensure that the emerging leaders of this decolonization and development process would not heed the siren call of communism, and to ensure that they would turn to capitalism in meeting the system requirements of national development. The

other was to defuse the revolutionary ferment associated with an emerging class struggle for land and social change ... against the forces of capitalist development.

The situation that capitalism and imperialism created in Kenya becomes clearer when seen in a global perspective, not only of imperialist exploitation, but resistance to it as well. Resistance also needs to be seen as a response to imperialism, a theory explained clearly by Cecil Rhodes as "an essential solution to the cries for bread among the unemployed working-class of England, since it was the responsibility of colonial statesmen to acquire lands to settle the surplus population and create markets for goods from British factories" (Tharoor, 2016). In the process, the needs, the land, the resources, the labour and the very lives of people in the colonies were sacrificed in an unprecedented system of brutality.

However, there needs to be caution when discussing who benefits from colonialism and imperialism. It is often assumed that everyone in imperialist countries benefited equally from colonial and imperialist plunder. However, while it is true that some resources were shared between the poor and working people, the reality is that most of the gains are enjoyed by a small minority of those in power and their friends in finance, business and the industrial-military complex. Aaronovitch (1947) answers the question "Who gains from the policy of imperialism?" thus:

> Not the British people, but at all times the financiers and industrialists who stand behind the Tory Party. They are opposed to the advance of democracy everywhere, and especially in the colonies. It is from the colonies that they draw much of their wealth and power. Theirs is the policy now continued by the Labour Government. Its results can only be disastrous for the British people. .. A new anti-imperialist policy is vital for our peace and prosperity.

An all-inclusive, dynamic approach to understanding historical events would make it clear that the massacres, murders, systematic sexual violence, burning and looting of property and livestock, the destruction of agriculture and industries, the stealing of land and natural resources in colonies were not isolated incidents but were at the very heart of the system of exploitation and oppression that resulted from colonialism and imperialism - in Kenya, in India and in other colonies. British colonialism not only controlled these aspects during colonialism, but planted the seeds of imperialist exploitation *after* formal independence, as will be examined later in the book.

However, the events in Kenya as well as in British Empire around the world need to be seen in the context of imperialist exploitation. The rather long quote below from Conboy, Lugo-Ocando and Eldridge (2014) shows a number of key issues in understanding how colonial actions make an impact that continues through time, and touches upon how the history of colonialism has been distorted:

> If truth be told, Empire was a disaster for those under colonial rule. For Africans themselves, the British Empire was a holocaust followed by genocide. It represented the destruction of entire societies, followed by perpetual oppression and exploitation. Moreover, after the end of slavery the Empire inserted Africa as a colonial market into the capitalist system, which still reproduces relations of dependency and exploitation in the name of modernity and civilisation. This insertion of Africa into the world markets consolidated in the 19th and 20th centuries the structures of wealth distribution and inequalities that still today define the relationships between Africa and the West.

-

The recounting of history, clichéd as it may sound, is an accordion which contracts and expands; playing conveniently to the tune of those in power. It is easy now for the West to blame all Africa's problems on corruption and to point fingers at the 'tribal' nature of its politics. In so doing, it is able to dismiss historical continuums and ignore direct links between the historical accumulation of wealth in Europe and the United States, and poverty and exclusion in Africa.

Indeed, too often those playing history as a justificatory instrument forget that many of the contemporary issues in Africa are directly linked to the colonial legacy and the structures that were left in place by European empires: from the most recent Arab Spring and the preceding authoritarian regimes, to the now not-so-recent problems such as land reform and its consequences in Zimbabwe, the conflict in the Congo and environmental degradation in Nigeria.

These same voices which now try to revive the legitimacy of colonial rule also tend to deliberately ignore the reality that the British Empire was made possible not only through the use of military force, but also by those widely spread narratives that kidnapped and raped the popular imagination of the public in Europe – a discursive travesty that presented the British Empire as an emerging adventure of discovery and a quest for progress, modernity and civilisation.

An imperialist record of history sees events as isolated, unconnected to other events happening at the same time. It tends to view some events as spontaneous actions by the few, brought on because some good or bad people (as defined by imperialism) drove them to it. This line of thinking encourages the destruction of progressive people and glorifies those who side with imperialism. Kenyan history - and indeed, African history - needs to be examined to check whether it is indeed an objective record of events and actions or it is a distorted version subtly glorifying or justifying imperialist plunder.

Three Pillars of Resistance

> Mr. Lennox-Boyd plans a new "Devil's Island" in the middle of Lake Victoria. He plans to transport there 10,000 or more "unredeemable" Kikuyus. The island is at present completely uninhabited and the Kikuyu will serve no fixed prison sentence. They will stay there until they die and because most of them are illiterate, they will be cut off from everyone and everything they know. 10-10-54 - Kenya Committee for Democratic Rights for Kenya (1952-60) quoting from press reports.

Mau Mau is perhaps not unique in being seen from differing and often opposing perspectives. That is a reflection of class divisions in the capitalist world where each class interprets history in keeping with its class interest, often ignoring facts or creating false ones. Ndegwa (1977) shows how different people interpret Mau Mau in Kenya:

As with any armed struggle against oppression, Mau Mau has been, and still seems to be, a very controversial subject. Various groups of Kenyan population viewed Mau Mau differently. To the Freedom Fighters and the ordinary wananchi, the Mau Mau movement was a noble and patriotic cause that required dedication and devotion to one's country to the extent of giving one's life for it. They viewed Mau Mau as a last resort to a long struggle against the humiliation, oppression and degradation of colonialism; and seemed the only way to restore back, fast disappearing land, lost pride and dignity, and [address] foreign domination. Violence became a last resort to calling attention to the movement.

To the Missionary, and the African Christians, Mau Mau was an evil and heathen rejection of Christianity and a return to the [supposed?] savagery and barbarism that Christianity was trying to root out.

But to the settler and the Colonial administrator, Mau Mau was viewed as a move back to tribal brutality and cruelty; a rejection of civilization and progress. The settler and the administrator could not possibly understand why a people for whom so much had been done and sacrificed would want to revolt against, and reject, what could only be good for them. Each group, therefore, viewed Mau Mau from whichever angle benefited them in their varied interests and so each group fought for what they believed to be right and just.

When Field Marshal Muthoni (2007) was asked why people like her participated in the War of Independence, she replied:

> To fight, of course... My father worked for a settler. I was brought up in a Settlers' farm. Once you had lived with them, you knew you had to fight. We felt it was better to die in the forest fighting them, than to live without our freedom. We wanted our land, and we wanted our freedom, that is what we wanted.

She continued:

> We were in the forest fighting for our freedom. Our fellow black man was not our enemy, not even those who collaborated with the white man. Those who collaborated we knew did so because of their ignorance. The white man was not our enemy because of the colour of his skin. No. It was because of what he had done. He had come and taken our land and was oppressing us in our own land. That is what we fought for: our land and our freedom.

Misunderstandings and distortion of what Mau Mau and the War of Independence were all about sometimes arises from looking at the struggle in a one-dimensional, static way. Mau Mau and the War of Independence were different things at different times and involved many struggles within a larger anti-imperialist war. The particularities of each period and in each part of the country differed, but the overall aim throughout was to get rid of the system of exploitation and looting that colonialism and imperialism brought to Kenya. At the same time, different struggles contributed to and fed into the larger aim. In this it was no different from the Cuban Revolution, as Cushion (2016) says:

> In common with many conflict situations, a number of parallel struggles took place in the revolution, and most combatants participated in some elements but not others according to their political beliefs and class interests. The insurrection was a civil war, a class struggle, an anti-imperialist movement, a democratic revolution, a fight for national independence against neocolonialism, a campaign against corruption, and an episode in the Cold War.

Mau Mau needs to be seen in the overall context of Kenya's War of Independence so as to understand the contribution of different streams of resistance that joined together to make up the overall flow. These streams included the active guerrilla armies in towns and forests, the non-combatant wing of Mau Mau, the different nationalities participating at different levels in the struggle, the organised and unorganised working class and their struggles for economic and political rights. It included those who saw armed resistance as the only way to fight colonialism and imperialism and others who were pacifists and wanted to wage a non-violent struggle. It included those who saw their struggles in single issues, such as education or religion, as their contribution to the War of Independence. The earlier peasant and nationalities-based struggle for land, as well as struggles for labour, economic and political rights in later years were all aspects of the War of Independence. One cannot identify any one of these as the overall determining factor in the achievement of independence - all played their part to differing degrees.

Thus in essence, the War of Independence was a movement built on three pillars of resistance to colonialism and imperialism. These can be seen as Mau Mau (which included the armed and people's forces with participants from the other two pillars), the trade union movement (including all organised workers in towns and rural areas) and the people's forces consisting of peasants, national and nationality political and social organisations from across the country who supported the War of Independence in different ways, not necessarily always supporting armed resistance.

Missing from many history books is the revolutionary role played by Kenya's peasants and pastoralists as partners with workers in the struggle for independence and later, in the post-independence period, as forces resisting neo-colonialism for land and against exploitation of their labour and produce. The period of the first invasion of Kenya by colonial plunderers saw massive peasant resistance and this militancy continued right up to, and beyond, independence. Colonialism found it necessary to hide the peasant militancy as aspects of tribalism and primitiveness. Yet it remains true that workers, on their own, could not have driven colonialism out of Kenya. The support of peasants provided a solid foundation for a united worker-peasant front against a powerful enemy. Davis (2017) relates the role of peasant-worker alliance during the foundation of the Soviet Union and sees this alliance as crucial in wars against colonialism:

> The practical application of the concept of a worker-peasant alliance proved not only to be critical in Russian conditions, but has also been central to liberation struggles in colonial and post-colonial countries. It was an original development of Marxist theory because hitherto the peasantry had been written off as a reactionary force.

And yet, Kenya's official history ignores the crucial role of the united force of peasants and workers in the victory over colonialism.

Colonial history, and those who follow its conclusions, did not show these three pillars standing together; many may recognise one or more in isolation but do not see them working together as part of an overall, complex reality. They therefore created an incorrect or incomplete history of the country, and it is this incomplete interpretation has then permeated the minds of Kenyans even today.

Similarly, a lack of clarity about the struggles also led to confusion and misunderstanding about the different methods used to fight the common enemy. Some fought with guns, other with ideas, others with newspapers and publication, songs, religion, education

Economic and Political System

An important clue as what Mau Mau stood for is in the name it chose when it resorted to armed struggle: Kenya Land and Freedom Army. Thus land and freedom for the people of Kenya were the aims of the movement, and as the British repression became even more intensive, the only method of struggle left was through an armed struggle. There was a long period before the Second Imperialist World War when the people of Kenya had sought to bring about change through peaceful means through petitions and pleas to the British Government, but these brought no results. Thus, as the Ghadar movement seeking freedom from colonialism in India said in 1913, "the time will soon come when rifles and blood will take the place of pens and ink" (Josh, 1977). While many organisations had started preparations by the late 1940s, the time for rifles and blood in Kenya was brutally ushered in by intensified repression through the declaration of the Emergency in 1952. The TJRC Report (2013) highlights the background to the militant stage of the War of Independence:

> The creation of reserves in areas deemed unsuitable for European settlement had far-reaching implications, both for the natives and the colonial administration. Underlying them was a policy of exploitation and oppression against the colonized people accentuated

by land alienation, forced male labour mobilization, overcrowding, insecurity, stagnation in African agricultural production, massive landlessness and rapid land deterioration due to fragmentation, overstocking and soil erosion.

In the long term, the problems in the reserves led to unrest and eventually to a political uprising – the Mau Mau resistance movement that organized around the issue of foreign rule, land alienation and political and economic inequality.

Maloba (1998) provides the background to the contradictions created by colonialism in Kenya and also links the economic with political issues:

> ... colonialism, and with it the introduction of capitalist relations of production in Central Province, caused the destruction of the traditional political economy. The resultant economic hardships, especially of displaced peasants and former tenants and squatters, complicated rural social relations and generated tension both in the rural and urban centers. But these economic problems were never viewed as distinct from political struggles by Mau Mau supporters. To them it was manifestly clear that the colonial state and its multiple demands and requirements were responsible for both the economic and political problems in the country. The colonial state's identification with European Settlers was complete. In these circumstances, it would have been impossible to distinguish economic needs from political needs, for neither could be satisfied independent of the other. In Kenya, there was a problem of distinguishing between economic and political causes of the revolt; for after all, political and economic injustice were intricately intertwined.

Roseberg and Nottingham (1966) explain the stages of resistance against colonialism that culminated in Mau Mau:

> At first Africans sought to obtain redress for their grievances within the framework of the settler orientated colonial state; following the Second World War, however, many came to challenge its very legitimacy. A nationalism of petition and constitutional protest ultimately gave way to a militant nationalism employing direct action

in seeking a new political and social order.

Mau Mau thus represented a fundamental shift from a passive, "within-the-system" peaceful approach to an armed revolutionary movement to overthrow colonialism and imperialism. It sought to establish a new equitable society based on principles of social and economic justice and to address the imbalance in power between different classes. Colonialism's response to this revolutionary approach by Mau Mau was threefold: first, it attacked Mau Mau with a massive build-up of military hardware; secondly, it waged propaganda and spin warfare to misinform people in Kenya and Britain about what Mau Mau stood for. Thirdly, it encouraged divisions among people of Kenya along "tribal" and class lines and created antagonism among people by creating the privileged Homeguard force to undermine national unity. All these responses have had a lasting negative legacy from which Kenya suffers even today. The court cases by Mau Mau veterans highlight the effects of the colonial government's military response to Mau Mau; the effects of the other responses – misinformation and implanted disunity and tribalism - are also obvious in Kenyan where national consciousness, moulded by mass media, the education system and policies of the comprador regimes, is not fully aware of the reality that was the War of Independence and also the reality of how the elite were groomed, encouraged and supported by the departing British colonial government to seize power in the interest of the elite and imperialism. While the British courts have accepted the "grave abuses suffered" by the veterans, only a people's court is in a position to pass judgement on British colonialism for the damage it has inflicted in other ways.

Colonialism and capitalism created unfair and unequal economic conditions and social relations during the colonial period which could only be resolved through an armed, revolutionary movement. It simultaneously failed to create suitable political systems and structures, which could perhaps have mitigated the harsh economic and political reality faced by the people. It was the failure of the political process which ensured that the only way of resolving social contradiction was through an armed resistance movement. Newsinger (2006) explains the failures of colonial policies:

> What drove the Kikuyu down the road to rebellion was the failure of the Labour government elected with an overwhelming majority in

1945 to offer any hope of improvement or advance ... the moderate Kenya African Union (KAU) repeatedly requested that the African people be given 12 elected representatives in the Legislative Council. Instead [James] Griffiths [the Colonial Secretary] offered to increase African representation from four to five. This left 30,000 Settlers with 14 elected representatives, the 100,000 Asians with six, the 24,000 Arabs with one and the five million Africans with five nominees. Even the Settlers were astonished at how reactionary the Labour government proved to be. This shattering of hopes for peaceful change fatally compromised the influence of the moderates and strengthened the hand of the revolutionaries.

This made armed resistance almost an inevitability. Woolf (1944) sums up the contradictions of the colonial policy and practice in Kenya, a contradiction well hidden by a colonial interpretation of history:

> In Kenya our professed principles and our political practice have contradicted each other ever since the beginning of the century. For forty years the interests of three million Africans have been sacrificed to those of a handful of Europeans.

But these "handful of Europeans" were not the working class from Britain. As WFTU (1952) points out about composition of the European population in Kenya:

> The sort of people who constitute the white population of Kenya amply justify the comment of Negley Farson... who says of the colony that "It has the greatest proportion among its inhabitants of ex-soldiers, generals, colonels, majors, of any country in the world.

It is thus the British military establishment, which indirectly influenced power, and policies that the colonial government wielded on behalf of the Settlers - together with some poorer, working-class British Settlers who benefited to a much lesser extent. But the corporations were not far behind. Besides individuals like Lord Delamere, the leader of the Settlers who acquired over 100,000 acres of the best land and Lord Francis Scott, "huge tracts were alienated in favour of plantation companies: the East African Syndicate was given 320,000 acres, the Uplands of East Africa Syndicate

350,000 acres and the Grogan Forest Concession 200,000 acres", as WFTU (1952) says.

It is clear that the entire colonial adventure was used to benefit the UK Establishment as a whole and the "handful of Europeans" were allowed to take their share in return for managing the colony on behalf of capitalism. Woolf (1944) recognised the presence of hidden but powerful forces behind the Settlers and the Kenya colonial government:

> It is not the Settlers, but the system, economic and political, and the Government which maintains that system, on whom the blame for this situation must rest.

It was this force of capitalism that dictated colonial plunder, murder and massacres that became the norm in Kenya even after independence. It is the conditions they created that could end only in violence.

And yet not everybody in Britain who sided with the Establishment point of view on Kenya. Brockway (1953), for example, shows that there were people in Britain who understood the reasons for the rise of Mau Mau. Fenner Brockway was an MP in the UK and became determined to show the reality in Kenya following a visit with another MP, Leslie Hale. As this is a clear indication of what drove people to an armed struggle in Kenya, it is worth quoting Brockway (1953) in depth as he identifies the reasons for the rise of Mau Mau:

> Mau Mau arises from a deep and continuing frustration - a frustration which is social, economic and psychological - a frustration from which the African can never escape.

> It is inconceivable that the British Government was not aware of these facts set out by Brockway as early as 1953 as follows:

Social

> The British have destroyed the old tribal system through which African instincts, thoughts, and emotions found expression and have failed to replace it by a satisfying substitute.

The clan was compact and small. At its head was an elected Council of Elders ... The Kikuyus were among the most democratic of African tribes. They did not have Chiefs because they objected to personal power. We have destroyed these democratic communities. Instead, the tribes are administered by British District Officers and Chiefs whom the British select...They are regarded [by the Kikuyu people] as the tools of an alien administration.

Economic

Whenever one asked an African in Kenya what grievance he felt most deeply, the answer came without a moment's hesitation: "Land Hunger".... To the African, land is life. Livelihood depends upon it. Land hunger in Kenya is equivalent to unemployment in Britain - unemployment without benefits, children's allowances or other social services.

Of the one and a quarter million Kikuyus, half a million have had to leave their reserve because there is no land from which they can gain a living. Over extensive areas there are from 500 to 1,000 people per square mile.... The despair which arises from the physical suffering of land hunger becomes bitterness when the Kikuyus look from their congested reserves to the neighbouring European areas, the White Highlands. Their [European] "reserve" contains twelve thousand square miles of cultivatable land: that is one European to a square mile. The bitterness of this comparison is intensified by the memory of how the Europeans obtained their land.

Land hunger, supplemented by racial discrimination in how land is used, is the root economic frustration of the African population in Kenya. [italics in the original].

Brockway (1953) then explains the plight of the "squatters" on the European farms - "the half-million Kikuyus who have been driven from their land" - before looking at the third aspect of the "deep and continuing frustration - psychological":

When I first heard the name I thought they must be trespassers. Not so. They are the labourers on the farms. The name should be "serfs" rather than squatters. I know of no labour conditions in the British sphere of Africa closer to slavery.

Psychological

Racial discrimination permeates every sphere of life in Kenya... Everywhere there is racial segregation.

This is the source of the psychological frustration of the African people. It is probable that the humiliations of the colour bar cause the deepest wounds of bitterness.

Thus the stealing of land was one of the key factors that united people in their struggle against colonialism. It remains one of the unresolved causes of social tension in Kenya even today. A brief look at the land issue may therefore provide a better understanding of the land issue in Kenya and the underlying reasons for resistance in Kenya.

WHY DO WE KNOW SO LITTLE ABOUT OUR HISTORY?

Kenya's War of Independence

Explosion Inevitable - Resistance Before Mau Mau

> The climate of much of the territory [Kenya] is excellent for agriculture, and it is free from tropical diseases. These conditions, however, have encouraged the settlement of Europeans who have invaded the healthy areas and alienated the land formally owned and tilled by Africans. The African population must now either perish or work for starvation wages on the farms they and their parents owned for countless generations. In addition they are compelled to pay a Poll Tax to sustain the Administration which has deprived them of their land.
>
> This situation has precipitated events which have since come to [be known] as Mau Mau, for when Human Rights are denied to any people, an explosion is inevitable - Frida Laski (1954?)

The struggle for land, labour and economic, social and political freedoms started long before Mau Mau which carried on the earlier struggles to new heights by adding organised, armed resistance to earlier methods. Koinange (1952) provides documents from various nationalities showing their grievances against "British imperialism". A few points from these are reproduced below to show resistance before Mau Mau:

> The Kipsigis grievances [include] the power to intervene in countries where a *minority* (Settlers) are oppressing a *majority* (Africans) and create the kind of instability that leads to trouble... The first District Commissioner of Jericho at about 1911-1914 evicted indigenous people from all these inhabited parts...While evicting people the Government Officials set fire to their huts. All their goods were burnt, properties were destroyed ... In conclusion, [we have been deprived of land] leaving only 1/4 of our land in 1921 up to 1940...About 3/4 has gone to Europeans.

Koinange and Oneko (1952) show the sham legal methods that the British Government used to dispossess African of their lands:

> His Majesty's Government had no power, under Protectorate Law in East Africa, to extinguish the rights of land ownership of the Africans...And yet this was taken. There was enacted the Crown

> Lands Ordinance ... This dispossession meant the alienation ("alienate means to dispossess Africans of the land of their birth and to give it to the Europeans") of 16,000 square miles to 2,000 European Settlers and the "reservation" of 50,000 square miles for five and a half million Africans.

Koinange and Oneko (1952) further show one of the consequences of the British take-over of Kenyan land:

> Thus we see in Kenya the creation of a European aristocracy which is founded not on innate superiority, but on monopoly of the best and healthiest land. A large part of the Africans, by contrast, must live in lands that are dry, hot and unhealthy - in lands too small and too infertile to support their population.

This creation of aristocracy and immense class inequality that started under British rule is continuing to this date, although the European aristocracy is now joined by the elite African aristocracy created and nurtured by British policies as part of the independence "settlement". Again, this is another aspect of the colonial legacy in Kenya which has received little or no attention.

One expression of the people's demands for land was shown at a mass meeting of 30,000 people in Githunguri in July, 1952 when "people came from all over the country in lorries", as narrated by Koinange (1952) who provides the words of the song people sang at the meeting:

> Our fight for the land will never cease.
> It was ours, and it will be ours, forever and ever.
> We do not fear those who speak behind our backs,
> If they scorn us they will not be here forever.
>
> We look for the day to arrive
> When great jubilation will reign everywhere
> And the children of black men throughout the world
> Will know happiness in the return of their rights.

Slaughter (1999) explains the land grievance that forced the people of Kenya to take up arms:

> By the end of the Second World War, 3,000 European Settlers owned 43,000 square kilometres of the most fertile land, only 6 per cent of which they cultivated. The African population of 5.25 million occupied, without ownership rights, less than 135,000 square kilometres of the poorest land. On the "native reserves" much of the land was unsuitable for agriculture.

The colonial divide and rule policies affected not only the lives of people but resistance to colonialism as well. Maloba (1998) looks at how such policies affected local and national politics in Kenya:

> The development of African nationalism was complicated further by the establishment of the African reserves in 1915. Each reserve occupied, as far as possible, a separate ethnic group. This had the effect of emphasizing "the distinctiveness of each tribal grouping" and limiting any chances of solidarity. Separateness led to suspicion and ill feeling, some deliberately fostered by the British in their strategy of divide and rule. Problems affecting each community tended to be viewed in local terms, with almost no consideration given to their national dimension. This was officially sanctioned parochialism, and it was to be many years before territorial nationalism emerged in Kenya.

Thus driven into regions, the struggle against colonialism was nevertheless waged in every part of Kenya. As the land grab had been the most severe in the land of the Gikuyu people, the fiercest resistance was also centred there. Newsinger (2006) provides details of how the land grab by Settlers affected the Gikuyu nationality:

> By 1948 one and a quarter million Kikuyu were restricted to landholdings in 2,000 square miles of tribal reserve, while the 30,000 white Settlers held 12,000 square miles, including most of the best farmland. In the reserves there was considerable poverty, with almost half of the population landless. Only a small class of collaborators prospered ... Outside the reserves some 120,000 Kikuyu lived as

squatters on the white farms, receiving a small patch of land in return for their labour, in effect a form of serfdom.

The resulting resistance by the Gikuyu – and other nationalities – was inevitable, given the harsh reality of what colonialism was doing to people. Cheche Kenya (1982) provides some background:

> By the late 1930s and early 1940s there were organisational links between the [trade] unions in the towns and the majority of our people in the countryside. Resistance to various aspects of colonial policy was often nation-wide. For instance, the trade unions, and such organisations as the Kenya African Union, the Kavirondo Taxpayers Welfare Association, the Ukamba Members Association, the Taita Hills Association, and the North Kavirondo Central Association, all took up the issue of land alienation and demanded a better deal for the African people. Protests became more militant after World War II. Nationalist feelings nurtured by such bodies as the Forty Group, the Action Group within KAU, and the unions under Chege Kibachia and Makhan Singh, must be seen as a part of a general world-wide Afro-American movement against colonial domination.

Such historical analyses from a working class perspective have begun to emerge and needs to be seen as a legitimate interpretation of Kenyan history. Among recent revelations are documents that show how the British government manipulated land deals favourable to imperialism and to the incoming comprador regime. Land grabbing by the successive KANU regimes of Kenyatta and Moi has been confirmed in the archives of the last Colonial Governor of Kenya, Malcolm MacDonald and those of the former Vice President of Kenya, Joseph Murumbi.

The Kenya Human Rights Commission (n.d.) sums up the methods and effects of the colonial land policy as recorded by the Truth, Justice and Reconciliation Commission (TJRC, 2013):

> The TJRC report identified that the colonial administration used irregular and/or illegal methods to obtain land from local communities such as: the establishment of native reserves; forced evictions of the Talai, Pokot, Turkana, and Sabaot communities; land alienation by

multinational corporations and coercive measures such as forced African labour, forced taxation and forced military service. These colonial policies, laws and practices had both immediate and long term effects on African communities, including permanent displacement. The colonial system created ethno-specific boundaries, which gave the impression that land rights within particular boundaries could only be enjoyed by certain communities, in certain areas. These ethnic ties to land continue to affect Kenya to date.

These practices were then handed over to, and continued in, the post-independence era. The Truth Justice and Reconciliation Commission (2013) sums up how the land settlement benefited the elite:

> The ex-Mau Mau fighters were thus short-changed after independence. Even when the settlement schemes were initiated between 1963 and 1967, the Maasai who suffered the most got nothing and the Kalenjin received small areas around Sotik and Nandi. The squatters were not any better in their continued demand for cultivatable land across the highlands. Those living in the former White Highlands were evicted. In the majority of the settlement schemes in Nakuru and Nyandarua, the existing squatters were simply removed by force, with new claimants chosen to occupy the plots. The situation of the landless did not improve with the sale of larger farms under the 'willing buyer, willing seller' model. A decade after the implementation, one sixth of the settler lands were found to have been sold intact to the emerging African elite comprising Kenyatta, his wife, children and close associates. These elites did not even need much money to buy settler farms, as they were also able to raise loans from government bodies such as the Agricultural Finance Corporation (AFC) and the Land and Agriculture Bank.

While the return of their land was the most important issue for Kenyans, it was not the only one, as Koinange and Oneko (1952) point out:

> Colonial development which seeks merely to produce more food and raw material for export, without reference to African needs, will fail. Cheap colonial food that relies on cheap colonial labour is not a contribution to development. Wages are already very low ... The

lives and destinies of more than five million Africans are controlled arbitrarily by 29,000 Europeans in general, and 3,000 European Settlers in particular. This arbitrary rule by a small minority raises many questions ... Believing in full democracy, we aim at a common roll for all the peoples of Kenya, to eliminate racial, religious and colour discrimination ... With these discriminations, there are others: so that in education, health, and many other aspects of life, the Africans of Kenya are placed in a position of relentless inferiority. They, alone of the inhabitants of Kenya, have to carry passes which control and restrict their freedom of movement.

And these demands were the same that people all over Kenya had been making right from the time that British colonialism put the first step in Kenya. But such demands, mostly passed on by word of mouth or appeals in memoranda, went unheeded. Arming themselves in order to achieve these basic rights remained the only way to ensure real "development" for the people of Kenya. In January 1952, before the British colonial government declared a State of War on the people of Kenya, Koinange and Oneko (1952) saw the consequences of continuing such colonial arrogance:

The African people are no longer prepared to be diverted by minor political or economic reforms. Although they look to world opinion and especially the British people for support, they realise that fundamentally they must rely on themselves for the achievement of full equality. In spite of all forms of oppression and persecution, the political consciousness of the people of Kenya has been growing rapidly.

And it was this political consciousness and the realisation that they must rely on themselves that made Mau Mau armed liberation movement inevitable.

As serious as all the above factors were, there was an even more serious principal at stake – the right of Kenyan people to life. Colonialism paid no heed to this fundamental right. On the contrary: while paying lip service to the tenet of Article 1 of the Universal Declaration of Human Rights (1948) that "All human beings are born free and equal in dignity and rights", the very existence of capitalism and British Empire defied this principal. Colonialism and imperialism made systematic and regular use of massacres, murders, the use of concentration camps, illegal imprisonment and murders of the colonised people, in addition to creating conditions of starvation in which hundreds of thousands of people perished. This happened not only in Kenya but in other colonies as well, notably India and Malaysia. Colonialism could not have survived without violence - no people would ever willingly give up their land, resources, labour and lives to enrich foreign elite.

Millner (1954?) recalls that Mr. P.M. Koinange, "a former representative in London of the now suppressed Kenya African Union", accused the British government of genocide, i.e., "the murder of his people". Millner (1954?) examines this accusation with reference to the Convention on the Prevention and Punishment of the Crime of Genocide, adopted by the General Assembly of U.N.O. on the 9th December, 1948. He examines the actions of the British government and its laws, and mentions the killings and forced starvation and ends with a question for readers: "These terrible ordeals are being inflicted...upon an African population... If you were an African, particularly a Kikuyu, would *you* call it genocide?".

The tragedy for Kenya and its people is that there is no global power that can freely examine facts and decide whether the British government was responsible for genocide there. Individuals can appeal to British courts for personal compensation for crimes of British governments, but relatives of victims of genocide have few chances of being heard. The moral responsibility of the past and current British governments remains. Millner (1954?) concludes, "British government flouts its moral obligation to observe recognised standards of civilised conduct".

It is not within the scope of this book to examine the policies of the White Settlers who supported and pushed the colonial government to even more extreme measures. It is within scope to look at their role in depriving people of Kenya of their land and driving peasants to provide cheap labour for the Settlers' farms, and how the effects of this should not be under-estimated in understanding the situation the Mau Mau faced. The Settlers also made up a large proportion of the Police Reserve Force who were infamous for abusing their powers in torturing African people. But this was not because of a few isolated individuals getting out of control. It was directly the result of their policy of "neutralisation or liquidation" of "certain African leaders". This was indicated, for example, in a letter dated August 7, 1952 from the

Electors' Union, signed by its Executive Officer, Kendall Ward:

> The Executive Committee were very strongly of the opinion that the first task of government should be the neutralisation of all known leaders of subversive organisations or any African leaders who are suspected of being leaders of subversive organisations ... The Executive Committee accordingly were of the opinion that this action should be given first priority.8 [Italics added].

Progressive people in the world today are shocked by the use of such methods by the Government of the United States against those they judge to be or suspect of being "terrorists". But colonialism had already fine-tuned this tool in an arsenal against liberation struggles around the world, decades before their use by USA.

Any objective study of history or politics leads to the conclusion that no-self respecting people would indefinitely accept the poverty and humiliation ruthlessly enforced on the Kenyan Africans.

- Pankhurst (1954?)

Resisting Colonial Violence

Resistance started during the earliest days of colonialism, even going back to the period of Portuguese colonialism and continuing under the British. From the earliest times, people of every nationality took up arms at one time or another to overthrow intrusion. It was only the colonialists' brutal use of superior firepower and inhuman measures such as massacres, murders, imprisonment, concentration camps, torture, forced labour and confiscation of land and livestock that enabled them to maintain their bloody rule over Kenyan people. The Truth Justice and Reconciliation Commission of Kenya (2013) records:

> The conquest of state and territory for British settlement and exploitation in Kenya was achieved through colonial violence. To force Africans into submission, the colonial administration in Kenya

---

8 The letter is reproduced in Kenya Committee for Democratic Rights for Kenya (1952-60).

conducted 'punitive expeditions' in the 1890s against what they called 'recalcitrant tribes'. There were military expeditions against the Nandi in 1901, 1905, and 1906, against the Embu in 1905, against the Abagusii in 1904, 1908, and 1914, against the Kipsigis in 1905 and against the Abagishu and Kabras in 1907 ... Practically everywhere in Kenya, as was the case in the rest of Africa, the imposition of colonial rule was resisted. Such resistance inevitably provoked military retaliation from the colonial powers. Better armed and employing crack shot mercenaries, colonial powers imposed their rule by violence and/or military expeditions. This was particularly the case between 1895 and 1914; a phase of pacification of 'recalcitrant tribes' fighting for the preservation of their political, cultural and economic independence. The period was thus characterized by an unimaginable degree of human rights abuses against defenceless Africans. The military expeditions were accompanied by crimes such as theft, rape, death and destruction of property by the colonial soldiers or their associates. Such actions defy the view that the British colonialist used humane and gentle methods to impose their rule in Kenya.

Saleh Mamon (2014) provides further details of these early struggles in Appendix C. The struggles of the earlier periods had taught the people valuable lessons in resistance. Some examples of such resistance are given below to indicate the scope of the resistance before Mau Mau.

Resistance at the Coast

It is important to see all resistance against foreign invaders as part of the larger resistance of the people of Kenya as a whole. This point is well made by Umoja (1987b):

> The British invasion of Kenya was resisted by many nationalities of Kenya. Between the formal declaration of a "protectorate" in 1895 and the outbreak of the first Imperialist War in 1914, the British colonial regime had faced armed resistance by forces led by heroic figures like Mbaruk bin Rashid at the Coast, Waiyaki and Gakunju in Central Kenya. Koitalel in the Rift Valley, Lowalal and Kotetiang in Northern

Rift Valley, Ahmed Megan and Mohamed Abdille Hassan in North Eastern Kenya, and Me Katilili in the Coast. These forces represented Waswahili, Mijikenda, Gikuyu, Turkana, Nandi, Somali, to mention just a few. Taken together, these nationality anti-imperialist forces amount to an all-Kenyan national movement against a common enemy.

These heroic foundations of modern Kenya are the aspects of our history which have been suppressed. Indeed, the collaborationist. loyalist sell-outs like Mumia, Kinyanjui, Ali bin Salim, Lenana, Ombata, Kitoto, Ngenyo wa Mvua and the others are the ones which the colonialists promoted.

Recalling Me Katilili and the 1913-1915 Giriama Resistance, Umoja (1987b) recalls resistance by the Giriama which was very similar in aims and strategy to those of the Somali (examined later) and Mau Mau in later times:

> The British wanted the land. They wanted the labour to work on the land. They wanted capital to develop the land. They wanted political power for the smooth running of labour on the land. The land grabbing and political power were to be gained by military conquests. The second and the third ... were to be gained through the actual exercise of political power. But no economic control or political control could be complete without cultural control. Under imperialist capitalism, free labour had, as it were, to acquiesce to its own enslavement.

> It was to the credit of Me Katilili, this incredibly gifted organiser and orator, that she saw all this and acted to give the Giriama people's resistance a coherent political form. She had witnessed the British drive for land and labour and taxation. She had seen how the British were eating into the Giriama political power system by undermining the Giriama national government by appointing servile headmen. She had seen how the colonialists were carefully exploiting any signs of disunity between the youth and the elders. and between the different nationalities. She had witnessed the British intensify disunity among the Giriama by undermining their culture. Above all, she saw the dangerous role the collaborators like Nyongo wa Mwavuo, Mkowo

wa Gobwe, Ziro wa Luganje, Tsuma wa Iha, Baya we Kadio, played. Me Katllili started to organise the women and the youth. She called the people's assembly, the Kaya.

> At this assembly, people took oaths and swore to defend their land, their labour and their culture. They denounced the colonial administration and the local henchmen. The assembly installed a people's government and administration led by the three patriotic elders: Wanje, Pembe and Bogosho. The youth swore to arm themselves for self-defence. The people denounced Christian bourgeois anti-people culture exhibited by the few who had been to mission schools and churches. The people were told not to continue paying taxes to the colonial government; and the assembly swore people to an insurrection. The collaborators were terrorised into silence.

The people of the Coast have played critical roles in resisting Portuguese as well as British colonialism. Yet they suffer the loss of land and resources to this day.

Resistance in Northern Kenya: The Somali Nationality

The Somali nationality are one of the minority nationalities ignored in Kenyan history and their contribution to the War of Independence has not been fully explored. It is for this reason that this section provides a little background on these aspects, although they fall outside the scope of the period this book deals with. Nevertheless, their contribution in earlier years definitely strengthened Kenyan people's resistance to colonialism and so contributed in no small measure to the achievement of independence. The policies of all Kenya Governments since independence have termed the Somali nationality in Kenya as "enemies of the people" and made it very difficult, if not impossible, to research or write an objective history..

Umoja (1987c) provides some details:

> From the first day the British set foot on Northern Kenya in the 1890s until their departure in 1963, they encountered unprecedented

opposition with heavy losses on the part of the [British] enemy. Casualties could only be sustained by the continuous supply of recruits from other countries such as India, Sudan, Uganda, Nyasaland and Aden.

Such intense activities in Northern Kenya must surely have weakened British forces so that other nationalities could have taken advantage and launched stronger attacks. This is confirmed by Umoja (1987c) in connection with Mohamed Abdille Hassan:

> Mohamed Abdille Hassan waged what is undoubtedly one of the biggest challenges to colonial rule in Africa. He visited Nairobi in 1890, then a growing colonial outpost. He was shocked by the presence of white colonial officials there. He quickly returned to the interior to mobilise the people against the colonialists and "stop them doing what they had done to Nairobi". Mohamed Abdille Hassan founded a politico-military front known as the Darwish against the British, the Italian and feudal Abyssinia... The British and Italian suffered defeats at the hands of the gallant Darwish fighters. In the battle of Dulmadobe in 1914, they trounced the Camel Constabulary and killed its commanding officer... The British beat a hasty retreat and moved their families and personnel across the sea to Aden.... Winston Churchill, then an officer in the colonial office... recommended an evacuation in the face of Mohamed Abdille Hassan's attacks.

Umoja (1987c) takes up the story that then links with Mau Mau and the War of Independence:

> ... Political activity, however, continued underground. In 1957, a secret movement known as Horseed (the Vanguard) came to light. Like KLFA [Kenya Land and Freedom Army, Mau Mau], Horseed instituted oath taking in Garissa and Isiolo. The development directly connected the NFD [North Frontier District of Kenya] resistance to that of Mau Mau which was known to have used oathing as part of its organisational authority in the war of independence.

There cannot be a clearer reading of history than this to see the War of Independence in Kenya as a national movement with linked organisations growing up in different parts, all having the same aims and all contributing to the eventual achievement of independence.

The Truth Justice and Reconciliation Commission of Kenya (2013) recalls some aspects of activism among the Somali people and their organisations, beginning with the early period of British colonialism:

> From 1893 to about 1918, various Somali groups engaged in primary resistance to the colonial powers. Resistance at this stage lacked an explicitly positive political objective and instead centred on resistance to the British invasion of previously independent territories.

It then goes on to examine Somali activism at a later period:

> The third phase of pre-independence political activity in Northern Kenya has more direct connections to the Shifta War. In May 1943, the innocuously named Somali Youth Club was founded in Mogadishu. Four years later, branches were opened in Wajir, Mandera and Isiolo. The club changed its name to the Somali Youth League (SYL). Membership was primarily Somali and more specifically, Herti. Large numbers of non-Somali Northerners, such as the Burji and the Borana, were also drawn to the SYL by a seductive and progressive manifesto that included promises to fight for better educational and health facilities. The paucity of schools and hospitals in the region was as much a concern in the 1940s as it is today; the roots of social and economic marginalisation ran very deep. There was a political edge to some of the League's other objectives. For instance, SYL leaders sought to "foster Islam". Although no further information was available as to what would be done to foster Islam, colonial officials came to view with a great deal of suspicion any efforts to increase the profile of Islam in the colonies.

The colonial authorities deemed the Somali Youth League dangerous to its rule and declared it illegal "and its leaders were deported to Lokitaung in the Turkana District" (Singh, 1969). And the reasons are clear when one considers the political campaigns of the SYL. The Truth Justice and Reconciliation Commission of Kenya (2013) says, "by the late 1950s, The Somali Youth League was most certainly in decline' adding some details:

The SYL branches in Kenya busied themselves with more local campaigns. While presenting itself as a social, charitable and quasi-religious organisation, the League's activities from 1948 onwards were more overtly political. SYL leaders began to advocate non-compliance with colonial policies, regulations and laws. They urged followers not to take orders from government-appointed headmen. All matters relating to Somali affairs (marriage, disputes, debt, etc.) would instead be handled by SYL-approved appointees.

Umoja (1987c) provides a deeper understanding of the Somali Youth League's activities:

> By the end of 1947, the Garissa Somali Youth League was urging the people to prepare to take over the running of their country. During the first half of 1948, the activities of the SYL brought the whole region to a standstill. The party opposed colonial grazing control schemes and encouraged disregard of nationality boundaries. They also undermined the system of ethnic control through government appointed headmen and totally destroyed the confidence of the provincial administration. The people refused to pay taxes and the SYL set up courts and institutions which directly challenged the colonial system.

Similarities between the actions of the SYL and Mau Mau are clear here. But it went further as the progression to armed struggle also matched. Umoja (1987c) continues:

> More alarming for the colonialists was the training of youths in the use of firearms. Former members of the Kenya Police Force and the King's African Rifles were involved in drilling [the YSL army]. It is important to note this was the period when the Kenya Land and Freedom Army [Mau Mau] emerged in Central Kenya. The SYL recruited from the police, the army and civil service and was instrumental in the police strike of 1947. Kenyan workers were vigorously organising to confront economic exploitation, political subordination and racial discrimination. In Mombasa, the workers staged the general strike in 1947.

The political organisation of the people tightened, the colonial government intervened by proscribing the SYL at the end of 1948. The state of emergency which was temporarily relaxed after war was renewed. The NDF [Northern Frontier District] was sealed off. This included the removal of all other Kenyans and people from Ethiopia, Sudan and Somalia from the region.

The SYL can legitimately be seen as a sister organisation of Mau Mau and the struggle of the Somali and other nationalities in the region needs to be seen as part of the Kenyan people's War of Independence. Umoja (1987c) sums up people's struggle:

> The protected resistance of Somali, Boran, Orma, Rendille and the Turkana nationalities symbolises our people's heroic struggle against colonialism. Foreign intruders describe the Somali as resistors par excellence, and indeed the NFD is full of examples of the gallant stand of our people and the failure of the imperialists to consolidate their influence in the region.

It is this militancy that also explains why USA imperialism found it necessary to reduce Somalia to a state of chaos, pitting one group against another and creating poverty in a region that has survived for centuries in harsh conditions. It also explains the current Kenyan government actions in Somalia in answer to a "call to duty" from USA and Britain in return for their support. The Kenyan regime is also worried about its own staying power in the face of the militant Somali people's resistance to imperialism and their allies.

This section highlights the need for more research on the resistance activities among all regions of Kenya and among all nationalities. Just because colonial, imperialist and the comprador governments have refused to explore such resistance does not mean that the resistance did not exist. Progressive historians and activists need to investigate such resistance and also to find linkages of these resistance activities with the Mau Mau resistance. Given the resistance history of people of all nationalities, it is not surprising that people of different nationalities were active in militant trade union activities and in Mau Mau.

Contradictions Sharpen: Settlers & Homeguards Create Chaos

The contradictions in the Kenyan society between colonialism and Settlers on the one hand and people of Kenya on the other were sharpening even more by the middle of the 20th Century, with each side taking on more militant position. The colonial government had always sided with the White Settler community in Kenya and the outcome was very likely to be what was already happening in Southern and Central Africa, with an apartheid government becoming an "independent" country. The political movement of the African people was getting stronger and organised under the Kenya African Union. Militant South Asian people had been challenging white domination in Kenya over a long period and their activities supported the African struggle against the settler-colonial government establishment. Added to this was the emergence of a militant trade union movement, as shown by Makhan Singh (1969 and 1980). These anti-colonial forces became stronger and began to threaten the colonial status quo. It was then that the Settlers - with the support of the British Establishment - sought to nip the growing resistance movement in the bud and engineered the State of Emergency (War) against the people of Kenya. Pankhurst (1954?) examines these opposing forces:

> For the last thirty years the Kenya African, in the face of the bitterest settler oppression, had gradually succeeded in evolving a democratic constitutional challenge to the settler system. In the post-war years this challenge was embodied in the Kenya African Union, which provided the broad mental climate of African nationalism.

This peaceful move towards a majority African rule was seen by the Settlers as a threat to their continued rule and to their hopes of a settler-dominated government in Kenya. At the same time, there was an emerging militancy among many Africans who saw the slow progress made by the Kenya African Union (KAU) as a reason to take up arms against the colonial forces as the only way to achieve their aims. Such views were held by many who were active in the trade union movement. The Settlers underestimated the power of the organisation, ideology and activities of the trade union movement coming together with the progressive nationalist forces when they sought to challenge their growing militancy. Pankhurst (1954?) takes up the story:

... Mau Mau was already several years old when in the middle of 1952 it was overnight seized upon by the Settlers, who sought to use its existence as a manoeuvre in their long campaign to secure independence from Whitehall.

While the settlers may have used the emergence of Mau Mau as a way to force the issue to destroy them, they certainly underestimated the strength of feelings as well as the organisational capacity on the part of Kenyans to end colonialism and with it, the Settler domination of power and resources in Kenya. Inadvertently, they may have lit the fuse that blew apart the entire colonial experiment.

The Kenyan people faced not only the might of British armed forces when they sought to liberate themselves. As is the custom of colonialists and imperialists wherever they go on their plundering trips, they create artificial divisions among people and set a thousand fires to drain the strength of local forces. Thus, besides the military might, British colonialism introduced the Settlers in Kenya and they were the first internal hurdle that people faced when seeking liberation. The second hurdle was even more damaging as it created internal divisions among the people and which has had lasting impact on Kenya. These were the Homeguards, the comprador class aligned to colonialism and imperialism. Imperialism trusted the homeguards to safeguard their economic interest when the militancy of the people made independence inevitable. It was to this British-created entity that Britain handed over the country at independence and they have ever remained faithful to their imperial masters. With the support of colonialism they survived to ensure that Mau Mau activists were marginalised at independence or soon after. Kenyans saw the danger that the country faced from the Homeguards and alerted people in Britain to the danger in a letter entitled *The Kenya Terror* which was published in the *Daily Worker* (London) on September 7, 1953. The London-based Kenya Committee For Democratic Rights for Kenya Africans reproduced the letter in its Press Briefings (1952-60). Relevant sections are reproduced below:

> This letter is to greet you and to give you news from here.
>
> Things here have grown terribly bad and I am sure that you don't get the whole truth of how things are here...

The Homeguards you hear about are the greatest enemy of the country because of what those people have done together with the white Settlers, a thing which no one will forget for many hundreds of years to come.

Those among the Homeguards who had previously had disputes about land or cash crops or of any kind, took advantage of the emergency to eliminate their adversaries.

If you happen to be well off and a certain Homeguard happens to be jealous of you, this is the time when they get rid of you. They find this is a good time to exterminate these people. The Homeguards are given permission to do whatever they like, to kill anybody without reference to any higher authority.

Such things were happening more in places where people are less educated like Githunguri, Kiamuangi and Gatundu.

In their meeting the Homeguards jot down names of those of who they want to kill, take it to show the district officer who gives them a motor car at night, and then they fetch every man from his home, put them in the car and then shoot them, some in the car, others at cross-roads, leaving the bodies there, and others they take to the forests and shoot them there. Some of the bodies they take to Kiambu and in the morning they are said to be terrorists.

This sort of thing has been going on for a long time and those who are doing that work are both Homeguards and white Kenya Police Reserves.

.... Another thing is that of people who have been detained in camps like Githunguri, Kiamuangi, Uplands. Every night two or four of them are taken out by ... the Kenya Police Reserve, to be shot. Three young men from Mbari ya Kihara were shot on July 18. These bad things are still going on.

The post-independent Kenya Government, consisting of many Homeguards thus feels comfortable using the same colonial methods to eliminate those they want to deprive of life, land, property or power. The seeds of impunity were planted under colonialism.

The Necessity For Armed Resistance

Besides the economic and political reasons, there was another reason why Britain needed to keep its hold on Kenya: military needs of controlling a vast colonial empire. In addition to the need to recruit Kenyan labour for its military needs in Ethiopia and Burma, Britain saw Kenya as a strategically important base, which needed to be controlled at all cost. Aaronovitch, S. & K. (1947) examine the military needs of Britain:

> In the eyes of the imperialists the whole of Africa today is a vast military base. East Africa assumes a special importance. The strength of the national movements in India and Egypt has made Britain seek additional means of maintaining strategic control of the Indian Ocean and the Suez Canal. For control of the Suez Canal East Africa shares with Palestine the "honour" of being a key base, "The important matter is to have an agreement with the Egyptian Government whereby we can maintain base installations in Egypt and can fly in British reinforcements, say from Kenya or Palestine at short notice in an emergency." [Quoting Lt. General H. G. Martin].

The military aspect is made clear by Lord Tweedsmuir, here quoted from Aaronovitch (1947):

> ". . . In Mombasa and Freetown we have two great Imperial bases. . . . Given time and patience, we can build up a first-class African army. Who pays does not matter; at all costs, the War Office must command and control it." Lord Tweedsmuir (quoted from *African Transcripts* by Aaronovitch (1947), May, 1946).

> "Two-thirds of that empire lies in the African continent. That continent is now of vital strategic significance, and whatever the upshot of the talks with the people of India and Egypt, it will not detract from that significance, but may very well enhance it." (quoting from *East Africa and Rhodesia*, December 12th 1946).

Thus for all these reasons - land, resources, control over labour, economy, strategic and military - Britain saw a necessity to put down, by whatever force was necessary, any serious attempt on the part of the people of Kenya for independence. The people of Kenya had realised as much over the entire period of British colonialism. Thus armed war was inevitable, as Kenyans had reached a point where subjugation by colonialism was not an option.

Kaggia (1975) provides one of the answers to the question why Mau Mau found it necessary to wage armed struggle:

> Far from being a Kikuyu primitive organisation, as portrayed by our enemies, Mau Mau was an organisation formed by KAU militants who had lost faith in constitutional methods of fighting for independence. The strength of the colonial government and their vested interests in Kenya were well known to us. It was clear that the government would never give way in Kenya without a struggle. For a long time KCA [Kikuyu Central Association] and later KAU [Kenya African Union] followed constitutional methods. But instead of the Settlers or the colonial government granting any concessions, behind the scenes policies were being enacted by the government to maintain settler control. Instead of gradually introducing changes to give Africans self-rule, the government was passing harsh laws whose only purpose was to curtail African political activity. In the reserves forced labour trench-digging was introduced to keep people from political activity. Chiefs were given the authority to ban meetings and public gatherings. The government was doing everything to suppress the political independence of Africans.

Colonialism continued to consolidate its iron rule over Kenya. As the settler community's claim over land began to be seen as their natural right, and as peaceful means failed to change the situation, armed resistance became the only way to challenge the colonial status quo. Of necessity, Mau Mau had to operate underground as colonial authorities banned not only countrywide democratic political organisations, but refused to tolerate any indication of a revolutionary demand for land and freedom. Kaggia (1975) explains:

A new way of fighting had to be found. Given the settler's hold on Kenya, the resistance movement had to be secret and underground. The oath ensured secrecy of membership and activities.

Mau Mau operated underground, but used resources from legally allowed political organisations to meet its aims. Kaggia (1975) again provides an explanation:

> The secret movement had to have a way of organising. That is why we decided to hide under the umbrella of KAU.

Adekson (2007) is correct in saying that the colonial government, by creating "conditions of siege" provoked the "final armed confrontation with the government for which the revolutionary forces were unprepared". Adekson (2007) explains further:

> ... a guerrilla action is the last stage in the development of modern revolutionary warfare, and it is not provoked until much has been achieved by the leadership by way of (a) efficient underground organization, which aims at securing effective links with the population (b) adequate training of substantial numbers of cadres in the art of modem guerrilla warfare and psychological manipulation; and (c) adequate accumulation of weapons and their continued supply from certain outside sources.
>
> Until the above objectives are achieved, a revolutionary leadership is invariably content with merely building upon the dissatisfaction of the population, gradually converting this dissatisfaction into subversive action and sabotage, but never large-scale guerrilla activity.

Why, then, did the Mau Mau irregulars seek to regularize the conflict without being prepared in terms of the above three criteria? One explanation is that the emergency of October 1952 and the events following it, especially the arrest of Jomo Kenyatta and other political leaders which precipitated the armed conflict, took the revolutionary leadership by surprise. It allowed very little time for the Generals and Field Marshals of the Land Freedom Army to train and arm their men, and as the enemy closed in on the forest where they were based, the Mau Mau guerrillas had to choose between fighting and being killed. Naturally they chose the former, which meant regularising the armed conflict without as yet having an infrastructure strong enough to sustain effective guerrilla activity.

Maloba (1998) noting that Bildad Kaggia "suggests that when the Emergency was declared in October 1952, Mau Mau had not finalised its preparations for an armed uprising" goes on:

> Everything seems to have been in the preparatory stage, with emphasis placed on building intricate lines of communication and a chain of command originating from Nairobi slums and extending to far-flung rural areas of central Kenya.

At the same time, it should be noted that Mau Mau was not entirely unprepared for a final armed confrontation with the colonial forces. As is indicated in other parts of the book, preparations for an armed conflict had been on-going some years before the Declaration of Emergency, and in fact, the very act of Declaration of Emergency was itself an indication that Mau Mau forces were preparing for armed struggle in a different way. Given an ideal situation, they would have waited until all the conditions for armed conflict were in place and in this sense Adekson's analysis is correct.

The scene was thus set for an armed confrontation between the largest military might at that time and a determined guerrilla force with the support of the people and a long history of resistance.

Terrorists or Freedom Fighters?

Anderson (2017) wants to see Britain hold an open debate and discussion of what happened in Kenya in the 1950s:

> There has been a serious debate over Algeria in France over the past couple of years, after admissions that the army was involved in torture and other violations. If the French can do it, so should we.

Kenyans who disagree on other aspects of the conflict concur: .

> There is a sense of national denigration and anger, whether people were Mau Mau or not, that the British have never admitted the importance of what happened. The British Government should recognise that it was a war and not merely a civil disorder, admit to the suppression that took place and apologise", David Anderson (2005b) says.

In the absence of an open debate, Mau Mau has been presented as terrorists by colonialists. So the question of who was the real terrorist in the Kenya's War of Independence becomes an important question.. Field Marshall Muthoni gives Mau Mau's perspectives on this and McGhie looks at archival records to show what the British actually did in Kenya. The answer to the question, "Who were terrorists in Kenya under colonialism" then becomes obvious.

First, Mau Mau's Field Marshall Muthoni (2007) poses a question for all:

> Who is the terrorist? Is it the one that fights back for their land and dignity through whatever means are available, or is it the one who forcefully takes that which belongs to another and treats them like dirt?

Kenyans or Mau Mau never took any land belonging to Britain, but had to fight "for their land and dignity through whatever means are available", she added Such actions are not considered terrorism under international laws, which see them as legitimate struggles to fight enemy aggression and invasion.

On the other side are the actions of the British government. Earlier sections of the book looked at the stealing of Kenyan land by British colonial authorities who then gave it to European Settlers free of charge or at a very low price, leaving the real owners landless. But British acts of terrorism do not end there. The brutality of the colonialists, hidden for decades, gradually began to be released and exposed as the real acts of terrorism in Kenya. Many records and books support this: first, Monbiot (2012) provides a succinct summary from Elkins (2005):

Elkins reveals that the British detained not 80,000 Kikuyu, as the official histories maintained, but almost the entire population of one and a half million people, in camps and fortified villages. There, thousands were beaten to death or died from malnutrition, typhoid, tuberculosis and dysentery. In some camps almost all the children died.

The inmates were used as slave labour. Above the gates were edifying slogans, such as "Labour and freedom" and "He who helps himself will also be helped". Loudspeakers broadcast the national anthem and patriotic exhortations. People deemed to have disobeyed the rules were killed in front of the others. The survivors were forced to dig mass graves, which were quickly filled. Unless you have a strong stomach I advise you to skip the next paragraph.

Interrogation under torture was widespread. Many of the men were anally raped, using knives, broken bottles, rifle barrels, snakes and scorpions. A favourite technique was to hold a man upside down, his head in a bucket of water, while sand was rammed into his rectum with a stick. Women were gang-raped by the guards. People were mauled by dogs and electrocuted. The British devised a special tool which they used for first crushing and then ripping off testicles. They used pliers to mutilate women's breasts. They cut off inmates' ears and fingers and gouged out their eyes. They dragged people behind Land Rovers until their bodies disintegrated. Men were rolled up in barbed wire and kicked around the compound.

Elkins provides a wealth of evidence to show that the horrors of the camps were endorsed at the highest levels. The governor of Kenya, Sir Evelyn Baring, regularly intervened to prevent the perpetrators from being brought to justice. The colonial secretary, Alan Lennox-Boyd, repeatedly lied to the House of Commons. This is a vast, systematic crime for which there has been no reckoning.

McGhie (2002) quotes John Nottingham:

John Nottingham, a district colonial officer at the time who stayed on in Kenya, said compensation could not wait because the victims were now mostly in their 80s."What went on in the Kenya camps, the Kenya villages was brutal, savage torture by people who have to be condemned as war criminals. I feel ashamed to have come from a Britain that did what it did."

The word "terrorism" is perhaps inadequate to describe what Britain did in Kenya as it does not reflect the level of organised massacres, looting and torture on an industrial scale. Mau Mau activists and today's workers, peasants and progressive individuals are clear about the crimes committed by Britain in Kenya. But the ruling elite would rather the question about who is a terrorist remain unanswered - or even unasked. The question goes to the very essence of the Kenyan War of Independence and Mau Mau's role in it. Ignorance, misunderstanding and imperialist propaganda have created incorrect and misleading perceptions about both. Hence, it is necessary to see events and history based on evidence and facts so a rational and critical assessment can be made about the struggle in which thousands perished and millions are suffering even to this day.

The colonial crimes against people of the world need to be seen in their totality, not as individual events. Richard Gott (2001) sums up the essence of British Empire:

> We now know that the British Empire was essentially a Hitlerian project on a grand scale, involving military conquest and dictatorship, extermination and genocide, martial law and "special courts", slavery and forced labour, and, of course, concentration camps and the transoceanic migration of peoples. Whatever way we now look at Empire, this vision must remain dominant.

Kenya's experience of this "Hitlerian project" needs to be seen in its overall context of what Britain was up to with its tool of exploitation - the British Empire. Its impact on India is well captured by Tharoor (2016). Yet the atrocities of the British Empire itself need to be seen in the context of those of the other European colonial powers such as Belgium in the Congo and Germany in Namibia and Tanganyika (Mainland Tanzania). Taken together, all these provide a realistic history of how Europe exploited and destroyed countries around the world. This explains the rise of Europe as a world economic leader with innovative industries. But the raw materials, labour and resources came from the rest of the world which was then condemned to centuries of underdevelopment. This is graphically illustrated in the case of India by Tharoor (2016):

> At the beginning of the eighteenth century ... India's share of the world economy was 23 per cent, as large as all of Europe put together. (It had been 27 per cent in 1700, when the Mughal Emperor Aurangzeb's treasury raked in £100 million in tax revenues alone.) By the time British departed India, it had dropped to just over 3 per cent; The reason was simple: India was governed for the benefit of Britain. Britain's rise for 200 years was financed by its depredations in India ... Britain's Industrial Revolution was built on the destruction of India's thriving manufacturing industries.

Just as the British colonial depredation in Kenya needs to be seen in a broader perspective, in terms of actions in India, and also in the context of European plunder around the world, so does the resistance to these attacks need to be seen in their global and historical context. Mau Mau and the Kenyan War of Independence should be seen in the context of resistance to colonialism in Africa. The nearest comparison is the Algerian War of Independence, which took place at around the same time (1954-62). Adekson (2007) compares the approaches of FLN (National Liberation Front or Front de Libération Nationale, FLN) in Algeria and Mau Mau in Kenya:

> Mau Mau in Kenya surely was as revolutionary in its approach as FLN in Algeria. Differences certainly existed between the two, but these differences were of degree rather than of kind. And once the basic point is accepted that the Mau Mau activity and the FLN revolt were both examples of revolutionary wars, we can then proceed to analyze whatever similarities and differences existed between them.

Adekson (2007) continues:

> ... both the Mau Mau and the Algerian revolts had one objective goal, which was to secure, through armed revolt, the independence of the territories concerned from the colonial and imperial power.

It is necessary if one is to understand the reality of Mau Mau to see it in its geographical and historical context. Clearing minds of colonial-inspired propaganda about people's resistance is the first step. The next step is to investigate facts and evidence to establish the reality of people's resistance to colonialism and imperialism.

Illustrations 1: Colonial Violence

British Camel Constabulary. Forces of Mohamed Abdille Hassan's Darwish Front "trounced the Camel Constabulary and killed its commanding Officer in 1914" (Umoja, 1987c).

Kenya Colonial Police Air Wing

Trade Unions Light A Spark

Trade Unions and Mau Mau

Documenting mass dissemination of crimes of colonialism, capitalism and imperialism have become easier today with the use of social media which are bringing to light hidden facts. Dissemination of facts about the atrocities and crimes committed by the imperialism, whether in Ireland, Malaysia, Vietnam or Kenya, has become part of the daily dose of information available to the millions using Twitter and Facebook. Some examples on Twitter are Crimes of Colonialism (@crimesofcolonialism), Crimes of Britain (@crimesofbrits), Crimes of the US (@crimesofUS), Crimes of France (@crimesoffrance), Empire Exposed (@empireExposed). They bring the reality of imperialist exploitation to a generation not taught the real history that has shaped their lives. The publication of the book, Crimes of Britain: the Book in 2017 takes this information to the print medium. It is not only the crimes of colonialism that are getting wider publicity. People's resistance to colonialism and imperialism, hidden expertly by imperialism, is also now becoming part of people's consciousness. Among important media that have helped to reshape and correct people's understanding of their past, as well as the real meaning of the current exploitative workings of the military-industrial partnership led by USA, are teleSUR, Sputnik, RT, CGTN and PressTV among others. It is for this reason that many of these are under attack by imperialism. Imperialism tries to hide a real understanding of history of capitalism and people's struggles, as Petras and Veltmeyer (2018) point out:

> The history of capitalism is a history of class struggle. This is because each advance in the march of capital, every assault made on working people in the quest for private profit - the driving force of capitalist development - brings about a strategic political response in the popular sector, resistance against the destructive forces engendered by this development.

"The book explores the history of the British Empire and how Britain's foreign policy of today is rooted in it. It chronologically goes through the history of every country Britain has colonised, invaded and subverted" – Book publicity on Twitter [Accessed: 13-11-17).

An important aspect of people's resistance that imperialism seeks to hide is the role of trade unions in the fight for the liberation of workers from capitalist exploitation. What is often forgotten. What is often ignored or forgotten is the key role that the trade unions played in the War of Independence. Working class activism helped build anti-imperialist solidarity and gave an ideological framework that eventually became the economic and political demands of the War of Independence. The working class came from all parts of the country and from all nationalities and their participation in the struggles made this a national struggle. It suited colonialism and imperialism, as part of the divide and rule policy, to ignore that the working class had anything to do with the War of Independence. And it is no surprise that Kenyan comprador governments after independence, reflecting imperialist interests, have similarly ignored the role of trade unions. Trade unions were early targets of the Kenyatta government. Indeed, the concept of class is all but absent from imperialist interpretation of colonial history. This then leads to a misrepresentation of the aims and methods used by the liberation forces. But Kenya is not alone in the role of the working class being ignored and underplayed. It is the same situation for the Cuban Revolution where imperialism seeks to downplay this class resistance. As this is an important issue that affects perhaps all struggles against imperialism, it is appropriate to dwell a little on the Cuban experience as it has many similarities to the situation in Kenya. First, Quinn (2015) provides the context:

> ... there remains surprisingly little documented and systematic analysis of the contribution of Cuban workers to the eventual overthrow of the detested Batista regime. Yet, as this engaging and meticulously researched book [Cushion, 2016] amply demonstrates, a militant and well-organized movement, often operating independently of union leaders, played a pivotal role in the victory of the Cuban insurrection, not only through the final coup de grace of the 1959 general strike, but in myriad actions that served to defend workers' interests, resist state repression, and materially support the armed struggle. Thus there was a third arm to the revolutionary forces, a movement, which has been consistently ignored by general public and historians of Cuba alike.

Quinn (2015) then addresses another issue that is relevant to Kenya too. This is to do with the buying out of trade union leaders by imperialism in order to render the unions ineffective in resisting oppression. This aspect becomes particularly important in the post-independence history of Kenya when shop stewards took over leadership of union activities. Many of the strikes and other actions by workers as documented in Mwakenya's *Register of Resistance* (1986), were organised and led by shop stewards when KANU imposed leaders favourable to itself on the trade union movement. In this context, Quinn (2015) reinforces Cushion (2016)'s definition of "organised labour":

> Steve Cushion's work calls for a broader definition of organized labour, looking beyond the formal structures of the trade union federation to include the multiplicity of unofficial, informal structures through which ordinary workers defend their interests. This includes the activities of shop stewards, independent minded union officials, as well as clandestine networks of militants, all of which make up the wider labour movement and interact together to produce the dynamic of industrial action.

Viewed within this expanded definition of organised labour, the record of working class in Kenya acquires a new perspective, particularly in the period before unions became better organised and led. Just as in the case of Cuba as Quinn (2015) records, in Kenya also "the final victory of the revolutionary forces should be viewed as the result of a combination of armed guerrilla action and mass support". However, the working class and Mau Mau in Kenya were overpowered by the British military presence and imperialism's use of its creation, the comprador class, programmed to prevent a revolutionary change.

And yet the part played by the organised working class was crucial in driving colonialism out of Kenya and instilling ideas of anti-imperialist struggles among people. The missing link of the contribution of organised working class was the aim of Cushion (2016) when he says:

> This book therefore challenges the notion that the revolution emerged from a rural guerrilla struggle in which the organized workers played no role and that the workers who did participate did as individual citizens rather than as part of an organized labour movement ... It is my intention to give organized labour its due credit for the role it

played in the overthrow of the Batista dictatorship.

And that is the challenge to all activists and historians - "to give organised labour in Kenya the due respect for the role it played" (Cushion, 2016) in the War of Independence in Kenya. And that can be done only within the context of class analysis and class struggles before and after independence. At particular times in Kenyan history, the class aspect was not the dominant one. But the involvement of working class in that struggle was partly an aspect of their struggle against capitalism, which imposed poor and life-threatening working conditions. Release from this capitalist bondage required, first of all, national independence. It was the all-important contribution of the trade union movement, and of Makhan Singh in particular, that linked workers' economic demands with political demands as part of a working class agenda.

British colonial policy and the White Settler politics had both been focused on the need to ensure that cheap labour was regularly available for plantations, industries, settler farms and colonial government needs. This fact has again not been given the significant role it played in the political development in Kenya. While colonialism needed to take away land from peasants, they also needed labour for the capitalist venture to survive and prosper. Clayton and Savage (1974) describe these aspects graphically:

> The history of a country can be likened to a rope composed of strands of several different colours, at any one section of the rope one or two strands may appear on the surface, a third and fourth may lie below to reappear a little distance away. In Kenya's colonial history three strands form the rope - land, labour and the action and reaction of races to one another, expressed consciously in politics. All three strands are necessary for a complete understanding of Kenyan history, but while the land and racial political strands in various periods have been the subject of close study, the study of labour has not yet received the same attention.

Thus land and labour issues in Kenya had a profound influence on Kenyan politics, not only in terms of what the Kenyan resistance forces did, but also what colonialism did and what policies they used to support their economic interests. Again, Clayton and Savage (1974) fill in the historical gaps in conventional telling of Kenyan history:

The need to induce Africans to work, to leave their tribal societies and customs and to hire themselves to immigrant, largely British, employers also produced the very widest consequences at the local level. The size of the tribal land units, known as reserves, was the subject of early controversy, European farmers pressing for small reserves with limited funds spent on their development in order to maintain a supply of men who were obliged to work elsewhere. Taxation, instituted initially as a normal feature of administration, was used as a tool to increase labour supply. Personal identity documents were framed with labour retention and discipline as their aim. African education for many years was planned only to equip men for the semi-skilled labour market, and for a long time social services of various types existed primarily to assist the labour supply. The degree of compulsion retained by the government for the supply of its own labour needs was on occasions planned with an eye to indirect assistance to the local private employer. Trade union, minimum wage and workmen's compensation legislation were all introduced later than in other British African territories. Even relatively minor matters, the size of a proposed coinage, railway freight charges, restrictions on African dances, pass laws, and the appointment, promotion or transfer of Colonial Service officials were often influenced by the politics of the labour market.

Britain introduced capitalism and with it came classes, class divisions and, unintentionally perhaps, class struggles to Kenya. It created a vastly unequal society and then obscured the very existence of what they had created. The real beneficiaries of capitalism were well-hidden thousands of miles away in London, New York and various Western European capitals. Their local allies, initially the Settlers and later the Black elite of independence, also benefited from this imperialist venture. The Settlers were gifted land and were then able to use their unfairly acquired wealth to venture into other areas of the economy in manufacturing, import and export, banking and finance with the support of Western banking and finance. On the other side, Kenyan peasants and workers became the victims of these new class divisions, losing their land and being forced into either a serf-like situation in the countryside or as super-exploited workers tied to the Settlers as cheap labour — in the earlier period they were physically tied down with the hated kipande[9] around their

9 Kipande: "The registration card that all African males were required to carry under

necks. South Asians communities were allowed to become petty traders, civil servants and skilled workers in many industries as their skills were needed for capitalist exploitation. They became the buffers for European domination against the African population of workers, landless peasants, the newly created "squatters" and the under-employed or unemployed workers. It was this class formation that the British sought to hide from the people. They encouraged a colour, racial or tribal interpretation of what was happening in the society, as these divisions were easier to exploit than divisions by class. This enabled them to divide Kenyan people along tribal lines as part of the new social set-up, also encouraging the African peasants and workers to see the South Asians as their enemy. At the time of independence, they used this distorted interpretation of social reality to gradually incorporate the new petty-bourgeoisie into the power structure as a way of defeating the ideology of Mau Mau and undermining trade union aspirations.

The struggle of working class in Kenya has a long history and is linked with the politics of struggle for independence – and beyond. It is also linked to the input from South Asian Kenyans in terms of working class struggles from India. Gupta (1981) traces some aspects of this history and the links with India:

> Ever since its origin the trade-union movement in Kenya had a sharply pronounced anti-colonial character; it developed in the struggle for national independence, for political rights and freedom. During the absence of political parties, workers' organisations were the only mass organisations representing and defending the interest of the broad masses. Struggle for the rights of the workers tended to be the struggle against the foreign capitalists who controlled the means of production.
>
> For many years it was difficult to separate the trade-union movement from political struggle against colonialism. During the post second world war period, particularly during emergency (1952-61) many trade-union functionaries developed into prominent political leaders and later became high ranking statesmen of Kenya.

---

the 1915 Registration Ordinance...the primary purpose was to enhance labour recruitment and control". Maxon and Ofcansky (2000).

Unlike many other Asian and African countries, trade unionism in Kenya originated under the influence and direct participation of Asian trade unionists, specifically Makhan Singh. The African unionists learnt union activities and assimilated the ideology and methods of the Asians. During the emergency, i.e., 1952-1961, Kenyan trade-union movement came under the influence of right-wing Socialist and Christian trade unions of Britain and the USA. The International Confederation of Free Trade Unions, through finances and advisers, gained control over the movement.

That explains the progressive period of the trade union movement before independence and its subversion by imperialism after independence.

Organising for Economic and Political Rights

There are two key strands to Kenya's War of Independence: Mau Mau and the trade union movement. The contribution of both to independence and to the struggle for rights of working class have been hidden and distorted. While the two complemented each other and fought together to undermine colonialism, imperialism has managed to give them separate identities running parallel to each other, never influencing and supporting each other. The question raised later in the book is why did Mau Mau succeed in getting independence when the earlier nationality-based resistance did not. Part of the answer is that class formation and class resistance were consolidated in the latter period. This resulted in the involvement of a militant trade union movement in the War of Independence, which then provided nation-wide perspective lacked by the nationality-based struggles of the earlier times. In addition, the trade union movement brought the perspective of class and class struggle to the forefront and this overcame the colonial-inspired divisions into "tribes" and ethnic groups.

And yet workers' and trade union activities were not confined to the rights of workers in terms of wages and conditions of employment. True, these were the essence of trade unionism, but they realised that these rights could not be achieved without active participation in the national political movement. Given the vacuum created by colonial laws which restricted nation-wide political organisations, the trade union movement filled this vacuum to give a boost to political demands of all Kenyans. In this way, workers' struggles were very closely linked to national politics and gave an impetus and guidance to national political movements. In addition, it supplied many leaders of national political organisations, who came with experience in trade unionism and awareness of classes, class contradictions and class struggles. This was greatest contribution of the trade union movement to the War of Independence and to Mau Mau. While this book does not focus on trade unions as such, it is important to see their involvement in national politics and national political organisation so as to understand better the War of Independence and the activities of Mau Mau. It should be noted that working class activism began almost as soon as capitalism created working class in Kenya, as Makhan Singh (1979) shows. Here it is important to look at some organisational aspects of organised trade union movement. The following section summarises some national political organisational work of the trade union movement. Strikes in individual industries as well as general strikes (across industries or county-wide) were key tools for organising workers politically and this experience created conditions of national political activism. The following section is based on Gupta (1981) and aims to indicate the political aspects of trade unions and how it fed into the work of national political organisations and into Mau Mau.

1921

The Kenyan workers demonstrated their strength in 1921 by forming the first politico trade-union organization, the East African Association (EAA) under the leadership of a telephone operator, Harry Thuku. The East African Association (EAA) organised the resistance of plantation workers to fight against the employers' proposal, to reduce wages from 4 pence to 2.5 pence daily. There was also a government proposal to raise the Poll Tax. The Africans called their first protest meeting at Dagoretti on 24 June 1921 to protest against these proposals. This was followed by many meetings attended by thousands of Africans. In one meeting at Nairobi 20,000 workers enrolled as members of East African Association. Encouraged by this response the EAA gave a call for the first African general strike. The strike was a great success as "Thousands quit their jobs. Workers on European farms and plantations stopped work. Domestic servants refused to cook and serve food for their British employers".

1930s

In the 1930s, the trade-union movement amongst the African workers took a new turn. Under the leadership of Makhan Singh, a Marxist, an Asian worker union was set up in 1934 on East African level - the Labour Trade Union of East Africa (LTUEA). Ever since the inception of LTUEA, Makhan Singh attempted to unite African and Asian workers. This was a difficult task. Because the Asians were identified with the exploiters and were paid higher salaries. In most cases the interests of African workers clashed with those of the Asian workers. Naturally the Asian-African workers' unity could not be achieved but Makhan Singh succeeded in making the African workers conscious of trade unionism. The Asian workers' struggle influenced the African workers.

1937

Various strikes led by LTUEA took place, including one for 62 days in April. A settlement was reached with employers agreeing to a wage-increase of between 15-22%, an eight-hour week and reinstatement of all workers. [Makhan Singh,1969].

In April 1937 all Indian artisans employed in the building works demanded higher wages and to press their demand stopped all works on the new buildings in the towns. The Africans took keen interest in the struggle of the Indian workers. The Native Affairs Department Annual Report for 1937 recording this change states: "Natives have as yet no organised trade unions but there is no doubt that they took a great interest in the Indian strikes and not long after they would endeavour to form their own Union."

This struggle of the Indians helped the African political leaders realise the importance of trade unionism. So far their trade union activities were compounded with political activities. The KCA was active among workers as well. Soon they formed trade unions. Scattered workers in various industrial and service units were collected and organised under professional umbrellas. These groups became centres of class struggle, playing the historical role of economic emancipation of the working class. Initially trade unions developed out of spontaneous attempts of the workers to fight for better living conditions and higher wages. [Thus there was a] spontaneous general strike in Mombasa in 1939...

1939

Realising the importance of labour organisation, the KCA was cooperating with the Labour Trade Union of East Africa. African workers joined the Union in large numbers. In 1939 Makhan Singh celebrated May Day. This was the first time that a workers meeting was held on the workers day. The KCA President, Jesse Kariuki joined the meeting along with African workers and spoke on the occasion. Similarly three months later in July 1939 some of the KCA leaders attended the 3rd Conference of the Labour Trade Unions of East Africa. Jesse Kariuki and George K. Ndegwa, Secretary of the KCA were elected members of LTUEA.

The most significant development in Kenya trade-union movement was the August 1939 Mombasa strike. The strike began with the municipality workers for higher wages, and quickly spread to electricity, docks, post and telegraph workers in the town. Nearly 6000 African and Asian workers stopped work. The strike was sponsored by the LTUEA and supported by KCA. The LTUEA and the KCA held a solidarity meeting of Asian and African workers in Nairobi. To break the strike the government used all the high-handed methods. One hundred and fifty workers were arrested. However, the strike was a success and ended in workers' favour.

The African working class gained an invaluable experience from the Mombasa strike. It was reflected in the subsequent years' struggles. Mombasa workers provided most militant, bold and far-sighted leaders capable of leading the working class in uncompromising struggle against imperialism and exploitation of both local and foreign capitalism.

1945 - POST-SECOND WORLD WAR DEVELOPMENTS

The trade union movement in Kenya grew faster after the Second World War. The anti-imperialist movement throughout the world had gathered great momentum and working-class consciousness had greatly increased. During and after the war, there was a phenomenal rise in the urban population. Similarly there was a development of industries and other new fields of employment. The changes increased the numerical strength of the wage earning working class. On the other hand, paucity of land in the reserves pushed more and more Africans to towns.

...

The 1940s also saw the growth of nationalist movement. The ideas of democratic reforms bred by British pronouncements during the war and accession to power of the Labour Party in England helped generate political consciousness and confidence. During this period the African nationalism succeeded in over-stepping the tribal limits. The trade unions, which helped in deviating the movement from taking tribal form, gained both in strength and membership. As Barnett points out there was "a good deal of overlap in both the leadership and rank and file membership of Kenya's African political, trade union and Church school movements. Their "cross-linking" was tending to produce a single movement." The government reports also refer to the close link of trade unions and political movement. This can be seen in 1946-47 Report of the African Affairs Department of Kenya (page 49). It is stated that "For the first time Africans began to hold meetings, numbering frequently as many as 5000 people, in the Open spaces in the location (African areas)... At first these meetings were concerned chiefly with labour conditions of Africans in Nairobi but they gradually became more and more political and concerned principally with conditions outside Nairobi."

Trade-union leaders were not silent observers to Kenyan armed struggle during Mau Mau movement. The Land and Freedom Army's General China commended their work. He writes: "At that time the trade unions had the most militant leaders and were the most active groups working for independence in the city" (Itote, 1967).

1948-52

...Despite the obstacles there was a vigorous growth of trade union organisations in Kenya during 1948-52...

The rapid development of the trade-union movement made Kenyan government extremely nervous. Workers were posing threat to Settlers as well as colonial system. European Settlers charged that trade unions were being used as a weapon of political agitation and asked the government to check this tendency. Bills after bills were rushed through the Legislative Council to limit the possibilities of the growth of trade union organisations and activities. Arrests, sentences, banishment, "frame ups" and the armed force were utilised by the imperialists in a vain attempt to crush the spirit of workers of Kenya. In 1948 the hands of the Registrar of Societies were strengthened through amendment to Trade Unions and Trade Disputes Act...

The Settlers were very worried. The trade union militants were dominating national politics. Their influence on struggle for independence was increasing every day. In September 1948, Makhan Singh, the Secretary of Labour Trade Union of East Africa organised a cost of living and wages conference, the first of its kind ever held in Kenya. Delegates from more than 16 trade unions and associations participated, representing more than 10,000 African and Asian workers. The British government struck at the trade-union movement by the immediate arrest of Makhan Singh. A deportation order was made out against him despite the fact that he was a legal citizen of Kenya having been resident in Kenya since 1927 apart from a short stay in India.

In January 1949 the government and railway administration workers were banned from taking part in political activity or joining political association which, in effect seriously hampered their participation in trade-union activity and organisation. Importing of trade-union journals and periodicals from Europe and other parts of the world was also prohibited.

These restrictions had been introduced because the working class had become champions of national forces and was consistently raising the demand for loosening the fetters of British colonialism, for ending racial inequalities and privileges of the immigrant groups. The urban working class was becoming the leading factor in the development of nationalist uprising for independence. On the rural scene the landless farm workers were growing in numbers and intensifying the class contradictions. The rural and urban working classes provided the basis for the freedom movement, as they increasingly fought against colonial relationship and economic exploitation.

The increase in the number of trade-union membership pointed to a trend in political radicalism amongst the working classes. During this period trade-union leaders expressed their preference for militant nationalism. They emphasised the need for a demand for total liberation and armed struggle to achieve it. Those who supported this trend associated themselves with Mau Mau movement and the others remained at the periphery of the national struggle with commitment for independence but not for armed struggle. Kenyatta, belonged to the latter group. Bildad Kaggia, Fred Kubai, Makhan Singh, belonged to the former group.

The struggle against imperialism thus objectively became the primary aim of the Kenyan proletariat. To them imperialism was represented by the European farmers, businessmen and bureaucrats.

In Kenya the national liberation movement and working class struggle for the better conditions were interwoven and cannot be separated. Every struggle of the working class was struggle against colonial subjugation.

During the emergency in Kenya trade union movement made most rapid strides. Unfortunately, the KFL'S [Kenya Federation of

Labour] financial development was financially linked with ICFTU [International Confederation of Free Trade Unions].

The above section indicates the need for bringing the resistance against colonialism right from its first steps in Kenya so as to get a better perspective of the Mau Mau period of resistance.

Classes and Class Struggle

While the British and Settler interests may have helped to hide the class divisions in the Kenya they had created, the objective facts on the ground could not be denied. Workers of all nationalities and "colours" had acted in their class interest and fought the capitalist system so as to gain their rights as workers and as an exploited class. Trade unions, ironically, got their militant outlook and organisational strength from South Asian Kenyan workers some of who were imported for their skills from colonial India to build the railways. Little did the colonialists realise that among the skills and experience that these workers would bring would include resistance to capitalism and colonialism. They came not only with their various skills needed by colonialism, but also with the ideology and experience from the struggles of the Indian working class against British and Portuguese colonialism in India. Thus capitalism created the proletariat, which, when organised as a militant force, became the source of a major challenge to colonialism, capitalism and imperialism. When this force joined hands with the militant nationalist and political forces in Kenya, the end of colonialism became inevitable. Had the armed stage not been forced upon the people of Kenya by the declaration of the Emergency, this new force would have carried on the anti-colonial, anti-capitalist struggle in Kenya perhaps with different weapons and with different results.

It is perhaps appropriate to ask why the earlier anti-colonial struggles of Kenyan nationalities did not succeed in defeating colonialism and why Mau Mau succeeded in doing so. After all, the former were fierce in their resistance, had the support of all people and had won important battles against colonialism.

What distinguishes the early resistance to colonialism from that in the 20th Century is the entry of workers and their resistance, *as a class*, against colonialism. This resistance had a number of distinguishing features that proved critical in the struggle against colonialism and imperialism. First, the organised workers saw their struggle as not only against colonialism but against capitalism and imperialism as well. This clear identification of the enemy helped them to focus on key aspects of their struggle. They also benefited from ideas and experiences of struggles from USSR and India, among others. They learnt from the earlier Ghadar struggles in Kenya and worldwide as well as participating in the Second Imperialist War. This gave them a class as well as national and an internationalist perspective. It provided them with links with international labour movements and organisations, which again added a new dimension to the Kenyan struggle.

Another impact of the entry of working class into the War of Independence was that workers were spread all over the country and so could not be so easily isolated and defeated in one part of the country. Any attack on them became a national attack against all workers throughout the country.

In addition, the lessons of organisation and experiences in class struggles in one part of the country spread all over the country, with the railway network and railway workers carrying messages of worker resistance and strikes to workers all over the country. The aspect of trade union and Mau Mau communication systems is looked at further by Durrani, S. (2006). This gave the working class solidarity and a national perspective. It also meant that colonialism could no longer impose docile leaders on workers who had established the principle of democratic elections long before colonialism was forced to do so countrywide at a political level.

At the same time, the working class movement had strong support from peasants who had struggled over a very long time against colonialism. On its own, peasant resistance had been isolated and suppressed by colonialism. However, when the peasant militancy was added to national working class militancy, the united resistance became a mighty force that colonialism could not contain. A new dimension in the countryside is plantation and farm workers who could no longer be isolated as they got solidarity and support from trade unions.

The trade union movement and Mau Mau also benefited from the nationality-based political work of earlier generation. Harry Thuku and later KAU leaders had addressed mass meetings and formed organisations that formed the basis of later struggles. They politicised people at mass meetings and through newspapers. The establishment of independent schools movement provided a new generation of young people who were literate and were able to play an active role in different ways. Similarly, independent churches had challenged the monopoly of Christian churches, which received the blessings of colonial administration. It is therefore important not to see the War of Independence and Mau Mau and the contribution of trade unions in isolation from these earlier strands of resistance. The earlier struggles, including the massive resistance of peasants, had provided fertile ground on which the new ideas, organisations and leadership flourished.

The working class movement's contribution to the national struggle was evident in other ways too. By its very nature, it was able to transcend the artificial enmity created by colonialism between nationalities, races, gender and other divisive tactics. Workers came from all nationalities and included men and women and had national consciousness and could act nationally.

Colonialism attacked nationalities and peasants by taking away their land; workers had no land; colonialism burnt and looted peasant properties: workers had none; colonialism confiscated peasant livestock and threatened their livelihood: workers had no livestock. Colonialism's only answer to people's resistance was brute force and imprisonment in concentration camps of entire populations. While this brought much suffering to communities, it also exposed the real nature of colonialism and created a resistance mentality in people.

Just as it had no answer to people's resistance and struggle for independence in India, colonialism had no answer when trade unions in Kenya used their class weapons to challenge capitalism and colonialism and joined hands with other forces opposed to colonialism. The only weapon in the colonial arsenal, which they used against workers, was brute force. But the workers' response began to hurt their profits.

It would seem that imperialists learn no lessons from history as their solution to any of their perceived problems even today - as in Afghanistan, Iraq,

Syria, Libya, Somalia - is to use their armed forces rather than seek political solutions. This approach perhaps keeps their economies going via military spending, but causes untold damage to lives of people around the world, including in imperialist countries themselves.

In the case of Kenya, the use of such military tactics *before* Mau Mau took up arms indicates that the British government had decided in advance to suppress people's demands for independence by force, as they did in Malaysia and other places. Referring to Mau Mau as terrorists was simply a way of hiding the colonial government's own military and colonial ambitions. But attacking workers in this way was counter-productive. It was like hitting themselves as, in attacking workers, they attacked their own economic interests. Their profits were based on exploiting the labour of workers and if workers stopped producing, this also stopped profits for capitalists. Thus capitalism had created a weapon that workers could use against capitalism itself. The greatest weapon that the working class brought to the colonial battlefield - potentially more powerful than the colonial armoured cars and planes — was the actual and threatened withdrawal of their labour on which capitalist exploitation was based.

But these potential advantages that the resistance movement possessed were not enough, on their own, to weaken or defeat colonialism which was strong and could not be overcome so easily. There was a need for critical ingredients, which could act as a spark to ignite a national liberation movement. And the trade unions provided this critical catalyst: working class ideology, organisation and experience from active struggles. As Singh (1969) says:

> Kenya's trade union movement has always been a part of her national struggle for resisting British imperialist colonial rule, for winning national independence, for consolidating the independence after winning it, and for bringing prosperity to the workers and peoples of Kenya.

However this truth about trade union contribution has not been accepted in many Kenyan history books. Maloba (1998) recognises the link between trade union movement and the political movement for independence:

The political energies of Nairobi African residence was again aroused in 1949 with the formation of the East African Trade Union Congress by Makhan Singh and Fred Kubai. This union would be banned in 1950. The significance of this phase of trade unionism is that it led to a revitalization of the KAU in Nairobi, the center of widespread urban discontent. This onslaught on the KAU's complacency was led by two young trade union activists, Bildad Kaggia and Fred Kubai. Both of these men were closer in temperament and radicalism to the youth in the Nairobi slums than to the established African elite in the KAU, the churches, and the administration.

Although Maloba comes closer to understanding Mau Mau than many earlier studies, he does not extend this to see the overall picture of the behind-the-scene impact of organised labour movement as an important contributory factor in the War of Independence.

It was the trade union movement that saw the links between worker struggles and national liberation as the only way of resolving the contradiction between capitalists and workers. Their awareness of the nature of their enemy is indicated in a 1936 leaflet by the Labour Trade Union of Kenya, reproduced below from Makhan Singh (1969):

The struggle between capitalists and workers has started in earnest

Our worker comrades! Come forward! March ahead! If you do not march ahead today, then remember that you will be crushed under the heels of capitalists tomorrow. Workers should have a united stand and should stand up strongly against the capitalists so that they should not ever have courage to attempt to exploit workers again, nor to take away workers' rights from them.

Note: The workers of M/s Karsan Ladha have gone on strike for higher wages. It has been reported that the strike situation is becoming serious. This has now become a question of life or death for workers'

Labour Trade Union of Kenya November 1936

But this was not the first strike in Kenya. Singh (1969) records some of the earliest strikes by workers - of all nationalities and races - in Kenya, for example:

- 1900: Railway workers strike – interestingly, this was initiated by European subordinate staff and later on "probably joined by some Indian and African workers". The strike started in Mombasa and spread to other centres along the railway line.

- 1902: Strike by African police constables.

- 1908: Strikes of African workers at a Government farm at Mazeras and those engaged in loading railway engines.

- 1908: Strike of railway Indian workers at Kilindini harbour.

- 1908: Strike by rickshaw-pullers in Nairobi.

- 1912: Strike by African boat workers in Mombasa.

- 1912: Strike by employees of the railway goods shed in Nairobi.

- 1912: Persistent refusal by thousands of African workers on Settlers' farms.

There is perhaps no better record of the struggle waged by workers and their organisations than the two pioneering books by Makhan Singh (1969 and 1980). These books provide evidence of workers' militancy, which then fed into the liberation movement. It is a commentary of today's neo-colonial state of Kenya that instead of making the books part of the curricula in schools, colleges and universities, they have been allowed to go out of print.

Gachihi (1986) looks at the contribution of trade unions:

> Trade unionism among the African workers grew as a result of the appalling conditions that these workers found themselves in. The need arose to form a strong front that could represent the workers' interests effectively. In 1947 the African Workers Federation was formed under the presidency of Chege Kibachia, an African veteran

trade unionist. Sporadic strikes continued right through 1947 with demands for better working conditions for African workers. These protests were flung countrywide, unlike other associations whose influence would only be strong locally. In that year, for instance, Mombasa was paralysed when the entire African labour force downed its tools in a strike.

Some highlights from the history of the labour movement may provide a better understanding of the role of the trade union movement in Kenya's liberation struggle. The Kenya Committee For Democratic Rights (1952-60) provides details of some action during the 1955 strike in Mombasa:

- 10,000 dockworkers and others strike at Mombasa. Troops move into docks while police patrol town and docks. Troops unload military stores. Strike spread to oil companies, brewery, transport firms and aluminum companies. 4-3-55.

- European office workers help unload liner, Kenya Castle. 5-3-55.

- 200 Striking dockworkers stone European Mombasa Club and European cars. They also stop buses and force passengers to leave. Police reinforcements called out, two companies of the Royal Iniskilling Fusiliers leave Nairobi by train for Mombasa, and further police drafted into the port. 7-3-55.

Such strikes angered employers, the colonial government and their capitalist backers. They relentlessly attacked worker organisations and their leaders. For example, Chege Kibachia was detained for ten years for his trade union activities, as Maxon and Ofcansky (2000) relate:

Kibachia, (1920-). Trade unionist. Born in Kiambu and educated at Alliance High School (1939-42). In 1945, Kibachia came to national attention after he moved to Mombasa to work for the East African Clothing Factory. When a general strike began in Mombasa in January 1947, the African Workers Federation was formed to articulate the demands of the strikers. Kibachia quickly emerged as its leader, first as executive officer and after March as president. As a result of Kibachia's leadership Mombasa workers won an increase in wages, and the appeal of trade unionism and industrial action spread in the colony. In August 1947, Kibachia came to Nairobi to organize a branch for the federation there, but on the 27th he was arrested. He was detained at Kabarnet for the next 10 years.

Clayton and Savage (1974) add a political connection for Chege Kibachia, that he had been "a member of KAU [Kenya African Union] and editor of the *African Leader*" and that "Kibachia told the Thacker Tribunal that he had read widely including the works of Karl Marx.

It should be noted, however, that it was not the leadership of the African Workers Federation and the leadership of the Mombasa strike alone that made Kibachia the target of colonialist attacks. The colonialists' fear was that the workers might succeed in creating a nation-wide trade union organisation as Kibachia and the African Workers Federation (AWF) had opened a branch in Nairobi and planned to open branches in other towns, including Kisumu and Nakuru. In order to scupper nation-wide trade unions, colonialism came down hard on Kibachia. This eventually led to the end of active life of the AWF.

Enter Makhan Singh

And that is why the entry of Makhan Singh in the trade union movement and in Kenyan politics became so important. While the overall history of the trade union movement remains outside the scope of this book, those aspects of its history that relate to its impact on the War of Independence are still relevant. And it is in these aspects that Makhan Singh played a key role. Again, the life and achievements of Makhan Singh have been dealt with in other studies, but this section looks at his work in so far as it influenced the direction of the trade union movement and in national politics.

Makhan Singh's background in trade union work and in politics helps to understand the overall stand he took. He was elected the Secretary of the Indian Trade Union, which was founded in 1934, in March 1935 and influenced it to become the Labour Trade Union of Kenya, which was open to all workers irrespective of race, religion and colour in defiance of the divisive British colonial policy at that time. Having changed the Union from Labour Trade Union of Kenya into Labour Trade Union of East Africa (LTUEA), Makhan Singh organised a successful strike of 62 days in 1937 and achieved a wage increase of between 15-25%. As a result of the successful strike, the Union's membership rose to 2,500 in Kenya and Uganda. The colonial government was forced to accept the presence of the trade union movement in Kenya. It passed the 1937 Trade Union Ordinance under which LTUEA was registered. It is important to note that LTUEA was an overall umbrella body and the success of the strike encouraged unions to be affiliated to the LTUEA. By 1948, 16 trade unions were affiliated to LTUEA whose membership now stood at 10,000 workers. The existence of so many independent trade unions in itself is an indication of the militancy amount workers.

This was a significant achievement on the part of the TU movement. Makhan Singh then had to go to India in 1939 and "within six months of his arrival [in India], he was arrested by the British government for his political activities and imprisoned for two and a half years in India. He was further restricted for two years on his release in January 1945" (Singh, 1963). During his stay in India, he studied working class conditions and the workings of the trade union movement. His work and experience in India equipped him for the coming battles in Kenya as Durrani, S. (2015b) says:

> It was during his detention [in India] that he strengthened his links with communist, socialist and other revolutionary leaders from all over India. He then worked as a sub-editor of Jang-i-Azadi [Struggle for Freedom], the weekly organ of the Punjab Committee of the Communist Party of India, until he left for Kenya in August 1947 ... His exposure to new ideas, to experiences in organisational work and mass action in India had prepared him for the struggle in Kenya, both at the level of trade unionism and in the freedom struggle. The experiences with which Makhan Singh came to Kenya enriched and developed the anti-colonial and anti-imperialist struggles in Kenya.

Makhan Singh was subsequently able to influence the trade union movement in Kenya based on his experiences and ideas he acquired in India. Among these, a few are mentioned by Durrani (2015b):

> Makhan Singh saw class divisions and class struggles as the primary

aspects of resistance to colonialism and to ensuring that the interests of workers, peasants and people of Kenya were in the forefront of an independent country. This was a turning point in the struggle for liberation in Kenya. Colonialism had succeeded in previous periods to divide people's struggles into "tribal" attacks on aspects of colonialism or limit them to specific locations or on specific issues, thereby dividing forces of resistance. Makhan Singh was able to see through such divisive tactics. He had learnt lessons from his studies of Marxist literature and from his practice in India. He saw that the need in Kenya was to politicise the working class, unite them with other progressive classes and wage a struggle that would remove the causes of poverty and injustice from the country.

A particularly important contribution that Makhan Singh made, and which influenced the trade union movement as well as the War of Independence, was mentioned by Durrani, S (2015b):

> An important contribution that Makhan Singh made to the struggle for liberation in Kenya was to link the two aspects of a liberation struggle that imperialism sought to keep separate. These were economic and political aspects. Makhan Singh believed that in order to meet the economic demands of working people, it was essential to win political power first. It was only thus that foundations for an entirely different society could be laid. Makhan Singh saw the connections between economic demands of workers and the struggle for national liberation.

These and other revolutionary ideas and practices that Makhan Singh introduced into the trade union and political movements then became the mainstream of political demands of the War of Independence. Chandan (2015) mentions one such link:

> By the 1950s, new unions were forming, strikes were frequent and Makhan Singh directed trade unionism towards anti-colonial nationalist struggle, indeed the labour movement effectively turned into a militant vehicle for African political aspirations.

Newsinger (2006) also sees the radicalisation of the liberation movement as coming from the trade union movement:

> The movement [Mau Mau] was radicalised by a militant leadership that emerged from the trade union movement in Nairobi. Here the Transport and Allied Workers Union led by Fred Kubai and the Clerks and Commercial Workers Union led by Bildad Kaggia were at the heart of the resistance. Most accounts of the Mau Mau movement either ignore or play down the role of the trade unions in the struggle, but the fact is that without their participation a sustained revolt would not have been possible.

Similarly, Kaggia (1975) examines the links between the trade union and the national political movements:

> People in Nairobi looked to the trade unions for leadership, not to the 'political' leaders of KAU [Kenya African Union]. Encouraged by this support, the trade unions decided to try and capture the political leadership as well. We would begin by taking over the Nairobi branch of KAU.

For Makhan Singh, Fred Kubai and Bildad Kaggia, the political role of trade unions was essential if the needs of working people were to be met. Clayton and Savage (1974) refer this approach in connection with the latter two:

> Both Fred Kubai and Bildad Kaggia regarded the E.A.T.U.C. as a ginger group to prod the K.A.U. into more dynamic political action. In practice this meant that the congress in the first four months of 1950 issued a stream of press releases and sponsored some twenty-five to thirty meetings, the tenor of which became more and more radical. It also meant that the congress supported three important strikes in 1949 and initiated a political demonstration early in 1950 which culminated a few months later in a general strike in Nairobi.

The strong links between the radical trade union movement and political organisations is what has provided strength to the War of Independence. The connection between economic and political activism, between peasant and worker struggles is highlighted by Leys (1975):

A significant group of the 'radicals' came from the trade-union movement. D. Kali and Bildad Kaggia had both worked with Kubai in the early 1950s, when a union-based group of Nairobi nationalists had tried to 'take over' KAU. Denis Akumu and O. O. Mak'anyengo were younger men, both from the historically militant and predominantly Luo dockworkers' union. Others reflected the problems of landlessness and insecurity in the countryside. This was certainly true of Kaggia, whose following was among squatters and labourers in the Rift Valley and among the landless and smaller landholders in his home area in Murang'a district, which had been a particularly bad case of malpractice in the process of land-consolidation and registration. More generally, the Kikuyu and Luo, besides being the two largest tribes in Kenya (20-7 per cent and 14-1 per cent respectively of the total African population in 1969) had experienced underdevelopment more extensively and for longer than most other tribes, though in different ways: more or less forced labour, the decimation of those conscripted for the East African campaign, restrictions on commodity production and trade and a growing land shortage in many locations. It was natural for the nationalist movement to be largely led by Kikuyu and Luo, and equally natural for some of these leaders to arrive at a socialist position.

And so it came to be that the trade union movement entered the political arena, which then fed into the broad movement of armed resistance, Mau Mau. It was this political work of trade unions that Kenyatta's government curtailed, as Clayton and Savage (1974) record:

> The advent of the Kenyatta government led to a curtailment, but not an abolition of the trade unions. The government moved slowly, its main object being to prevent the unions from becoming a quasi-political party in opposition to the authorities. This was achieved by transforming the K.F.L. into C.O.T.U. with direct role for the Kenya President in naming the leading officials of the federation [Union].... the bargaining power of individual unions was restrained by the creation of an Industrial Court...

But that was in the future. In the period before independence militant trade unions played a crucial role in the War of Independence and that was the reason that the comprador regime came down on it so strongly. That is why the CIA invested heavily in sponsoring and training its own brand of "trade unionism" in Kenya. The CIA saw EATUC as an enemy to be eliminated. An indication of the position of the trade unions and the intensity of the on-going class and national political struggles is given by examining the content of union publicity and communications. They also indicate the aspects of classes and class struggles that the working class introduced into the War of Independence.

Another important contribution that trade unions made to the War of Independence was the establishment of links with international trade unions and other progressive organisations. These proved useful not only for developing support for Kenyan trade unions but for Mau Mau whose struggles got a higher profile and support from such linkages. Singh (1963) mentions some of these relations:

> During 1938 the Union established relation with the British Trades Union Congress, South African Trades and Labour Council and the International Labour Office.

Such relations were in addition to those established by Makhan Singh, Pio Game Pinto and other activists with organisations in India as well as with progressive British anti-colonial organisations. Many of these organisations carried out their own research on Mau Mau and the situation in Kenya and published important publications which alerted world opinion about British oppressive behaviour in Kenya and on the struggles waged for independence by Mau Mau. Some of these publications are listed in the Bibliography and References and include S. and A. Aaronovitch, Philip Bolsover, Fenner Brockway, Frida Laski, Richard K. Pankhurst and Leonard Woolf. The publishers of such material include important political opinion-makers such as the Communist Party, the Congress of People Against Imperialism, Fabian Colonial Bureau, Kenya Committee for Democratic Rights for Kenya (London), the Union of Democratic Control and World Federation of Trade Unions. In addition, those on the mailing lists of organisations such as the Kenya Committee for Democratic Rights for Kenya (London) would have received regular newsletters, press cuttings and updates. Many activists in Kenya regularly sent reports of happenings in Kenya, particularly Pio Gama Pinto who sent regular news to his contacts in India, Mozambique and Britain where he sent these to Kenyans as well as to progressive British activists, such as Fenner Brockway. Aching Oneko, Joseph Murumbi and Mbiyu Koinange and Jomo Kenyatta were also kept well informed while in London and they passed on their new items to progressive British organisations.

The full impact of these individuals and organisations on public opinion overseas regarding Mau Mau has not been fully understood. Those who claim that Mau Mau had no external support or avenues of communications forget that there were three pillars of the War of Independence: Mau Mau, the trade unions and progressive people's force. Each made its own contribution and, taken together, provide the totality of the War of Independence.

Kenya's TUs in the Context of TU Struggles in Africa

Trade Unions in Kenya cannot be seen in isolation from the activities and experiences of Africa-wide trade union movement. At the same time, these activities and experiences were aspects of resistance to colonialism and imperialism. Imperialism realised the essential contribution that trade union movements were making in the people's struggles for political and economic liberation and in weakening imperialist control. While progressive trade unions and trade unionists were being banned and detained in Kenya, a similar attack on progressive trade unions in other parts of Africa was also taking place. Thus while imperialist historians failed to mention trade union contribution to the overall anti-colonial and anti-imperialist movements in Africa, imperialism was fully aware of the TU contributions. Thus they attacked not only the militant political movements but also the militant trade union movement in a silent acknowledgement of the essential unity between the two strands of people's struggles for liberation. So while on the one hand they downplayed the role of trade unions in the liberation struggle, on the other hand, they carried out covert and overt attacks on trade unions. In the case of Kenya, this involved detaining activists such as Chege Kibachia, Makhan Singh, Fred Kubai, Bildad Kaggia and Pio Gama Pinto, at the same time, banning progressive TU organisations such as the East African Trade Union Congress and African Workers Federation. The other side of the coin was to promote individuals and trade unions which opposed radical trade unions and were in more or less sympathy with the capitalist perspective on what trade unions' role should be. In the case of Kenya, this involved supporting trade unionists such as Tom Mboya and conservative trade union organisations such as the Kenya Federation of Labour.

Imperialism, however, had its own internal contradictions which saw the gradual decline of British influence on African trade unions which was then replaced by the influence of USA policies and aligned conservative trade union organisations, both national and international. Davies (1966) shows the intra-imperialist contradictions:

> Between 1953 and 1957 the Americans worked behind the scenes to erode the influence of the British in African affairs by increasing their own independent activity throughout Africa. During 1953 and 1954 the 'Mau Mau' war in Kenya provided them with an excellent opportunity.

The position of the EATUC in linking political with economic struggles was reflected on the African continent. Davies (1966) says: "Trade unionists in colonial Africa regarded the expulsion of foreign power as their primary purpose". He goes on to elaborate:

> The history of African trade unions to date is as much one of the reaction to imperial rule as to working conditions, and any study has to trace the major social changes introduced by European activity before discussing the role played in these by the unions themselves.

However, the advice from the British TUC to Kenyan trade unions was to avoid linking political with economic demands. Davis (1966) indicates the British TUC position:

> A British trade unionist was employed in Kenya as an adviser in the Labour Department, but in 1952 he was advising workers that 'a trade union is not an organization with political aims: it is an association which has as its object the regulation of relations between workers and their employers." This advice fell heavily on the ears of Kenyans whose political parties were banned and whose leaders were in detention, so that the only legal organization able to make political

comments was the Kenya Federation of Labour.

However the Kenya federation of Labour was heavily influenced by institutions and government of USA and did not support political role for trade unions. Davies (1966) explains how the USA support for conservative voice in the trade union movement was strengthened, once the progressive one was silenced by detentions and bans:

> From the Kenya labour leaders themselves the Americans possessed some distinct advantages. As representatives of the major non-communist power, they were in a position to compel respect from the British authorities. They had money ... and had an impressive network of publications and platforms which would enable the Kenya Africans to put their case before world opinion. Tom Mboya pulled out all the stops, using the international trade union press for his articles on conditions in Kenya and astutely drawing on the help of the AFL, the ICFTU, and the TUC to develop the organizational strength of the KFL and avoid a ban on its activities.

Thus was settled the role of trade unions in Kenya and Africa – removed from political struggles of people, it soon became a mechanism to ensure the smooth functioning of a capitalist state.

Workers and Peasants Unite for Armed Resistance

It was the linking of trade union activism with the radical national political movement that provided the spark that changed the direction of the War of Independence. This led to the emergence of the armed resistance movement, Mau Mau, as the new approach to defeat colonialism and imperialism. The trade union movement provided ideological clarity and national organisational experience; the militant national political organisations provided political structures and mass support developed over a long period. The former brought the working class to the struggle, the latter brought peasants, creating a national movement of all the exploited and oppressed people. Together they formed an iron fist that colonialism fought hard to defeat. It was this combination of resistance movements that linked economic, political and social demands of the people and decided on the path of armed resistance as the way to achieve national goals.

Gachihi (1986) provides a good overview of the role that the trade union movement played in the War of Independence and in Mau Mau:

> Another facet of the prelude to Mau Mau was the growth of militant and revolutionary spirit in the trade union activities under the veteran and radical trade unionist, Makhan Singh. The role of the trade unions was significant because KAU had faced a succession of failures in its bid to effect change. Out of this failure was created the Central Committee by men who interpreted this failure to mean that much more than a reformist approach had to be adopted. Radical Africans looked to the progressive and anti-imperialist trade union movement as a viable alternative because of its national outlook and the ability to deploy workers.
>
> This spate of strikes in 1947 was felt throughout Kenya, creating in turn, radical leadership for the workers in various urban centres. One of the advantages that the Mau Mau organizers received from this was the growth of the organizational ability among men who were to become chief architects of the Mau Mau movement — men like Fred Kubai, J. M. Mungai, Bildad Kaggia and others. This radicalism in trade unions was not at first taken as an ominous sign by the Administration, but was rather regarded as a nuisance to the smooth running of state affairs. Instead of recognizing this for what it was — a militant growth of African Nationalism, — they saw, instead, the growth of 'abnormal' behaviour among the Africans. Africans were not supposed to be capable of effectively organizing themselves. Corfield, for example, did not believe that Africans could have formed or joined trade union movements or political movements as an expression of political and economic protest.

The coming together of the trade union movement and the radical politics provided the spark that was to ignite Mau Mau's War of Independence. Kinyatti (2008) provides an appropriate summary of the contribution of the trade union movement to the War of Independence:

> The EATUC leadership is credited for deepening the anti-imperialist

resistance among the working class and for producing the Mau Mau revolutionary leadership. It is, therefore, important to note that the driving forces of the Mau Mau movement were the workers, the peasants and the patriotic petty-bourgeoisie. On every level of the struggle, the working class and its proletarian leadership played the leading role.

It suits colonial and imperialist-orientated historians as well as the Kenya Establishment to bury the role of radical, organized trade unions in the liberation as they prevent the workers, the oppressed and the poor people in today's Kenya from learning of the militant past of the trade union movement and of Mau Mau.

A final point to be noted is that while organized, urban militant workers were in the forefront of the trade union movement, they had active support of rural workers, including workers in plantations and in industries generated along the railway line. Such linkages provided a nation-wide perspective to the working class struggles, as did the coming together of workers from different nationalities in urban centres. Gupta 1981) makes this clear:

> The urban working class was becoming the leading factor in the development of nationalist uprising for independence. On the rural scene the landless farm workers were growing in numbers and intensifying the class contradictions. The rural and urban working classes provided the basis for the freedom movement as they increasingly fought against colonial relationship and economic exploitation.

Just as the role of peasants in the War of Independence has been sidelined by official histories, so has the contribution of rural workers not been recognised. Creating a working class and authentic history of Kenya requires all these different levels of struggles to be researched, documented and disseminated with active participation of all classes who participated in the War of Independence.

Illustrations 2: Trade Unions

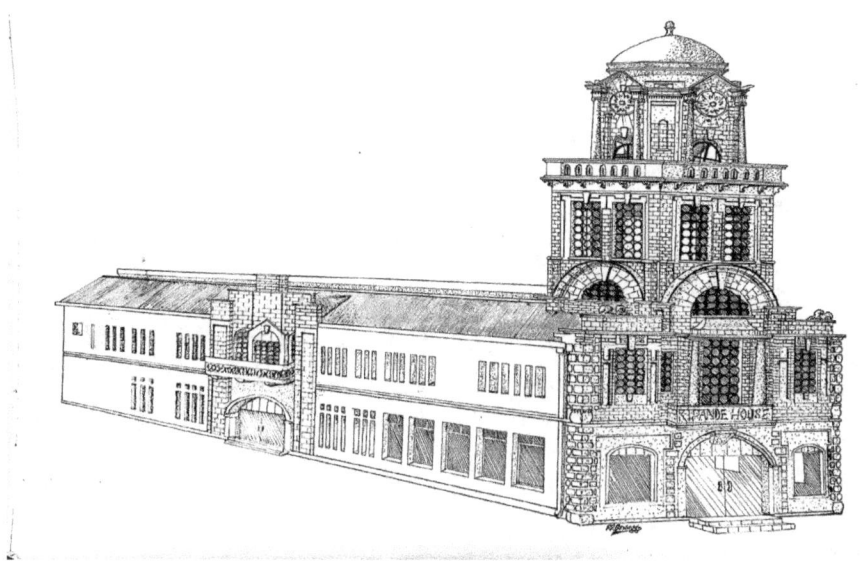

Kipande House drawn by Oswaggo, a member of the Sehemu ya Utungaji

Chege Kibachia

Bildad Kaggia

Makhan Singh   Fred Kubai

PART 2: MAU MAU, 1948-1960

> The worst illiterate is the political illiterate, he doesn't hear, doesn't speak, nor participates in the political events. He doesn't know the cost of life, the price of the bean, of the fish, of the flour, of the rent, of the shoes and of the medicine, all depends on political decisions. The political illiterate is so stupid that he is proud and swells his chest saying that he hates politics. The imbecile doesn't know that, from his political ignorance is born the prostitute, the abandoned child, and the worst thieves of all, the bad politician, corrupted and flunky of the national and multinational companies. - Bertolt Brecht 10

Mau Mau, The Revolutionary Force

Preparations for Armed Struggle

Soon after the Second World Imperialist War, the hopes of peaceful removal of colonialism from Kenya began to fade. The revolutionary line of armed, organised people's war began to emerge by around 1948. The lessons of the past struggles were clear to the advanced workers: the contradiction with colonialism and imperialism could not be resolved without an organised, armed confrontation. This realisation began to be put into practice gradually as the subjective and objective conditions developed. It was becoming clear that in the meantime, intense working class struggles under Makhan Singh and Fred Kubai had developed ideas and experiences of working class struggles and organisations that added to the anti-capitalist arsenal at the disposal of working people. At the same time, social and political activists had decided that the formation of a new organisation was necessary to meet new challenges of fighting colonialism. Thus was born Mau Mau. The name came later, but its organisation, its ideology, its vision, its strategies were all decided by the conditions of the time in the struggle against a foreign power that had captured people's land, people's labour, the country's resources and had created an unequal and unjust system to maintain their power, to exploit, to oppress and to govern.

10 Available at: https://www.goodreads.com/author/quotes/26853.Bertolt_Brecht [Accessed: 16-10-17].

The requirement at the beginning was to organise secretly when the need for unity was paramount among the active combatants. One of the ways of achieving unity was to organise an oath for active fighters. Thus, thousands of people began to take the unity oath for Uhuru. By the end of 1950, over one hundred and forty had been prosecuted in colonial courts on charges related to oath taking. The colonial Government realised the strength behind the new organisation and banned 'Mau Mau' on August 12, 1950. Singh (1969) explains the aims and organisation of Mau Mau in those early days thus:

> A major development in the period following the general strike (of May, 1950) was the rapid progress of a secret mass organisation. The organisation, which previously had been in existence for some time, could be joined by persons of any (Kenyan nationality) who took an oath according to their customs, traditions and beliefs, pledging themselves to secrecy, dedication and sacrifice for the cause of land and freedom of Kenya. The aim of the Uhuru-oath organisation was to unite and mobilise the African people of Kenya in the struggle for independence and to resort to armed struggle against the colonialists if and when it became obvious to the organisation that there was no other way of achieving independence of Kenya.
>
> In the course of some court cases, which took place during and after June, 1950, the Uhuru-oath organisation began to be called Mau Mau. Later, when the Organisation had to resort to armed struggle against the colonialists it began to be called the Kenya Land and Freedom Army.

There was a period of transition on the political front as people began to realise that the moderate approach of peaceful petitions to gain rights and justice was not likely to lead to independence and the settlement of land and freedom issues. Gachihi (1968) indicates the role of the trade union movement in making this transition to armed resistance possible:

> The change of policy from petitioning to violence came with a militant, younger and uncompromising leadership that had begun to emerge in the ranks of KAU, having realized the futility of peaceful negotiations. This corresponded with the ban imposed on trade

union activities in 1950 after a general strike. Many staunch trade unionists found in KAU a venue to vent their energy and militant attitude formerly exercised in trade union activities. They revived KAU's Nairobi branch and its activities countrywide. From this there developed a very intricate relationship between KAU and Mau Mau. An important development in the party occurred with these new and militant supporters who called not just vaguely for 'Independence', but "Independence now!" Three notable trade unionists-namely Fred Kubai, Bildad Kaggia and J. M. Mungai - stood out and were easily chosen to lead the Nairobi Branch of KAU with Kubai as the Chairman, Mungai as the Vice Chairman and B. Kaggia as its Secretary. These men were to bring with them into KAU's new phase the discipline and trade union tactics that they were so familiar with. Violence, long simmering in African circles, began to find a new venue in KAU. Clandestine oathing ceremonies that had started in the Rift Valley, where the squatters had sharply felt the effects of colonial rule, began to spread in Nairobi and its environs, taking an increasingly important role in the union's main branch in Nairobi. This oath was different in the sense that it was different in form and context from the traditional oaths or those taken by the KCA members. In Olenguruone, this "new" oath called for "freedom" and participants were thoroughly lectured on the purpose and meaning of the oath. KAU militants aimed at harnessing all oathing activities and, as a first step, intensifying it in the African locations in Nairobi and its environs. The decision by F. Kubai and Mungai to take the oath and to bring some of their 'most trusted associates' was significant in the development of the Mau Mau in that from this group was to be formed the 'Action group'. The so-called "trusted associates" were at first ten in number. Later 24 trade union joined and they all saw the founding of the Action Group. With the formation of this group, one begins to see organized violence and acts of terrorism. Particular groups of people were oathed and commissioned to carry out particular tasks. Taxi men, for example, were used for ferrying people to and from oathing places. Arms collection began to be accelerated and according to F. Kubai, even Nairobi prostitutes had their role to play. He says, "Some four hundred prostitutes from Nairobi African areas of Pumwani and Eastleigh were oathed and told to collect whatever information would help the movement.

It will be seen that workers not only provided the leadership of this new, radical movement but also they were in the forefront of providing active support to the movement. Capitalism had created conditions for a mass dislocation of people who were left without adequate means of survival. From among those rose the Anake a 40 organisation which was to play an important political role in the struggle for independence. Furedi (1973) provides a background of the organisation:

> The Anake a 40 was founded by Dominic Gatu and a number of young, dissatisfied Nairobi Kikuyu. Its first members were the unemployed, petty traders, thieves, prostitutes and others of the lumpen proletariat of Nairobi. Many of the leaders were ex-soldiers and traders who felt that within the colonial system there was little scope for their skills and ambitions. Many of the leaders saw the 40 Age Group as the vanguard of the African nationalist movement. According to one of its leaders, '. . . we felt that K.A.U. was going too slow and that the only way to change things was through violence. This was why we started armed robberies. Most of the Africans in Nairobi were behind us and they would not inform the police of our activities.'

The organization established links with the trade union movement as well as with the radical wings of KAU. It "played a central role in the movement which the government called the Mau Mau" Furedi (1973) and established links with working class people in Nairobi as well as in the so-called Reserves created by colonialism. They continued to play an important role after the Declaration of Emergency, as Furedy 1973) records: "During the early part of 1953 their main activity was to supply ammunition, medical supplies and recruits for the fighters in the forest". Furedi (1973) concludes:

> They played a pivotal role in the organizing and financing of the 'Mau Mau' throughout Kenya, and thus the role of the Nairobi populist movement in the nationalist struggle cannot be underemphasized.

A study of the differing forms of organisation of Mau Mau reveals that changing conditions at different stages of the struggle gave rise to corresponding changes in the resistance organisation accompanied by a refinement of ideologies, which then resolved the particular problems of the day. Thus the organisation of the revolutionary movement was quite different in its early years (i.e. before October, 1952) from that which evolved after 1952, which again was different from that which emerged by 1955 and again by 1960.

In the early years, new cadres were recruited and given political education in preparation for the time when they would become fully active in resistance. Prospective members were placed under observation, then given the first oath, that of unity. They were then given specific tasks to test their commitment. At the same time, they were placed in an underground cell structure and assigned to work at a democratic level in legal organisations. Many of these became part of the Mau Mau intelligence-gathering network.

The task of military preparation was not being ignored even at the early stage, although the time for armed struggle was not considered ready yet. Many cadres were being given military training in the forests and the procurement of arms and ammunition was also going on. As early as 1948, arms were being captured from enemy forces and kept in readiness for the time when conditions made an armed struggle inevitable.

The particular form of organisation of Mau Mau during this period reflected existing conditions. A somewhat decentralised organisation was necessary so as to allow maximum security and room for building up leadership and organisational qualities among new recruits by allowing greater opportunity for local initiative. At the same time, it was still possible to operate without much harassment from the colonial armed forces, as they were not really aware of the extent of the preparations being made. Furedi (1989) looks at the transformation of the "loose network of militant activists" into Mau Mau when conditions required a stronger central organisation:

> The transformation of a loose network of militant activists into the movement known as Mau Mau came through a process of experimentation and adaptation to the external environment. The breakdown of the uneasy alliance with the moderate wing of the KCA was a result of frustration with its lack of effectiveness. Since it appeared that the colonial government was in no mood to

compromise, the militant option seemed the only way forward to the younger generations. The split with the moderate elements was consolidated through the establishment of separate committees of militant activists, an initiative that came from Nairobi. Their spread to the White Highlands in early 1950 indicated the close links forged with activists in Nairobi. Until that time the squatter movement had operated through area branches loosely linked together through the KCA. Now the formation of separate committees provided the organizational foundation for more militant forms of action.

It suited the colonial interests to ignore such organisational developments and continue its propaganda that Mau Mau was an "illegitimate, perverted force" (Furedi, 1989).

The War Begins

A new situation developed after 1947 under increasing activities by the trade union movement. There was a general strike in Mombasa on January 13, 1947 when over 15,000 workers took part and led to the formation of the African Workers Union, later renamed the African Workers' Federation. The strike "started with dock workers and railwaymen, and quickly spread to virtually all Africans including the houseboys and sugar workers at Ramisi on the mainland", according to Clayton and Savage (1974).

Following the Mombasa strike, workers in other parts of Kenya "came to the conclusion that unless they themselves went on strike, no notice would be taken of their demands" (Singh, 1969). There were strikes in Kisumu, Kisii, Mason, Luanda, Asembo Bay and other towns.

The colonial Government was fast losing its control over events and people. It reacted by arresting the trade union leaders. In 1951, the working class replied by staging a boycott of colonial buses and foreign beer in protest against colonial repression, supported by Mau Mau. Mau Mau forces began to attack traitors, Homeguards and other enemy targets. Fearing it would soon become totally ineffective, the colonial government declared a State of Emergency in October 1952 thus acknowledging its inability to govern without open military suppression. Immediately, about one hundred and eight political and trade union leaders were detained. British battalions poured into Kenya and the British ship *Kenya* docked at Mombasa. As Makhan Singh (1969) said: "A new chapter had begun. A new imperialist colonial war was now on against the people of Kenya".

Mau Mau had made some preparations for such an eventuality. It had already started early preparing for the armed stage of the struggle. It still had to adjust to this new situation and prepare for active resistance. It was no longer possible to be active in the above-ground movements. Although many of its activists had been detained, it had prepared for such an emergency. Every responsible cadre had a second in command who would take over the work if the former were detained. This enabled Mau Mau to continue its work in this new period. It is also true that to some extent, the Declaration of Emergency and the subsequent attacks on people forced many to become armed fighters and others to join people's forces. Many had no training for this new phase and this caused disruption to organisational structures and discipline in Mau Mau.

The military aspect became the principle one in this period. All activities were geared to serving this new demand. This included more urgent procurement of arms and ammunition; a new network of cadres to ensure the safe conduct of cadres and supplies to the newly established forest headquarters; the supply of intelligence on the strength and movement of enemy forces; acquisition of technicians and technologies to establish armament and other factories and facilities in the liberated areas in the city and in the forest headquarters; the establishment of underground hospitals for the treatment of wounded guerrillas. All these and other urgent tasks demanded a close-knit, efficient organisation. In addition, the presence of heavily armed enemy military occupation forces made it essential that security of cadres and organisation itself were given priority.

The changed situation resulted in organisational strengthening in Mau Mau. The basic level of organisation was via a network of small cells of just a few members who, for security reasons, did not know members of other cells or any members at higher levels. A number of such cells, represented by its leader, formed the next unit. A number of such units then formed a locality unit, which again sent representatives to the District Committees. At the head came the Central Committee, which oversaw the whole struggle through various committees.

In the meantime, there was a shift in the balance of power at an organisational level between the moderate KAU approach and the approach of radical groups influenced by involvement in trade union and other progressive activities. The radical groups took over the powerful Nairobi branch of KAU, but this was not happening only in the capital. It was fast turning into a national programme, as Furedi (1989) shows:

> Under grassroots pressure the KAU men were forced to take on a radical posture. In Elburgon and Thomson's Falls matters went further when the KAU branches were taken over by young militants in 1952 during the months leading up to the declaration of a State of Emergency. In these areas at least the very character of KAU had changed as the old leadership lost control over the organization it had created.

The developments below would not have been possible without this radical transition in the organisation.

The Establishment of Liberated Territories

The years that followed the Declaration of Emergency by the colonial government saw dramatic changes in the political and military situation and the establishment of liberated territories by Mau Mau as seen in the following a brief review. Barnett and Njama (1966) sum up the position by the first half of 1954:

> It was certainly true that after almost a year and a half of fighting, and with vastly superior weapons, the (Colonial) Government seemed no closer to defeating the insurgent forces. In fact, guerrilla strength seemed to be growing, with Kenya Levellation Army units more active than ever in the reserve, a Nairobi Land and Freedom Army formed and was very active, supplies flowing from the city into the forests, and Government apparently unable to launch a winning offensive against the guerrilla armies of Nyandarwa and Mt. Kenya

A report in the *Manchester Guardian*[11] revealed the extent of Mau Mau
11 Quoted from the Kenya Committee for Democratic Rights Press Briefings. 2-5-55.

control, as seen by the British Establishment:

> In June 1953 things were going badly in Kenya. Parts of Kikuyuland were virtually Mau Mau republics, and the great majority of the Kikuyu were passive supporters of Mau Mau. The gangs in the forests of the Aberdares and Mount Kenya were living fairly comfortably. They were well supplied with food and clothing, with stolen arms and ammunitions, with women to tend for them, and with information of the movements of the security forces. They had effective communications by couriers with Nairobi. They were able to raid, murder and to pillage over most of Kikuyuland and into the surrounding settled areas. Nairobi was a hot-bed of Mau Mau. The greater part of the population of the city was intimidated, living in terror of the gangsters. Mau Mau were able to enforce a boycott of the buses, and on the smoking of cigarettes, and the drinking of beer.

So successful had Mau Mau been that large areas of land and people had been liberated from colonial rule. These included not only the forest bases in Nyandarwa and Mount Kenya which were "impregnable to the (colonial) army" (Odinga, 1967); there were semi-liberated rural areas in the settler farms and in the so called "reserves". In addition, there were liberated and semi-liberated areas in Nairobi itself, which was the centre of colonial rule in Kenya. Large parts of the city of Nairobi were under the rule of the guerrilla forces; others were controlled by the colonial army by day but were taken over by the Mau Mau by night.

The full extent of Mau Mau control in Nairobi became known to the colonial authorities towards the end of 1954 as the followings reports show:

> A severe blow was struck at the Mau Mau movement by the destruction of their base in Nairobi during "Operation Anvil". Since then, Mau Mau leaders and organisers had been unable to send the recruits, the money, the food, the weapons and ammunition, and the messages to the forest gangs and to those who belonged to the elaborate organisation in African Reserves and farming areas ... At times a large roving gang could still strike a severe blow.12

---

12 East African Standard, 15 October, 1954.

Another report indicated the infrastructure set up by Mau Mau in the liberated areas in the forests:

> Reports so far received (as part of Operation Hammer) (reveal) the significant feature of the first phase has been the large number of hideouts found (in the Aberdare forests), some considerable size and many were skilfully constructed. One consisted of four huts capable of holding 80 men and with a piped water supply from a waterfall 30 yards away. [13]

The guerrilla forces established their own government in these liberated areas, controlled law and order in the interest of Kenyan people, ran an effective administration with its own legal system and a policy for financial control with its own taxes to finance the war effort. It was this tax levied in liberated and semi-liberated areas in the enemy territory that bought guns, ammunition, food and other supplies for the guerrilla army. It established hospitals as well as factories for the manufacture of armaments and other necessities such as clothing. Some details of Mau Mau infrastructures are recorded later in the book.

Mau Mau forces had liberated large areas even before the Declaration of Emergency; in fact this was one of the reasons why the colonial administration felt the need to declare the Emergency. This process of liberation was recorded in the Corfield Report (1960). It admitted that by August 1952 in large parts of Central Province, which was the primary battleground in that period leading up to independence, colonial law and law courts "had virtually ceased to exist". Their function had been taken over by the emerging Mau Mau administration, which established revolutionary justice for the workers and peasants of Kenya and carried out sentences against colonial officers, saboteurs and other anti-people elements. Thus between May and October 1952 (before the Declaration of Emergency) fifty-nine Homeguard traitors, including the colonial Chief Waruhiu had been sentenced by the liberation courts and the sentences were carried out by the armed forces of the people.

As the armed struggle advanced after 1952, so did increase the areas that were liberated by Mau Mau forces. They began to control large administrative machinery, which had jurisdiction over vast areas with

---

13 *The Times* (London), 14 January, 1955.

hundreds of thousands of people for whose economy, welfare, education, health and security they were responsible. An official report (Great Britain. Colonial Office. Parliamentary Delegation to Kenya. Report, 1954) admitted the control established by Mau Mau:

> It is our view based upon all the evidence available to us, both from official and responsible unofficial sources, that the influence of Mau Mau in the Kikuyu area (i.e. the whole of Central Province and parts of Rift Valley and the Highlands), except in certain localities, has not declined; it has, on the contrary, increased; in this respect the situation has deteriorated and the danger of infection outside the Kikuyu area is now greater, not less, than it was at the beginning of the State of Emergency ... In Nairobi, the situation is both grave and acute. Mau Mau orders are carried out in the heart of the city, Mau Mau courts sit in judgement and their sentences are carried out. There is evidence that the revenues collected by (Mau Mau), which may be considerable are used for the purposes of bribery as well as for purchasing Mau Mau supplies ... There is also a passive resistance movement among Africans, an example of which is a bus boycott under which Africans have for several months boycotted European-owned buses.

In addition, Mau Mau's organisation, structures and influence had reached outside the borders of Kenya. Thus the Government of Tanganyika [now Tanzania] declared a state of emergency in North Tanganyika, and Kenyans from North Tanganyika and Zanzibar were returned in increasing numbers for fear of spreading liberation ideas in these areas and to cut off the supply structures to Kenyan liberation forces. The Tanganyika government set up a detention centre at Urembo in Tanganyika for Kenyan detainees.[14] Some other details on the situation are also recorded by Kenya Committee's Press Extracts:

- The Tanganyika Government arrested and expelled Kenyans living in the Kilimanjaro area on the Kenya border.[15]

- Over 1500 Kikuyus arrested in northern Tanganyika – a Kenyan officer taking part in the arrests had already

---
14 Kenya Committee. Press Extracts, Vol.1 (2 January, 1954), p. 49.
15 Kenya Committee. Press Extracts, Vol.1 (10 November, 1952), p. 14.

been sentenced [by Mau Mau] for the torture of captured Kikuyu[16]

- Tanganyika Government announces that Kikuyu women and children in the Northern Province – about 5000 in all – would be sent to new restricted areas in the colony.[17]

- The Tanganyika Government declares a state of emergency in the Northern Province. [18]

- 44 Wakamba were arrested in Tanganyika and returned to Kenya during a police round up in the Northern Province. [19]

- There were Mau Mau cells in Mombasa, Pemba, Zanzibar, and other coastal regions. In Tanzania, the movement [Mau Mau] succeeded in winning over hundreds of Kenyan migrant workers. Mau Mau cells were established mainly in northern and Tanga regions where the bulk of these Kenyan migrant labourers worked and resided. In their attempt to contain the spread of the anti-imperialist resistance in Uganda and Tanzania, the colonial authorities in both countries banned the Mau Mau Organisation and severe punishments were meted out to those who were suspected of being members. In Tanzania, a state of emergency was declared in the northern and Tanga regions and police and army were ordered to round up Gikuyu, Embu, Meru and Kamba (GEMK) workers and put them in concentration camps. Thousands were arrested, tortured and then deported to Kenya where they were further brutalised and then sent to Manyani concentration camp. In Uganda, all the GEMK students attending Makerere University were arrested, interrogated and then deported to Kenya. The GEMK traders who had established business in Uganda were also subjected to the same brutality. Both colonies worked with the colonial regime in Kenya to fight the Mau Mau forces.

---

16 Kenya Committee. Press Extracts, Vol.1 (11 January, 1954), p. 49.
17 Kenya Committee. Press Extracts, Vol.1 (14 January, 1954), p.50.
18 Kenya Committee. Press Extracts, Vol.1 (14 January, 1954), p.50.
19 Kenya Committee. Press Extracts, Vol.1 (17 June, 1955), p. 142.

> They supplied the colonial Kenya with intelligence, men and war material. [20]

- The Ethiopian intelligence is aware of what is going on in Kenya. Mau Mau and its causes are subjects about which they frequently ask questions. On the face of it there seems to be a parallel with their own mountain rebels, the Shiftas.[21]

- Mau Mau influence reached South Africa as well, as shown by a letter from A.J. Simpson who wrote: "I am on holiday in S. Africa where it is considered there is an underground movement by the natives to overthrow established Government throughout Africa and this is certainly the idea of Mau Mau". [22]

These facts, although well documented, remain outside general awareness about Mau Mau. It should be noted that military preparations had been taking place after the Second Imperialist World War and many military trainers of Mau Mau guerrillas were veterans of that war. Kabubi (2002), for instance, replies to the question *Tell us about your military training* thus:

> I was, like all the Mau Mau guerrillas, trained by a World War II veteran. His name was Mbithi Manyuira. was trained in the use of the 303 Enfield rifle, the Bren gun, and the Sten gun, and also in gaturauhoro -"a big gun to kill elephant."

> Once again, the history of Mau Mau lacks details about its military preparations, trainers and gun and ammunition factories, which then leads to misunderstanding the armed resistance movement.

The Birth of Kenya Defence Council (1953)

After the declaration of a state of war (called the 'Emergency' by the colonial government) in October 1952,[23] the stage of armed resistance began

---

20   Kinyatti (2008): The quote here and later from this source are taken from an early draft.
21   Manchester Guardian. 12 January, 1955.
22   Kenya Weekly News. 19 November, 1954.
23   A KLFA struggle-song records the event: When the war was declared in 1952, our

in earnest. The guerrilla forces established their new military headquarters in the forests from where the armed battles were planned and executed. This military need was felt at the level of organisation as well. Many small and large guerrilla units had entered the forests and waged battles against the enemy in their local areas. Mau Mau recognised the need to co-ordinate the activities of these different fighting units and to form an umbrella military organisation that could control the overall strategy of warfare in the face of a well-armed and equipped enemy.

After about eight months of armed warfare, during which valuable military and guerrilla warfare experience had been gained, it was decided to call a representative meeting of the various units. The meeting was held in August 1953 near the Mwathe River and came to be known as the Mwathe Conference. After an exchange of ideas and long discussions, it was decided to form the Kenya Defence Council as the highest military and political organ of the armed struggle. In keeping with the needs of the armed struggle, the Kenya Defence Council resolved the contradictions between a central authority and the need for local units to have a certain amount of autonomy so as to become more effective in the war situation. Thus, as Barnett and Njama (1966) say, while the Kenya Defence Council had the "power to formulate overall strategy and policy, enact rules and regulations and sit as the highest judicial body, the authority to implement and enforce its rulings rested largely with the individual leader-members or section and camp heads." [24]

The other important task of the Mwathe Conference was the election of the leadership of the Kenya Defence Council and also the organisation of all the fighting forces into eight armies. Kimathi was elected the President of the Kenya Defence Council, with Gen. Macharia Kimemia as vice-president, Gen. Kahiu-Itina as the Treasurer and Brig. Gathitu as Secretary.

Because of the particular needs of combining the military and political aspects of the anti-colonial armed struggle, there was a considerable overlap between the military and political leadership. Thus Kimathi was not only the

---

country was turned into a huge prison. Innocent people, men, women and children were herded into concentration camps under all kinds of harsh repression. - Kinyatti (1980).
24 Bernett and Njama (1966). The following account on Kenya Defence Council and the Kenya Parliament are based on the this source.

President of the Kenya Defence Council; he was also the highest military authority as Field Marshal. The leadership was thus charged with the overall planning, organisation, and execution of both the aspects of the struggle, military and political.

The military force was divided into eight armies as follows:

1. Ituma Ndemi Army. Operating in the Nyeri District, commanded by Gen. Stanley Mathenge.

2. Gikuyu Iregi Army. Operating in the Murang'a District, commanded by Gen. Macaria Kimemia.

3. Kenya Inoro Army. Operating in the Kiambu District, commanded by Gen. Waruingi.

4. Mei Mathathi Army. Operating in the Mt. Kenya area, commanded by Gen. China.

5. Mburu Ngebo Army. Operating in the Rift Valley, commanded by Gen. Kimbo.

6. The Townwatch Battalions. Operating in all the urban areas. The fighters carried on normal civilian lives by day, but undertook active armed struggles at night or whenever necessary. Commanders varied from town to town and from time to time, in keeping with needs of warfare and security.

7. Gikuyu na Mumbi Trinity Army. Operated throughout the country and consisted of all Mau Mau sympathisers, and also those who supported the struggle in different ways. It was this Army that helped with supplies and information on enemy activities. The actual participation of members varied.

8. Kenya Levellation Army. A complementary Army to the Townwatch Army, operating in the rural areas. The name implies the ideology of the freedom fighters, equality for all in society achieved through an armed struggle.

The Mwathe Conference was an important development. Not only did it put the armed forces on an organised war footing; it created a new united organisation which became the central policy making and administrative body with responsibilities covering the whole country, both over military and political matters. This was particularly important as the colonial regime had sought to kill the armed struggle by striking at the leadership and through them at the whole organisation without which the movement, they hoped, would just wither away.

By the formation of the Kenya Defence Council, Mau Mau created a new democratic political and military authority, which organised all the freedom fighters, their supporters and sympathisers. It was to the Kenya Defence Council that the struggling people looked as the new legal entity, which replaced the authority of the colonial administration. The Kenya Defence Council became the new beacon of hope for Kenyans under attack from a fierce, desperate enemy. It grew from the experiences of the previous years of struggle, suffering, imprisonment, torture, land and livestock confiscation and death. It also provided a foundation for the development of the future Kenya Parliament.

Soon after its formation, the Kenya Defence Council assessed the political situation and took action to support forces fighting colonialism. There had been a lot of adverse enemy propaganda condemning the freedom struggle as a backward movement. In order to give the correct picture and to achieve a greater unity among the freedom fighters and its supporters, it published a Charter, which set out its demands and aims. It was prepared by Kimathi under the authority of the Kenya Defence Council and came to be known as the Kimathi Charter. The Charter, reproduced below from Singh (1980), was widely circulated and it publicly and openly showed what Mau Mau and the people of Kenya were fighting for:

Kimathi Charter - We Reject Colonialism

We demand African self-government in Kenya.

We demand an African Magistrate's Court in full authority which will judge lawfully and righteously. We demand to know who hands over the money for land from Settlers and where the money goes.

We demand to know why many different Christian missions with different laws are brought to Kenya. Can one mission not suffice?

We demand authorities of gold, markets, roads, co-operative societies, and auctions to be in the hands of Africans.

We claim the full authority of making fire-arms and various kinds of weapons.

We demand that the European foreigners, rascals, troops and police should be withdrawn from Kenya African Reserves.

We reject imprisonment over Mau Mau.

We reject criminal or death cases to be judged by foreigners.

We condemn the dropping of poisons from the air as the colonialists in Kenya are doing to the African population.

We reject the foreign laws in Kenya, for they were not made for Kenya and are not righteous.

We reject being called terrorists when demanding our people's rights.

We demand a stop to the raping by foreigners of our wives and daughters; also female imprisonment and carrying of passes.

We reject foreign Attorney-General in Kenya, for he deals with appearance rather than righteousness. We reject the colonisation of Kenya, for in that state we are turned into slaves and beggars.

The publication of the Kimathi Charter by the Kenya Defence Council proved of immense importance in mobilising the people's forces to continue their anti-imperialist struggle. Thousands of workers and peasants had taken up arms against exploitation of their labour and stealing of their land and the Kimathi Charter articulated their demands. The Kenya Committee For Democratic Rights for Kenya Africans (1952-60) records the following from British press:

> The publication of the Kimathi Charter was timed to coincide with an important mass struggle being waged by the Kenya Land and Freedom Army. This was the bus boycott which was a protest against various aspects of imperialist control over the lives of people, and aimed at mobilising popular support to advance and promote the armed struggle. 23-9-53.

Singh (1980) sums up the importance of the Kimathi Charter and the bus boycott:

> The Charter gave great encouragement to the people of Kenya. It also gave impetus to the great demonstration of national unity and national struggle that was taking place at that time in Nairobi. This was the Bus Boycott which started on 23 September, 1953. Initiated by the Mau Mau freedom fighters, the Bus Boycott involved all the patriotic people. It was a national protest against the oppressive Emergency Regulations including: the introduction of History of Employment Cards (Green Cards); keeping African buses out of many locations in Nairobi; closer control over all Africans by forcing them into 'villages' (detention camps) surrounded by barbed wire with a police post in each 'village'; cancellation of (many) drivers' passes in the Rift Valley areas; restrictions on travelling; painting of names on bicycles; the order for yellow band 'marked' taxis.
>
> Above all, it was a protest against the imprisonment and detention of tens of thousands of patriots; against (Colonial) government's refusal to release the imprisoned and detained national leaders; and against the policies of the European Settlers' Organisation and the Electors Union, the main point of which was to "build a strong and prosperous state which will be a bulwark of the Commonwealth in British Africa maintaining British traditions of loyalty to the Crown." The Bus Boycott continued for many months.

Thus by these various means, the Kenya Defence Council carried the struggle in the military field as well as at the popular mass-level to new heights. These led to many victories, which forced the colonialists to make token offers of reform, hoping thereby to divert the attention of the struggle. But the struggle continued.

The Kenya Parliament Takes Control - Kimathi is Prime Minister (1954)

As the armed conflict intensified, new contradictions, both antagonistic ones against the enemy, and non-antagonistic ones within Mau Mau, developed. Certain weaknesses of the Kenya Defence Council also emerged. It was found that in an attempt to make the Kenya Defence Council more democratic and representative, it had been made too large to be able to function efficiently in a war situation.

A meeting of the Kenya Defence Council was held in February 1954 in order to address these shortcomings. Eight hundred delegates attended the meeting and after intensive discussions, a decision was taken to replace the Kenya Defence Council by a new body - the Kenya Parliament. This was a change of fundamental importance. The Kenya Parliament was the first legitimate African Government of Kenya. Its aims were to separate political and military aspects of the struggle, making the former paramount, to emphasise the national character of the freedom movement, to ensure the representation of all Kenyan nationalities, and to assume authority over liberated and semi-liberated areas and people. Militarily, it established its authority over all fighting units and prepared a new military offensive. It also formulated a foreign policy and sent representatives to foreign governments.

Twelve members were elected to the Kenya Parliament, and Kimathi was elected the first Prime Minister. Their first loyalty was to the Kenya Parliament and not to their former armies. A new Field Marshal was elected. He was Macharia Kimemia. Kimathi was now free to devote full attention to the political sphere and to the affairs of Kenya Parliament. In addition, all the thirty-three districts of Kenya were represented in the Kenya Parliament, thus making it a national body.

One of the delegates at the meeting summed up the argument for the formation of the Kenya Parliament and saw its potential role, as recorded by Njama (Barnett and Njama, 1966):

> ...the thing we lack is a Kenya central (political) organisation which should be the Government. I think it is high time we elected our Kenya Parliament members and let them run the country ... the little we would have done (by this action) would be of great importance in Kenya's history, which will (record) that the Kenya Parliament was formed and maintained by warriors in Nyandarwa for so many years. As the Kenya Parliament shall govern Kenya, the founders' names shall live as long as the Kenya independent Government shall live.

The following were the first members of Kenya Parliament (in effect, the first Cabinet; other levels represented Kenyan districts):

Kimathi wa Waciuri - Prime Minister

Brig. Gen. Kahiu-Itina - Deputy Prime Minister

Gen. Kimbo Mutuku - Minister for Finances

Karari Njama - Chief Secretary

Gen. Ndiritu Thuita - Deputy Chief Secretary

Gen. Abdulla - Deputy Minister for Finance

Major Vindo*

Gen. Kirihinya*

Col. Kahii ka Arume*

Brig. Gathitu Waithaka*

Gen. Muraya Mbuthia*

Major Omera*

Gen. Rui*

varying responsibilities according to the needs at particular times.

One major crisis that faced the Kenya Parliament was the capture of General China by the colonial forces and his subsequent betrayal to the enemy. The Kenya Parliament held a special session to discuss the crisis and to reply to the colonial government's offer to negotiate an end to hostilities. The reply is important for it sets out clearly the aims of the struggle and conditions for starting negotiations. The reply also demonstrated the strength of the armed forces. Among points made in the reply in February, 1954 (Barnett and Njama, 1966) were:

Land and Freedom Now

> We are fighting for our lands - the Kenya Highlands which were stolen from the Africans by the Crown through the Orders in Council 1915, of the Crown Lands Ordinance which evicted Africans from their lands at present occupied by the Settlers or reserved for their future generations while landless Africans are starving of hunger or surviving on the same land as cheap labourers to the Settlers who were granted that land by the Crown.

> Before we come out of the forest, the British Government must grant Kenya full independence under the African leadership, and also hand over all the alienated lands to Kenya African Government which will redistribute the land to its citizens.

> If we do not get land and freedom now, we will continue to fight till the Government yields or the last drop of blood of our last fighter is spilt.

> Now it is wartime; and war means destruction of everything without recognising children or their parents. War simply means taking away lives and wealth. The most civilised and advanced nations have failed to stop war as they believe that war is the only safeguard against slavery, oppression and exploitation by others.

> It is now almost one and a half years since the declaration of the emergency. Every day since then you have been trying your best to destroy us completely, using nearly 100,000 strong forces and dropping thousands of bombs on us from your jet fighters, Harvards and the heavy Lincoln bombers. All your forces work day and night trying to finish us off, but you have not been successful, and you will not succeed. Though you think we are unarmed compared to your strength, we stand for right, we are confident of our victory. You may

lose your empire in the course of impeding Kenya's independence.

The formation of the Kenya Parliament and the installation of Kimathi as the first Prime Minister of Kenya were events of great historical importance not only for Kenya, but for Africa as a whole and for the anti-colonial struggle generally.

Colonialism sought to suppress the dissemination of information about the formation of the free Government of Kenya under Kenya Parliament from fear that other colonies would also do the same. Yet the example of the Kenya Parliament remains forever as the greatest achievement of the Kenyan people in their anti-colonial warfare. The events of 1954 in Kenya were a herald of the events to come in other colonies: the final independence from colonialism as a result of fierce struggles. That this new historical era saw its first expression in Kenya was no small an achievement, given that colonialism had seen Kenya as a country of permanent European settlement and colonial control. The freedom fighters of Kenya showed by their total commitment and sacrifice for the cause of national liberation, that no oppressed people can be exploited forever. Such was the magnitude of the achievement of Mau Mau forces. And Mau Mau's statement that "You may lose your empire in the course of impeding Kenya's independence" contained much truth, as events were to show.

Venys (1970) provides an overview of Mau Mau:

The whole movement was organised in great detail and was very complex. It had two main wings which were usually called the "active wing" and the "passive wing". The former consisted of a number of fighting units forming together the Kenya Land Freedom Armies which finally concentrated in three main areas: the Aberdares, Mt. Kenya and Nairobi. The "passive wing" comprised various committees which were scattered all over the Kikuyu Land Unit as well as the capital. The movement had its headquarters in a central committee situated in Nairobi.

Mau Mau fighters and the people who worked with the armed forces sacrificed their property, the future of their families, faced colonial torture and suffered in colonial concentration camps and many perished under intense military attacks by the British forces. Their full history needs to be fully researched and made known to all.

Elements of Mau Mau Governance

The establishment of the Kenya Defence Council and particularly the Kenya Parliament with a Prime Minister and a cabinet were not mere trappings of power. They reflected Mau Mau's power over territories, people and institutions needed for exercising functions of a state. These included legal institutions, finance and taxation, communications, education, health and welfare of citizens, policing, security and military affairs, as reflected in the Cabinet of the Kenya Parliament. Mau Mau needed constitutional and policy frameworks to ensure it was capable of meeting needs of the people it controlled as well as the needs of waging a war - in the same way as the colonial government needed these. Its policies were reflected by, and were implemented through, its ideology, organisation, strategies and other related areas, which are examined below. These are the features that defined it as a civil administration as well as a fighting force. These two aspects - political and military - were clearly demarcated by the establishment of the Kenya Parliament. It is doubtful if the Mau Mau could have survived for years unless it has these essential elements of governance, which also looked forward to a post-independence Kenya. Alam and Gachihi (2007) reflect on the twin requirements of any revolutionary movement:

> For any revolutionary movement to succeed there must be plans [for] both organizational and military [aspects]. Mau Mau was no exception. It was a revolutionary movement against colonial oppression. The first phase of the movement involved establishing a network, contacts and a support base. Afterwards, the revolt was gradually transformed into a military campaign. These two phases are inseparable. Indeed, the success of the latter depends on the former.

Anti-Imperialist Ideology

The three strands of Mau Mau's ideological stand were anti-colonialism, anti-imperialism and a proletarian world outlook in the struggle against capitalism. They thus represented the unity of workers and peasants and all those who were not allied to the colonialists. This stand was derived from peasants' anti-colonial struggles and from the trade union movement and working class struggles in the liberation struggle as well as from the nationalist forces resisting colonialism through political organisations over a long period.

Different aspects of the ideology became dominant at different times and freedom fighters responded differently at different times depending on the particular needs of each period. Just as at the political level different organisational structures were created in response to specific needs, so at the ideological level, different perspectives came to prominence in keeping with the specific contradictions and needs in the struggle at the specific times.

The ideological stand of the Kenya Defence Council and the Kenya Parliament were seen earlier. As time went on, there was a gradual shift in the struggle from an anti-colonial phase to an anti-neo-colonial one. This change in ideology reflected a change in the material condition at the time. In the period leading to independence and the period after independence, imperialism, the main force that Mau Mau fought, changed from colonialism to neo-colonialism. In keeping with this change, Mau Mau also changed its political and military priorities.

The class stand of Mau Mau was clear right from the beginning. The enemy was not seen in terms of the colour of their skin, as the colonialist propaganda had insisted, and in effect encouraged. Indeed, black Homeguard collaborators were prime target of revolutionary wrath. Kimathi explained in a letter he wrote from his headquarters in Nyandarwa in 1953, "the poor are the Mau Mau." Poverty can be stopped, he explained, "but not by bombs and weapons from the imperialists. Only the revolutionary justice of the struggles of the poor could end poverty for Kenyans" as Kimathi stated in his letter to the Nairobi newspaper, *Habari za Dunia.* (Odinga, 1967). Thus the movement was not against European people or Black people, but against colonialism and capitalism. It is also clear that Kimathi and the movement were taking a definite class stand.

Mau Mau was aware of the dangers that face a society when a rich minority sought privileges for itself at the expense of peasants and the workers. One high official in the Kenya Parliament warned of the dangers of such a situation, in a session in 1954 (Barnett and Njama, 1966):

> Some of us may seek privileges, but by the time we achieve our freedom you will have learnt to share a grain of maize or a bean amongst several people, feeling selfishness as an evil; and the hate of oppressing others would be so developed in you that you will not like to become another class of 'Black' European ready to oppress and exploit others just like the system we are fighting against.

Thus the battle was against oppression and exploitation. It is a reflection of the maturity of Mau Mau and of its deep understanding of imperialism and its grip on countries in the South that it was able to foresee the danger of imperialist control over newly independent countries in Africa even as it fought colonialism.

As the colonial phase was coming to an end, Mau Mau began to raise the concerns about its replacement by neo-colonialism. This brought the ideological battle to the forefront. It became necessary to place before the people a correct analysis of historical events, and to emphasise the need to continue the struggle. This was done in the form of a Policy Document, which was widely circulated. It was also presented at the Conference of the Kenya African National Union held in Nairobi in December 1961, where contradictions were developing about the need to combat neo-colonialism. The Document, entitled *The Future of Kenya* was the clearest statement on the dangers of neo-colonialism. It is reproduced in Appendix B with a note by one of the writers. A brief selected section below provides clarity about what the ideological stand of activists in the War of Independence was:

> The struggle for Kenya's future is being waged today on three distinct though interrelated levels - political, racial and economic. It seems to us that we Africans are being allowed to "win" in the first two spheres as long as we don't contest the battle being waged on the third, all-important economic level.

It is this ideological stand of the War of Independence and of Mau Mau that the departing colonialists and the arriving neo-colonialists have sought to shut out from history books and from people's consciousness. It is the "properly indoctrinated group of the 'right kind' of Africans" who are today overseeing the process of averting a *"genuine* social revolution" but which still remains the goal of those struggling for liberation to this day.

Barnett and Njama (1966) sum up the importance of organisation and ideology in a revolution - the two aspects of Mau Mau's work:

> Just as any revolution requires a certain minimum amount of organization, a people in revolt requires an ideology. Without a set of ideas and ideals, few people are willing to risk their lives in revolutionary action. In Kenya, it is unlikely that the revolution would have occurred but for the integrative ideology developed over a period of thirty-odd years by numerous political, educational and trade union associations which articulated and brought in focus various grievances and set forward certain political, economic and social objectives.

Furedi (1989) looks at the links between a strong ideology and a strong organisation that Mau Mau demonstrated:

> Interpretations which portray Mau Mau as a centrally organized institution find their strongest support on the level of ideology. All sections of the movement articulated a similar ideology. Public pronouncements and petitions used similar language and put forward shared objectives whether from Nairobi, Nyeri or Elburgon.

It is this ideological stand and the organisational strength of Mau Mau that neo-colonialism and the comprador regime find difficult to accept.

Organisation

No struggle as large and facing a vastly superior military power as did Mau Mau could have existed without a strong organisation. The organisational strength of the movement needs to be recognised. Edgerton (1990) provides a succulent summary of Mau Mau's organisational structure:

The Mau Mau movement was directed by what they usually called "Muhimu," or the Central Committee. The Central Committee consisted of 12 men, including Kubai and Kaggia, with Eliud Mutonyi as its chairman. When the police began to make arrests at oathing ceremonies, the Central Committee created another group, known as the "30 Committee," to direct oathing and to shield the true directorate from government detection. Under the direction of Fred Kubai, the 30 men on this committee were responsible for coordinating the activities of local leaders in the tribal reserves and townships. In addition, the leaders of Man Mau were advised by what they called the KAU Study Circle, a kind of brain trust composed of four or five KAU members and an equal number of outsiders who were sympathetic to KAU's stated goals. These men prepared background research on policy matters that the Central Committee might need to address in Kenya, as well as international concerns, especially ways of attracting foreign support.

At the same time, Edgerton (1990) provides records that show that Mau Mau was more interested in their political principles and in working class interests rather than racial background in their organisation or outlook:

> Curious as it may seem in retrospect, the leaders of Mau Mau allowed three non Africans to serve on the Study Circle. One, Pio de Gama Pinto, was a Goan. Two were Europeans: Peter Wright, a former professor of history at Cawnpore, India, who served as a Lieutenant-Colonel in the British Intelligence Corps during World War II, and John P. B. Miller, a former Royal Navy Lieutenant Commander, then a resident of Kenya. The Study Circle originally met in the Nairobi offices of the Indian National Congress, and later, as police surveillance tightened, in private homes.

The formation of the Kenya Defence Council and of the Kenya Parliament indicates the importance that Mau Mau gave to organisations at national level. Its organisational structures at other levels have also been well documented, for example by Barnett and Njama (1966) and Mathu (1974).

Further evidence of Mau Mau's strong organizational structure is provided by Edgerton (1990):

> No rebels fought from forest camps. The rebellion also depended on the support of sympathizers in the reserves, and in Nairobi and other towns. Until mid-1954, the Central Committee and its War Council still purchased weapons, organized food supplies, and recruited new fighters for the forest armies. These new recruits were issued special identification cards in order to prevent infiltration by government informers. Meanwhile, men and women in the Kikuyu, Embu, and Meru reserves continued to supply money, information, food, and weapons. Many risked their lives as often as those who fought in the forest. In fact, much of the actual fighting was done by men and women who lived in the reserves, and in Nairobi or smaller towns. Units from the forests often entered the reserves at night, and spent the day sleeping in the houses of sympathizers or hiding in a secluded area, before carrying out their raids and returning to camp. But others who had never entered the forests were sometimes called into action by a local leader, usually with the approval of higher Mau Mau authority. Sometimes they were ordered to kill a Kikuyu traitor, at other times to raid a Homeguard or police post for weapons.

This is a far cry from the picture of Mau Mau painted by colonial propaganda of "local white Settlers who painted it as dark and satanic in content and inspiration" (Maloba, 1998).

Strategy

The strategy that Mau Mau used against a militarily stronger enemy was crucial in its struggle. Mau Mau saw Kenyan peoples' contradiction with imperialism as an antagonistic one, which could not be resolved peacefully. It thus used the method of armed struggle, guerrilla warfare and people's struggle against imperialism. But it made a distinction between the three aspects of the enemy. Against the colonial military forces, it used the method of guerrilla warfare and military battles (both offensive and defensive), which included attacks on military targets, on prisons to free captured guerrilla fighters, and on arsenals to procure arms.

The other 'face' of the enemy was white Settlers, many of whom benefited from free or cheap land and who had taken up arms against the people of Kenya. The Mau Mau movement used another method to deal with this threat. The Settlers' main concern was to protect 'their' property on which their wealth depended. Indeed, their main aim in settling in Kenya was to appropriate, or acquire very cheaply, peasant land and labour and use it to produce wealth for themselves. The freedom fighters attacked them where it hurt most: the property itself. This served not only to threaten the very economic base of the Settlers; it also helped the guerrillas to procure food and rations they needed to continue their armed struggle, thus providing the material base for the armed Revolution.

Mau Mau used yet another method against the third face of the enemy, the African Homeguards. Considering that many had been forced either by economic reasons or through force or ignorance to become collaborators, many of those considered capable of reforming were given advance warnings to stop betraying the cause of national liberation. Only when these were ignored was action taken against them, depending on the seriousness of their collaboration, but sanctioned by Mau Mau courts. In this way many who had initially sided with the enemy were won over to the nationalist side and some of them then made important contribution to the anti-imperialist struggle. Many whose economic base was tied too strongly to imperialism refused to reform and had to be dealt with more severely in order that they did not pose a threat to the armed resistance forces.

Another tactic used against the collaborators involved information warfare aimed at demoralising them. An example of this was spreading favourable news about guerrilla successes in enemy held territory. Pinning large notices on trees and walls near schools, police stations and social halls was one such way. It was not only the message of these posters that put fear in the enemy but the very fact that such notices could be placed in areas under colonial control. Despite the fact that strict security measures were taken by the colonial armed forces, the Mau Mau activists managed to reach areas in the very heart of the city to pin these posters thus showing their strength and demoralising enemy soldiers and civilians.

It would be wrong to deny that there were contradictions among the ranks of Mau Mau fighters and among the people. These became sharper under enemy attack. But these were not antagonistic ones, at least at the beginning, and were resolved by the use of non-violent means. In the main, democratic methods were used to resolve these contradictions. One of the aims of Mau Mau was to form a democratic society where everyone would have equal rights and duties and an equal access to the wealth produced by their joint labour. They put their ideas into practice in the liberated areas even as they engaged the enemy in a fierce battle.

The democratic method involved the use of meetings, conferences, and congresses where free discussions could be held and ideas could be expressed without fear of persecution. After long discussions, decisions would be taken on basis of majority vote. Questions of leadership were settled through secret ballots and elections were held at every level in so far as war conditions allowed. An example of such a conference was the Mwathe conference mentioned earlier. Elections were held, for example, when Kimathi was elected the Prime Minister. These democratic discussions and elections helped to formulate new policies and to resolve many contradictions. In addition, free exchange of ideas was encouraged to allow the people a chance to hear views of their leaders and to give their views to the leadership.

Mau Mau's military strategy ensured that the military might of the greatest military power at the time was kept at bay for over four years. Some aspects of this are discussed in other parts of the book. Kaggia, B, Leeuw and Kaggia, M (2012) sum up their achievements:

> In the battle Mau Mau soldiers distinguished themselves as great guerrilla fighters. General Sir George Erskine, a British general advised his Government that Mau Mau could not be stamped out by force. Although the general was soon to be removed from command, what he said was true and the Government eventually had to accept it in practice. The British couldn't crush Mau Mau with all their sophisticated weapons. Considering the difficult conditions under which the Mau Mau soldiers fought and lived, it is impossible to ignore their greatness. They managed to fight the war for more than four years.
>
> Mau Mau's political and military strategy were well aligned to its

overall vision of creating a nation free from foreign domination and with policies meeting the needs of its people, not corporations and Settlers.

Utavumilia Kifo? - A Mau Mau song 25

Watoto wa Kenya huishi mwituni
Wakinyeshewa na mvua
Wakipata njaa,
mateso na baridi nyingi
Kwa upendo wa udongo.

Uui, iiyai, uui, iiyai
Kuuawa na taabu na kufungwa
Mara Nyingi
Je, utavumilia?

Na akina nani hao wanaimba kwa sauti kubwa
Ngambo ya pili ya mto
Wakiwaimbia Kago na Mbaria
Watafutaji wa haki.

English translation:

'Are You Ready to Face Death?'

---

25 This Mau Mau song was released by the Tamaduni Players of Nairobi during their production of Mzalendo Kimathi, a play on the Kenyan struggle written by Ngugi wa Thiong'o and Micere Githae Mugo (1978). The Tamaduni Production performed at the University of Nairobi in early 1980s.

Kenya's children live in forests
they are soaked in heavy rains
they go hungry, endure hardships
they live through cold days and nights
all because of the love of their country

Woe! Woe! Woe! Woe!
Are you ready to endure all these hardships?
Are you ready to face prisons and detention camps?
Tell me, are you ready to face death?

Whose are those voices raised in song
from across the river
singing praises of Kago and Mbaria
champions of truth, fighters for democratic right
whose are those voices?

Infrastructure

There is no doubt that Mau Mau was well organised as a military and as a political organisation. The colonialists were aware of their abilities, as they had discovered many examples of infrastructure in towns and forests even as the War of Independence was going on. They deliberately chose to hide these facts and set out to destroy such evidence so as to continue their myth that Mau Mau was a primitive group of people who had nothing to do with the War of Liberation. Such structures included hospitals, libraries, social halls as well as rules and regulations and records of civil and legal practice that guided the movement. Some such examples are given in the book. Additional ones, given below, are taken from the Press Briefings compiled by Kenya Committee For Democratic Rights for Kenya Africans (1952-60):

- During Operation Epsom… a large encampment furnished as a high court, and also a well built installation like a barracks, with numbered rooms and a well-equipped kitchen with accommodation for 60 people was discovered. (19-6-53).

- An army patrol following in the tracks of freedom fighters discovered a 40 bed hospital with complete medical kits. A Government communiqué said the hospital was 5 miles east of Mount Kinangop. 13-7-54.

- A Rifle Brigade tracker team in the N.E. Aberdare discovered a thatched building with a notice "Government House" written on it, and found 25 bicouacs, a structure resembling a church, with seating for 90 people, and a hide-out. 27-5-55.

- Security Forces searching the Aberdare Forest found a deserted hospital which had apparently been evacuated a few days before, also a Council Chamber with accommodation for about 150. 6-6-55.

Newspaper and other reports build up a fuller picture, as quoted earlier in this book:

- Reports so far received (as part of Operation Hammer) (reveal) the significant feature of the first phase has been the large number of hideouts found (in the Aberdare forests), some considerable in size and many were skilfully constructed. One consisted of four huts capable of holding 80 men and with a piped water supply from a waterfall 30 yards away. [26] [p70]

- On the outskirts of Nairobi, Kikuyu guards and men of the Kenya Regiment, killed four freedom fighters, destroyed a Mau Mau hospital furnished with a supply of medicine and food, and arrested six women food carriers.[27] [p.70]

A number of reports on Mau Mau gun factories, conference facilities, as well as housing and water supply systems in liberated areas were carried in newspaper reports:

· East African Command headquarters announced today that a patrol

---

26 Times (London), 14 January, 1955.
27 Kenya Committee. Press Extracts, Vol.1 (25 September, 1954), pp. 82-83.

Kenya's War of Independence

of guards and police from the Meru (nationality) led by Officer Harry Hinde discovered and destroyed a Mau Mau arms factory in the Meru forest. [28]

· Police today discovered a Mau Mau gun shop and store in a part of Nairobi where the city's two hundred street sweepers live. [29]

· In early days the terrorist camps were well built. The sites were laid out with solidly constructed huts of split bamboo, with kitchens and stores, quarters for women and children and signboards indicating the commander of the camp ... from these camps, arms and ammunition, food, clothing and valuable documents have been recovered. [30]

The Kenya Committee Press Extracts summarises reports from contemporary papers about the destruction of Mau Mau hospitals by the British forces:

An army patrol following in the tracks of freedom fighters discovered a 40 bed Mau Mau hospital with complete medical kits. A Government communiqué said the hospital was 5 miles east of Mount Kinangop.[31]

*

Security Forces searching the Aberdare Forests found a deserted hospital which had apparently been evacuated a few days before, also a Council Chamber with accommodation for about 150.[32]

There are various accounts of Mau Mau gun factories and some of these are still available. Kinyatti (2008) says: "The Shauri Moyo and Pumwani bases played a special role as KLFA gun factories. Karura Forest was the main KFLA gun factory in Nairobi. It was also a KLFA major hospital." There were many South Asian skilled craftsmen who helped the establishment of such factories and training Mau Mau cadres in gun making. One such person was Jaswant Singh who was sentenced to death for illegally possessing two

---

28   Manchester Guardian. 29 Jan.1954.
29   Manchester Guardian. 23 Feb. 1954.
30   East African Standard. 20 August, 1954.
31   Kenya Committee. Press Extracts, Vol.1 (13 July, 1954), p.67.
32   Kenya Committee. Press Extracts, Vol. 1 (6 June, 1955), p.140.

rounds of ammunition. As the London *Times* noted: "...this was the first time that the supreme penalty has been imposed on a non-African under the emergency regulations."[33] Kinyatti, 2008) provides some details:

> Jaswant Singh was storing firearms for the Movement. His house was a safe haven for the Movement. In 1954, he was betrayed, arrested and sentenced to death for possession of firearm. Despite the savage torture he underwent he refused to betray the Movement.

Durrani, Nazmi (2017). provides further information on him:

> Jaswant Singh lived in Molo. By profession he was a carpenter, mason, plumber, electrician, builder, radio and motor mechanic, welder, lorry driver, tractor driver and gun maker (a karigar). He secretly supplied material to manufacture weapons, guns and ammunition to Mau Mau fighters active in the Rift Valley area.

Other reports of Mau Mau gun factories, conference facilities, as well as housing and water supply systems in liberated areas were carried in newspaper reports:

- East African Command headquarters announced today that a patrol of guards and police from the Meru (nationality) led by Officer Harry Hinde discovered and destroyed a Mau Mau arms factory in the Meru forest.[34]

- Police today discovered a Mau Mau gun shop and store in a part of Nairobi where the city's two hundred street sweepers live.[35]

- In early days the terrorist camps were well built. The sites were laid out with solidly constructed huts of split bamboo, with kitchens and stores, quarters for women and children and signboards indicating the commander of the camp ... from these camps, arms and ammunition, food, clothing and

---

33 Times (London). 31 July, 1954.
34 Manchester Guardian. 29 Jan.1954.
35 Manchester Guardian. 23 Feb. 1954.

valuable documents have been recovered.[36]

These are but a few examples of Mau Mau infrastructures. Other can be seen in the narratives of many books written by Mau Mau activists as well as in official colonial records. Here is an important area for research, particularly among surviving Mau Mau activists, to provide a fuller picture of this important aspect of Mau Mau organisation.

Politics of Information [37]

Mau Mau's information and communication strategy reflects different aspects of its overall work. Each of the elements of governance mentioned above, such as ideology, organisation and strategy, required effective flow of information between different units and parts of the resistance movement. This flow was the lifeblood of the organisation. This is essential in peacetime in any organisation, but was of particular significance in an underground movement facing a war situation against a heavily armed enemy. Survival depended on this life-giving process of flow of information and communication. And yet this was difficult to achieve in the war situation created by the imposition of the State of Emergency by British colonialism which relied not only on it military and political might but also on its experience of oppression in its other colonies, particularly India and Malaysia. The difficulties for Mau Mau were compounded by the absence of global networks such as the Internet and information embargoes by colonialism - experiences from the resistance forces in India and other countries were not easily available to the resistance organisation. It was to prevent the availability of such information that the Kenya colonial government banned various progressive publications, including many from USSR, Peoples Republic of China and India, as mentioned in Durrani, S. (2006).

> That Mau Mau managed to develop a sophisticated information policy and practice is a reflection of its strength as an advanced 20th Century resistance movement. This is again another area that requires much research. This section attempts a brief overview of its information and communication strategy.

36   East African Standard. 20 August, 1954.
37   This section includes material from Durrani, Shiraz (2006).

Communications

Mau Mau realised that any serious confrontation with a technically superior power required good organisation and planning. A key requirement to meet this was the establishment of an efficient and effective communications strategy. The information and communications structures had to be strong. These had to be created in secret and on a national scale. The task was made more difficult as the enemy they faced had the resources of its whole colonial empire. As the number of people involved in the anti-colonial struggle was very large and spread out over a vast area, the problems of communications had to be solved first. An organisation of this vast magnitude could not function unless its various components could communicate with each other: the leadership needed to get intelligence and other reports from the smallest units and pass down instructions for action. At the same time contacts with sympathetic masses of workers and peasants had to be maintained, together with links with nationalities from all parts of the country.

Different methods of communication were developed and used at different stages of the struggle and in different areas of the country, depending on the intensity of struggle in each area and on whether the area was liberated, semi-liberated or under British control. Mau Mau developed an information strategy, which included the following aspects:

1. Oral communications.
2. Revolutionary publishing.
3. Use of pamphlets and handbills.
4. Establishments of a people's press.
5. Information gathering and dissemination.[38]

At the time of the Declaration of Emergency, the need was to organise secretly. The colonialist regime had kept Kenyan nationalities in isolation from each other by banning Kenya-wide nationalist movements. This had been overcome at one level by various nationality-based organisations working closely together. But one of the first tasks of Mau Mau was to

38 Further details on Mau Mau's communications policy and practice are covered in Durrani, Shiraz (2006).

develop new communication links with all people of Kenya, and to do it secretly.

Mau Mau, using its organisational network which was based at Mathare Valley, a working class residential area in Nairobi, solved this problem. Since the largest concentration of workers was in Nairobi, communications and organisational networks reaching all parts of the country were organised from here. Workers of various nationalities were recruited from here. There were close links between the militant trade unions and the central command of Mau Mau. The advanced workers recruited in Nairobi acted not only as cadres in the city but they helped to set up powerful links with the peasants. Workers of different nationalities became in effect links between peasants, plantation and urban workers and Mau Mau. Particularly important was the information collected by workers in domestic service, offices, and plantations. Workers in government departments were particularly important as they collected information from conversations, official files, newspaper and other reports and passed these on to Mau Mau using oral means of communication. It was this flow of information that enabled Mau Mau to be more effective in all its work. Without such links the resistance movement could easily have been crushed by imperialism in a short time. Historical studies that see Mau Mau as a peasant movement only, miss this important aspect of working class input into the War of Independence.

The process of communications was made easy by using the central position of Nairobi as the transport hub of Kenya. The railways provided links from Mombasa to Kisumu and messages could be passed on by workers on the railways all along the path of the railway. Within urban areas, taxi drivers provided well-developed means of communications. In addition, Mau Mau developed bicycle networks to supplement other means of communicating and connecting its various support structures. Such an approach developed on the practices developed by the trade unions that had used such methods to gain strength during their strike and other activities and for recruiting members, as described by Makhan Singh (1969).

Kenya's experience in using transport facilities and workers involved in running them - taxi drivers, buses, trains etc - has a parallel with the experience in Cuba, as recalled by Quinn (2015):

Taken together, the workers' struggles provide a compelling account of how organized labour contributed directly and indirectly to help shape the course of revolutionary struggle in 1950s Cuba. As Cushion [2016] depicts so vividly here, workers provided valuable material support for the rebel guerrillas in a number of ways, including organizing significant strike action in support of the Granma landing and armed uprising in Santiago. Workers in shops, warehouses, and distribution depots proved valuable by large-scale pilfering of essentials, railway workers were able to move those supplies under the noses of the police, and bus drivers formed propaganda distribution networks, while telephone operators eavesdropped on police conversations, providing vital intelligence for those more directly engaged in the armed struggle. Others organized clandestine networks involved in acts of sabotage such as derailing an armoured train carrying soldiers sent to protect the vital railway system, and helping disaffected soldiers to desert. Such actions depended on a high degree of organization that reached its apotheosis in the revolutionary general strike of January 1, 1959. Overlooked in much of the literature, this strike is reassessed here for its decisive contribution to the triumph of the revolution ... Thus, for Cushion, the final victory of the revolutionary forces should be viewed as the result of a combination of armed guerrilla action and mass support.

Of course the situation of working class and the level of class struggles in Kenya were quite different from those in Cuba. Yet it is true that in Kenya, as in Cuba, resistance forces worked as a partnership between armed guerrilla units and mass support. Lessons in analysing Kenyan history can be learnt from the Cuban experience. Similarly, understanding the role of peasants in the revolutions in Vietnam, China and Cuba can find parallels in the experience in Kenya. The struggle against colonialism and imperialism is universal in many countries but the particular manifestations of these struggles vary from country to country. Within these boundaries, understanding the forces of resistance and oppression can help in learning lessons not only in how to conduct anti-imperialist struggles, but also how to understand and communicate information and history from a working class perspective.

After the Declaration of Emergency by the Colonial authorities, it became necessary for Mau Mau activists to go underground but the movement functioned very efficiently as an organisation. This is shown, for example, in its communication activities. The colonial administration took over total control over all the mass media upon Declaration of Emergency. Until then, Mau Mau had been publishing over fifty newspapers in Kiswahili and in various nationality languages, as well as a large number of struggle songs and other anti-colonial material. The Emergency measures were now used to suppress all these publications, which had functioned as important means of communication with the supporters of Mau Mau.

Mau Mau soon found alternative methods of communicating not only with the active fighters, but also with the masses who supported it and whose armed fist it was. Oral media were extensively used. Established printing presses, particularly those owned by progressive South Asian Kenyans were used. Cyclostyling machines were installed at their Mathare Valley Headquarters. All these were used to issue hand bills, posters and newspapers. Mau Mau published the *High Command* which was issued regularly between 1952 and 1957. Asian Kenyan cadres and supporters of Mau Mau initially printed this, as they could initially escape colonial suspicion. Later, it was printed at its Mathare Valley printing works. *High Command* was anti-imperialist in content and circulated underground among the 35,000 freedom fighters and provided a basic forum for the politicisation and advancement of the combatants. It informed them on the ideology, the organisation, the strategies, and activities of the Revolution. (Mirii, 1979).

One task facing Mau Mau was that of ensuring the political and ideological development of its cadres. The other was to demoralise the enemy troops and their White settler supporters. Many handbills and posters were issued and posted at prominent places in enemy areas. One pamphlet was issued just three days after the Declaration of Emergency. It was sent to many Settlers and posted on trees and walls in many areas of Nairobi. This shows the organisation commanded of the resistance forces. While the colonial armies were busy creating a reign of terror, cadres were printing and distributing important communications under enemy gunfire. One such pamphlet is important also for its content, which shows the clear understanding of the situation by Mau Mau. It was addressed to the "Murdering Colonialists" and was entitled *Fascism Has Come to Kenya*. It read:

Fascism Has Come to Kenya

> You must feel very happy at the outward success of your cruel operation. You arrested our leaders and a lot of other people. Thousands of Africans leading a normal life have been stopped, searched, beaten, humiliated and arrested. Creating the Emergency, you have brutally treated us and now you cannot claim democracy and freedom. Fascism has come to Kenya.
>
> We have been robbed of all freedom. You have destroyed our press by arresting our editors and suppressing our newspapers. But you cannot suppress the voice of the people. The brutality and oppression, the show of force and the rule of gun will not stop us from our goal. You cannot end our political wish by arresting our leaders. We have many more men with brains and will continue to fight you and achieve our freedom. This is the voice of new Africa. We have been forced to go underground. If we are known, you will murder us. We are not afraid. We ask how many of us you will imprison, how many of us you will kill? We are six million and power is in our numbers. We shall retaliate in the method you have employed. We shall not forget the bad treatment we are suffering. When our time comes we shall not show mercy, because you do not know what mercy is. We will kill you like are murdering us today. This is no threat. It is how we are feeling today. Africans unite! [39]

Oral Communications

The use of oral communication systems was well established before the colonial government declared a state of Emergency. Fred Kubai (1983) explains how this developed:

---

[39] A copy of the pamphlet was sent to the 'Kenya Committee for Democratic Rights for Kenya' in London, from whose files it is quoted here. The Committee was formed in solidarity with the people of Kenya in their struggle against imperialism. So alarmed were the Colonial Government authorities by the content of this pamphlet that the Colonial Attorney General, Mr. John Whyatt, prevented any newspaper from printing it 'on threat of prosecution'.

In November 1951 the colonialists and white settler newspapers stopped covering KAU public meetings. [In order to overcome] this, the militants started mouth-to-mouth bush-radio information service. Songs were composed carrying revolutionary and 'subversive' messages and were sung by both young and old. Kinuthia Mugia of Olenguroine became champion in the composition of new Kikuyu songs. J. J. Gakara, among others, printed the songs into 'hymn books'. Kikuyu and Kiswahili newspapers and pamphlets were started. I revived the official KAU organ, *Sauti-Ya-Mwafrika*. Other militant papers included *Afrika Mpya* which was edited by Kaggia, *Hindi ya Gikuyu* and *Muthamaki*, which were edited by Victor Wokabi, *Muramati, Mumenyereri*; *Kayu-ka-Embu, Wihuge, Gikuyu na Mumbi*.

The content of these publications reflect a high awareness of what imperialism meant for Kenya. For example, Kinyatti (2008) quotes from *Muthamaki* which explained the conditions which gave rise to Mau Mau in an article in July 1952:

> Mau Mau will never be destroyed by the imposition of fines, imprisonment or torture. Mau Mau is the product of the exploitation and racism which our people experience in their daily lives. Eliminate exploitation and racism and there will be no Mau Mau.

There was a need to organise secretly against colonialism. This was achieved by using oral communication, a method developed during an earlier period when the colonialist regime had banned Kenya-wide nationalist movements, in order to keep Kenyan nationalities in isolation from each other.

The problem of how to communicate effectively, but secretly, was solved by Mau Mau, using its organisational network, centred at Mathare Valley in Nairobi. Since the largest concentration of workers was in Nairobi, a new communication network was organised from here. Workers of various nationalities were recruited in Nairobi. One aspect of their work was to act as links with their nationality areas. Thus the worker-organised Mau Mau movement established deep roots among peasantry, without which the whole movement could have been crushed by imperialism within a short time.

This early organisational work, together with the task of establishment of communication links with the rest of the country, was done so secretly that it was almost five years before the colonial government became aware of the movement and were forced to declare a State of Emergency - in effect a state of war - against Kenyan workers and peasants in October, 1952.

Before the Emergency was declared, the nationalist and the worker forces had been using the "legal" press to organise and communicate, although this had to be done in coded languages which outsiders could not understand. One aspect of the political work was to organise mass political meetings, which could both organise people and give direction to the political movement. It was thus necessary to communicate times and places of such anti-imperialist meetings to the people who were ever eager to be active. Barton (1979) examines this early period to assess how the communication needs were satisfied:

> The mushrooming of the African press was an important factor in fostering political action in the urban centres of Kenya after the Second World War. Publications appeared in several (national) languages and also in English. Most of these were printed in Nairobi, although Mombassa had the *Coast African Express* and on the shores of Lake Victoria, in Kisumu, there was the *Nyanza Times*.
>
> All were nationalist and highly militant, expressing bitterness at colonial discrimination and poverty and insecurity of the African [people] against the affluence of the Settlers.
>
> The Kikuyu papers around Nairobi were the most successful, and the most influential was *Mumenyereri* ("Defender"). This was a weekly edited by the Kenya African Union's assistant general secretary, Henry Mworia, and with a sale of 10,000 was probably read by six times that number.
>
> As the tension grew which was to ignite finally in the Mau Mau, it became more and more uncompromising in its nationalism. The colonial government had banned political meetings but *Mumenyereri* was regularly referring to 'tea parties' in the shanty

towns (Mathare, Kariobangi, Bahati and Majengo worker areas) around Nairobi, which were, in fact, occasions for the secret [anti-imperialist] oathing ceremonies.

Kinyatti (2008) gives even a higher estimate of the circulation of *Mumenyereri*:

> As channels of political communications, and using our own languages, these anti-imperialist newspapers were vital in developing anti-imperialist consciousness amongst the Kenyan masses. Some of them were widely read and had great political influence in the country. For instance, Mumenyereri was the most popular paper in Central Kenya and the squatter areas of the Rift Valley, with an average circulation of 20,000 copies. It played a patriotic role in agitating against British colonial land and labour policy, vehemently opposed white racism and cultural imperialism, and supported the underground movement.

After the Declaration of Emergency by the Colonial authorities, it became necessary for the Mau Mau to reorganise as an underground movement. But it continued to function very efficiently as an organisation. This is shown, for example, in its communication activities. The colonial administration took over total control over all the mass media upon Declaration of Emergency. Until then, the Mau Mau had been publishing directly or indirectly over fifty newspapers in Kiswahili and in various nationality languages, and had published a large number of liberation songs and other anti-colonial material. The Emergency measures were now used by the colonial power to suppress all these publications, which had functioned as important means of communication for the liberation forces.

When the British colonial administration became aware of the full extent of the organisation with its specific ideology and strategies for liberation backed by a political and military power, it began to investigate the background and organisation of the movement. Leakey (1954) had this to say about Mau Mau's intelligence gathering, and its development and use of the oral medium:

> The value of good intelligence system has always been appreciated by

the Kenyan people. The Mau Mau organised a system of getting their own followers into key positions where they could find out what was happening and report to their leaders. Chosen men obtained positions as houseboys and chauffeurs in the household where there was the greatest likelihood of being able to learn things about the plans of Security Forces. Others were encouraged to get jobs in Government Offices, in the Police, and in the Homeguards and Telephone Service. Since the Kikuyu have always supplied a very high proportion of the employees of these categories in normal times and since there are generally loyal Kikuyu in such jobs, it was and still is very difficult indeed to distinguish between the spy and the genuine loyalist.

Moreover, by no means all those employed on such intelligence work were drawn from the ranks of the Kikuyu. Enough members of other tribes had been won over to the Mau Mau cause to make it possible to use members of these other tribes in this intelligence organisation.

It is interesting to note that when the colonial authorities wanted to minimise the national significance of Mau Mau, their propaganda described Mau Mau as purely a Gikuyu movement; yet, as the above clearly indicates, the national spread of the movement is freely acknowledged by colonial sources.

Oral communication was considered a safe means of communication by the liberation forces because of the high security risks in written communications. It was common for a team of two or more Mau Mau activists to carry messages from the Mau Mau High Command in the heart of Nyandarua to different Mau Mau centres, and its armies, or to the progressive workers and peasants throughout the country. The art of the progressive Wakamba wood carvers (carving no. 1) depicts the scene:

> Two couriers carrying orders from the Kenya Defence Council are caught in the enemy ambush. One courier rushes at the enemy so that the other may escape and deliver the orders. The dying fighter digs deep the soil and exhorts his companion to continue. The courier crosses many ridges and valleys across Kenya. (*History of Kenya*, 1976).

These activists performed many tasks: soldiers, librarians (with duties ranging from collection, storage and making available the intelligence from different units), social workers and hunters (to obtain food while on missions). The soldier-information workers avoided carrying any written material on their bodies. They had developed their memories and could carry detailed instructions in their heads. They were under specific instructions that should they meet the enemy, they were not to risk their lives but ensure that their messages were delivered. Many brave soldier-information workers gave their lives during the struggle while ensuring that communications lines were kept open.

The Mau Mau movement had developed a large number of such soldier-information workers who knew the land routes for safe travel. At the same time they had developed a network of small libraries and archival units in the liberated areas which contained much useful information. The colonial authorities found details of advanced Mau Mau practices in the course of one of their mass arrest campaigns, as quoted by the *Times* (London, 11-08-1954):

> Arrests made in operation "Broom"...The search revealed that the Mau Mau had begun to use as couriers persons not likely to be suspected, among them a large number of young boys and old men. One deformed elderly man who was identified as a collector of funds had £40 hidden among beggars' rags when arrested.

Again, the *Times* (London, 30-09-1954) reports:

> Brigadier Boyce, general secretary of the Save the Children Fund, said that in the reserves there are children whose fathers have been killed, others whose families had left their homes, and many more whose fathers had gone away. In Nairobi, it was estimated that there were up to 1,000 such children. "Many of the orphans and homeless boys are acting as food carriers and couriers to the Mau Mau gangs, and eventually become recruits to Mau Mau," he added.

Oral communication was used in other areas as well. It was particularly useful in working with the masses, for example, in passing messages about meetings or plans about specific military engagement. It was in this way that active and progressive workers and peasants passed on news about enemy movements to the military command. Children and women played a central part in this as, initially at least, they were not suspected to be Mau Mau activists. The use of resistance songs continued in detention camps. The *Kenya Committee Press Extracts* (Vol. 1, 07-05-1954) records:

> Most of the women showed quite openly their support for the freedom fighters while detained in screening camps. At one camp the women danced and sang Mau Mau songs. When some of them were escorted to the trains they hurled their rations of tinned meat, milk and biscuits at the railway staff.

The colonial administration was so concerned about singing of Mau Mau songs that it sentenced people to solitary confinement for this "crime", as the following report in the *Manchester Guardian* (30-05-1956) shows:

> ...Cases which Miss Eileen Fletcher (a former rehabilitation officer in Kenya) described yesterday included one in which Kikuyu women were given sixteen days' solitary confinement in small dark cells made of corrugated iron, for singing Mau Mau hymns.

Another aspect of Mau Mau's guerrilla and communications strategy was to feed incorrect information to the colonial forces. They also deprived the colonial forces of information altogether, so that often the colonial forces acted in total ignorance about Mau Mau movements, force strength and plans. This obviously could not have been achieved without the support of the masses in towns as well as in the countryside. This was acknowledged in the Kenya Police Annual Report for 1954:

> The year opened with the initiative in the hands of Mau Mau which... had virtually put a stop to the flow of information to the authorities. The vast majority of the Kikuyu (people) was either, actively or passively, assisting the Mau Mau movement.

This was confirmed by the British Parliamentary delegation, which visited Kenya. Its report, published on 23 February 1955 and quoted in the *Times* (24-02-1955), contrasts the use of information as a weapon by the two opposing forces:

The delegation considered that insufficient use is being made of the weapon of information and propaganda. To some extent, the Mau Mau by using the traditional African channel of spreading rumours, the "bush telegraph" held the initiative in this field.

Mau Mau also used creative communications as a way of achieving their political and military aims. They forged symbols of colonialism to infiltrate enemy lines. Their members with special skills supported them in this. The Kenya Committee provides details and commentary, which provide a glimpse into this aspect of Mau Mau strategy:

- African tailor, making white arm bands similar to Homeguards, arrested. Bands used by Freedom Fighters as disguise. (Vol. 1, 07-04-1953, p.29)

- New emergency regulations making it an offence for anyone to wear naval, military, air force, police and other official uniforms without authorisation. (Vol.1, 29-05-1953, p.33).[40]

- A number of fishing boats operating from villages on the Kavirondo Gulf have been the subject of a report to the authorities. The name "Jomo Kenyatta" is painted on one boat, another bears the name, "Mau Mau". (Vol.1, 08-07-1955, p.151).

- The Kenya Government announced today that a Kikuyu woman who had been crowned "Mau Mau Queen" on Coronation Day, June 2, had been imprisoned for ten years for taking the Mau Mau oath and for being chair of a women's terrorist movement. (Vol.1, 02-01-1954).

Language of Resistance

The need for oral communication led to the development of a special language of resistance that only the liberation forces could understand.

---

40 This was in response to the tactics used by Mau Mau combatants to launch attacks wearing British army uniforms. Kinyatti (2002) records an event in 1953: "the KFLA unit disguised in enemy uniform ambushed a patrol of the KAR traitors at Ihuririo in Uthaya killing three of them".

It thus became possible to pass on oral messages even in the presence on enemy forces and to use enemy controlled or censored newspapers for the same purpose. Even the colonial sources admitted the skilful use of such methods, as Leakey (1954) observes:

> In view of the risk of written messages being intercepted by security forces, documentary methods were only seldom used [by the Mau Mau cadres], and when they were, they were nearly always so worded as to be seemingly innocuous.
>
> To this end Mau Mau developed a most complex system of everyday words to indicate things other than what they seemed to mean and these code words were frequently changed. Examples of these code words are 'makara', which normally means charcoal, for ammunition; 'muti', which normally means a tree, for a gun; 'kamwaki', which means a little fire, for a revolver or pistol; and 'kihii', which means an overgrown boy, for a gunman.
>
> Constant communication was maintained between the army in the forests and various councils at upper level in Nairobi and elsewhere, responsible for collecting food, supplies, etc. [Additionally] an organisation was set up - mainly with women as couriers - to make and maintain contact with detained leaders in detention camps.
>
> As a part of the arms business, it became necessary to have all sorts of special code words, so that the verbal and written messages could be sent about the (procuring), hiding, or distribution of firearms, that would be clear to the recipient, but not appear in the least suspicious to the ordinary security investigator.

Further examples of the development of language to suit the needs of waging an armed guerrilla movement are given by Barnett and Njama (1966), most of these dealing with military terms:

Banda	Guerrilla terminology for home-made guns

Bebeta	Derived from the Swahili term *pepeta*, meaning to winnow or sift. It was the guerrilla term for Stan gun.
Gatheci	Literally, 'sharp instrument'. It was the guerrilla term for Homeguard, derived from the fact that Homeguards were initially armed with spears.
Gathugo	Literally, 'throwing weapon'. Guerrilla term for Homeguard.
Gatimu	Literally, 'small spear'. Guerrilla term for Homeguard, derived from the fact that Homeguards were initially armed with spears.
Gatua uhoro	Literally, 'the decider'. Guerrilla term for big-game shooting guns ranging from .375 to .450.
Gicakuri	Singular of *icakuri*, meaning 'heavy pitchfork'. Guerrilla term for any government personnel or European.
Gikonyo	Protruding navel'. Guerrilla term for British bombers, derived from the impression conveyed by the open bomb doors.
Ihii cia mititu	'Forest boys'. Guerrilla term for warriors.
Kamwaki	'Small fire'. Guerrilla term for pistol.
Kariiguru	'It is up'. Guerrilla term meaning that an airplane was approaching.
Kenya Ng'ombe	Guerrilla term for (British) Kenya Regiment personnel, derived from the fact that Ng'ombe (cow) was the KR symbol.
Kuri hono-i ndirara?	A guerrilla signal to camp guards signifying that one was not an enemy.
Makara	'Charcoal'. Guerrilla term for ammunition.
Mbuci	Guerrilla terminology for a camp, derived from the English 'bush'.
Muhimu	A code term for the Mau Mau, meaning 'most important' in Kiswahili.

Muingi	"Community" or "people" (as opposed to "enemy"). A term used by the Mau Mau for workers and peasants.
Muirigo	'A clear forest path'.
Nakombora	'The destroyer'. Guerrilla term for Bren gun.
Nyagikonyo	'The bearer of a protruding navel'. Guerrilla term for the Lincoln heavy bomber.
Nyamu Nditu	'The heavy animal'. Guerrilla term for the Mau Mau.
Tie-Ties	African white collar worker; a pejorative term for Europeanised Africans who were least likely to assist in the revolutionary struggle for land and freedom. Refers to those who wore ties, a symbol of foreign culture.
The Townwatch Battalions	The guerrilla term for all those who fought in the towns, most of whom carried on their normal jobs during the day and fought at night.

Communication in Detention Camps

Mau Mau activists in detention camps developed the use of oral communications further. The living conditions were very harsh, and lack of proper food, poor housing conditions and hard labour made the lives of the inmates even more difficult. They were also deprived of contact with the outside world. No newspapers, radios or any news from outside the detention camp were allowed.

But the detainees developed their own oral news services and oral newspapers, with regular news, and were thus able to communicate with each other and to get news about the struggle outside as well as world news. Kariuki (1975) describes some of these oral information services:

> In many ways the most important nourishment we had was from the two news services that we operated (at Manyani Detention Camp).

The Manyani Times was the news that was known to be true which had been picked up from newspapers by those cleaning in the warder's lines or had been heard on a wireless by someone working near an officer's house. We were extremely cunning at obtaining news without being seen to do so.

The Waya Times was the news that was largely speculation, rumours or light relief. In the evenings, after food, each 'club' in every compound would send a representative to the barbed wire partitions to get the news. We were extremely lucky in Compound 13 since we could converse with five other compounds. Anyone who had any news would stand up and say *giteo*, which is Kikuyu for 'respect' and brought instant silence all around him. Then he would say, "I now begin my words of Manyani Times (or Waya Times) which are that . . ." This immediately told his listeners how much credibility to place in what was coming. Waya Times news items might include the dismissal of the Governor, the date of Independence (never later than 1956), the revocation of unpleasant regulations by the Commissioner of Prisons, our imminent release...

The warders disliked our news service intensely and whenever they saw us eagerly listening to it someone would throw a few stones to break us up. The evening news hour was also used for throwing tobacco to friends in other compounds.

Other detention camps also had similar communications network, for example the *Kamongo Times at* Saiyusi Detention Centre and *The Mukoma Times* at Lodwar Detention Centre. Pio Gama Pinto and Ramogi Achieng Oneko's contribution to the development of oral communications in detention camp is also significant. Oneko (1966) gives an interesting insight:

[During detention on Manda Island] there came a time when the authorities had begun to engineer confusion in the camp in order to demoralise us. We realised that if we did not organise counter measures and propaganda many of us (numbering about two hundred) would be wrecked. We therefore started a counter propaganda move. Pio was one of the editors and played a big role in a well organised network. It was his job to dish out information to the Lower Camp by word of mouth to our own propagandists. To the astonishment and surprise of the Camp Administration the morale of the detainees was restored and we remained hard and impenetrable.

It is noteworthy that the detention centres came to be known as "Mau Mau Universities" (Kenya Weekly News, 18-03-1955) as there was a well-developed programme run by experienced cadres to educate new inmates on the ideology and world outlook of Mau Mau. They also acted as recruitment grounds for new members.

McGhie (2002) reveals yet another use of oral tradition in detention camps as a form of resistance and records the brutality with which the colonial regime treated such resistance. The incident below took place at the Mwea detention centre:

> Mr Gavaghan explained, however, that there had, in past intakes, been more persistent resistors who had been forcibly changed into camp clothing. Some of them had started the 'Mau Mau howl', a familiar cry which was taken up by the rest of the camp, representing a concerted and symbolic defiance of the camp authorities. In such cases it was essential to prevent the infection of this 'oath' spreading throughout the camp, and the 'resistor' who started it was put on the ground, a foot placed on his throat and mud stuffed in his mouth. In the last resort, a man whose resistance could not be broken down was knocked unconscious. [41]

More information about such atrocities by the occupying British forces are coming into public domain as part of the war crimes inquiry launched by the Scotland Yard following the move by the Mau Mau veterans to start a potentially huge legal action for compensation for atrocities during the war of liberation.

Songs

Revolutionary songs were another aspect of Mau Mau's use of people's oral culture. They served a number of purposes. Songs became a powerful expression of people's culture in the struggle against colonial culture. They broke the colonial monopoly over means of communication and took the

---
41   McGhie (2002).

anti-colonial message right into people's homes. The content reflected the political needs of the struggle. Songs were tools of organising people against colonialism, a rallying point for people to identify with. They encouraged people to oppose a common enemy in an organised way and as a united force. Songs became a source of information and a record of history, which was passed on to the new generation.

New songs were made to record Mau Mau activities and events. For example, General Kariba's soldiers of the Kenya Levellation Army composed and sung songs to commemorate the battle of the Tumu Tumu Hill. Songs were used to propagate ideas about liberation, which could not be openly published due to colonialist censorship. Describing the 26th July 1952 KAU meeting at the Nyeri Show grounds, attended by over 30,000 people, Njama (Barnet and Njama, 1966) says:

> The organisation (Mau Mau) was given considerable publicity because most of the organisers of the meeting were Mau Mau leaders and most of the (audience), Mau Mau members. They were given the opportunity to circulate Mau Mau propaganda songs when both coming and leaving the meeting ... As I was pushing my bicycle uphill towards Muthuaini School where I was teaching I enjoyed many Mau Mau songs which were sung by the crowd as they left the meeting.

There were still other types of songs, the *Marari*, which were warrior songs encouraging the people to fight for their rights. The Mau Mau published many such songs when the movement began to spread over larger areas. One Mau Mau song was used by the Tamaduni Players (1978):

Utavumilia Kifo?
Watoto wa Kenya huishi mwituni
Wakinyeshewa na mvua
Wakipata njaa, mateso na baridi nyingi
Kwa upendo wa udongo.

Uui, iiyai, uui iiyai
Kuuawa na taabu na kufungwa
Mara nyingi
Je utavumilia?

Ni akina nani hao wanaimba kwa sauti kubwa
Ngambo ya pili ya mto
Wakiwaimbia Kago na Mbaria
Watafutaji wa haki.

Uui, iiyai, uui iiyai
Kuuawa na taabu na kufungwa
Mara nyingi
Je utavumilia?

Are you prepared to face death?
Sons and daughters of Kenya
live in forests
enduring thunder, starvation,
for the love of their soil.

Uui, iiyai, uui iiyai

Enduring torture and jailings
time after time
Are you prepared?

> And who are those
> on the other side of the river
> singing in fearless voices
> praises and exploits of Kago and Mbaria
> Seekers of our rights.

Uui, iiyai, uui iiyai
enduring torture and jailings
time after time
Are you prepared?

Kinyatti (2008) discusses the importance, purpose, and content of songs and oral medium as used by the Mau Mau. He identifies three aspects of oral communications, which developed during the changing contradictions of the times:

> Within a span of five years the Mau Mau produced most formidable political songs which were used as a weapon to politicise and educate the Kenyan worker and peasant masses. This helped heighten the people's consciousness against the forces of the foreign occupiers, and, in the process, prepared them for armed struggle. The role of these songs in educating the workers and peasants against the dictatorship of the colonialists was an undeniable catalyst in the development and success of the movement.

> [The second aspect] consisted of detention and prison songs from the early war years. They highlight the suffering in the camps and prisons. They express the people's bitterness against the "Homeguard" traitors who were hunting, spying on and torturing them in the camps and who superintended their eviction from the Settlers' plantations. The songs make it clear to these traitors that they will pay with their lives for their treachery. Some of them also eulogise the Mau Mau guerrillas in the forests of their heroism and express their confidence and faith in Field Marshall Dedan Kimaathi's leadership. Finally, they articulate the people's optimism that they will win the struggle against the forces of the occupation.

> [The third aspect consisted of] lyrics by guerrillas. One can sense the very flames of war in them. They glorify the revolutionary aspects of the Movement: its dialectical relationship with the worker and peasant masses on the one hand and its principal contradiction with

British colonialism on the other.

One of the Mau Mau guerrilla songs reproduced by Kinyatti (1980) shows the freedom fighters' awareness of the sufferings of the people under colonialism; it mentions the fact that colonial laws were used to ban Kenyan newspapers; and the leadership's call "to unite and fight"; and the heroism of the people against the foreign enemy: the song is entitled *Declaration of War in Kenya*:

> When the war was declared in 1952
> Our country was turned into a huge prison.
> Innocent people, men, women and children,
> Were herded into concentration camps,
> Under all kinds of harsh repression.
>
> Our livestock were confiscated
> And our crops in the fields were destroyed.
> All public markets were closed down
> And all people's newspapers were banned.
>
> Meanwhile Kimaathi in Nyandarwa called for total mobilisation,
> He told people to unite and fight
> These foreign murderers with heroism
> And drive them out of the country.
>
> In spite of harsh enemy repression
> The revolutionary flame was maintained and developed.
> And people's hatred towards the British oppressors
> Grew day by day,
> And proudly they declared:
> "It would be better to die on our feet
> Than to live on our knees."

Many songs were written by Kinuthia wa Mugia, Muthee wa Cheche, Gakaara wa Wanjau, J. M. Kariuki, Karari wa Wanjau, and Mohamed Mathu. These songs were then circulated to people as orature. Many were also printed and published as booklets by activist organisations such as Gakaara Book Service. An example of a songbook is *Witikio*, which became extremely popular. Others were printed and distributed as individual cyclostyled sheets.

The effectiveness of the oral sources of information was proven when the highest level of confidential British information reached the Mau Mau before it became public knowledge. This happened, for example, when the colonial government declared a State of Emergency. The news had already reached the combatants through the organisation's well-placed activists, even before an official announcement was made. The Kenya Committee Press Extracts (1952, Vol.1 pp. 6-7) records the events:

> On Monday, October 20th, the State of Emergency was declared... over 100 African leaders were arrested...There was one hitch however in the Government's elaborate plans. News of the impending arrests leaked out causing the Government to advance the arrests by one hour. In spite of this advancement, many Africans on the list for arrest were warned in time to make their escape – most likely to the forests!

This was also the case when the colonial authorities made a surrender offer to Mau Mau in 1955. The London *Times* (17-01-1955) expresses colonial frustration at the ease with which information reached Mau Mau combatants before it was officially sent:

> In both cases, as now, there has been a breach of security, and the news of the impending offer has leaked out ahead of schedule. The fact that such leakages can still occur scarcely inspires confidence in the ability of the authorities to handle these surrender offers in the best circumstances.

Publishing

Revolutionary publishing of this period was aimed at satisfying the communication needs of the guerrilla army to maintain links among themselves, as well as with the masses which provided it support. Three different levels of publishing activities were used in keeping with the particular conditions of the time. These were:

1. The use of existing 'legal' newspapers which were sympathetic to the Movement to pass on their messages to the people and to receive intelligence reports through coded messages.

2. The establishment of many new publications which functioned 'legally' for a time before the colonial government suppressed them. Others would then be started to replace the suppressed ones.

3. The third level was the establishment of Mau Mau's own publishing industry with its own printing works, editors, reporters and technical experts. They developed a network of printing presses in liberated and semi liberated areas, which were under the control of the people's forces. An independent distribution network supplemented this.

"Legal" Publications

"Legal" publications were newspapers, books and other printed material, which were published under colonial laws. The colonial government was not, however, aware of the real purpose served by these publications. Although the intelligence branch of the colonial police censored these publications very strictly, the liberation forces managed to pass on much information to its supporters and also used them to create anti-colonial consciousness among people. An example is the use of *Mumenyereri* to pass on messages about anti-imperialist meetings to its supporters under the guise of "tea parties".

These 'legal' publications developed in contradiction to the colonial controlled publications. Specifically they helped the liberation forces to counter colonial propaganda broadcast over radio stations, newspapers, books and educational systems. It was the specific conditions of this period which shaped the publishing activities of this period.

It is important to realise the close co-operation during this period between progressive South Asian press workers and their African counterparts on the liberation front. Spencer (1983) records their contribution:

>...There were other Indians (besides Apa Pant) who did even more but whose importance has been overlooked. These were the men in the newspaper business: printers, publishers, and editors, whose machines produced the African papers. It would be difficult to overstate the significance of these new publications...all these papers helped build a political awareness that had not existed before. Because European printers obviously would not touch them and since, for several years after the War, no African could afford to publish them on their own, it was left to the Indians ... to print these new African papers.

The use of the existing publications was one way in which the revolutionary forces communicated with their supporters. Mau Mau did not control these but they managed to use whatever openings there were to pass on their messages through the columns of local papers. But given that they controlled large administrative machinery which had jurisdiction over vast areas with hundreds of thousands of people, other methods of communication had to be developed.

One such method used by Mau Mau was the establishment of 'legal' newspapers. This was possible in the late 1940s and early 1950s. By 1954, about fifty such newspapers were established by the liberation forces. As soon as the colonial administration became aware of the reality that Mau Mau controlled them, they were banned. Most of these were in one of the nationality languages or in Kiswahili and supported Mau Mau and the independence movement. They were in fact, directly or indirectly, controlled by the Mau Mau High Command through its Mathare Valley headquarters in Nairobi. Some of these are listed in Durrani, S. (2006).

Newspapers were started by Mau Mau for political reason, to give publicity to their political demands and to organise the masses behind Mau Mau ideology and programme. Mass meetings organised by KAU were becoming very popular with thousands attending. One way in which the colonial administration tried to stop these meetings was to cut off any publicity for them. The European-owned newspapers would not report these meetings and there thus developed an information gap, which needed to be addressed by Mau Mau. It did so by launching a number of newspapers in nationality languages, all indirectly controlled by the High Command and run by individuals who were not known by the government as belonging to

Mau Mau. Thus the organisation was protected from being known by the colonial administration and even when many newspapers were banned, the organisation remained intact.

Among papers started by activists were: *Inooro ria Gikuyu* (November 1951), *Afrika Mpya* (October 1952), *Gikuyu na Mumbi, Wihuge,* and *Wiyathi*. There were many songbooks, such as *Witikio*, all of which were spreading the same message. They gave a political interpretation to events and also publicised KAU activities.

Around this time, the old contradictions between the two ways of achieving independence sharpened. On the one hand were those who favoured petitioning the colonial government to 'grant' independence; on the other hand were those who maintained that the only way to remove imperialism from Kenya was through an armed struggle. The latter started preparations for an armed struggle soon after 1945 and represented the worker consciousness of the Kenyan proletariat. It was this line, which merged with militant nationalists and trade unionists to become Mau Mau.

Kaggia (1975) records the conditions of the time:

> My newspapers and the others founded during 1951 and 1952, catered for politically conscious readers. It was the period of great strides in oath administration; it was a period of change, when people were beginning to lose their faith in gradual constitutional progress. Many young initiates were very impatient. They were always asking when we were going to take up arms and fight for our rights. The newspaper editors had to write for this audience, even if it meant being prosecuted. We had only one aim: to arouse people to the point where they would be ready to do anything for Kenya. We didn't consider our own safety or welfare.

The activities of the African press had begun to worry the colonial authorities as early as 1946 from which time they sought to find ways, legal or otherwise, to suppress Kenyan publishing. A meeting of provincial commissioners held on 26th October, 1946 discussed the issue of newspapers and recommended that the following points be sent to the Secretary of State in Britain as recorded by Corfield (1960):

- That the present trend of the [African] press constituted a grave menace to the future of the Colony.

- That certain [African] newspapers were being financed and influenced by seditious minded Indians and that their object was purely anti-government and anti-European.

- That, as regards freedom of the press, liberty was being mistaken for licence, and that in addition to deliberate distortion of facts, many of the articles in such newspapers contained a most dangerous and pernicious form of anti-European propaganda.

- Asking for information as to what legislation existed in any other British Colony for the control of the Press, and suggesting consideration of the possibility of some form of supervision or censorship.

In the following months, even more local publications emerged and the message they carried became even more anti-imperialist and militant, demanding even more urgent changes. The colonialists' concern was voiced by the Acting Chief Native Commissioner to the Member for Law and Order and the Deputy Chief Secretary on 20th February, 1947, quoted in Corefield (1960):

> In my view the general tone of these tribal newspapers since the date of the provincial commissioners' meeting in October last year has steadily deteriorated and the situation which was urgent enough then is worse today. As you are aware, 18 months ago there was practically no (national) Press, with the exception of the Baraza, which is run by the East African Standard and which is, broadly speaking, moderate in tone. Since that date a number of newspapers edited by Africans and published in English, Swahili, and the vernacular languages has sprung up ... To my mind a serious cause of this cleavage is the continuous stream of lies, misrepresentation and colour consciousness which is pouring out from vernacular presses, and which is inspired by a few Africans, abetted by the owners of the Indian presses who produce these papers. In my view, if we are unable to control this unpleasant stream, we are bound to have trouble in this Colony, and

I do not think it is going too far to say that those troubles may well lead to bloodshed. If we are to avoid trouble, we have got to fight this deliberate attempt to drive a wedge between the African peoples and the Europeans in this country.

Thus the liberation forces faced the enemy not only on the battlefield; the powerful enemy propaganda machinery kept up a continuous attack to misrepresent the national struggle. The cause of the freedom fighters and their supporters was deliberately distorted by the colonial propaganda. This presented Mau Mau as a 'savage atavistic movement'. The 1950s was a period of war of independence in Kenya, but the colonial administration presented the events as acts of barbarism, as happened in all anti colonial wars. Odinga (1968) takes up the aspect of colonial propaganda against Mau Mau:

> The sensational anti-Mau Mau propaganda of the period is a gross insult to the leadership of Dedan Kimathi and the brave men he led who defied death in a guerrilla army for the freedom cause in Kenya.
>
> The propaganda against the Mau Mau as a "savage atavistic movement" – from sensational press reports, to government and army handouts and the British Government Corfield Commission – was so fierce...The Emergency was a time of revolutionary war in Kenya. For almost a decade in the fifties only one side in this battle was able to present its case and its account of events.

For its part, the Kenya Parliament, established by the liberation forces, continued to interpret events from the point of view of Kenyan masses and made it very clear what the fight against imperialism was all about (Odinga, 1968):

> We are fighting for all land stolen from us by the [British] Crown through its Orders in Council of 1915, according to which Africans have been evicted from the Kenya Highlands. The British Government must grant Kenya full independence under African leadership, and hand over all land previously alienated for distribution to the landless. We will fight until we achieve freedom or until the last of our warriors has shed their last drop of blood.

Dedan Kimathi explained in a letter, quoted by Odinga (1968) he wrote from his headquarters in Nyandarua in 1955 to the Nairobi newspaper *Habari za Dunia* that "the poor are the Mau Mau. Poverty can be stopped, but not by bombs and weapons from the imperialists. Only the revolutionary justice of the struggles of the poor can end poverty for Kenyans".

The Mau Mau High Command gave much importance to the communications aspect of the struggle. As Barnet and Njama (1966) record, in January 1955, when a secret meeting was held to make important organisational changes, various committees were formed with one of them being made responsible for information and publishing. The secret War Council, which had the overall responsibility for co-ordinating political and military activities, had its headquarters at Mathare in Nairobi in the mud and thatch houses among the trees. It was here that Mau Mau publishing and printing activities were located and from where its national publicity was organised.

The early period of active revolutionary anti-imperialist war saw the build-up of armed forces, which assumed control over a large part of the country. We saw earlier how some areas in Nairobi came under full control of the liberation forces. Many people like Corfield had to admit that by August, 1952, in large parts of Central Province which was the primary battlefield, colonial law and law courts "had virtually ceased to function." [42] Their functions were taken over by Mau Mau revolutionary courts, which established justice for workers and peasants and carried out sentences against colonial officers, saboteurs and other anti-people elements. Thus between May and October, 1952 (*before* the Declaration of Emergency) Homeguard comprador traitors including Chief Waruhiu had been sentenced by Mau Mau courts and the sentences were carried out by the armed liberation forces.

It was in this atmosphere that Mau Mau established over fifty newspapers, which were all banned by the colonial government using the 'emergency' powers after 1952.

Intelligence Gathering and Communications

Mau Mau organised an efficient intelligence-gathering system right from the beginning of the struggle. It was only later that the colonial regime came

---
42 Corfield (1960), p. 279.

to realise the full extent of this system.

Collecting information was only one aspect of intelligence work; another was ensuring that information was available to the Central Command and to the fighting units. This was also organised by Mau Mau. One of the most important methods was through oral communication, which was the safest, given the increased enemy surveillance activities. It was based on the orature developed over many generations by the people. This led to the development of special language that only the patriotic forces could understand. Thus it became possible to pass on oral messages even in the presence of enemy soldiers, or to pass on written messages using enemy controlled newspapers.

Not only was a constant communication system maintained between the Army in the forest and the various Councils at upper level in Nairobi and elsewhere that were responsible for collecting food, supplies, etc., an organisation was also set up - mainly with women as couriers - to make and maintain contact with detained leaders in detention camps.

Paul Maina (1977) explains the working of the Kenda Kenda Organisation set up by Mau Mau for its intelligence gathering activities:

> For the purpose of concealing Mau Mau activities in Nairobi and elsewhere an elaborate intelligence service called the Kenda Kenda (Nine Nine) Organisation was formed. This consisted of (people) from all walks of life in and around Nairobi. Its agents were the taxi drivers, European house servants, men working in big government offices and even beggars who sat at street corners all day. All information of value was passed on to the Kenda Kenda Organisation and then to the Central Committee. As a result of the success of the Kenda Kenda, Mau Mau activities went undetected in Nairobi until late in 1952.

Another aspect of information work was that of dealing with the training of cadres who would undertake politicisation work among the masses. This was an essential part of Mau Mau's work as without it, it would be difficult to continue receiving the people's support in their work. At the same time, it helped to train cadres who would assume important work in the years to come. Kaggia (1975) explains the importance of this work:

Other active groups of young men and women played equally important roles in our organisation and recruitment. These were the propagandists who went round telling people about the aims of the movement and selling our literature. Besides newspapers *like Inooro ria Gikuyu, Gikuyu na Mumbi, Wihuge, Wiyathi* and others, there were the many song books, such as *Witikio*, all of which were spreading the same message. All these had to be advertised and sold. Through the work of these dedicated people, as they dispensed literature and organised (national) dances, many young people who would otherwise not have been uninterested in politics were brought into our movement.

So important was this work of distribution of political books and politicisation of the masses that many Mau Mau leaders had at one time or another undertaken it. Kimathi himself had been involved in it. This was in connection with the distribution of *Witikio wa Gikuyu na Mumbi* which was published by Gakara wa Wanjau, who was detained by the Colonial regime from 1952 to 1959. Gakara recently recalled how his publications passed from hand to hand under the cover of darkness in the jungle among the guerrilla fighters and in cities and towns. One such publication was *Witikio* with its message of inalienable land rights of the people. It was printed on a four page card and was selling at twenty five cents each. It was intended only for those who had taken the oath of unity. It was this publication which Kimathi helped distribute. This was in the months of September and October 1952, when the Colonial administration declared a state of Emergency. At this time, Kimathi managed to take about 15,000 copies of *Witikio* in large baskets to the Rift Valley people within a period of two weeks.

Leadership

All the aspects of governance, the actual conduct of warfare, the political aspects of Kenya Parliament and other actions mentioned above were not spontaneous acts happening in a political, social and military vacuum. There was a guiding force behind them all. And that force was Mau Mau leadership, which is often ignored or minimised by historical studies. Mau Mau leadership needs to be seen in a dynamic level in all its aspects.

It is not possible to see Mau Mau leadership in the sense that one sees the leader of a Western country personalised in the person of a president or a prime minister. The reality of fighting against the superpower of the day with limited resources dictated that a different model of leadership had to be found if the movement was to succeed. At the same time, the War of Independence in Kenya was not directed by an organised political party as happened in Mozambique under FRELIMO or in Namibia under SWAPO. As seen earlier, forces in Kenya were coming together to form such a political-military organisation before British colonial government pre-empted the development with its excessive use of force under the guise of an emergency. Of necessity, Kenya's War of Independence was led and organised in a way that suited local conditions.

At the same time, as seen earlier, there were a number of aspects that came together to form the various strands of the War of Independence. These included the trade union movement, the nationalistic forces active over a long period, the peasant movements that had a long history of anti-colonialist struggles as well as members of public including taxi drivers, publishers, doctors and lawyers, not organised as trade unions but acting in sympathy with progressive forces. All these specific forces of resistance had their own leadership in terms of organisation and individual leaders. In a broad sense these gave organisational, ideological and individual leadership to the War of Independence. A comprehensive history of Kenya's War of Independence would probe the leadership at all these levels.

It has become customary in history under capitalism to see leaders only as those who stand at the top of political movements and parties. Whereas the reality in movements such as Mau Mau and Kenya's War of independence was that there was leadership at every level of organisation, with the smallest unit of organisation having its own leaders. Thus at the level of trade unions, shop stewards led many strikes in Kenya and were thus leaders in their own right. So were the leaders of the unions as a whole, with the overall body such as the East African Trade Union Congress leaders forming a national umbrella body of trade unions.

The same can be said about Mau Mau. While Kimathi and other leaders in the forest were no doubt leaders of the movement, it is not possible to ignore leaders at divisions, provinces and cell levels who propelled the movement.

It is appropriate to see history in terms of the spirit of the question posed by Brecht (1935):

Questions From a Worker Who Reads
Who built Thebes of the 7 gates?
In the books you will read the names of kings.
Did the kings haul up the lumps of rock?

And Babylon, many times demolished,
Who raised it up so many times ?

In what houses of gold glittering Lima did its builders live?

Where, the evening that the Great Wall of China was finished, did the masons go?

Great Rome is full of triumphal arches.
Who erected them?

Over whom did the Caesars triumph?

Had Byzantium, much praised in song, only palaces for its inhabitants?

Even in fabled Atlantis, the night that the ocean engulfed it,
The drowning still cried out for their slaves.

The young Alexander conquered India.
Was he alone?

Caesar defeated the Gauls.
Did he not even have a cook with him?

Philip of Spain wept when his armada went down.
Was he the only one to weep?

Frederick the 2nd won the 7 Years War.
Who else won it?

Every page a victory.
Who cooked the feast for the victors?

Every 10 years a great man.
Who paid the bill?

So many reports.
So many questions.

Leadership of the complex War of Independence in Kenya, if it is to do justice to every level of leadership, is a vast topic that needs to be examined in much greater detail than is possible within the scope of this book. At the same time, those who planned, fought and died in the course of the war cannot be forgotten. Kaggia, B.Leeum, and Kaggia, M (2012) mention a few leaders whose records need to be written fully:

> Besides Dedan Kimathi, whose leadership and influence kept the war going all the time, a number of truly great soldiers distinguished themselves by any war standards. I will mention only a few: Stanley Mathenge, Gitau Matenjagwo, Ihura Kareri, Manyeki Wangombe, Kago Mboko, Mbaria Kamu and Waruhiu Itote. These men were greatly revered by their fellow Mau Mau soldiers and by all Africans in general. They were feared by the British Government soldiers and their helpers.

Leaders such the ones mentioned above are essential in any social movement. Without them, Mau Mau could not have fought the strongest force in the world.

A Movement of All People

One of the long-term and intense damaging effects that colonialism engineered in Kenya – as in other places such as India – is the creation of artificial antagonistic divisions among people based on issues that had not divided people before colonialism. One such division was ethnic differences, which were not antagonistic but were rendered so by colonialism's "tribal" policies. Other divisions that colonialism used were based on regions, religions and gender. Capitalism was to add a yet more divisive factor along class lines.

Colonialism faced united opposition of all the people and nationalities to its rule. It had no weapons in its arsenal to face people's demand for liberation. Its strategy of dealing with this opposition was "divide and rule" which it had used in other parts of the world. Furedi (1989): explains this further:

> Although the administrators of Kenya were consummate practitioners of the policy of divide and rule, ethnicity only emerges as a political factor in the 1950s. In the White Highlands, an area of heterogeneous ethnic mix, there is evidence of ethnic identification throughout the period under consideration. However, it is only in the late 1950s that tribalism emerges as an important political influence.
>
> The evidence from our investigation suggests that tribalism is not the natural or inevitable consequence of ethnic identification. In the case of Kenya, a tribalist consciousness was strengthened through the implementation of policies designed to fragment nationalist politics. The expulsion of Kikuyu squatters became an invitation for other ethnic groups to take their place. When Kikuyu squatters returned to the White Highlands they were portrayed as intruders on the welfare of other ethnic groups. These local tensions were part of a national pattern. What colonial policies achieved was to create the impression that the interests of one ethnic group could only be enforced at the expense of another.

It is therefore important to see Kenya's War of Independence as a movement of all the people for liberation and not to fall into the colonial traps of artificial hostile divisions created by imperialism. This section looks at some aspects of people's unity in the war of independence.

The need for instruments of governance mentioned earlier implied that Mau Mau controlled the lives and territories of people in large parts of the country. The Kenyan War of Independence, led by Mau Mau, was a national movement for liberation. It served British colonial interests to present the movement as a tribal one and create the myth that it was not a national movement in which many nationalities participated. Nor did they want to show the reality of the involvement of workers from all nationalities and the trade union movement. While it is true that not every part of the country participated equally actively in the active stages of the struggle, this is by no means unique to Kenya. Resistance develops from small sparks where the pain of colonial exploitation is the greatest and where the oppressed people are in a position to struggle actively. However, it served British interests to further divide Kenyan people into the so-called Mau Mau and non-Mau Mau on the basis of those who fought for independence and those who did not. Yet evidence suggests many nationalities were active in the struggle. For example, Edgerton (1990):

> When Kenyatta said that "we all fought for Uhuru," he was repeating a politically expedient slogan, not a fact. Still, in reality many more Kenyans gave their support to Mau Mau and its call for freedom than the government liked, or wanted the world to realise. Information relating to the spread of Mau Mau was classified, and although some of it leaked to the press, the magnitude of the threat was not known to the public. Mau Mau attacks now took place anywhere in Kenya from Mombasa to Kisumu on Lake Victoria. While the spread of Mau Mau was indeed a threat to the colonial power and its local supporters, it was no threat to the majority of Kenyans who had nothing to lose but their colonised status. This brief section gives just a few examples of some groups who participated in the War of Independence. A complete history on this aspect also needs to be researched and written.

Warrant of Commitment on a Sentence of Imprisonment or Fine.

CRIMINAL No. 103

COLONY AND PROTECTORATE OF KENYA

In the **SUPREME** Court
at **NYERI.**

To the Superintendent of Prison,
N Y E R I.

WHEREAS on 27th day of November, 1956

DEDAN KIMATHI S/O WACHIURI
(Name of prisoner)

the (~~................~~) Prisoner in Criminal Case No. 46 of 1956 was convicted before me **Sir Kenneth O'Connor, Chief Justice**
(Name and official designation)

H.M. SUPREME COURT OF KENYA of the offence of Unlawful possession
(Mention the offence briefly)

of ammunitions

under ~~Section~~ Regulation 8A (1A) of the Emergency Regulations 1952

and was sentenced to Imprisonment for ~~three~~ Seven (7) Years with Hard Labour

This is to authorize and require you, the said Superintendent, to receive the said **DEDAN KIMATHI S/O WACHIURI**
(Prisoner's name)

into your custody in the said jail, together with this warrant, and there carry the aforesaid sentence into execution according to law.

Given under my hand and the Seal of the Court this 27th day of November, 1956

K. K. O'Connor
Chief Justice
H.M. Supreme Court of Kenya.

[P.T.O.]

ENDORSEMENT

I have the honour to inform you that I carried out the sentence of death upon .... DEDAN KIMATHI S/O WACHIURI, ... in the Prison at ...NAIROBI.............................. at 6............ a.m. this 18th. day of ...February,............. 19 57...

....
Superintendent of the Prison.

I hereby certify that I was present at the execution of ...DEDAN KIMATHI S/O WACHIURI. at about 6 a.m. ..... this morning and .... after the execution I examined the body of the deceased man and found life to be extinct. Death was caused by ...HANGING........................ and was * ...INSTANTANEOUS.

Dated at ...NAIROBI.............. this 18th........ day of ...February, 1957

....
K. E. ROBERTSON
Medical Officer

* Instantaneous.

copy to:-
The Hon. Chief Secretary, Nairobi.
The Registrar Supreme Court of Kenya, Nairobi.
The Commissioner of Prisons, Nairobi.

Women

In spite of such violence, or perhaps because of it, women played an active role in the War of Independence in many capacities, including active participation in almost all aspects of the armed struggle. They also enabled the struggle to continue over so many years by ensuring support for families where men had been detained or were on active duties in the forests and towns. Again, their military role landed many of them into colonial concentration camps.

It is regrettable that the important role of women in the War of Independence has not been fully understood or fully recorded. Alam (2007) notes this point and adds a possible reason for the lack of coverage of women's involvement in the struggle:

> Women's testimonies and autobiographies reveal extensive participation in the Mau Mau insurgency. Interestingly, there are certain silences in the narratives of women's roles in Mau Mau. There are gaps and contradictions not only in official discourse and insurgent accounts but also in male insurgent's accounts as well. Women in colonial Kenya have had a long tradition of resistance against colonialism, which, unfortunately, quite often remains unaccounted and hidden.

Women played critical roles in a number of areas that made Mau Mau sustainable. These include tasks that built and sustained Mau Mau's organisation as well as key duties in the forest as barriers and as activists in other work needed for survival in the forests. Gachihi (1986) provides a useful record of women's involvement in Mau Mau. She gives an overview of women's contribution:

> These women were assigned duties that were decisive in engagements between the Mau Mau fighters and the well-armed British forces, and especially in rallying the support of fellow women. Thus in the Mau Mau there emerged women leaders who organized fellow women to act as contacts with the other fighters. Zealous Mau Mau supporters were also found in the bulk of peasant women who shouldered heavy

burdens and executed dangerous tasks in the name of the movement. These are the women who fed and supplied Mau Mau contact groups with weapons and other provisions usually purloined or wrenched from the enemy. Other important tasks that these women carried out for the movement included smuggling such vital provisions as medicine and clothing while acting at the same time as couriers of information through many hazardous routes.

In addition to the specific roles mentioned above, women played their part in the War of Independence in many other ways as part of people's resistance. Thus they joined hands with men, children, older and young people whose united support for resistance provided the bedrock of resistance that Mau Mau built its strength on. Gachihi (1986) mentions yet another level of support that women and children provided to Mau Mau:

> Wives and daughters in Emergency villages became vital providers of food, shelter and information. All these people formed a formidable support group which nurtured the comparatively small number of combatants in the Nyandarua and Mount Kenya forest regions. Indeed, the Colonial Government realized that to crush out Mau Mau meant crushing out this support. The Government, therefore, adopted a broad policy in the Kikuyu reserves "to force, entice, the passive element into a change of heart". As a tacit conspiracy between the supporters and the fighters had already been firmly established, there was little prospect that the Government would succeed by enticement, and consequently, a lot of force was used. It is this support group behind the Mau Mau which reveals, to a great extent, why such a relatively poorly-equipped group of freedom fighters under such stringent conditions and pressure from the Government were able to sustain the struggle for at least four years.

Bruce-Lockhart (1914) records the establishment of women's concentration camps by the colonial authorities in specially created concentration camps:

> From 1954 to 1960, the British detained approximately 8000 women under the Emergency Powers imposed to combat the Mau Mau Rebellion in Kenya. Kamiti Detention Camp was the main site of women's incarceration, and its importance has been widely

acknowledged by scholars. However, new documentary evidence released from the Hanslope Park Archive since 2011 has revealed the existence of a second camp established for women at Gitamaiyu, created in 1958 explicitly to deal with the remaining "hardcore" female detainees.

However, it is important to understand the multiple dimension of women's resistance. There were specific conditions under colonialism that affected lives of women and which made them active in the struggle. (Umoja, 1987d) connects these conditions for peasant and worker women:

> Peasant women in their role as producers for subsistence were particularly affected by the changes brought about by colonialism. The forced migration of men led to changes in the pre-colonial division of labour between men and women, the women taking over a larger share of 'shamba' labour and marketing. Thus, peasant women were overburdened by having to carry out their domestic tasks in addition to doing the work previously done by men and producing for the domestic and international market.

As land became scarce, peasant women were forced to seek work on farms and as domestic labour in European homes, thus colonialism led to the emergence of women workers. Women were also forcibly recruited as labourers under the guise of "awaiting substitution by their male relatives". The conditions under which women worked were appalling. Apart from the exploitative low wages, women workers lived in deplorable housing, were provided with inadequate medical facilities and were denied all rights.

Kenyan women's role in the resistance to imperialism, therefore, has to be understood within the context of peasant and workers' struggles against imperialism.

Umoja (1987d) goes on to give a good number of examples of women leaders and activists in Mau Mau. These include the following:

> **Field Marshall Muthoni** who joined Mau Mau and went to the forest because she believed that the people had to get back their land from the white men who had grabbed it from them. Muthoni's bravery,

dedication and qualities of leadership earned her deep respect among her comrades and she rose to the rank of Field Marshall.

Salome Owiri from Ugenya, Siaya, was a Committee member of the Kenya African Union, the Treasurer of the East African Federation of Labour and was active in the struggle and "would organise secret delivery of food to those arrested for taking part in the freedom struggle". Salome was "detained numerous times for her activities in the liberation movement, was tortured and beaten in an effort to force her to reveal the secrets of Mau Mau, but she remained steadfast".

Some of the women held in Camp NO. 9 at Kamiti - the women's detention camp - were Rebeka Njeeri, Sera Serai, Cecilia Wanjiku, Wangui Gakuru, Priscilla Wambaki, Nyagiciru Mbote, Flora Wanjugu, Miriam Wanjiru Ndegwa. Wanjiku Gordan, Nyamacaki Kagondu and many others. In all there were more than 200 women detainees in this camp alone. Among them were wives of Mau Mau leaders like Mukami Kimathi, Muthoni wa Mathenge Mirugi and many others. These women are an inspiration for their dedication and courage in the struggle.

Muthoni Mathenge was born in 1926 in Kihome Gitugi Village, Nyeri. Her involvement in the struggle commenced during the oath taking which was done first in her compound and later in the forest. She mobilised women, men and children into joining the movement and urged them to take up arms and fight. She also mobilised young women and trained them in the methods of acquiring guns and bullets from the enemy and passing them on to the fighters. She was also involved in the administration of the oath and in composing Mau Mau songs that were used to mobilise people. Muthoni Mathenge was subjected to brutal torture by colonial police who wanted her to reveal the whereabouts of her husband General Mathenge. Some of the torture methods included the insertion of a glowing cigarette into her ear. This did not deter her and she went into the forest where she continued the struggle. She prepared food for the fighters and supplied them with medicine... Muthoni was arrested and detained at Kamiti prison in 1955. She spent more than four years in prison.

Hannah Kung'u was another woman fighter who devoted her entire youth to the struggle for independence. She was greatly influenced by her father Kung'u wa Gichia, who was himself an active freedom fighter and used to make guns at his home from water pipes. These home-made guns were then smuggled to the KLFA (Mau Mau) in the Mt. Kenya and Nyandarua forests. Hannah took her first oath of loyalty [to Mau Mau] while still a young woman. Hannah was active in mobilising people to sign petitions for the release of their detained leaders. Collecting signatures involved travelling the country and mobilising people to support the campaign. She was also involved in the various demonstrations called in protest at the imprisonment of people's leaders. At one such demonstration, the pregnant Hanna was kicked by colonial police, causing a premature birth. Hannah also acted as a courier carrying guns and food to the freedom fighters. She provided cover for the freedom fighters in her house. Hannah was jailed for her activities in the freedom movement.

Some of the women in the detention camps had been arrested for their activities in publishing underground resistance papers. One such woman was Judith Nyamurwa Mworia who had continued the work of publishing *Mumenyereri* after her husband Henry Mworia was sent on a nationalist delegation to London. Nyamurwa was arrested in the offices of the newspaper and was taken to detention camp with her baby son Kinyanjui.

Next to the women's detention camp at Kamiti was the women's prison for those Mau Mau women fighters who had been tried in court and given life sentences for their active participation in the war of liberation. Among the prisoners were guerrilla leaders like Wanjira wa Kimiti, Wambui Gacanja, Muthoni wa Gakuru and others. Their punishment involved burying convicted Mau Mau guerillas. In one last act of defiance, they used to bury their executed comrades with full military honours, facing Mount Kenya where they believed the God of Mau Mau resided. Despite brutal beatings by jail guards who were trying to prevent them from carrying this last act of honour for their fallen comrades, they persisted defiantly and their jailers were forced to concede defeat and let them carry on.

Women combatants proved to be as good as the men in the forest. A good example is provided by the attack on Kanyota Post at Kiamariga in Nyeri District. In July 1953, a woman, Wamuyu Gakuru, successfully led the attack on this post. The detention camp was completely demolished and 200 Mau Mau prisoners were freed. People were full of admiration of Wamuyu's commanding ability and were particularly impressed with her use of the Sten gun.

Wanjiku Waring'u, also known as Mama Kamenge. She served on the Mau Mau War Council, responsible for providing food, shelter, concealment for fighters in Nairobi, and transportation when they had to move to new bases. (Source: Nazmi Durrani, Nairobi, personal communications).

The Kenya Committee For Democratic Rights for Kenya Africans (1952-60) gave some more examples of women Mau Mau activists, some reproduced in the section on Mau Mau Infrastructure.

Such records in women's involvement in the War of Independence are not part of the history as it is taught in schools and colleges, nor are a majority of people aware of this aspect of the struggle. Yet this is an essential ingredient of social and political liberation. As Umoja (1987d) says: "The involvement of women in the Mau Mau war of liberation clearly shows that it is only when women are active participants in struggle against imperialism that the women question can begin to be tackled'.

At another level, many nationalities were active in the War of Independence, a fact that has been obscured by colonial propaganda that the War of Independence did not take place and that Mau Mau was a "tribal affair". The following section therefore provides brief glimpses from available literature about activism from different nationalists:

The Kamba Nationality

The involvement of the Kamba nationality in Mau Mau secures their place in the War of Independence. Their involvement was not only in terms of their nationality issues, but in their part of the Mau Mau movement. This makes it impossible for anyone to claim that only the Kikuyu nationality were involved in the War of Independence or in Mau Mau. The following section from Edgerton (1990) provides evidence of Kamba involvement in Mau Mau:

> During the first half of 1954, while large Mau Mau units battled security forces around the forest's edges, the government was alarmed by evidence that Mau Mau was spreading, especially to the 600,000 Kamba whose lands stretched south and east from the Kikuyu reserve. In May, Kenya's new police commissioner warned that the Kamba were drifting toward active Mau Mau involvement, and in June the Blundell-led War Council's greatest fear was the threatened spread of Mau Mau. After Operation Anvil cleared Nairobi of most Kikuyu residents, more than 20,000 Kamba moved to the city, becoming its majority African population. Many of these Kamba took Mau Mau oaths.
>
> In the past the Kamba had been enemies of the Kikuyu, but by 1952 they had come to share Kikuyu grievances against poverty, land shortage, population growth, and white racism. Several hundred young Kamba formed themselves into Mau Mau units, killing progovernment chiefs and headmen in the Kamba reserves, while others joined combat units in the Mt. Kenya forests. Still, the great majority of the Kamba population watched and waited to see how the rebellion would succeed. When government security forces had little visible success in defeating Mau Mau during 1953, the Kamba became more restless, and, by 1954, many thousands had taken the Mau Mau oath, and thousands more were openly on the verge of committing themselves to armed rebellion.
>
> The prospect of the Kamba was particularly frightening to the government because Kamba soldiers and policemen formed the backbone of both the K.A.R. and the Kenya Police. If these men with their military training and their weapons had joined the rebels, the result for white Kenya could have been disastrous. Many of these armed Kamba discussed joining Mau Mau, and some considered turning their weapons against their white officers; but concerned Kamba loyalists alerted the government and Baring wisely chose to respond not with threats but with benefits.

As the conflict developed, Mau Mau leaders quickly moved to recruit Kamba members. this recruitment was achieved through the Mau Mau oath. KAU Nairobi branch which had been run by Mau Mau militants since 1952 (Rosberg & Nottingham, Myth 1966), though dominated by Kikuyu, included members drawn from other ethnic groups. Paul Ngei, Assistant secretary of KAU, was Kamba and a member of the committee. Nag invited "politically-minded" Kamba to Kiburi House to take the oath. ... Thousands of Kamba took the oath.

Corfield (1960) details that when, in March 1954 security forces arrested a significant fighting force of Kamba Mau Mau, ten of the seventeen arrested were railway workers. Later that year, the government identified 253 known Kamba members of Mau Mau who were employed as railway workers.

As 1953 drew to a close, officials were concerned about the increasing penetration of Mau Mau among the Kamba. "The cancer is spreading", noted one. Officials estimated that the "vast majority" of Kamba in Nairobi had taken the oath. Kamba now began to take a greater part in the physical struggle. Security forces also found members of a Kamba oathing team in Arusha in northern Tanganyika, and discovered at least one Kamba Mau Mau "general" at the head of a battalion of over 1,000 Mau Mau in the Abedares of Central Province. (Quoting: TNA. PRO CO 822/780, "Infiltration of Mau Mau into Tribes other than the Gikuyu (Secret)"). One Mau Mau major from Meru recalled that a Kamba general named Kavyu ("knife") was in charge of his fighting unit, which operated in the forests around Mount Kenya. "In every fighting group of about thirty, there might be five or six Kambas," he noted (Quoting: Interview no. 77, Kirimara, 11 May 2009).

Kamba Mau Mau

- Kenya African Union Nairobi branch run by Mau Mau militants since 1952 included members from many ethnic groups. Paul Ngei, Assistant Secretary, a Kamba, invited "politically-minded" Kamba to take the oath. Thousands took it.

- 1953: officials concerned at penetration of Mau Mau among the Kamba. "The cancer is spreading", noted one. Officials estimated that the "vast majority" of Kamba in Nairobi had taken the oath. Security forces found members of a Kamba oathing team in Arusha in Tanganyika and discovered a Kamba Mau Mau "general" heading a battalion of 1,000 in the Abedares.

- 1954: security forces arrested a fighting force of Kamba Mau Mau. The government identified 253 Kamba members of Mau Mau, all railway workers.

- A Mau Mau major from Meru recalled that a Kamba general named Kavyu ("knife") was in charge of his fighting unit in the forests around Mount Kenya. "In every fighting group of about thirty, there might be five or six Kambas".

The Kenya Committee for Democratic Rights (1952-60) provides additional references:

- 44 Wakamba were arrested in Tanganyika and returned to Kenya during a police roundup. 17-6-55

The Maasai Nationality

- Mzee Paita was the leader of Mau Mau fighters in Kajiado in the 1950s. He was imprisoned alongside other big names during the struggle.

- Shomo News estimates that there are 50 Mau Mau veterans in Kajiado. Majority of them are Maasai. The group led by Mzee Paita and Aden Hassan Elmi narrate how they were evicted from their hideouts at Oldoinyo Orok in Namanga which was the base for Mau Mau along the Kenya-Tanzania border and a link to freedom fighters in Tanzania.

- Oldoinyo Orok hosted more than 2,000 Mau Mau freedom fighters by 1954 before the British overran them, detaining the fighters and taking thousands of livestock from communities that supported them. Most of the freedom fighters were held at Isinya detention camp.

Ole Kisio

Gen. ole Kisio (1)

- The Maasai played a vital role in the struggle. Young warriors sacrificed their lives for the country under the leadership of one of the most revered Mau Mau generals, the late Kurito ole Kisio. A defiant Kisio marshalled the Narok war front that heavily destabilised the colonialists, prompting them to put a heavy bounty on his head.

- His valour would later see his then pregnant wife, Miriam Enekurito, become the first person to be arrested for collusion with the Mau Mau. She was tortured until Kisio was killed in 1954.

- "They took oath and never looked back. They started raiding settler homes and detention camps across Narok in search of firearms," says Sironka ole Ketikai, who played the role of 'piki piki' (gun runner) for the Mau Mau in the 1950s. Then aged 19, he would ferry stolen guns, drugs, and military uniform and supplied those in Nyandarua with livestock for food. Under Kisio's leadership, and with Nkere, Nkapian and Nahangi as generals, the battalion caused the imperialists sleepless nights.

Gen. ole Kisio (2)

- Karari Njama says the Maasais were crucial in the resistance against the British. "Kisio led an army of more than 800 fighters in Nairegi Enkare. They would move all the way to Suswa and destabilised the Britons," he states. The warrior is said to have employed guerrilla tactics in raiding British facilities where they would release prisoners.

- It was during one such raid in Olololunga that Ketikai's uncle was captured by the 'lolonkana' (Homeguards).

Mau Mau influence spreads

- In Nairobi, the situation is grave and acute. Mau Mau orders are carried out in the heart of the city, Mau Mau courts sit in judgement and their sentences are carried out. The revenues collected by Mau Mau are used for bribery and Mau Mau supplies.

- 44 Wakamba were arrested in Tanganyika & returned to Kenya.

- There were Mau Mau cells in Mombasa, Pemba, Zanzibar, and other coastal regions. In Tanzania, Mau Mau succeeded in winning over hundreds of Kenyan migrant workers. The colonial authorities in both countries banned the Mau Mau.

- The Ethiopian intelligence is aware of what is going on in Kenya. Mau Mau and its causes is a subject about which they frequently asked questions... there seems a parallel with their own mountain rebels, the Shiftas.

- "In S. Africa it is considered there is an underground movement by the natives to overthrow established Government throughout Africa and this is certainly the idea of Mau Mau".

- Sources can be found in Durrani, S (2006).

Women Mau Mau

Without women's contributions nothing could have been achieved. It was the women who transported arms and food to the forest edge, who steered loyalists into the fighters' traps, who stole guns and bullets, who spied for the freedom fighters. The women as much as the men hazarded their lives to gain back a country. - Likimani (1985).

Wanja wa Johana and Wangui wa Kimani were the first KLFA women guerrillas to be sentenced to death in 1954 by the British. Wanja led a KLFA village detachment in Nyeri, which ambushed an enemy patrol. - Kinyatti (2008).

From 1954 to 1960, the British detained approximately 8000 women under the Emergency Powers. Kamiti Detention Camp was the main site of women's incarceration. New evidence has revealed the existence of a second camp established for women at Gitamaiyu, created in 1958 explicitly to deal with the remaining "hardcore" female detainees. The charge that hardcore women were "of unsound mind" was used for a variety of purposes in the late 1950s, including covering up the abuses in the camps. - Bruce-Lockharta (2014).

The Kenya Committee For Democratic Rights for Kenya Africans (1952-60) adds the following:

- Masai districts of Narok and Kajiado declared special areas. 23-9-53.

- Kenya government declares a prohibited area of 58,580 acres of the Masai Mara reserve, forests in the Narok District, about 70 miles from Nairobi. Security forces will be able to shoot on sight in the area. 20-7-54.

- A Masai, Mundet Ole Ngapien, among five executed in Nairobi for Mau Mau activities. 10-1-55.

South Asian Kenyans

One of the methods used by colonialism and imperialism to control people and countries include falsifying their history and creating divisions among people on the bases of class, race, religion, gender or any other social manifestations that could be used so that they get busy fighting these imperialist-lit small fires while forgetting the big blaze of imperialist looting and devastation which are in the very nature of capitalism. South Asian Kenyans also suffered from the divisive policies of colonialism, which created artificial divisions and distance between South Asian and African people. They were used as scapegoats for the poverty and inequality caused by capitalist exploitation.

In addition, just as the history of the Kenyan national liberation struggle and of Mau Mau was destroyed or secreted away in hidden hauls in England, the entire progressive contribution of South Asian communities to the liberation of Kenya has been hidden, marginalised or misinterpreted. This was done throughout the period of colonial and imperialist presence in Kenya, but particularly during the Mau Mau period. While many South Asian communities are aware of their contributions and regularly communicated these in publications such as the *Awaaz Magazine*[43] and on-line networks (such as Africana-Orientalia and EACircle groups), their deliberations remained outside the mainstream Kenyan or British lives. Some recent publications[44] have begun to re-examine the history of the contribution made by the South Asian communities in the liberation struggle in Kenya.

There are a number of strands to the struggles of the South Asian communities as a minority nationality in Kenya as well as part of the wider Kenyan anti-colonial, anti-imperialist struggles. One strand dates to the early part of the 19th Century, indicating that their involvement in Mau Mau was not an isolated event but followed a long period of anti-colonial, anti-imperialist activism. Such action included the activism in the Trade Union movements, recorded by Makhan Singh (1969 and 1980). Their contribution included involvement in the Ghadar movement for which some activists were sentenced to death and deported by the British colonials. Some aspects of

---

43 Available in print and on-line: http://www.awaazmagazine.com [Accessed: 20-11-16].
44 See for example Patel, Zarina (1997 and 2006), Aiyar, Sana (2015), Durrani, Shiraz (2015) and Durrani, Nazmi (2017).

their contribution in the publishing field, which was closely linked with their political activism is covered in a number of publications, including Durrani, Shiraz (2006).

Yet another strand was the activism and involvement of many South Asian Kenyans in India's struggle for independence which then influenced their activities in Kenya. Thus Makhan Singh was active in India where he was jailed by the British administration, Pio Gama Pinto was active in the Goan people's struggle against Portuguese colonialism, and many others were influenced by the sub-continents' liberation struggle. Some cases are mentioned in Durrani, Nazmi (2017). Pereira (2017) links the struggle for independence in India with that in Kenya:

> In the mid 1940s, the struggle for independence in India fanned the flames of nationalism in Africa. In Kenya, patriotic fervour brought an end to the Colonial governance duplicating the historic events on the Indian sub-continent thus taking a lead in Africa's struggle for independence. Most observers agree that South Asians of Kenya were catalysts in the rise of national self-determination in Africa.

The independence of India in 1947 provided an important boost for the Kenyan national struggle and for Mau Mau. Jawaharlal Nehru, India's first prime minister, "saw India's role as promoting freedom for all people, especially in Africa. Nehru positioned his new state to facilitate the emergence of 'one world where freedom is universal and there is equality of opportunity between races and peoples'" (Aiyar, 2015). This principled stand provided ideological strength to those Indians in Kenya who were involved in Kenya's War of Independence and also to Mau Mau. Nehru summed up his approach in 1953 when he announced that the "Indian sympathies were entirely with Africans 'in their struggle against exploitation, repression and colonialism'" (Aiyar, 2015). Apa Pant's position is summed up by Aiyar (2015) thus: "Pant had concluded that Mau Mau violence was a self-defensive reaction to the violence of the Settlers and colonial government"

In August 1948 Pant came to Kenya as the first Indian high commissioner. His work in supporting the cause of Kenya's independence is outside the scope of this book. But a mention can be made of his work with Pinto and other South Asians in Kenya and the fact that he was made a Kikuyu elder "at a secret ceremony attended by twelve elders, with Chief Koinange presiding" (Aiyar, 2015). This support extended to education, publishing and training.

Kinyatti (2008) quotes James Beauttah from a 1979 interview:

> James Beauttah tells us that Pant used his diplomatic privilege "to champion our anti-colonial struggle". For the six years that he served in Kenya, he conscientiously raised funds for our struggle. He was particularly successful in soliciting funds for the Kenya Teachers' College from the Indian community and also obtained scholarships for Kenyan students to study in India. He also gave political advice to the movement and publicly supported Kenya's anti-imperialist leadership.'

Kinyatti (2008) continues the narrative:

> When the armed struggle started, according to Beauttah, his [Pant's] office became a political base where messages and documents were received and transmitted and his house a center of political meetings and a place where Kenyans and Indian supporters could secretly meet.

Such support for the liberation struggle was extremely important as no other major country had supported the Kenyan people's struggle for liberation.

It was India's support that Pio Gama Pinto used to aid the struggle, including funds for setting up of the Lumumba Institute which was later destroyed by Jomo Kenyatta.

One area that has not been adequately explored is the role of South Asians' support for Mau Mau. But just as Kenyan history as a whole and in particular the history of Mau Mau has been seen as isolated incidents, unrelated and uninfluenced by each other, so has the history of South Asian revolutionary movement in Kenya been seen as a series of isolated individuals and events that happen as individual spark points, not related to any bigger picture. It is the bigger picture that is missing from the current history of South Asian presence in Kenya. But while the recent release of colonial papers in Britain has enabled a fresh approach to understanding the history of Mau

Mau and Kenya, the history of South Asians in Kenya has not experienced a similar renaissance. But there is evidence, for example in the work of Aiyar (2015), that there is material in the colonial files that can help to create a correct and a more complete picture. It remains for committed historians and researchers to travel the long path of painstaking toil in these papers to create the bigger picture.

As little attention has been paid to the militant South Asian history in Kenya, the following section recalls these strands of the South Asian struggles in Kenya. While the isolated facts have been accepted, the overall picture created by these facts has not been fully seen or appreciated. A process of joining the dots to make the picture clear is perhaps what is needed now. The start of the process of South Asians' arrival in Kenya and its impact on Kenya is explained by Durrani, Naila (2017):

> They came without a penny but with a political understanding and experience more potent than gold. They brought with them a wealth of experience of militant class struggles. They came armed with the knowledge of the weapons of organisation and of the power of newspapers, handbills, newsletters, pamphlets and such other means of raising worker consciousness and of forging unity along class lines.

From this early start, the involvement of South Asians in the national liberation movement was but a short step. It is in this field that Aiyar (2015) throws light on this rarely discussed or researched topic and her work provides some interesting facts mentioned below. This is supplemented by material from Durrani, Nazmi (2017). Together, they provide an altogether different picture from the "norm" of the South Asian involvement in the liberation struggle. It is not that information on this is not available. Aiyar (2015) quotes from Kenya Government Intelligence Reports which were specifically on South Asians. Such reports, as well as oral testimonies from those active at the time (again, as used by Aiyar) remain an under-used resource. Aiyar (2015) quotes below from the Kenya Government Intelligence Reports:

> By February 1953, [Kenya Colonial Government Intelligence] reports from Nyanza pointed to more specific and direct involvement

[in Mau Mau]. A "Punjabi auctioneer" from Kisumu, where about 5,000 Indians lived, "expressed sympathy and support... for Kikuyu terrorism" and had joined "a number of Indians from Nairobi" to tour the colony with the aim of encouraging other Indians to support the Mau Mau. An Indian in Kisii, another town in Nyanza with an Indian population of less than 350, was publicly "advocating Kikuyu terrorist methods" as the only hope for "African freedom". Intelligence officers identified six Indian railway employees who were supporting Mau Mau activities "as the best way to prevent European 'domination.' " In Nyeri, the Kikuyu reserve in Kiambu where 604 Indians lived, the Patel Brotherhood, an association of Gujarati Hindus, was found to be "actively" assisting the Mau Mau. Intelligence summaries reported that even in Mombasa, which was far from the epicentre of the rebellion, Hindus had announced their support for "the Kikuyu cause and its efforts to secure its rights"... Although no Indian ever became a Mau Mau guerrilla forest fighter, others helped rebels in direct ways.

At another level, Aiyar (2015) finds a well-organised network of South Asian activists:

With the arrest of almost 200 KAU members, activists in Nairobi organised themselves into a number of different groups. This group included [Pio Gama] Pinto, who was the liaison between the rebels, detainees, Indian lawyers, and [Apa] Pant. Pinto not only organised political defences for the detainees but also supplied arms and money to fighters in the forest from supply lines in Nairobi. This led to his arrest on June 19, 1954. He was detained without trial in Takwa camp, Manda Island, until July 1959, when his restriction orders were revoked. Pinto was joined by at least five other Indians in this camp, which was set up especially for non-Kikuyu considered "hardcore" - a term used by the security forces for Mau Mau detainees they were unable to "break" (i.e. force to confess to taking Mau Mau oaths) in the pipeline system. These included Jaswant Singh, Jaswant Singh Bharaj, Babubhai Patel, and Bakshish Singh. In addition, Makhan Singh, who had been arrested two years before the emergency, was kept detained for its entire duration.

The fact that the contribution of South Asians to the War of Independence in general, and to Mau Mau in particular, has been sidelined is due to yet another factor, not just the deliberate actions of the colonial divide and rule tactics and policy of "stealing people's history". Aiyar (2015) interprets this in the following way:

> In the early 1970s, Mau Mau memories published by forest fighters and their supporters in postcolonial Kenya usurped the narrative of the rebellion that the state refused to acknowledge. Pio Gama Pinto found a place in this history, but he was presented as an exceptional individual who was against the grain of mainstream Indian politics. Both Kaggia and Odinga claimed that he was "regarded by many Africans not as an Asian but as a real African." Insisting that Pio did not represent Indian politics in any way, Kaggia was emphatic that Pinto was the only Indian detained during the emergency.

Aiyar (2015) is correct that the perspective promoted through such memorials by Mau Mau fighters did influence the history of the liberation struggle in Kenya and of Mau Mau. At the same time, it is necessary to look deeper into the reasons why such "narratives were usurped". It would not be surprising if the colonial policy of creating and nurturing strife along racial and "tribal" lines found fertile ground among some activists themselves. This affected the narrative, not only of South Asians, but nationalities other than Kikuyu as the colonialist propaganda promoted the myth that the liberation struggle was a "kikuyu affair". Thus, in common with South Asians, other nationalities such as the Maasai, Kamba, Luo, Somali as well as coastal and other people are also seen as not having played a part in Mau Mau.

But there are likely to be other reasons why the history of Mau Mau ignores and marginalised the participation of South Asians. One such reason may relate to the need for secrecy which Mau Mau as an organisation established in order to struggle against a superior enemy. Thus Mau Mau organisation was along the lines of "kundi" - cell structures - so as to ensure that only a small group of people knew other members and few knew who the leaders were. This is a common practice in other guerrilla movements. While such a structure no doubt protected the organisation against the enemy, it resulted in many combatants and activists not knowing who other combatants and activists were. This was particularly true where activists had taken oaths to preserve organisational secrecy. Perhaps this may explain the perspective of Odinga and Kaggia as expressed by Aiyar (2015).

Another point to note is that those who took the Mau Mau oaths were sworn to secrecy till death and many combatants to this day are reluctant to talk about their experiences fully, particularly when it comes to naming others who fought with them. The political atmosphere in Kenya after independence has again not been conducive to talking openly about Mau Mau and naming others may condemn them in the eyes of Kenya governments who have been hostile to Mau Mau and its egalitarian goals.

At the same time, many South Asian activists belonged to political organisations - in India or other parts of the world - which had strong codes of discipline and secrecy. These included the Ghadhar movement, the Indian Communist Party as well as the movements for liberation in India and Goa. Such activists then maintained their silence about their political work as part of their organisational commitment and discipline. In addition, people like Makhan Singh belonged to the Sikh community which again emphasised service to others without seeking self glory. It may be for these reasons that Makhan Singh's two books on history of trade union movement in Kenya (Singh, Makhan, 1969,1980) hardly mention his own role in trade union and political struggles.

All the above may explain the lack of South Asian presence in the history of Mau Mau. In addition, there is some oral evidence requiring further research that a number of South Asians were members of Mau Mau. A Mau Mau veteran in his 80s gave this information to the author and two others in an interview in Nairobi. The veteran clarified that his and his group's Mau Mau oath still had validity and that any information about their activities could be revealed to the public only if the group agreed. The interview took place in a Nairobi hotel on August 5, 2013 and was videoed. Some points from it are mentioned below. The veteran remains nameless and will be referred to here as Mzee WM[45]. He first gives some facts about his life as it

---

45 Sad news update on Mzee WM: " ... Lakini Mzee [WM] ametuwacha [*But Mzee* has left *us*]. He fell down where he was staying and after that he was unable to walk. Akapelekwa hos.[*He was taken to Hospital*]. Familia wakamtoa [*His family had to have him released from hospital*] before he was well due to finances. He died on Friday at his place". [Message to the author from GM, Nairobi, 05-09-17, 6:41 pm].

throws light on the lives of Mau Mau activists:

- Born in 1931.

- We were poor. Father was a member of KCA [Kikuyu Central Association]. Food, school fees difficult; sold animals to survive; everyday fear. Father's land taken by government, but still have no shamba.

- Mau Mau [MM] Kiapo [Oath]: very serious matter. Love of land, binadamu; this is *our* land. Oath is forever, for life, even today.

- Pio Gama Pinto and I were in one *kundi* (Mau Mau cell). Issac GW gave me the Mau Mau oath in 1946. My sister and mother knew Pinto. Pinto's work was to *kuungana makabila* [bring together different nationalities], establish links with like-minded people who shared goals.

- Question: Why silent all these years? Reply: Talk to who? Can't see the President. There have been three governments from the time of independence; *nifanye nini [What can I do?]*? Tell me, who do I see?

- General Ndungu died recently; compensation in London to only 5,000. What about the rest? and those who died? 7 years in the forest, I am angry day and night, 20,000 Mau Mau still alive in Taita, Ukambani, Nairobi. Francis Muthee fled from Manyani [Detention Centre] to the forest, he is selling onions now. Active in World War II, no *shambas* [farms], we got nothing.

- Makhan Singh took the highest Mau Mau oath, the seventh oath and the highest one, and top secret: preparing for future wars, for neo-colonial stage; after colonialism, another enemy may come. Oath not to return from battle, die but do not surrender. Oath taken at Shauri Moyo.

- Makhan Singh was a member a long time with _____ who brought Makhan Singh [MS] to the movement. MS took 2nd & 3rd oaths in Pumwani, behind social hall, at Mama W's. He was a member before going to India.

Kenya's War of Independence

- Inspector Bian Singh, *Mkubwa* [Head] of Prison, was a Mau Mau member and helped the struggle; knew which Mau Mau members were in danger and allowed them to escape.
- Makhan Singh had lots of contacts, brought other Asians, had an Asian *kundi* [political cell] brought money and medicine.
- Ambu Patel worked with MS.
- MS worked with a doctor and arranged medical service via "ugali communications".
- Mau Mau guidance if facing death:
- *Mtu apende nchi yake* [A person should love his/her country]
- *Makabila yote bila bagua* [People of all nationalities, without discrimination].
- Don't sell your country.
- Don't sell your rights.

As mentioned earlier, the above information needs to be further investigated together with that from other veterans. Mzee WM is no longer with us and many other veterans are dying with the passage of time. The urgency of this work cannot be over-emphasised.

Besides the above possible reasons relating to lack of information about the participation of South Asians in Mau Mau, Durrani, Shiraz (forthcoming) suggests, in the context of Pio Gama Pinto, another possible reason:

> Another significant reason why information about Pinto is not available can perhaps be found in the fact that Pinto belonged to a minority ethnic community - South Asian Kenyans. In a situation where not only the British colonial authorities, but the independent Kenyan government and the elite nurtured by imperialism encouraged divide-and-rule policies against South Asian minority communities, Pinto's achievements were actively hidden from masses of people on whose behalf he fought. Again, there was not a mass population of progressive South Asian communities which would seek to ensure that one of their own sons was given due recognition for their contribution to national freedom. In any case, class formation among South Asian Kenyans had progressed further than among other

Kenyans and the petty bourgeois Asians certainly did not support Pinto's call for equality nor his active involvement in the national liberation struggle. For example, *Drum* (1965) comments:

> Few people except those who, like Pinto, are regarded as misfits or even traitors to their own community, can know just how much courage he needed to act as he did... Spurned and often ostracised by his fellow Goans for throwing his lot in with the Africans, only absolute conviction in the rightness of his cause could have carried Pinto through those difficult years.

Pinto's own temperament, which sought hard work for himself and glory for others, often came to Sbe taken for granted and hid his real achievements from many people. Thus, forces of both race and class conspired to maintain a blanket of silence about Pinto, his politics, his contribution and about his political work.

Durrani S. (forthcoming book on Pinto) mentions the following:

> ...yet another reason for lack of information on Pinto ... is related to racism and anti-race struggles within the progressive circles. It remains a matter of speculation whether one of the reasons that Pinto remained "a hand behind the curtain" and did not come out centre stage was because of racism within the liberation forces. Similarly, it is not clear whether some aspects of his achievement remain unknown because of efforts by some to sideline him because of his racial background. While not much has been written about this aspect, a glimpse of racism towards Asian and European activists in the Kenyan is provided by Kaggia (2012):
>
>> One of the most notable event organised by the Study Circle was the "April 6th as the day for South Africa" in 1952 ... Before the Conference began, it was proposed that the non-Africans must leave. The two non-Africans at the conference, Pio Gama Pinto and Peter Wright, were members of the Study Circle which convened the conference in the first place... Eventually...the conference [chaired by Jomo Kenyatta, President of KAU] continued without our two friends.

Kaggia does not mention the name of the person who raised the objections, but mentions that he and Joseph Murumbi opposed the proposal, implying that the others supported the proposal. It is also unclear what the position of the Chair on this matter was.

The same forces of race and class apply to Makhan Singh and Ambubhai Patel, among others. Makhan Singh was the driving force behind setting up the radical trade union movement, its activities and ideological direction. In his histories of the trade union movement or in any of his writings, he does not talk about his own role or actions. Even his brief autobiographical piece is written in the third person. This is also the case with Ambubhai Patel who was active in many dangerous activities including collecting photographs of Mau Mau fighters, yet there is almost no reference to his own contribution.

It is therefore not surprising that very little is known about South Asian activities in Mau Mau. But this does not imply that they were absent. Although Patel, Z. (2006) says that Makhan Singh "never took the Mau Mau oath", she also says that Achieng Oneko in an interview in 2005 "stated categorically that Makhan Singh was Mau Mau". This would confirm what Mzee WM also said. Edgerton (1990) says "Even during the Emergency some Indians risked their lives to help the rebels, while others like Makhan Singh and Pio de Gama Pinto played important roles in launching the movement". At the same time, Kinyatti (2008) says:

> The progressive, anti-imperialist group in the Indian community, men like Pio Gama Pinto, Jaswant Singh Bharaj and others, played a very important role in supplying KLFA with firearms, intelligence, funds, medicine, and helped the movement to produce revolutionary literature. Jaswant Singh not only supplied the movement with firearms, his house was also a safe haven for the KLFA guerrillas... Ambu Patel also played a significant role in the Mau Mau movement. He collected funds for the movement and made his house in Nairobi, a safe haven for the movement. He and Pinto were involved in the production of the Mau Mau organ, The High Command.

It is inconceivable that those involved in the production of such a key publication of a movement such as Mau Mau would be given this responsibility unless they were highly trusted members of the organisation. It is thus important to examine a little further into the involvement of the South Asian communities in Mau Mau and in the War of Independence. This is best provided by brief portraits of activists from the minority community. This section looks at only the first category that Seidenberg (1983) mentions, the "radicals", as the other two categories, the conservatives and the moderates, are not within the scope of this book:

> The Asians, in their response to Mau Mau, tended to fit into three categories. There were no Asians who fought in the forest, but one group which might be called the radicals was strongly sympathetic and gave covert aid to the movement. Although some of these radicals had been active before 1952, many of the new activists were second generation Asians who had left their fathers' businesses and been educated abroad. Whether in India or Britain or even in North America, they were influenced by the libertarian ideals of John Stuart Mill and the socialist precepts of Karl Marx.

Edgerton (1990) mentions three non-Africans as playing an important part in advisory capacity for policy development for Mau Mau. Interestingly, it is not only the presence of South Asians that is missing from the history of Kenya's War of Independence: Europeans are almost absent, but there have been many progressive Europeans, some as civil servants, whose contribution still needs to be researched and acknowledged:

> Curious as it may seem in retrospect, the leaders of Mau Mau allowed three non Africans to serve on the Study Circle. One, Pio de Gama Pinto, was a Goan. Two were Europeans: Peter Wright, a former professor of history at Cawnpore, India, who served as a Lieutenant-Colonel in the British Intelligence Corps during World War II, and John P. B. Miller, a former Royal Navy Lieutenant Commander, then a resident of Kenya. The Study Circle originally met in the Nairobi offices of the Indian National Congress, and later, as police surveillance tightened, in private homes.

The following extracts are from Seidenberg (1983)

> **Ambu H. Patel:** Other individual Asians manifested a radical response to Mau Mau by carrying on underground assistance to the patriots in the forest or to the families of Mau Mau detainees. Ambu

H. Patel, a staunch follower of Gandhi who had been imprisoned in India for this anti-colonial stand, was a man with a mission "who made many sacrifices for Kenya" (quoting Hon. Clement Lubembe]. Throughout the Emergency, Patel collected funds for food and clothing for Mau Mau fighters and published leaflets and books concerned with Kenya's independence struggle. Patel also looked after Kenyatta's daughter, Margaret, while Kenyatta was in detention, and at great personal risk sent him clothes, food, and shoes when no-one else would or did.

Yacoob-Deen, owner of a sawmill located near Karatina in Mau Mau territory, gave the patriots generous supplies of food, boots, medicines and bandages until he was tipped off that he was going to be arrested and hanged by the British police. He took the first plane "going anywhere" and landed in Karachi where he remained for twelve years. After Kenya independence, he returned on a special pass and became a citizen.

Apa Pant Militant African nationalism was greatly aided not only by individual Asians residing in Kenya but also by Shri Apa Pant, the Indian High Commissioner, and his wife, Nalinidevi. As Prime Minister Nehru's emissary in East Africa from 1948 to 1954, Pant befriended African leaders and promulgated the African cause among Asians in Kenya. At any opportunity - tea parties, at openings of football matches and schools, and at large, independent gatherings organized at his home - he propounded his views on the freedom of Kenya. His spirited, anti-colonial stand was in fact so appreciated by African leaders that Senior Chief Mbiu Koinange, a prominent Kikuyu headman, adopted him as his eighth son, and gave him land in Kiambu. Pant exhorted the Asians to fight against racialism, sectarianism, and communalism, and to give shelter to Africans during Mau Mau; and encouraged them to take up citizenship in their country of adoption. As a result of his activities, a great deal of pressure was put on the Government by the Settlers to oust Pant and his staff. Consequently, this chief representative was declared *persona non grata* and left Kenya in May 1953.

Patel, Ambu (1963) provides further information on some other activists::

> **Jaswant Singh Bharaj** ... This [bad treatment and insults at the Kenya Police Reserve] made him a sympathiser of the anti-White section among the Mau Mau and he commenced manufacturing and supplying them arms, ammunition and other material. He supplied piping to the Mau Mau Bush Fighters for making guns and taught to a few of them the art of gun-making ... He was arrested in May, 1954, tried and sentenced to be hanged. In the appeal, the sentence was reduced to life imprisonment but he was released in 1958 after serving four and a half years in Takwa Detention Camp, off Mombasa, along with other detainees such as Messrs. John Mbiyu Koinange, Mr. Achieng Oneko and Mr. M. C. Chokwe. He is a sincere and selfless supporter of the African struggle for freedom and intends serving Africa and the African in every way possible. By profession he is a Carpenter, Mason, Plumber, Electrician, Builder, Radio and Motor Mechanic, Welder, Lorry Driver, Tractor Driver and Gunmaker. Today he is earning his bread in a temporary job by labouring as a carpenter in Nairobi.

Durrani, Nazmi (2017) provides some details of activities of Manilal A. Desai, Makhan Singh, Ambubhai Patel, Pio Gama Pinto and Jaswant Singh Bharaj. These few examples point to the need for more research and also better dissemination of these facts so that they are part of people's consciousness about Kenya's history and the active involvement of different nationalities and people in the War of Independence.

Illustrations 3: Mau Mau

Dedan Kimathi   Kavote and Peter Nthirima in 1963

SAUTI YA KAMUKUNJI

INSIDE
— University Workers - N.S.S.F. Deduction
— Where to From Campus?
— Maji Maji Rebellion
— Workers Corner
— Is SONU dying a Natural Death?
— Jailed Students Fund Lauched

General Kago

Field Marshal Dedan Kimathi

General Kariba

Muthoni Kirima

Mbaria Kaniu

Karari Njama

Field Marshal Mutungi

Kavote

from their sources of supply and support in the reserves. *Below:* A Lincoln heavy bomber on a raid over the Aberdares. Photos: Kenya Information Services

Kenya's War of Independence

Emergency Village

Travelling in long convoys of vehicles under tight
Screening and Detention Camp

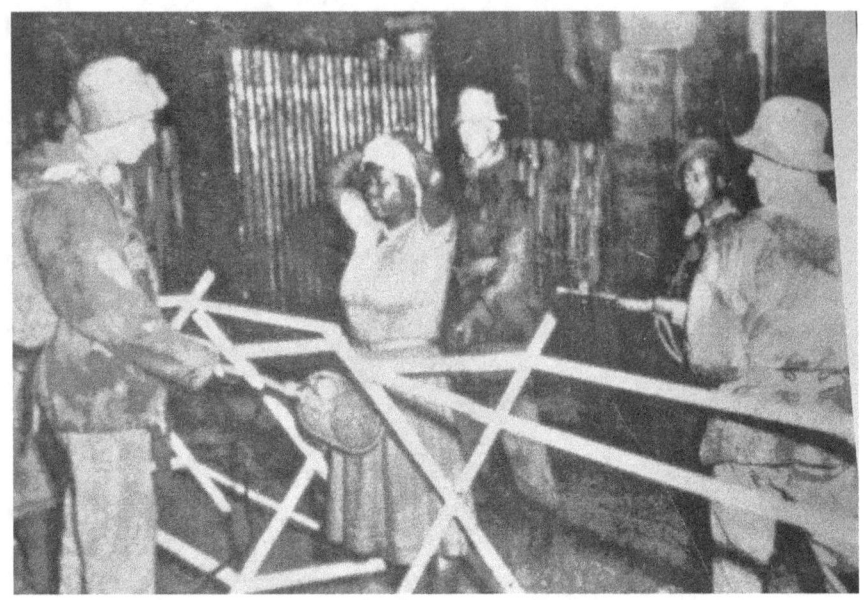

Security suspect arrive at the screening and possible Detention Camp

Field Marshal Mwariama N'Kirigua, 1963

Mau Mau General Inspects troops in the forest

General Tanganyika (Muriuki Kamotho)

The Final Stage: Battles Lost, Battles Won

The two opposing forces engaged in the War of Independence were, on the one hand, the British army, navy and air force - the most powerful superpower in the world at the time; on the other hand were Kenyan people's forces with limited armaments, some stolen from their enemies, some basic ones manufactured by themselves in make-shift factories. However, they were armed with total commitment to "die on their feet" while seeking the return of their land and freedom. The question is whether or not they succeeded in their aims.

Kaggia, B., Leeuw and M. Kaggia (2012) record the achievements of Mau Mau as fighters:

> In the battle Mau Mau soldiers distinguish themselves as great guerrilla fighters. General Sir George Erskine, a British general, advised his Government that Mau Mau could not be stamped out by force. Although the General was soon to be removed from command, what he said was true and the Government eventually had to accept it in practice. The British couldn't crash Mau Mau with all their sophisticated weapons. Considering the difficult conditions under which the Mau Mau soldiers fought and lived, it is impossible to ignore their greatness. They managed to fight the war for more than four years. Besides Dedan Kimathi, whose leadership and influence kept the war going all the time, a number of truly great soldiers distinguished themselves by any war standards. I will mention only a few: Stanley Mathenge, Gitau Matenjagwo, Ihuru Kareri, Manyeki Wangombe, Kago Mboko, Mbaria Kaniu and Waruhiu Itote. These men were greatly revered by their fellow Mau Mau soldiers and by all Africans in general. They were feared by the British Government soldiers and their helpers.

A fuller understanding of the battles and their impact can perhaps emerge once all the recently released "lost" files of the British Government are analysed. Yet the picture is by no means unclear. Newsinger (2006) gives figures of casualties on both sides of the conflict:

The official British figure of rebels killed in action was 11,503, but the real figure was much higher. Some estimates go as high as 50,000, and this is much closer to the truth. The casualties suffered by the [British] security forces were considerably lower: only 12 European soldiers and 52 European police were killed, three Asians and 524 African soldiers and police. ... as for settler casualties, only 32 were killed in the course of the emergency, less than died in traffic accidents in Nairobi in the same period. What was successfully portrayed by the British government as a pogrom against the white Settlers was in fact a pogrom against the Kikuyu.

This excludes civilian suffering in Kenya. Again, Newsinger (2006) provides further insight:

Unofficial repression was accompanied by the most ferocious repression. As well as tens of thousands interned without trial (the best estimate is that over 160,000 people were interned during the course of the emergency), even more were imprisoned for emergency offences. Between 1952 and 1958 over 34,000 women were to be imprisoned for Mau Mau offences, and the number of men imprisoned was probably ten times that figure. According to one historian [Anderson, 2005], "at least one in four Kikuyu adult males was imprisoned or detained by the British colonial administration.

But this was not the end of the story, as Dowden (2005) records:

But the British also deployed an even more fatal if effective method, the one they had used against Afrikaner civilians in the Boer war, the concentration camp. Both Anderson and Elkins draw convincing parallels with Nazi concentration camps and Stalin's gulags. More than 1m people were crammed into heavily guarded camps where starvation and disease killed thousands.

On the outside, the army used the same tactics that the Sudanese government has been using against the rebels in Darfur: they armed the local enemies of the rebellion and encouraged them to kill, rape and loot at will. When accounts of British atrocities leaked out, officials in Nairobi and London lied to deny them. When a few brave souls spoke out or even resigned, they were persuaded to keep quiet. When at last some of the truth came out the game was up.

These examples of colonial brutality were not an unintended outcome of a dirty war, nor "collateral damage" of a larger war. It was an integral part of a well-planned strategy, as *Hunting the Mau Mau* (2013) confirms:

> Other measures included the setting up of controlled villagers as a punitive measure against areas suspected of being solidly behind the Mau Mau. By early 1955 over a million Kikuyu had been settled in these villages.

Such brutality was the norm from the earliest days of European colonialism in Africa. And the global records of slavery, elimination of native people, the looting and confiscation of people's land and property are all parts of the same picture of how colonialism and imperialism shaped the lives of people around the world. Tharoor (2016) explores the colonial looting and brutality in India. The experience in China and other countries is no different. Kenya's is but a small part of a global picture of colonial and imperialist plunder, looting, massacres and "sinning quietly".

Mau Mau and their supporters made many sacrifices in their struggle to achieve Kenya's independence. They were shown no humanity nor given a peaceful way of addressing their concerns. Brutality, economic strangulations, massacres and torture were the response of the occupying colonial government. The occupiers eventually lost out by having to give in to demands for independence; yet they won in the long run by ensuring that imperialism flourished in Kenya. Mau Mau won the moral, and belatedly, the legal battle. In this they were not the first, nor will they be the last, resistance movements against colonialism and imperialism. The battles may be over, but the wars of total liberation rage on - in Kenya as elsewhere in the world.

There are lessons to be learnt from the Kenyan War of Independence - for Kenyans as well as for people around the world: how did the resistance movement survive so long against the vastly superior military machinery of British colonialists and how were they finally side-lined. The defeat of France and USA in Vietnam taught its own lessons on people's struggle for liberation. Kenya stands proudly in the long list of "teachers of liberation".

Forces of Repression

Following the declaration of a state of war (officially called the "Emergency") by the colonial authorities in October 1952, the stage of armed resistance began in earnest. The guerrilla forces established their new military headquarters in the forests from where the armed battles were planned and executed. Many small and large guerrilla units had entered the forests and waged battles against the enemy in their local areas. It is to the credit of Mau Mau that it recognised the need to co-ordinate the activities of these different fighting units and to form an umbrella military organisation that could control the overall strategy of warfare in the face of a well-armed and equipped enemy.

It is useful to see the strength of British forces that Mau Mau had to confront. Too often Mau Mau is seen in isolation as if they were fighting some unseen, imaginary force in the sky. This robs them of an acknowledgement of their achievement of fighting a major superpower of the day. A brief look at British strategy and military strength can provide a better perspective on the Kenyan War of Independence. The strength of the British forces in 1953 is recorded by Barnett and Njama (1966):

> To implement this new offensive strategy, [British] security force strength was greatly increased and, by September [1953], included 39th Brigade of Buffs and Devons, the 49th Brigade of Royal Northumberland and Inniskilling Fusiliers, the East African Brigade of six KAR [Kenya African Rifles] battalions, the Lancashire Fusiliers, the Kenya Regiment and two East African units, an armoured car division and a squadron of Lincolns – a total of eleven battalions and over 10,000 soldiers. In addition, the police force was increased to 21,000 men and the Kikuyu guard units to a somewhat higher figure. During the third quarter of 1953, then, the British and Kenya Governments were employing a force of well over 50,000 men against the Mau Mau insurgents.

Barnett and Njama (1966) mention the use by the British forces of bombing by Harvard and Lincoln bombers and recount the effects of 1,000 lb. bombs dropped on Mau Mau combatants and the countryside. The tactics used by the British armed forces were the tried and tested ones all around the Empire. "Hunting the Mau Mau" website provides some useful insight on the strength and tactics used:

> The British forces in Kenya employed the tried and tested tactics which had worked so well in the counter-insurgency operations in Malaya. The problem was to balance the wealth of knowledge with the flexibility of response, allowing the knowledge of past experience to meld with what was needed in the theatre, but not to rigidly apply that knowledge to the exclusion of ingenuity and individual experience. This knowledge dates back to the Boer War and beyond to colonial operations ... In the British army's war against Mau Mau it was evident from the start that both branches of the government were agreed that "Mau Mau had to be suppressed; political negotiations were totally inconceivable."

The website goes on to record the strength of the British armed forces lined up against Mau Mau:

After the declaration of the State of Emergency it soon became clear that the colonial government had no strategy for dealing with the revolt and unrest. The governor requested and obtained British and African troops including the King's African Rifles. The troops were composed of:

1st Lancashire Fusiliers (from the Canal Zone)
4th KAR (from Uganda)
6th KAR (from Tanganyika)
Local KAR Battalions

The site also provides details of British forces under Royal Air Force, Army, Royal Navy and local forces. It will thus be seen that the Mau Mau forces were so well organised that all branches of the British armed forces had to be mobilised in order to defeat them. Newsinger (2006) sums up the balance of forces during this period:

> The [white] Settlers dreamed of a permanent white supremacist regime in Kenya ... Mau Mau, however, had shown that the Settlers did not have the strength to survive on their own. Without the British government coming to their assistance in the 1950s, Mau Mau would have won.

When the armed stage began in 1952, Mau Mau maintained over 35,000 active fighters in the forests, and many thousands more in urban areas. It maintained friendly relations with thousands of peasants and workers. Its influence extended over a large part of the country, from Mombasa on the Coast to Kisumu in western Kenya. It even extended over parts of Tanganyika (now mainland Tanzania) where the British authorities were forced to declare a state of Emergency in Northern Tanganyika at the same time as it was declared over Kenya.

As one of Mau Mau struggle songs, "we are everywhere" (Maina, P., 1977) made clear, the presence of the guerrilla forces was felt everywhere:

> If you go to Nairobi
> We are there.
> If you go to Mombasa,
> We are there.
> And if you go to Kisumu
> We are there.
> We are so many
> That we are everywhere.

These facts indicate that the Mau Mau must have had a vast organisational network to be able to keep the large British military machinery on the run.

Mau Mau faced defeat not at the hands of British colonial forces, but at the hands of the government of an independent Kenya led by Jomo Kenyatta, handed over this responsibility in the interest of imperialism. But the colonial administration ensured it provided ample ammunition to the Kenyatta government to fulfil this task successfully. Angelo (2017), for example, records one aspect of this support:

> Most of the prominent members of Kenyatta's government were selected and trained within colonial administrative system (re)shaped during the Emergency, and part and parcel of the Mau Mau counter-insurgency. Those who were appointed provincial commissioners at independence had been trained by T. J. F. Gavaghan, the brains behind the brutal rehabilitation politics during the Mau Mau war and later appointed in 1961 as training officer of the Kenyan provincial administration. By 1965, two top members of the Office of the President were renowned loyalists: Duncan Ndegwa (Permanent Secretary) and Jeremiah Kiereini Under-Secretary in charge of the provincial administration.

That was only one aspect of the Kenyatta Government's efforts in attacking Mau Mau. A more brutal approach was the elimination of Mau Mau leadership, reminiscent of the worst excesses of colonialism, as Angelo (2017) shows:

Around the time of independence (1961–1965), Kenya's African nationalist government organized the continued repression of the remaining Mau Mau fighters who had refused to surrender after the ending of the Emergency in January 1960. [One such case focused] on Meru district, in Eastern Province, where Mau Mau fighters gathered under the leadership of Field Marshalls Mwariama and Baimungi. Documents from the Kenyan National Archives, in particular the correspondence of the provincial administration and security reports, show that politicians and officials alike saw the remaining fighters in Meru as a potent political threat to the nationalist government of Jomo Kenyatta. Kenya's government sought to deal with the Mau Mau threat by co-opting its leaders, while Kenyatta carefully distanced the presidency from the government's choice of repressive politics. A symbolic propaganda campaign was organized to maintain the myth that Kenyatta had always been the Mau Mau leader the British arrested and jailed in 1953, despite the reality of Kenyatta's repeated denunciation of the movement. After 1963, the President continued to ignore Mau Mau fighters' fundamental claims over land redistribution... the Kenya government organized a violent repression of Mau Mau in order to deprive freedom fighters of their leaders and to force them to retreat into silence.

Among the leaders killed were Field Marshall Baimungi and Chui "believed to be the most dangerous leaders" (Angelo, 2017), both "killed by police in a dawn swoop on the forest"[46]

Primary Aim

The primary aim of the War of Independence - as the name suggests - was independence for Kenya. And that aim was achieved. Without an armed struggle, Kenya's independence would have been delayed at best, and the European Settlers would have increased their power and perhaps even been granted independence on their own terms. The Settlers in Southern Rhodesia achieved such a "victory" after its Universal Declaration of Independence in 1965. That singular achievement of Mau Mau tends to be ignored in colonial interpretation of Kenyan history. The comprador regime after independence accepted this version of Kenya's history and saw Mau Mau as an enemy just as Britain had done. While Mau Mau would have been an enemy of the elite which took over power to serve their own interests, it was no enemy of the people of Kenya whose demands during the War of Independence was land and freedom as part of independence. As Tandon 2017b says, "Political independence is a significant stage in the fight against imperialism. The 'common man' is brought into the democratic process directly". There can then be no doubt that independence was the first step in the total liberation from imperialism which Kenyan people have been struggling for generations.

There is, however, a legitimate question to be answered as to whether Mau Mau can be referred to as a revolution or whether it was just a revolt or a resistance. It certainly was not a revolution in the sense of the Russian or the Chinese Revolutions, which overthrew the old class order and ushered in working class into power. Yet it was revolutionary in the sense that it led to the withdrawal of British colonialism and cleared the way for Kenya's independence. Defeat of colonialism is not seen as revolutions, whether in India or countries in Africa. Academics and historians can debate the appropriate words to describe the defeat of colonialism, but the term, as used in this book, has the limited meaning of overthrowing the colonial

---

46   *Daily Nation*, 27-01-1965, quoted by Angelo, 2017.

regime and its replacement by a government of an independent country. It is recognised that there needs to be a struggle for economic liberation from imperialism when working people come to power in a truly revolutionary change. In that sense Mau Mau and the War of Independence were not revolutionary wars. Ndegwa (2017) sees the battle as being lost, but the war was won:

> However, although the Freedom Fighters are said to have lost the, battle it could be said that they won the war. Soon after the end of the state of emergency, Kenya's independence was declared in December 1963.
>
> Mau Mau had made the British think again about the people they had colonized. It had made them realize that the local people were a force to reckon with. It was not surprising that the British were ready to see the Kenyan people in a different light; they were no longer the meek, obedient and good natives they had always been, but people who knew what they wanted and had ideas of how to get it.

Much was achieved by the struggle, however one describes it. Independence would not have been possible in 1963 without the input from Mau Mau. In addition, Kaggia, B., Leeuw and Kaggia, M (2012) set out other achievements of Mau Mau succinctly:

> Mau Mau was an organization formed to achieve what KAU had failed to achieve through constitutional means. It was ready to achieve its objective by any means. It was a movement determined to achieve Kenya's real liberation at any cost. As to what Mau Mau achieved, only blind people could fail to appreciate the many concessions which the British Government granted Kenya. These concessions were what KAU had been demanding for years. During the early months of the Emergency the Colonial Secretary said no change would be possible until the revolt was squashed, and before the beginning of the armed struggle, there was no sign of any change being granted. The British Government followed one concession by another, and it was clear that while the British tried on the one hand to discredit Mau Mau as a primitive organization whose only aim was to return the tribe to the past, at another level the Government accepted the fact that Mau

Mau was political and that hostilities would only end with political advancement for Africans.

Even before independence, Mau Mau had changed the political climate in Kenya. Kaggia, B. Leeuw and M. Kaggia (2012) point to some other achievements:

As a result of the Mau Mau armed struggle, the following changes were effected by the British government within a short time. These changes paved the way to independence:

1. In 1954 a new constitution (the Lyttelton plan) started by giving Africans, for the first time in Kenya's history, one minister in the government.

2. In 1955 the Coutts Commission was appointed to work on demarcation of African constituencies and to devise a method of voting for Africans.

3. In the same year the ban on political parties was lifted and Africans were allowed to form district political parties.

4. In 1956 two portfolios were given to Africans.

5. In 1957 limited voting rights were given to Africans and the number of African members of Parliament increased to 8.

6. In 1958 the number of African members of Parliament increased to 14.

7. In 1959 Emergency Governor, Sir Evelyn Baring, was removed from office. He had vowed for years to crash Mau Mau.

8. Britain agreed to a round table conference with the African members to decide on Kenya's future.

Venys (1970) sums up the overall achievements of Mau Mau:

> It was the first conscious attempt at an armed anti-colonial revolt in Africa which had no analogy on the continent at that time... The Mau Mau movement has held a unique position in the modern history of Africa as it was the first anti-colonial movement of its kind that produced an armed uprising and persisted for such a long time against the superior force of the colonial power. It was the first manifestation of the strength of subjugated Africans and became a turning point in Kenya's struggle for uhuru ... the movement influenced the subsequent political development of Kenya. It helped the African masses involved in the movement get out of political passivity, providing them with a chance to experience the first lesson in the fight against colonialism. It forced the colonial government [to admit] that the times when the African could be considered nothing but a "poor uncivilised thing" had passed and that there were enormous potentiality hidden in Kenya Africans. The colonialists came to realise that the time had come when Africans must be allowed to participate in the ruling of the country and eventually to run it by themselves. The insurrection was a serious warning indicating that there was something corrupt in the Colony of Kenya and that colonialism in its old shape had ceased to function.

It was Uganda's then Prime Minister Milton Obote who summed up the achievement of Mau Mau in a speech when Kenya achieved independence:

> Today is the day on which Kenya formally joins Algeria at the high rank of being the hero of colonial Africa. The struggle in Kenya was bitter. Many people lost their lives ... The past cannot be forgotten ... It cannot be forgotten because it is the past not only of Kenya but of world history. [47]

And it cannot be forgotten because the aims for which many lives were lost are as valid today as they were then. Nor can the example of the brave warriors be forgotten, warriors who, as one of the Mau Mau struggle song records, declared:

---

[47] Daily Nation (Nairobi) December 13, 1963.

It is better to die on our feet

Than to live on our knees.

Kaggia, B., Leeum and Kaggia, M (2012) provide a fitting tribute to Mau Mau:

> The Mau Mau struggle, whether one likes it or not, will stand in history as one of the greatest liberation struggles in Africa. It was the first of its kind on the continent. Its heroes will be remembered by generations to come ... The greatness of the Mau Mau struggle becomes more striking when one remembers that the fighters had no outside contacts, arms supplies or money. Mau Mau relied on its own resources. Money was collected from followers and supporters. In addition to capturing arms, the soldiers manufactured their own. It is time to recognize their achievements. Long live Mau Mau! Long live the freedom of Kenya, which the Mau Mau fought for and brought about.

Mathu (1974) looked back at the movement some years after hostilities ceased and sounds a warning about lack of change:

> Looking back on "Mau Mau" today, I still consider it to have been a just and courageous struggle for freedom. Though mistakes were made and some people entered the revolt for narrow or selfish interests, the Kikuyu people as a whole fought and suffered bravely and I am proud of them. Our fight against British colonialism, by throwing fear into the hearts of the imperialists and Settlers, quickened the pace of political development and independence in Kenya. I should like to remind those African leaders who now condemn Mau Mau and tell us to forget our past struggles and suffering, that their present positions of power in the Legislative Council and elsewhere would not have been realized except for our sacrifices. I would also warn them that we did not make these sacrifices just to have Africans step into the shoes of our former European masters.

Mathu thus points to the unfinished work of the War of Independence: "Are the masses of people simply to become the slaves of a handful of wealthy

Black men?" Pio Gama Pinto's (1963a) suggestion now needs to be taken up seriously:

> The sacrifices of the hundreds of thousands of Kenya's freedom fighters must be honoured by the effective implementation of the policy - a democratic, African, socialist state in which the people have the right to be free from economic exploitation and the right to social equality. Kenya's uhuru [independence] must not be transformed into freedom to exploit, or freedom to be hungry and live in ignorance. Uhuru must be uhuru for the masses - uhuru from exploitation, from ignorance, disease and poverty.

Mukami Kimathi, Dedan Kimathi's wife and a Mau Mau warrior in her own right, also a detainee at Kamiti Prison where her husband was killed, assessed Mau Mau and called for restoration of justice (Venys, 1970):

> Dedan Kimathi's wife took the platform (on the day of Uhuru celebration, December 12, 1963) and declared emphatically that the bloodshed by Mau Mau in the forest had brought Kenya's independence and all land confiscated by the colonial government from former Mau Mau fighters should be returned to them.

Barnett and Njama (1966) sum up the transition to neo-colonialism:

> The revolt of the Kikuyu peasantry lasted for more than three years. Though defeated militarily, few objective observers would deny that there was more than mere coincidence in the fact that the official end of the State of Emergency in January 1960 occurred while British colonial officials at the Lancaster House Conference were agreeing to an African majority in the Kenya Legislative Council and eventual independence for Kenya under African rule. The lowering of the Union Jack in Kenya on 12 December 1963 was unquestionably the culmination of political forces set in motion by the 1953-56 peasant revolution called 'Mau Mau'.

Furedi (1989) provides an overview of the significance of Mau Mau within an African context:

The weakness of political coherence should not obscure the important achievements of the Mau Mau leadership. In contrast to general experience in colonial Africa the mass movement emerged with its own plebeian leadership. This represented a major innovation in the history of Kenyan nationalism. With Mau Mau, for the first time the mass movement acted independently of the educated middle-class leadership. Consequently, here was a mass movement not susceptible to co-optation. The colonial administration had no choice but to destroy it. The growth of Mau Mau can be seen not merely as the result of the strength of the mass movement but also as a symptom of the weakness of the middle-class moderate nationalists. A central theme of colonial policy in the subsequent period was to make sure that this would never happen in the future.

The stage was set for the next phase of resistance to neo-colonialism and imperialism.

Advice for Someone Going into Prison

You must insist on living,

There may not be happiness

but it is your binding duty

to resist the enemy,

and live one extra day.

Inside, ten years, or fifteen years

Or even more can be got through

they really can:

Enough that you never let the precious stone

under your left breast grow dull.

- Nazim Hikmet (1949)[48]

---

[48] Nazim Hikmet, A Sad State of Freedom. Translated from the Turkish by Taner Baybars and Richard McKane. 1990. Warwick: The Grenville Press.

Possible Shape of a Mau Mau Government

There can be no doubt that without colonial interference in the process of transition to independence, a government led or influenced by Mau Mau would have come to power. Given that peasants were an important part of Mau Mau, the first acts of such a truly independent government would have been to redress the land issue which was one of the main aims of the War of Independence. This is also the view of Kabubi (2007), a Mau Mau warrior active on the battlefield, when she replied to the question, "What kind of Kenya would have come if Mau Mau had succeeded?":

> I think land distribution would have been given priority. The government posts would have been filled by the patriots who fought for independence, not by loyalists who collaborated with the British".

If peasants and land were one essential foundation of Mau Mau, "Freedom" was the other one. This included political, social and economic freedom from colonial and imperialist interference. Given that trade unions and working classes played a key role in the War of Independence as a whole and in Mau Mau in particular, it takes no leap of imagination to conclude that a Mau Mau-led government would have strengthened workers' rights and circumscribed those of transnational corporations and reduced or eliminated the influence of foreign governments in deciding government policies. Social and political rights of nationalities, women, working people generally would have been protected.

However an objective assessment of Mau Mau needs to examine what Mau Mau did not achieve. It did not achieve the two aims of "land and freedom". Here the freedom is defined not in terms of independence only but in the broader sense of power and control over policies that would change the life chances of working people. The return of the stolen land to their rightful owners was a key demand of the War of Independence. It has been removed from national agenda by the independence government with the connivance of the colonial government. Added to this is the scuppering of the agenda set out by the trade union movement under the East African Trade Union Congress (EATUC). The colonial government and the comprador government sidelined the demands of EATUC by restricting trade union rights and curtailing the political aspects of trade union activities while co-opting the trade union movement as part of the comprador government.

The question then arises whether there was anything that Mau Mau could have done to ensure success in meeting its broader objective. Maloba (1989) mentions that Mau Mau lacked a strong political party which could have completed the work that political and military activists had carried out in the country. While there was a political structure that was beginning to emerge with the Kenya Parliament, this process had not reached fruition by the time the British colonial government decided that independence with moderate elements it had nurtured was a better option than delayed independence, which would allow the full force of Mau Mau's revolutionary programme to develop. This was one of the reasons for the rush to independence that was instigated by the last Governor of Kenya, Sir Malcolm McDonald as seen elsewhere the book. Just as at an earlier stage, British colonialism had prevented the full preparation of the military development of Mau Mau, in the late 1950s and early 1960s, it similarly scuppered the normal political development that could possibly have seen the emergence of a Mau Mau political Party with aims as set out by Pinto (1963a) above. In the absence of such a militant party, the way was clear for conservative politicians nurtured by colonialism to become the rulers to replace colonialism. The marginalisation of Mau Mau in these two aspects - the military and political - can be seen as the long term victory of imperialism over the people of Kenya.

And yet it would be unfair to judge Mau Mau on the basis that it did not achieve the results whose time had not come during their period. The contradiction of the time was with European Settlers and colonial government and that was certainly settled in the favour of Mau Mau as the British military and political manoeuvring could not delay independence. The battle against neo-colonialism could not be waged in the period of colonialism. It is to the credit of Mau Mau that it highlighted and started preparing for the fight against the new face of imperialism even as it was succeeding in its anti-colonial battles. Its military preparedness, ideological struggles and communications strategy were once again gearing up for the new struggles ahead. And the long term war against imperialism was set to continue after independence, this time by successors of Mau Mau.

Reparation

British colonialism has ended. It has left major problems for Kenya in a similar way it did in India, as Tharoor (2016c) says:

> British rule de-industrialised India, created landlessness and poverty, drained our country's resources, exploited, enslaved, exiled and oppressed millions, sowed seeds of division and inter-communal hatred that led to the country's partitioning into two hostile states, and was directly responsible for the deaths of 35 million people in unnecessary and mismanaged famines as well as of thousands in massacres and killings. That just skims the surface of the havoc wreaked by British colonialism. The British conquered one of the richest countries in the world and reduced it to one of the poorest.

So is it time to think of reparations that Britain needs to make to people of Kenya - and India and other former colonies - for the damage it has done? Tharoor (2016c) does not think so, but it seems only for technical reasons:

> But I don't in fact ask for reparations, as the Oxford debate did. How do you place a monetary value on all that India suffered and lost under British rule? There's really no compensation that would even begin to be adequate, or credible. The symbolic pound-a-year I'd suggested would be a nightmare to administer.

And there are other difficulties in getting reparation. Quantifying damage in a situation that is highlighted by Bufacchi (2017) can be a daunting task:

> Any debate about the best way to rectify historical injustice must take into account the violence at the heart of the injustice, its arbitrariness, and enduring qualities ... in the context of colonialism the violence is fundamentally different from the violence that one finds in a democracy. The difference is the arbitrary nature of colonial violence, and arbitrariness is what makes colonialism not just wrong but distinctively so.

Similarly, Tharoor (2016a) raises another legacy of colonialism that is difficult to address in the neo-colonial phase:

Empire might have gone, but it endures in the imitative elites it left behind in the developing world, the 'mimic men', in Naipaul's phrase, trying hard to be what the imperial power had not allowed them to be, while subjecting themselves and their societies to the persistent domination of corporations based mainly in the metropole. The East India Company has collapsed but globalization has ensured that its modern-day successors in the former imperial states remain the predominant instruments of capitalism.

And yet the crimes of colonialism cannot be allowed to do permanent damage to the former colonised peoples and not pay for its crimes. We need to separate the technical and other difficulties in getting reparation from the moral case for making reparations. And it should not be a few individuals who can decide if and how reparations need to be made. It is for the people of former colonies to decide in partnership with the people of the countries that colonised them - certainly not the elite and not the corporations in both the countries which benefited from decades of exploitation and repression. History is on their side.

Neo-colonialism, the Legacy of Colonialism

The War of Independence was waged against the system of exploitation. This system itself had undergone changes in response to the military attacks of Mau Mau. By about 1956-57, it became clear that colonialism was no longer sustainable in Kenya. The departure of British colonialism was a matter of time. In just a few years of warfare, Mau Mau had changed the balance of power, although it had to pay a heavy price for this change, with many combatants injured, dead, in detention or maimed. Many others had lost their land, livestock and means of livelihood, their children having to grow up without adequate food, clothing, housing or education. The new independent Government of Kenya cast them aside even as the new power holders, who had played insignificance or no part in the struggle for independence, became the new rich class with power, wealth, land, jobs and education denied to Mau Mau activists and their children. But Mau Mau militants had realised quite early the danger of colonialist tentacles returning to take control of the country in a new form. They clearly saw colonialists "going from the door, only to return through the window" as neo-colonialists.

From that initial realisation of the new threat to the young Kenyan nation right up to and beyond the time of formal independence in 1963, all the energies of Mau Mau cadres was poured into making people aware of the new danger facing the revolution. Ideological and military preparations had to be made for another struggle before final victory could be achieved.

These renewed Mau Mau preparations were admitted by the colonial regime in the last years of its existence. Thus the colonial minister of Internal Security and Defence (the ministry charged with fighting Mau Mau), Mr Swann, had to admit that "for the last three months of 1962, operations have progressed to curb the activities of the Kenya Land and Freedom Army." He revealed that the colonial government was detaining more people "to avoid a second emergency in Kenya". Mr Swann said that the purpose of Mau Mau was to take over power in Kenya. "An emergency would be inevitable if we had not taken any action this year", he added.

Mr Swann admitted that in spite of the vast military intervention of top military forces in Kenya since 1952 and even earlier "he did not hope to stamp out the type of activity typified by Mau Mau and the Kenya Land and Freedom Army ... this activity will never stop". He made a number of observations in this period which shows that Mau Mau continued its organisational and military activities in this new period of neo-colonialism. Below are some of his comments, and reports from newspapers of the time taken from Kenya Committee's Press Extracts:

> It was hoped to secure the help of Jomo Kenyatta after his release. "We have discussed the Kenya Land and Freedom Army with Kenyatta and he is certainly not in favour of it", Mr. Swann said. "I hope to enlist him as well as other leaders".
>
> ...
>
> The reorganized Kenya Land and Freedom Army consisted of a Committee representing various parts of Kenya, and it (is) the Supreme Command ... It revived also among Mau Mau detainees in Mbagathi prison in 1957. They started work on the organization.
>
> ...
>
> The Kenya Land and Freedom Army was still organizing, and had launched a recruiting campaign. Its cry was not for action now but in the future. It could be planned for the end of the year, for internal self-government, or for independence. The idea is to secure more members and more weapons now.
>
> ...
>
> The pattern of oathing was the same - to preserve secrecy, maintain unity, never cooperate with the [colonial] government ... steal arms and ammunition and money ... commit murder when ordered and to obtain land. (Mathu, 1974).

Mau Mau was preparing, thus the renewed organisational structures, revised ideologies and new military tactics in the period before 1963. Perhaps the most important work in the early years was to warn the people against the new danger. The neo-colonialist allies were constantly pouring forth lies and falsehoods through their mass media with their message that independence was just round the corner, hence there was no need to struggle any more. The goals of the struggle for independence were won, they said; Africanisation and multiracialism were here, they proclaimed, so there was no longer a need to continue the fight.

It thus became necessary to bring the ideological battle to the forefront. It became necessary to place before the people a correct analysis of historical events, and to emphasise the need to continue the struggle. This was done in the form of a Policy Document which was widely circulated. It was also presented at the Conference of the Kenya African National Union held in Nairobi in December 1961, where contradictions were developing about the need to combat neo-colonialism. The Document, entitled "The Struggle for Kenya's Future" was the clearest statement on the dangers of neo-colonialism. It is reproduced in Appendix B.

Some aspects of this struggle for the future of Kenya are examined in the rest of the book.

A Prison Without Walls[49]

There are no walls
In this prison
It is built on a foundation of fear, intimidation, and threats.

Keep the history book closed, keep the historian in prison

The prison without walls
Has room for many.

How to subdue
The anger of millions
Who see their sweat and blood enriching but a few?

Concentration camps and stone prisons are never enough.
Gallows will not silence them
They are too many, far too many.

---

[49] Written by the author in London on October 20, 1984 to mark Mau Mau Freedom Fighters' Day.

Quick, open the gates
Gates of the prison without walls. Create a terror
Worse than death.

No evidence of violence
No, not even a scratched forehead. Yet opposition is silenced
Millions are struck dumb.

Blame the victim
Make the innocent guilty for questioning their misery, for being.

Interrogations, threats, and insults.
Why think? Why not be an animal? Threaten by suggestions, intimidate by looks

Will your child be safe?

The prison without walls
Is never full
Bring in more and still more
Until the whole country becomes
A prison house without a single wall.

And yet
Questions keep coming
Voices of protest keep singing, minds keep working, day and night, day and night

The prison without walls
Will never solve the problem. Only the united will

Of the people will.

Kenya became independent on December 12, 1963. Now an African Prime Minister and an African government ruled the country. The old order had given way to the new. And that achievement was due entirely to Mau Mau.

And yet it was not the independence that those who participated in the War of Independence had fought for. The changes were soon seen for what they were: the replacement of colonialism by neo-colonialism, the replacement of European Settlers by African "owners" of land. European Settlers remained, as did multinational corporations as the rulers behind the scene. Government policies were handed down by the "independent" government in Nairobi but directed by imperialist forces in London and New York. Policy guidance came from IMF and the World Bank. The only aspect that did not change was the condition of working class, the situation of those who fought in the war of independence. It was, in effect, independence of the ruling classes (black and white this time) to rule, kill, massacre, suppress and loot as they pleased. And suppress, kill and massacre they needed in order to remain in power as the people who had sacrificed all were not yet ready to hand over control to new masters with the same agenda. But the new masters were fully backed by the same imperialist powers which had engineered their coming to power.

Field Marshal Muthoni (2007) has no hesitation in identifying this neo-colonialist hijacking of Kenya's independence:

> It's like a competitive match. We were the team. We played valiantly, sacrificially, against the opposing team. We sweated. We gave our lives. Then, at the end of the match, when we had won, the spectators ran away with the trophy.

Field Marshal Muthoni (2007) explains what happened at the time of independence with clarity and understanding:

> Come independence, 1963 is when the injustice of the system began to set in. Mau Mau readily gave up their weapons and returned to

their villages. The struggle, after all, had been won. Reality proved somewhat less than ideal. They found that, while they were in the forest fighting the enemy, land consolidation had taken place in 1960. Those who were absent had had their land taken away from them and given to others. They found that, while they were fighting, those they had left in the villages had been educating themselves and educating their children. The fledgling government needed this educated cadre as it began to establish itself. So therefore, it was the children of those who did not fight who were offered positions of influence in government on account of their experience and education.

And these things happened not as an accident but as a result of a carefully planned exit of colonialism which eased the way for the smooth entry of neo-colonialism. Mau Mau achieved one of the key aims of the War of Independence which was to defeat colonialism and achieve independence for Kenya. In this, it also changed British colonial policy and perhaps hastened the independence of other African countries. Yet gaining political independence was not the only aim of the War of Independence as the document, *The Future of Kenya*,[50] made clear:

> The struggle for Kenya's future is being waged today on three distinct though interrelated levels - political, racial and economic. It seems to us that we Africans are being allowed to "win" in the first two spheres as long as we don't contest the battle being waged on the third, all-important economic level.

An indication of things to come after independence was given by Jomo Kenyatta, as Venys (1970) records:

> Within six months of Uhuru, Kenyatta was publicly denouncing activities of the rebels. He found it necessary to travel in the affected areas warning people against oath-taking and supporting the forest rebels to whom he referred as "vagabonds". Kenyatta continued the policies of the now departed colonialists and had General Baimungi, General Chui and other Mau Mau leaders assassinated in 1965. He described Mau Mau as "…a disease which has been eradicated and must never be remembered again" (*East African Standard, September*

---

50   Reproduced in Appendix B.

10, 1962).

The fear that the imperialist enemy would go from the door only to return through the window came to pass in the form of an "enemy within". Kenya provides a good example of what Thomsen (2017) refers to as "the attempt of imperialism to turn back the wheel of history to colonial times". While this may not have happened in all its details, the oppression of working class was certainly reimposed. Given that the oppression and exploitation continued after independence, the War of Independence entered its second phase on the attainment of independence.

But the situation that Kenyans found themselves in was not unique as imperialism was well prepared to combat people's resistance. Thus it was not only in Kenya that imperialism eliminated resistance leaders and planted seeds of division among people. The experience of South Africa at a later time was similar to what happened in Kenya, as Kasrils (2013) recalls:

> South Africa's liberation struggle reached a high point but not its zenith when we overcame apartheid rule. Back then, our hopes were high for our country given its modern industrial economy, strategic mineral resources (not only gold and diamonds), and a working class and organised trade union movement with a rich tradition of struggle. But that optimism overlooked the tenacity of the international capitalist system. From 1991 to 1996 the battle for the ANC's soul got under way, and was eventually lost to corporate power: we were entrapped by the neoliberal economy – or, as some today cry out, we "sold our people down the river".

But the subversion of African liberation and the elimination of leaders who stood against imperialism also indicates that there was a systematic plan to eliminate all progressive movements and leaders, as the article, *Every Leader Who Stood Up...* (2017) in *How Africa News* records:

> One by one, our most steadfast leaders have been eliminated, to the point where Africa is hard-pressed to point out more than three people who are advancing the continental agenda for economic freedom. Almost every single leader who has stood up for Africa's right to economic self- determination has been eliminated – either physically

or politically.

The process did not start within the 20th Century, nor with the elimination of Kwame Nkrumah in Ghana and Patrice Lumumba in the Congo. It started right at the beginning of colonialism itself and continued with the elimination of Dedan Kimathi and systematic attacks on Mau Mau. And it continues unabated today.

The response in Kenya, as elsewhere in Africa, is the continuation of the struggle for total liberation, particularly in the economic field. The War of Economic Independence is continued by the political successors of Mau Mau.

Sina Habari, Mwanangu: I have No News, My Child[51]

> I have no news, my child
> no news at all
> Except
> news of troubles, torture and death.
>
> I have no news, people of my land
> no news at all
> If you want land, food, shelter, clothing
> no news at all
> Except
> News of bullets and wars.
>
> I have no news, patriot
> no news at all
> If you want freedom, liberation, liberty
> I have no news
> Except
> News of struggle and struggles

---

51 Translation of Sina Habari, Mwanangu (Kiswahili) by Shiraz Durrani (1985).

Colonialism's Secret Weapon

In the long run, the tactic that appears to have ended Mau Mau's armed resistance was the British Government's use of Homeguard force to divide Kenyan people and to infiltrate ranks of resistance. In what was to develop in later years as contra-forces and similar local mercenary forces under US imperialism, British colonialism used an early version of the same disruptive force. Anderson (2016) shows that this use was not confined to Kenya:

> In all the wars of decolonization fought across Africa and Asia from the 1940s until the 1970s, European colonial powers deployed local forces to battle against armed nationalist groups. These local allied combatants, variously known as auxiliaries, militias or loyalists when drawn together in irregular forces, or sometimes more formally recruited to swell the ranks of police or military reserves, often became a critically important component of colonial counter-insurgencies.

While such loyalist forces were used against the armed combatants of Mau Mau, they were also used as a weapon to overcome the militancy of Kenyan War of Independence at economic and political levels. The use of divisive politics by Britain continued as they sought to ensure a situation favourable to imperialism, as Wasserman (1976) explains:

> When the fighting war came to an end, loyalist leaders were therefore consolidated as a ruling elite in Central Province, given control of administrative positions as local government was restored from 1956, and then shepherded into government as Kenya's decolonization got underway from 1959. Their monopoly of local politics was secured by laws that prevented known rebels from participating in elections, and once in positions of authority they were able to exclude former Mau Mau from many areas of public life, while also blocking any attempt they made to restore their lost property or to recover their forfeited land.

> Kikuyu loyalists were the building blocks with which Kenya's post-colonial state was constructed in Central Province, and in the 1960s

they even came to dominate the political economy of the entire country.

A Brief Recap

A brief recap of what Britain did in Kenya would help set the background to understanding the impact colonialism had on people and the country and what imperialism sets out to do after independence. Leigh Day (2016) summarises British brutality:

> On 24 April 1954, the Colonial Administration launched an assault on the Mau Mau which was known as "Operation Anvil", whereby 17,000 Mau Mau suspects were rounded up and incarcerated in detention camps without trial. Detainees were moved from one camp to another, where the treatment was of increasing or decreasing severity depending on the detainee's willingness to cooperate and denounce the Mau Mau. In particular, detainees were expected to confess that they had taken "the Mau Mau oath" and to repent of having done so.
>
> In 1954, a process known as "villagisation" was initiated and with approximately 1 million Kenyans were forced to burn their homes and rounded up for six years in 854 villages fenced with barbed wire where acts of brutality by colonial guards were widespread.
>
> It is estimated by historians that, over the years which followed, as many as 150,000 suspected Mau Mau members and sympathisers were detained without trial in a labyrinth of about 150 detention camps and 'screening centres' littered around Kenya known as 'the Pipeline'.
>
> From the inception of the detention camps, the Colonial Administration engaged in widespread acts of brutality. Detainees were subjected to arbitrary killings, severe physical assaults and extreme acts of inhuman and degrading treatment.
>
> The acts of torture included castration and sexual assaults which, in many cases, entailed the insertion of broken bottles into the vaginas

of female detainees.

Camp guards engaged in regular severe beatings and assaults, often resulting in death. In the course of interrogations in some cases guards would hang detainees upside down and insert sand and water into their anuses.

In 1957, the Colonial Administration decided to subject the detainees who still refused to cooperate and comply with orders to a torture technique known as 'the dilution technique'. The technique involved the systematic use of brute force to overpower the Mau Mau adherents, using fists, clubs, truncheons and whips.

This brutality would continue until the detainees cooperated with orders and ultimately confessed and repented of their alleged Mau Mau allegiance.

Leigh Day (2016) goes on to quote Professor Elkins who adds to this grim picture:

There is no record of how many people died as a result of torture, hard labour, sexual abuse, malnutrition, and starvation. We can make an informed evaluation of the official statistic of eleven thousand Mau Mau killed by reviewing the historical evidence we know ... The impact of the detention camps and villages goes well beyond statistics. Hundreds of thousands of men and women have quietly lived with the damage - physical, psychological, and economic - that was inflicted upon them during the Mau Mau war.

And it is even worse than this. The seeds of destruction of a peaceful development of Kenya were planted right at the beginning of British colonialism. It is necessary for those who resist imperialism today to be equipped with appropriate information about how their country was sold out to imperialism by colonialism and its chosen Kenyan elite. The following brief section documents this process which needs more additional research and analysis.

Neo-colonialism Entrenched

As far as the British Establishment is concerned, Mau Mau is a closed chapter, the War of Independence did not take place, Kenya was "given" independence by Britain. And so imperialism can carry on its work, freed from colonial baggage. But the adverse effects of the colonial manipulation on the working people of the former colonies continue to this day. It actively planned Kenya's future so that the colonial aims were achieved under imperialism, which is now led by USA. African elite now are the local delivery boys and girls of the imperialist enterprise.

From the time that it was realised around 1959 that the War of Independence under Mau Mau leadership would force colonialism out of Kenya and that independence was inevitable, colonialists actively organised a "friendly coup" to enable takeover of power by an elite favourably inclined towards the new imperialist alliance, USA and Britain. The political position was to ensure that moderate leaders groomed by colonialism came to power at independence and to marginalise and eliminate (physically in some cases) those who supported or represented Mau Mau's radical programme for land and freedom. That this was well planned and delivered by the British Government is obvious as the following section from an early draft of Durrani, Shiraz (forthcoming) indicates:

> But the radical wing of KANU in the years before independence and its subsequent development into the Kenya People's Union under Oginga Odinga faced not only internal but external enemies too. The departing colonial power, Britain, now joined by the new imperialist superpower, USA, had already decided to ensure that independent Kenya would be run by the moderates. They fully supported the Kenyatta moderate wing as a way of stopping the radicals who, in effect, were carrying on the revolutionary agenda of Mau Mau. While the elimination of the radical wing was supposedly done by the Kenyatta moderates, the power behind their actions was the colonial government which cleverly dispatched a so-called progressive to be the Governor of Kenya to oversee the transition of the colony to a Western neo-colony under the guise of independence. The last Governor of Kenya, Malcolm MacDonald (MacDonald, 1976b) - self proclaimed Moderate Socialist - explains the thinking of the colonial

government regarding the moderate-radical contradiction in Kenya in response to the question, "I remember you saying earlier that it was wise for the British Government to support Kenyatta because he was a moderate":

> I thought that if the moderates ... came into power in independent Kenya they would not only be moderate in their national policies, in economic and social and political affairs, but on the side of moderation in international affairs, and for example not go communist and not come under the influence of any other communist anti-British anti-Western power.

The significance of this support of colonial power goes beyond the control over Kenyan politics after independence. It helped to overturn the entire Mau Mau programme of change and their quest for land, freedom and justice. The radicals were well aware of this neo-colonial danger as they pointed out in 1961 in their document The *Struggle for Kenya's Future*, quoted earlier. The British support for the moderates was crucial in ensuring that a regime compliant with Western interests came to power and remains in power to date. This support for the moderates included the suppression of progressive trade unions, political parties and social movements as well as marginalisation and undermining of radical leaders.

And the last British Governor in Kenya and the British Government met their objectives of selecting Jomo Kenyatta as the first Prime Minister of Kenya. The land grabbing by the successive KANU regimes of Kenyatta and Moi has been confirmed in recently available documents of the last Colonial Governor of Kenya, Sir Malcolm MacDonald and those of the former Vice President of Kenya, Joseph Murumbi. Ng'otho (2008) reveals the land issue from both these sources:

> Fresh evidence pieced together by the Sunday Nation confirms widespread speculation that Kenya's first president Jomo Kenyatta entered a secret pact with the British government not to interfere with the skewed land distribution at independence. In return, the British would clear his way as independent Kenya's first leader which looked impossible only three years to freedom. Kenyatta would later extract a similar pledge from his successor, retired president Daniel arap

Moi.

And Kenyatta duly fulfils his side of the colonial bargain with his colonial masters, as the Truth Justice and Reconciliation Commission (TJRC,2013) records:

> In his independence speech, Jomo Kenyatta did not suggest any substantial change in the colonial structures. The colonial state would remain intact – despite the fact that the fight for national independence had been dominated by demands for social justice, egalitarian reforms, participatory democracy, prosecution of those who had committed mass killings and other forms of crimes during the war of independence, and the abolition of the colonial state and its oppressive institutions ... Also, in his independence speech, Jomo Kenyatta never mentioned the heroism of the Mau Mau movement. No Mau Mau freedom songs were sung, no KLFA leaders was allowed to speak during the historic day. Instead, Kenyatta asked the people to forget the past – to forgive and forget the atrocities committed against them by the British and their Kenyan supporters during the war of independence.

That sums up the imperialist plot against the people of Kenya, with the connivance of the elite groomed by colonialism. Wasserman (1976) completes the story:

> Mau Mau remained banned until 2003. Public silence about Mau Mau was a means to avoid discussion of the unfinished business of the Emergency, and a way to prevent claims being made against loyalists. The loyalist bargain therefore consolidated the authority of the independent Kenyan state, first shaping the settlement that was made in the process of decolonization, and then securing the position of the political elite who governed the country. And impunity was not an idea confined to colonial Kenya. In 1970, Kenyatta's loyalist Attorney General, Charles Njonjo, would pass into law the Indemnity Act, to 'protect the activities of government officials and security officers.' This was specifically aimed at thwarting the prosecution of soldiers and police for acts of atrocity committed in northern Kenya, between 1962 and 1967, during the Shifta War against Somali

insurgents. Until its annulment in 2010, this act came to represent 'the institutionalisation of impunity in Kenya.'

Thus colonialism handed over to the independent government of Kenya some of the most poisonous weapons that were directed against the people demanding what Mau Mau had always demanded.

Oppression and Exploitation: Gifts of the British Empire

The British colonial government's legacy of impunity as it massacred, murdered and tortured people at will was then bequeathed to the governments it set up after independence. The lesson that colonialism passed on to the comprador regime would seem to be that it is acceptable to eliminate and destroy people who oppose their policies and government for the elite and imperialism. Pio Gama Pinto was the first martyr in a long line of leaders eliminated. And individuals were not the only targets: entire communities and populations were "cleansed" and made refugees when they refused to support the elite rulers. And massacres and genocide were also part of this imperialist arsenal. The armed forces, officially serving the people, became their oppressors and a weapon of the elite against the people. The TJRC (2013, Vo.IIA, 72) records the events of the time:

> Kenyatta, having realized that he would not be able to meet the needs and expectations of all Kenyans, engaged in measures that would ensure political survival and self sustenance of his government. This lead to a strengthening of the role of the security agencies similar to the role they played during the colonial period, and particularly aimed at controlling, and suppressing dissent and organized political opposition. In brief, in the words of Charles Hornsby, 'the Independent State soon echoed its colonial parents repressive attitudes to dissent'.

The three governments after independence continued to use political assassinations of those they perceived as enemies as a normal practice. With the support at a national level of police and army and implicit agreement of USA and UK governments at international level, the use of such assassinations became a normal way of dealing with political issues. TJRC Report (2013) says:

Political assassinations have occurred under each of the three successive governments since independence. The motives associated with these assassinations have varied, from getting rid of political competition, weeding out ambitious politicians, and removing perceived "dissidents" of the government or those who posed as "threats" to power. Evidence of state involvement and subsequent cover-ups is evident in the majority of political murders. Propaganda and commissions of inquiry are often used as smokescreens to get to "the bottom of the matter," and often have the effect of masking the motives and faces behind the assassinations. Prominent figures in government are said to be implicated. Key witnesses into the assassinations disappear or die mysteriously. No real perpetrators have ever been prosecuted, much less effectively investigated. (TJRC Final Report, Vol.IIA).

The Truth, Justice and Reconciliation Commission (TJRC, 1913) documented extra-judicial killings, stretching back to the colonial period when an estimated 90,000 people were executed, tortured or injured during the crackdown against the Mau Mau uprising. During those operations, over 160,000 people were detained in appalling conditions.

Upon attaining independence, the country witnessed political assassinations during President Jomo Kenyatta's tenure, says, TJRC Report, "Kenyatta was president during the deaths of Field Marshall Baimungi (1964), Pio Gama Pinto (1965), Kungu Karumba (who disappeared since June 14 1974), Tom Mboya (July 5 1975), Ronald Ngala (12 December 1972), J.M Kariuki (March 2 1975) and Argwings Kodhek (1969) ... The investigations into these deaths were quite cursory. The lack of serious investigation into these killings created the public perception that the truth about these killings was yet to be established".

During the post-Jomo Kenyatta era, the political assassinations continued, according to TJRC. "Extra-judicial killings during this time also took place in the form of shooting and killing of political dissidents, as well as deaths during detention," says the commission. The commission cited instances where people were killed for questioning extra-judicial killings by police.

Repression by the regime ensured that there was no public outcry against such official action. The support of USA and Britain ensured that the regime was let off the hook internationally too. But the seeds of massacres and murders had been sown by the departing colonial regime and the favoured leaders after independence used the same colonial methods to stay in power.

Durrani, Shiraz (forthcoming) looks at the machinations behind the scenes that Britain used to ensure their favoured politicians came to power after independence:

> By bringing in the Cold War logic into the Kenyan situation, the Governor [Malcolm MacDonald] and the British Government succeeded in ensuring the moderates they could trust and work with became the new Government of independent Kenya. But this was no last minute planning. MacDonald, upon arriving in Kenya 1962, decided to speed up the process of independence planned by London for late 1964 or early 1965. His reasons for early independence in 1963 makes interesting reading as they relate to ensuring that the moderates came to power at independence. MacDonald (1976a) says:

> The reason why I thought the transition should be speeded up was that the "moderates" were in control of both KANU and KADU. Jomo Kenyatta was not supposed to be a "moderate", but I decided within a few days that he was one… I felt that if independence didn't come as quickly as they wanted, they would lose influence with a lot of their supporters, and the more extreme, less reasonable and capable politicians would take over. I thought it would be a great mistake to allow that to happen.

This manipulation of Kenyan political process is what led to the line of Mau Mau, progressed by the militant wing of KANU, losing out to the moderates who went on to be one of the most corrupt governments in Africa.

The tactics of "disappearing" people continues to date as Gumbihi (2016) reports:

> A report by Human Rights Watch released in July 2016 indicated that 34 people, including two women, were missing. They were arrested in

counter-terrorism crackdowns in northern Kenya between 2013 and 2015. "Kenyan authorities have denied knowledge of the missing people, failed to acknowledge credible evidence of abuses during counterterrorism operations, failed to investigate the allegations and in some instances, intimidate and harass those seeking information and accountability," states the report. The organisation also established that bodies of at least 11 people previously arrested by State agents were found in the last two years.

Britain handed over to the comprador rulers of her former colonies around the world the lasting legacy of British Empire: tools of economic exploitation and political repression, all backed up by armies usually set up and maintained by imperialism.

Stealing Land "legally": Corruption Entrenched

Land always was, and still remains, the biggest grievance that Kenyan people have and it still remains unresolved thanks to British colonial policies which independent governments have continued to uphold. But the colonial economic aims in Kenya were to ensure that moderate leaders groomed by colonialism came to power at independence and to marginalise and eliminate (physically in some cases) those who supported or represented Mau Mau's radical programme for land and freedom. Land was, and remains, a crucial issue in Kenya. It was the key demand under colonialism and is at the centre of tension today. It is an issue that cannot be ignored or swept under the carpet.

Truth, Justice and Reconciliation Commission Report (TJRC, 2013, Vol. IIB) examined the land situation in the colonial period:

> ... the establishment of the reserves was another tool applied by the British colonial administration to further alienate local communities' prime land, thereby exposing communities, over time, to land scarcity and landlessness ... The British administration's efforts to alienate land in mainland Kenya accelerated after World War I, when former British soldiers were encouraged to settle and engage

in agricultural production activities and for that purpose, they were allowed to acquire land, ostensibly from the Crown, at concessionary rates. Settlement of ex-soldiers was facilitated by the Ex-Soldier Settlement Scheme and backed by the Crown Lands (Discharged Soldiers Settlement) Ordinance of 1921, Kenya having been declared a British colony in 1920. However, only a limited amount of 'Crown Land' was suitable for settler cultivation and this provided impetus for the colonial government to alienate more land from indigenous Africans, in areas that were deemed to be of high agricultural potential by establishing and confining African communities to what were referred to as "native reserves."

The Report goes on to examine the colonial practice of acquiring land through "coercive measures" and "forced evictions" before looking at an important cause of land shortage that has not been given the prominence it deserves. On "land alienation and displacement by multinational corporations" the report says:

> Apart from the colonial administration and its white settler demand for land, multinational corporations, many of which had European origin, also contributed to displacement and landlessness of African communities, especially in Kericho and other parts of the Rift Valley. In various parts of Rift Valley, especially in Kericho, such companies acquired large tracts of land that was initially meant for the resettlement of African communities in the area for cultivation of tea.

The Report also shows the extent of such land policies of the British Government, tying down land deals with 999 year-leases:

> Companies that were allocated most of the productive land in the Rift Valley in 1923 on lease for 999 years were, notably: James Finlay Company Limited (formerly the African Highlands Produce Company Ltd) and Unilever Kenya Ltd (formerly Brooke Bond). These companies, among others, acquired land at the expense of the local landless Africans in the affected areas.

The Truth, Justice and Reconciliation Commission Report (TJRC, 2013, Vol.

IIB) provides evidence of how the British Government used the so-called emergency to intensify its land alienation policy:

> Repressive tendencies of the British, especially forced eviction of Africans from their homelands, coupled with alienation of evictees' land, which was made worse by, among other things, the suffering of Africans in squalid conditions in the overpopulated reserves and restrictions on African commodity production, precipitated an African freedom movement in the nature of a land and freedom army, known as Mau Mau. The Mau Mau, which comprised members of a number of African ethnic communities that had, among other things, been dispossessed of their land, under the leadership of members of the Kikuyu community, launched several violent assaults against officers serving the colonial administration in Kenya and their African collaborators, in a bid to recover their land and regain freedom from oppression. Attacks organized largely in forest areas and staged by the Mau Mau prompted the colonial government to declare a 'State of Emergency' in Kenya in 1952 and that provided the colonial administration another chance to unjustifiably alienate Africans' land.
>
> During the emergency period, persons suspected to be members of the Mau Mau movement were either killed, detained or repatriated from their settlement schemes, including Olenguruone Settlement Scheme in Nakuru, Rift Valley, from which some of the members of the Mau Mau were repatriated to Central Province. Under the guise of the declared State of Emergency, the British colonial administration took draconian measures against Africans, including repatriation from their settlements, arrest and detention of members or sympathizers of the Mau Mau. Land was alienated from those associated with the Mau Mau and allocated to those who were loyal to the administration as a punishment for what it considered as acts of terror against the settler community. Thus the Mau Mau movement attracted further African land alienation by the colonial administration and attendant landlessness and destitution because when Mau Mau fighters and their collaborators returned from war, they found that their land and other property had been confiscated by British administration loyalists including 'Homeguards' and the provincial administration.

It is noted that the Declaration of Emergency also, as a colonial measure, permitted the colonial administration to suspend hearing and determination of land-related suits in African courts through the enactment of the 1957 African Courts (Suspension of Land Suits) Ordinance, which made it impossible for affected Africans to present their claims in court for redress and thus foreclosed their right to justice in respect of land ownership and utilization in the colonial period.

The TJRC Final Report (2013, Vol.IIB) examines land issues in different parts of the country, including the explosive situation at the coast:

> ... most of the individuals, families and communities at the Coast ended up living as 'squatters' on land that had either been acquired by Arabs or the British such that by the time Kenya attained independence, many at the Coast had no titles to their land.

The Report highlights the fact that the unequal land policy of British colonialism led to inter-ethnic conflicts which have continued in the period after independence as a lasting legacy of colonialism, reinforced by the refusal of Kenyan governments to change these policies. This refusal is, in fact, part of the independence settlement agreed upon the British government and its favoured "leaders" at independence.

The TJRC Final Report (2013, Vol.IIB) records that the corruption and injustice of the colonial era continued after independence:

> Official corruption in the acquisition, allocation, ownership and disposal of land in Kenyatta's era continued unabated regardless of the existence of applicable laws and policies that were intended to govern dealings in land ... the coastal region has the largest number of landless people and has been severely marginalized in terms of land adjudication, consolidation and registration. Because of the myriad land problems, the majority of people at the Coast remain very poor; it is the region where land acquisition by individuals and other bodies from outside of the indigenous ethnic communities (considered as up country people) has been the largest. It is also the region where land-related injustices appear to have been the gravest

and the longest lasting.

In keeping with his promise of following in the footsteps of Kenyatta, Moi continued Kenyatta's policies on repression and maintaining the rule of the elite minority by force of arms, but particularly on corruption. The TJRC Final Report (2013, Vol.IIB) notes his continuing corruption on land issues:

> In August 1978, Daniel arap Moi took over as the second President of the Republic of Kenya following the death of Jomo Kenyatta. He promised to follow the footsteps of his predecessor. Moi's 'Fuata Nyayo' philosophy literally meant that he would follow in the footsteps of his predecessor in critical aspects of policy and governance, including approval of illegal land allocations, and he did, with the exception of minor policy departures, especially in relation to his pro-pastoralist policy and his new focus on the development of arid and semi-arid lands. During his tenure, every category of government-owned land including military establishments, road reserves, public parks, bus parks, public toilets, forests and cemeteries as well as trust lands were illegally acquired in what became publicly known as the widespread phenomenon of land grabbing, mainly by the president himself, his family, officials in his administration, politicians, civil servants, and military officers. In the process, more than 200,000 illegal title deeds were acquired which ought to be revoked.

The effect of these policies was a massive build-up of wealth and power in the hands of a minority which also controlled state power. Class divisions became sharper. The policies of successive Kenyan governments to entrench illegal wealth transfer have ensured that no revocation of illegal title deeds suggested by the Truth, Justice, Reconciliation Commission takes place. Mau Mau's struggle for land and economic freedom continues in the post-independence period.

What Might Have Been: Independence Without Imperialism

British colonialism used extreme measures such as the declaration of the so-called Emergency, the use of military might, the creation of Homeguard comprador class (both in military and political fields), the use of legal and illegal measures of repression - all to defeat the vision that Mau Mau and Kenya's War of Independence had. It ensured that individuals and political organisations supporting the struggle against imperialism were marginalised, banned, destroyed or eliminated. This colonial programme, aimed at Mau Mau, was also used against militant trade unions, progressive educational institutions, political parties, social movements, newspapers and mass media. No individuals, no social force that did not support imperialism was spared. In Mau Mau, it had a particularly difficult opponent who refused to cave in even in the face of the military might of the British Empire and continued its struggle even when colonialism had created a new pro-imperialism ideology, leadership and political organisations seen as "safe" for imperialism.

The question then arises: what would Kenya have looked like if the democratic, radical forces fighting colonialism and imperialism had not been thwarted by imperialist machinations? Some military and political aspects of the War of Independence and Mau Mau, examined earlier, point to the type of society they were aspiring to. It is important to put such glimpses into a fuller picture of what a society and government, guided by Mau Mau's vision, would have looked like had imperialism not disrupted the natural development of society in Kenya. While, by its very nature, such an endeavour has to be speculative as the process was not allowed to reach fruition, there is enough evidence to indicate what type of society would have emerged under Mau Mau. The recently released colonial files, more primary research on Mau Mau and a careful study of material already in the public domain would, perhaps, build up a fuller picture. It is for this reason, among others, that there is an urgent need to set up a Mau Mau Research and Documentation Centre which could provide answers to the above question.

All that is possible within the scope of this book is to provide a brief glimpse into what Mau Mau and the War of Independence's policies, practices and vision could possibly have evolved into if they had not been scuppered by imperialism and its local allies in Kenya.

Among social fabric that colonialism destroyed, using the excuse of the Emergency, was civic society painstakingly developed by Kenyans. Millner (1954?) mentions some early developments at political and social levels that would have continued into and beyond independence had they not been disrupted by Britain, whose aim, far from "civilising the natives", was to make people dependent on colonialism forever, in material terms as well as mentally:

> In order to press their modest and reasonable demands - the African's land hunger, wages questions, education, health services, colour bar and the constitutional issue - the Africans created their own political party - the Kenya African Union, which by 1952 had a membership of 100,000.
>
> To assist them in their struggle for better terms of employment African workers formed trade unions, the most important of which was the Labour Trade Union of East Africa; and in 1949 they formed the East African Trade Union Congress.
>
> To meet their thirst and longing for education they built their own schools and set up educational associations. By the end of 1952 there were nearly 200 African independent schools which had been organised by two bodies known as Kikuyu Independent Schools' Association and the Kikuyu Karing'a Educational Association.
>
> Africans published their own newspapers and other printed material in order that their wishes and needs could be publicly expressed.
>
> *Every one of these ordinary democratic activities has been crushed by the British rulers of Kenya* by means of a series of laws, apparently intended to stifle completely the expression of his views by the African and deny him any and every form of association and organisation which can help him in his struggle. [italics added].

Gachihi (1986) provides a good analysis of the role played by independent schools and the reasons the colonial government closed them down:

> Young boys and girls were recruited from the ranks of the Independent Schools that were managed by the Kikuyu Independent Schools Association, a factor that led to the closure by Government order of thirty one such schools on 19th November, 1953.

This was an attempt to attack those aspects that had the potential to create a democratic society based on principles of justice and equality after independence. Had these achievements been allowed to survive and develop, they would certainly have been part of a future government, possibly led by a Mau Mau Party. But the colonial practice was to eliminate entire nations as in USA and Australia, chop off fingers, thumbs and hands of skilled workers - as in India as shown by Tharoor (2016) - or to force-feed people with opium - as in China - so as to ensure that the achievements of people were destroyed and then render them powerless and dependent on imperialism for their lives and livelihood.

Mwakenya (1987a) sums up the failed attempts for democratic opposition to the neo-colonial solution followed by the comprador KANU party:

> Organised resistance against neo-colonial rule started with organisations like KKM (Kiama Kia Muingi), which after realising the neo-colonial betrayal, attempted to regroup ex-freedom fighters to continue fighting for their land and freedom. This organisation was ruthlessly suppressed and many of its members brutally murdered by the new KANU regime. It took our people less than three years after the flag independence to organise an opposition political party. K. P. U. (Kenya Peoples Union), formed in 1966. It was a legal opposition party which advocated land reform in Kenya and some socialist policies. The ruling neo-colonial regime banned K. P. U. in 1969 massacred and ruthlessly repressed its members and supporters. Leaders like Oginga Odinga were detained without trial and others like Bildad Kaggia silenced.
>
> Although there were various types of resistance including armed struggle by Mau Mau, some of whom had returned to the mountains, and by N.P.P. in the North, the democratic resistance in this period 1963 - 1970 was typified by K.P.U. K.P.U. took the standpoint of the betrayed masses of the entire Kenya and advocated disengagement from foreign domination as the only basis of real economic take-off. It also advocated the socialist path of development. K.P.U. was the genuine inheritor and continuation of radical nationalism in Kenya.

It was, however, clear that the KANU government would allow no democratic expression and feared facing KPU in a fair general election.

Trade Unions

It was seen earlier that it was the radical trade union organisations which had injected working class ideology and leadership into the liberation struggle. As Durrani (2015) points out:

> The working class, organised around trade union movements, played a critical role in the struggle for independence as well as in achieving the rights of working people.

Both these forces, imperialism and the neo-colonial regimes in Kenya, saw the liberation movement as a whole and the trade union movement as threats to their minority rules. Millner (1954?) explains further the reasons for attacks on the trade union movement:

> The trade union movement has been subjected to a series of attacks, over a number of years, calculated to remove all independence of thought and action and render it totally impotent.
>
> Trade union leaders were arrested and deported, and repressive legislation was passed, culminating in the Trade Union Ordinance, 1952, which placed the trade unions under strict control of the Government. Introduced the infamous system of "probationary" trade unions and contained elaborate provisions intended to encourage the creation of docile "employees' associations" in place of genuine trade unions.

It is clear that had a Mau Mau government come to power, it would have championed the cause of the working class and its organisation, the trade unions. This could have checked or prevented the wholesale sell-out of national wealth to comprador and corporations and prevented the continued exploitation of labour.

Democracy

Besides the various Mau Mau documents that indicate the movement's approach to democracy, there is evidence in many reports from activists about the democratic practices that were invoked whenever Mau Mau were in control of small or large groups of people. It should, however, be noted that the conditions created by colonialism and its constant attacks under which it operated were harsh and yet even under these situations, democracy prevailed. An example is that of Mau Mau democratic practices in the way it was organised nationally, as well as in concentration/detention centres. Barnett and Njama (1966) provide evidence of the former. Mathu (1974) shows the organisation and democracy even at Athi River Detention camp:

> Within each compound a leader was elected to represent the detainees in dealing with the camp commander. In the hardcore compounds men were chosen for their loyalty to the Movement and ability to speak English.
>
> Apart from this elected leader we had a secret organization within the four hardcore compounds. It was organized by grouping the men within each compound according to their location, division and district. In each compound there were committees representing the three Kikuyu districts plus Embu and Meru. At the top was a central committee of members from each compound and district. A system was set up in which notes, written on scraps of paper, were passed between leaders of the compounds. Where a decision had to be reached by the central committee, notes were wrapped around a stone and thrown from compound to compound. Each member would indicate his agreement with what had already been written or add his own ideas. This continued until a unanimous decision was reached... A number of rules existed... elders and disabled men had to be respected and given easy jobs...

Similarly, Muchai (1973) provides another example of Mau Mau organisation and democracy in the forest even as the "repressive measures of [the British Colonial] Government increased":

> In June 1953 a new Kiambu District Committee was formed. It consisted of 24 members who stayed in the Limuru European-settled area. I was elected with another man from my location to represent Kiambaa. Two members were elected from each of the three division committees and from each of Kiambu's nine locations. Our people in Nairobi also sent two members to attend important meetings.

While the appointments made in the forest for over-all Mau Mau posts such as those for the Kenya Parliament were based on elections, sometimes involving thousands of participants, even at the lowest and local levels, such appointments were made by elections. This contrasts with the British practice of rule by appointing District Commissioners and Chiefs who were given powers including for confiscating property and for death sentences. And Muchai (1973) records, the Mau Mau practice was to elect committees and spokesmen. "We also elected cooks and allocated the various jobs involved in cleaning up and maintaining the camp", he adds. Surely it was the British who needed a lesson on democracy from the Kenyan resistance movement.

Millner (1954?) points out that "under the 'Emergency' the Governor has power (over and above the powers of the Council of Ministers) to make laws by decree, and he has been given the assistance of a War Council". It is these illegal and arbitrary powers that colonialism had given itself that were used to suppress the achievements of Mau Mau and earlier resistance movements.

The various declarations and statements from Mau Mau, including the document, "The Struggle for Kenya's Future" and others reproduced in Appendix B gave a clear picture of the type of society that would have emerged under a progressive agenda supported by Mau Mau. That this aspect has not been explored fully is an indication of the control over information and communication imposed on Kenyan minds by imperialism and their comprador agents in Kenya.

End the Conspiracy of Silence

Perhaps the greatest difficulty faced by Mau Mau veterans and those who even today support its aims is the lack of correct information among the public about the movement, its leadership, its vision and action. This is highlighted by a number of people who have in-depth knowledge about the movement. They say:

Our plea to break the conspiracy of silence about the Kenya Land

and Freedom Army struggle includes also a plea for a more serious study of the history of Kenya since the Second World War and more particularly since 1952.[52]

It is only in recent years that this conspiracy is being challenged as new material, interpretations and analyses of the movement become available. But biographies and other historical records by Kenyan historians and Mau Mau activists have existed over a long period – easily ignored by those seeking to suppress the reality of atrocities.

Breaking the silence will reveal truth about British colonialism all over the world as highlighted by Tharoor (2016):

> "You cannot quantify the wrongs done," he told the PTI news agency.
>
> The dehumanisation of Africans and the Caribbeans, the (mass) of psychological damage, the undermining of social traditions, our property rights, authority structures of these societies all in the interest of British colonialism. The fact remains that many of today's problems in these countries, including the persistence - in some cases the creation – of racial, ethnic and religious tensions were the direct result of colonialism.. There is a moral debt to be paid.

It is only those guilty of stealing and continuing to benefit from the theft of national wealth who would oppose breaking the silence. Unfortunately, they are in positions of power - both nationally and internationally - and so would rather imprison history than let the full light of truth shine on historical facts.

It is not only the silence about history that imperialism has imposed in Kenya that needs to be attacked. A society based on wealth and power for a minority elite needs to be attacked and a new social order created that ensures justice and equality for the majority of people. That is the challenge in Kenya today as much as it is in Britain.

Colonialism does not end on the day of independence, as if it was a switch to turn a light on or off. The attitudes, power-relations, classes and class

---

52 The plea is made by Bildad Kaggia, Fred Kubai, Joseph Murumbi, and Achieng Oneko. See Barnett, Donald and Njama, Karari (1966): op. cit. Preface. p. ii.

struggles from the past are carried on into the future unless there has been a thoroughgoing revolution which alone can replace capitalism with socialism. This certainly did not happen in Kenya. Bolivian President Evo Morales established a Vice Ministry of Decolonization to address this issue. The Vice Minister Felix Cardenas is quoted by *Lessons from Latin America on Fighting Colonialism* (2016):

> It's not sufficient to go somewhere and say, 'I declare you decolonized!' and that's it, they're decolonized. No. It's a question of changing mentality, behaviour, of life philosophy, and to do this at an individual level, or at a communitarian level, a national level, we have an obligation to first ask 'what is Bolivia?' If we don't clearly understand what Bolivia is, then we don't know what needs to be done.

In the case of Kenya, the question, "What is Kenya?" needs to be answered by understanding its history of colonialism, by making a class analysis of its people, by examining class struggles and by examining the impact and activities of foreign governments and corporations in exploiting the country and influencing government policies. The question also needs to be answered by knowing on behalf of which class are government policies, the mass media, the education system and other social institutions run. And all this needs to be seen in the context of the way imperialism affects not only Kenya, but the entire continent of Africa. The context for the imperialist exploitation of Africa, for example, is given by *Honest Accounts* (2017):

> Much more wealth is leaving the world's most impoverished continent than is entering it, according to new research into total financial flows into and out of Africa. The study finds that African countries receive $161.6 billion in resources such as loans, remittances and aid each year, but lose $203 billion through factors including tax avoidance, debt payments and resource extraction, creating an annual net financial deficit of over $40 billion.

The only way to address such massive exploitation of "independent" Africa is through a well organised, united, Africa-wide resistance movement guided by anti-imperialist ideology. One of the reasons that imperialism invaded Libya which led to the murder of Muammar Gaddafi was that he had the vision and the resources to develop an anti-imperialist Africa. Earlier murders of Patrice Lumumba, the overthrow of Kwame Nkrumah were not enough to silence Africa's demand for liberation from imperialism.

British colonialism in Kenya was resisted by all nationalists. It would be strange if the resistance was then not continued after independence in the neo-colonial stage. The War of Independence had broader aims than just the achievement of independence. The struggle for liberation thus continued after independence as these aims had been subverted by colonialism in alliance with the newly created local elites. The context is set by Umoja Co-ordinator (1987):

> The route to real changes in Africa is not through coup d'états, whether progressive or not, but through the liberation forces completely rooted in the people. Power to the people has to mean a people's armed forces that would defend real changes which would liberate our economy, our politics, and our culture from neo-colonial control. The organised power of the alliance of the working class and the peasantry is the only basis of real changes. This is something that cannot come about simply by itself or spontaneously or through pious words and correct slogans - it is a goal to be worked for deliberately and consciously.

And that was the route taken by various progressive organisations, including Mau Mau, in the War of Independence. And that was also the route taken by people *after* independence.

The future of independent Kenya was charted out by the departing colonial government by ensuring that the new government would follow a pro-capitalist, pro-imperialist path. And in deepening internal divisions along class lines in terms of wealth, income and property, it also set out fertile grounds for resistance to the new government's policies. Anderson (2016) sums up the scenario clearly:

> At Kenya's independence in 1963, following the suppression of the rebellion, it was the loyalists who claimed the political victory and filled the ranks of the new African government. In a critical move that was intended first to ensure victory in the counter-insurgency

war, the British made a bargain with their African loyalist allies that involved agreement over the safe surrender of Mau Mau fighters, and that gave amnesty and impunity from prosecution for both rebels and loyalist militia.

> ... British commitment to their loyalist allies was such that they could not conceive of how to govern Kenya without them. Despite the noise made by European Settlers over the precipitous British decision to 'scuttle and run' from Kenya after 1959, it was the Kikuyu loyalists, and not the white highlanders, whose interests the departing colonialists would work hard to secure: white Settlers were expendable, Kikuyu loyalist allies were not.

It should be noted that Britain managed to gain the support of loyalists by means of bribery, looting, corruption and killing. It thereby legitimised the use of such methods for the in-coming government of Kenya. And, interestingly, it did not use British resources to achieve its aims. It was the land of Kenyan peasants, the labour of Kenyan workers, it was the resources of Kenyan people that were allowed to be looted so that a government loyal to neo-colonialism could be placed in position of power. It was a cheap bargain for imperialism. It had developed this method of using colonies' own resources for colonial plunder from its practice in India, among other places. What Tharoor (2016) says in relation to India and British colonialism, applies equally to the case of Kenya and British colonialism. "We literally paid for our own oppression", he says. The legacy of lasting poverty and landlessness affects Kenyan working people to this day. And in the same way, the legacy of killing, jailing, torture and massacres that Britain passed on to independent Kenya is happily endorsed by the successors of the loyalist government but this time using Kenyan armed forces to suppress and subdue people. Britain is quietly out of the picture, happily enjoying the fruits of its neo-colonial policies.

That the legacy of resistance to oppression and exploitation by British colonialism has continued in independent Kenya is not a matter of surprise. It was the conditions created by capitalism that created resistance to it. Those conditions have not changed and they have had an everlasting consequences on the lives of the people.

PART 3: TRANSITION TO NEO-COLONIALISM

> Nowadays, anyone who wishes to combat lies and ignorance and to write the truth must overcome at least five difficulties. He must have the courage to write the truth when truth is everywhere opposed; the keenness to recognize it, although it is everywhere concealed; the skill to manipulate it as a weapon; the judgment to select those in whose hands it will be effective; and the running to spread the truth among such persons. - Bertolt Brecht (Galileo)53.

Kenya's transition to neo-colonialism was carried out in accordance with a well planned, organised and executed programme by imperialism which changed the earlier colonial era tactics to new ones to suit the qualitatively different stage of class struggles in the country, just as working people had changed their tactics in keeping with new contradictions and conditions. These changes in imperialism's methods are explained by Petras and Veltmeyer (2018) in the Latin American context, but their analysis applies to Kenya as well:

> From the 1950s to the 1970s the class struggle was primarily a matter of land and labour, while in the 1990s, after a decade-long interregnum in which the forces of resistance that had been brought to ground or dispersed were rebuilt, the class struggle took the form of uprisings and widespread resistance against the neo-liberal agenda of structural reform in macroeconomic public policy. In the new millennium the class struggle once again has assumed a different form under conditions of several epoch-defining changes in the global economy and the demise of neo-liberalism as an economic doctrine and development model. Under these conditions and the expansion of extractive or resource-seeking capital the class struggle went in several different directions. First, the struggle to some extent was internationalized or globalized as multinational corporations, international financial organizations and imperial states intervened, directly or by proxy with the assistance and connivance of collaborator

---

53 Available at: https://www.goodreads.com/author/quotes/26853.Bertolt_Brecht [Accessed: 16-10-17].

states, in the class struggle between labour and capital.

The political and military actions of Mau Mau forced Britain to review its colonial policy. However, colonialism had years of experience of subverting people's struggles for liberation by using whatever force was necessary, as in India and Malaysia. And it was not about to give up its imperialist ambitions in Kenya, however hard the people fought. It worked out a strategy of making a smooth transition from colonialism to neo-colonialism and to continue its economic stranglehold over Kenya. One aspect of this was the military campaign against people, whether armed or not. Another was the political aim of grooming a leadership that would be favourable to imperialist aims. Furedi (1989) explains this:

> The question was no longer whether Kenya would become independent but when, and under what conditions. It was clear that changes had to be made in the forms of political relations through which the colony was governed. It was also evident that British socio-economic interests could not for long be preserved through white minority rule. The declaration of a State of Emergency can be seen as a first step in the construction of a system of political institutions through which the existing social relations could be perpetuated in the post-colonial era. The key element in the government's post-Emergency strategy was to provide the conditions for the emergence of a moderate nationalist leadership. The crushing of Mau Mau provided an opportunity for the emergence of a moderate nationalist option. But that option had first to be created. The nationalist parties that arose in the post-emergency period owed their existence above all to the colonial regime. These parties had no historical roots, nor did they evolve from any manifestation of grassroots pressure. It was on the initiative of the colonial administration that the new political system was born.

That new political system has been remarkably successful from the point of view of colonialism. It has survived to this day and delivered the economic control to corporations and foreign governments that Mau Mau sought to end. At the same time, colonial manipulation of the political process ensured that the key demand of the independence movement, the return of land to rightful owners, was also resolved in favour of capitalism as it handed over land and political power to the "indigenous capitalist class" as Furedi (1989) explains:

> It took nearly four years before the Kenyatta government was able to establish stability on the land. During this period, the conflict between the ex-squatters and the state took on a class character, as those without land tried to fight the new group of African capitalist farmers. By the end of 1968, this struggle had come to an end, with the new landlords clearly in ascendancy. A chapter in the struggle for land had come to an end. The emergence of protest in the late 1920s which matured into a mass movement in the 1940s and armed struggle in the early 1950s was finally destroyed by the Kenyan African ruling class in the late 1960s.

This British policy cemented class relations and class contradictions that have become increasingly sharp over the years. In order to achieve its aims, Britain undertook what Furedi (1989) calls "controlled decolonization" which required:

> ...the exclusion of the masses from political life. The defeat of Mau Mau and the containment of radical nationalists in the early 1960s were preconditions for the realization of this process. But the stabilization of capitalism in post-colonial Kenya also required the neutralization of grassroots aspirations towards social change. In the sphere of politics the main priority of the Kenyatta regime was to ensure that the urban and rural proletariat should be deprived of its own organizational and political voice.

It is important to understand the two struggles taking place in Kenya. On the one hand, it was an anti-colonialist struggle waged by people of Kenya. That has been well understood and recognised in history books and in people's consciousness. It is the second struggle that has been obscured by imperialism and colonialism: this is the class struggle that started with the introduction of capitalism in Kenya. A key aspect of Kenya's War of independence was the struggle to regain land lost to settlers and local capitalists. This struggle for land was an essential aspect of class struggle but is not often seen as such. Furedi (1989) sees the class aspect very clearly:

The creation of the new African nationalist movement in the 1950s was paralleled by the stabilization of the economic position of the indigenous capitalist class. Land consolidation in Central Province benefited the landowning collaborators. As M.P.K. Sorrenson argues, the colonial administration hoped that this class 'would be too interested in farming to be seduced by Kikuyu politicians into further subversion'. In other parts of Kenya the same process was under way. By the time Uhuru had arrived it was clear that the African nationalist leadership would fiercely resist any attempt to change the prevailing socio-economic institutions.

The victory of Kenyatta and the conservative Kanu government against the radical politics of Mau Mau at the time of independence was gained with active support from the colonial British state. The conservative forces would most likely have been defeated otherwise, as the radical wing of Kanu had the support of peasants and workers. And the outcome in favour of the conservatives, led by Kenyatta, had implications far beyond Kenya, as Maloba (2017) says:

> The struggle between the radical nationalists and the conservatives is without doubt one of the most important periods in the history of post-colonial Africa. The ideological struggle in Kenya was one of the most intense and sustained in Africa. Hence, the eventual defeat of the radical nationalists in Kenya had both local and continental implications. .. this defeat required intense political, economic and strategic coordination between Kenyatta (and his government) and Western intelligence services and governments... Kenyatta's government, with active and strategic support from the West, sought to project capitalism as an African ideology, and communism (or socialism) as alien and dangerous. This was yet another critical transformation in post-colonial Kenya. Imperialism, which had colonized, humiliated, and plundered Kenya, was now to be seen as the country's indispensable friend and savior. Capitalism would move Kenya to development and social justice. But why had it not done so in the past?

The struggle in Kenya between the two groups was an important ideological struggle between capitalism and socialism, between running the country in the interest of a local elite backed by imperialism, on the one hand, and socialism in the interest of the working people, on the other. Imperialism could not let socialist ideas and programmes win, not in Kenya, not anywhere else it had control. It waged this battle with Cuba over 50 years after Cuban independence. So would it have done in Kenya if the socialist forces had prevailed. The struggle in Kenya was played out against a global landscape.

The issue of the ideological struggle and the winners and losers are not merely an academic exercise. The results had real impact on lives of people, particularly those who lost out. Kitching (1980) sets out who the winners and losers were:

> Those who benefited from Mau-Mau were essentially 'loyalist' and their interests were well protected and deed enhanced by the colonial regime during the Emergency, while the poor, who had lost out badly in the preceding period, made up the majority of the forest fighters and in the end gained very little economically for their sacrifices.

It is a sobering fact that Britain's controlled decolonisation project was such a success that its effects have not been unravelled even after 50 years. A brief look at the beneficiaries of the "controlled decolonisation would indicate the real tragedy for Mau Mau and the working class in Kenya" says Tandon (2017b) as he looks at what finance capital gained:

> My understanding is that independence is an important achievement, but it manifests itself only at the political level and that, too, only partially. The economy is still not liberated from the control of the empire, and so even its politics are compromised. I would state unhesitatingly that Kenya is a neo-colonial state. There is convincing evidence that the economy is still largely in the hands of imperial finance capital, even if there are pockets of "national" capital in the little market left to the indigenous people.

Maina, K. (2016) looks at beneficiaries of Kenyan land:

In a country where owning a small plot of land 50 x 100 metres is many people's elusive dream, you'll be surprised that there is a small group of natives and foreigners who own land so big the eyes cannot see the end. A few families, stretching from colonial times, to this day control thousands upon thousands of acres. The one place they've been able to acquire endless tracts of land is Laikipia. Laikipia plateau is estimated to be about 10,000 sq km or roughly 2.5 million acres. It has the biggest number of white landowners concentrated in one place in Kenya. The plateau stretches from Mt Kenya in the east to the Rift Valley in the west. The Maasai community here numbers less than 50,000. They are squashed on different patches of the land, which totals 281,587 acres. The rest (more than 2 million acres) is owned by foreigners comprising mostly the British and American "aristocratic" class and a few white natives. Private ranches range from 'small' parcels measuring about 5000 acres, to endless horizons of massive land -properties that are over 100,000 acres.

It is not a surprise that economic, social and political tensions in Kenya today are at bursting points. The two key pillars of Kenyan resistance, peasants and urban and rural workers were the main forces behind continued resistance in the post-independence period as they were in the colonial period. In both forces, what Petras and Veltmeyer (2018) say about Latin America in the period 1950-70s, applies equally to the situation in Kenya. "In the countryside", they say, "the semi-proletarianized peasants resisted the advance of capital and engaged in a protracted struggle for the land and land reform".

The other force of resistance was the radical, organised trade unions which imperialism rendered ineffective as part of the independence deal with the in-coming comprador parties and leaders, aided by White Settlers who were given power over the independence settlement. They used laws, repression and side-lining of radical trade unions so as to weaken leadership and organisation of the previously militant movement. Makhan Singh was detained; Bildad Kaggia and Fred Kubai were marginalised. Imperialism also created a compliant trade union movement under Tom Mboya with financial and political support from USA. This brought about qualitative changes in the work of trade unions, the key one being to break the unity of political demands of workers from their economic demands – a unity that the trade union movement under Makhan Singh had fought hard to establish.

And yet, neo-colonialism could not eliminate class divisions, class differences and class struggles. In the changed circumstances of the post-independence Kenya, new forms of resistance emerged, as examined later in this book.

Independence but "Not Yet Uhuru"

> The essence of neo-colonialism is that the State which is subject to it is, in theory, independent and has all the outward trappings of international sovereignty. In reality its economic system and thus its political policy is directed from outside.- Nkrumah, Kwame (1965)

The fear of neo-colonialism expressed by progressive forces in *The Struggle For Kenya's Future* (1973) became a reality after independence. *Africa Events* (1990b) sets the scene:

> In 1966, just three years after Kenya attained its independence, some of the prominent personalities in the Kenya's struggle against the British were of the opinion that the party they had founded to steer the country to true independence, the Kenya African National Party (KANU), had diverted from the previously agreed path and, in the words of one of its founders, 'had started to let in neo-colonialism through the back door.' Some tried to correct things from within the party and government, but were frustrated, and their criticism not tolerated.

Such efforts to defeat neo-colonialism were constantly under attack by imperialism. Tandon (2017c) highlights the danger for former colonies:

> Political independence exposes the internal class contradictions - class oppression and class struggle - more clearly. The danger is that these are interpreted in ethnic, religious and other identities, which are then presented by the political elite to the people as "principal"

contradictions. They are not. They are "secondary" contradictions among the people, and exploited by the empire for its own ends.

Kenya is not alone in having its ambitions of equality and justice scuppered by imperialism. Other African countries face similar fate. Lehulere (2017) sees a very similar situation in South Africa:

> Monopoly capitalists and their allies in the ANC [African National Congress] have corrupted something very precious in South Africa's history – the proud and militant tradition of struggle for social justice. They have corrupted the dream of a free and egalitarian nation. For over two decades, the ANC has presided over entrenched corruption, which must now be resisted. But that struggle will constitute a whole new historical epoch.

Prominent members of the government had openly condemned Mau Mau before independence. They were well aware of the power that the movement once had. Its control over mass media, above and under-ground newspapers and books, oral medium and songs and educational institutions had given it strength to overcome the superior media control of the colonialists. This lesson was not lost on the new leaders of the government. Among its first moves was to make it extremely difficult to publish newspapers and books. Various legal difficulties were imposed to ensure that only a few, controlled newspapers and publishing houses could function. Even under the harsh colonial rule, it was possible for Mau Mau to publish fifty newspapers, but under the neo-colonial government after independence, all such avenues were blocked. Large deposits were now needed to publish newspapers and this meant that few Kenyans could afford to be in media business. Censorship laws and self-censorship ensured by the government meant there was little freedom to express independent, alternative ideas, let alone taking democratic action for change.

December 12th - Poem by Nazmi Durrani [54]

- The struggle for December 12th
started long ago at the dawn of the century
and before

---
54 Poem by Nazmi Durrani. *The Nairobi Law Monthly*. No.16, May/June 1989.

when the sun had set
and the dense night

of colonial conquest
started spreading
across the land
from the ocean coast
to the lake shore.
As the darkness
of foreign oppression spread

so did the light of resistance.
As the inordinate appropriation
of land and livestock and labour
relentlessly covered the country
so did the sparks of rebellion

fly across the dark sky
giving hope of the new day
that must down
in a year, decade, century
but dawn it must.
From every corner of the country

the cry went up
the cry for freedom
the cry of struggle.
The cry of Mazrui, Fumo Bakari,
Me Katilili, Mwangeka at the coast
was taken, up by Itumo Muka,
Sendeu, Mutero, Njama, Waiyaki
across the plains and mountains
further strengthened by Koitalel, Lo walel, Gem, Bonariri
right to the shores of the great lake.
The conqueror answered
pillage murder and massacre
the light was dimmed
but the spark
was not to be put out so easily.

From that one spark
new fires were lit.
Each fire put out with
greater force, greater brutality
only from the embers of each
a bigger fire to emerge
giving out more light

to show the way to the patriots
who followed the shining path;
giving out more heat to test
the resolve of the fighters.
to forge a new generation
which would undertake a new
the journey on the road
of sacrifice and martyrdom
towards the beacon far ahead
that beckoned them forward.

One hundred and fifty
following Muthoni Nyanjiru
faced death at the Norfolk massacre.
Thousands led by Muindi Mbingu
braving heat and dust
hunger and thirst
marched from Ukambani
to protest the taking away
by force of their cattle.
The cry from Olenguruone
against the confiscation of land
was strengthened from Murang'a
against forced labour.
From towns across the country
workers added their voice
to the song of resistance
conducted by Makhan Singh,
Kaggia, Kibacia, Kubai, Pinto
calling for a just return for their sweat

demanding the end
to foreign exploitation.

And so the flame of struggle
reached new heights
the brilliance of its light
the crackle of its fire
inspiring a new
more powerful chorus
calling for
total liberation.

Before the echo died
the cry of earlier warriors
was taken up by their
sons and daughters
each generation adding
its own thunder
till it became
the mighty roar of the '50s
that made the enemy tremble
that shook the foundation of the empire.
The roaring fire was kindled
from the undying spark
by Kimathi who held aloft
the torch that once again
lit the way on the road to
December 12th
that held out hope, promise
Of a new dawn, a new age
when the fire of freedom
would burn forever.-

Nazmi Durrani, Nairobi.

Three Pillars of Resistance Attacked

The three pillars of resistance – Mau Mau, trade union organisations and people's forces - that were responsible for the achievement of independence were systematically attacked by imperialism and rendered powerless in order to ease the establishment of neo-colonialism. Mau Mau fighters in the forests were killed in large numbers by colonial military forces and those who continued the struggle were hunted down and killed; others who came out in good faith at independence were ruthlessly murdered by independent Kenya's armed forces.

The trade union movement was weakened by legal attacks on militant trade union movement and the banning of the EATUC and the detention of its militant leaders. But the colonial government had to use its military to supress the working class movement, just as it had done against Mau Mau guerrillas. Gupta (1981) says:

> On 28 April, the EATUC, in a 200,000 strong meeting demanded the complete independence for East African territories. Later the government refused permission to hold May Day rally. In the preceding weeks government declared the EATUC 'not a registered body', and arrested Makhan Singh and Fred Kubai on charge of being officials of an unregistered trade union." Following the arrest of Fred Kubai and Makhan Singh, within a matter of hours, the workers of Nairobi struck work. This strike and the consequent demonstration was one of the greatest in the history of Kenyan labour movement. Unprecedented armed force was used against the workers. One would have thought a war had broken out. Not content with baton charges and tear gas, the government employed Auster spotter aircraft, RAF planes, Bren-gun carriers, armoured cars and armoured trucks. By 28 May, it was reported in the Press that at least 800 workers were behind bars.

At the same time, money from USA poured in to create a compliant trade union movement under Tom Mboya. This charted a non-militant role for trade unions and strengthened the earlier colonial policy of diverting trade-union movement from political struggle for independence.

The third pillar, people's forces, had been under attack by colonialism with moves such as the construction of concentration camps, detention and terror by the Homeguard and Police Reserve forces.

Thus all the avenues of militant political action were banned. The banning of opposition political parties followed. In 1969, the Kenya People's Union, the only opposition party ever to be registered in Kenya, was banned, its leadership arrested and detained. Thus ended the one chance of open politics in Kenya. All political activities now went underground as did the expression of any independent ideas and opinions. The murder of Pio Gama Pinto at his house in Nairobi in 1965 had signalled this new period of repression in Kenya. The banning of KPU completed this phase of silencing any opposition by legal or illegal means. Henceforth the battlefield shifted to the underground level.

Opposition Continues

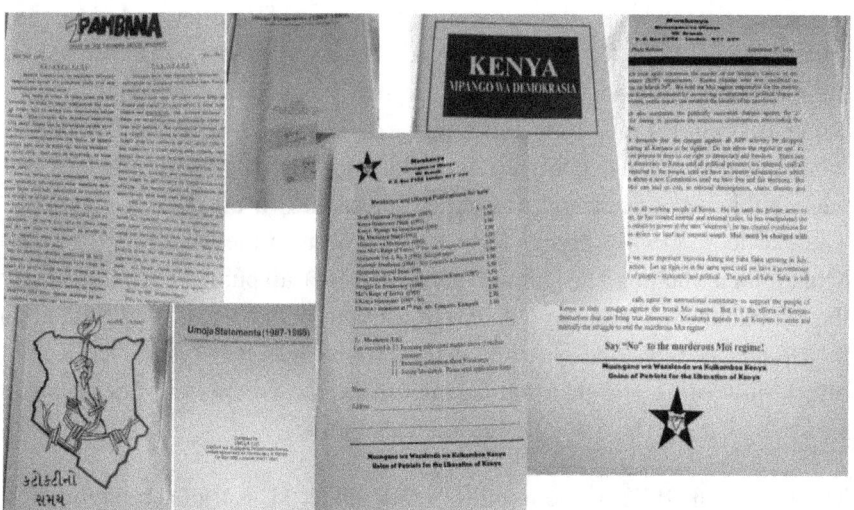

INFORMATION RESISTANCE

Throughout the 1970s underground groups flourished and articulated their vision of a Kenya free from capitalism and imperialism, issuing various underground pamphlets. These included *Mwanguzi* and *Kenya Twendapi* which questioned the direction Kenya was taking after independence under the new elite. Many former Mau Mau combatants began to recount their experiences and stated that they had not suffered during the anti-colonial struggles merely to see a minority elite getting all the benefits of independence. Many such views could not be published within Kenya and were published overseas. Among the best known are Karigo Muchai's The Hardcore (1973), Ngugi Kabiro's The Man in the Middle (1973) and Mohammed Mathu's The Urban Guerrilla (1974), all published in Canada by the Liberation Information Centre (LSC) with path-breaking introductions by Donald Barnett, the Director of LSC, who was part of the "collective effort" in writing and distributing one of the most important document in Kenya's history, The Struggle for Kenya's Future. [55]

The murder in 1975 of the popular politician, J. M. Kariuki, brought out a national unanimity in anti-government feelings. It also saw the publication and distribution of a large number of underground leaflets in support of basic human and democratic rights.

The popularity of songs and plays performed at the Kamiriithu Community Centre in 1977 once again showed that the Kenyan people had rejected the

---

55   The document is reproduced in Appendix B.

elite politics and culture promoted by the government but were in support of progressive content in politics, art and drama. Events were to show that the government would not tolerate such expression of free ideas. Ngugi wa Thiong'o, one of the authors of the play performed at Kamiriithu, was detained and the open-air theatre constructed by workers and peasants was razed to ground by government bulldozers. This was the largest open-air theatre in Africa and had the added attraction that it was far from urban centres, in the countryside with peasants and local plantation and other workers forming the actors, audience and sponsors of the cultural activities. It now became clear to all that no public expression of any ideas or opinion not in agreement with imperialism was possible in Kenya. Such expression had of necessity to go underground. This lesson bore fruit in the late 1970s and 1980s when a popular underground press flourished, with a large number of leaflets being issued.

In general, the underground leaflets of 1970s reflected the contradictions of the times. Many were written by school, college and university students who played an important role in mobilising public opinion on important issues. The writers of these leaflets were also conscious, as *Africa Events* (1990a) put it, "of the class dimensions of the post-colonial Kenya society and they often tried to show the connections between Kenya's problems - not in tribal or personality lines - but in terms of what they called 'the neo-colonial path' of development opted for by the government. The leaflets bearing Kiswahili names became part of a vigorous underground press that took a very different line on national and international affairs from that of the established press."

Gradually resistance became an everyday feature of life. The extent and strength of this resistance may not immediately be obvious to a casual observer, hidden as they are by the silence of the official and corporate media. Such resistance can be examined at three levels. First, the resistance of workers, peasants, students and that of the 'whole nation'. This is the general response of the working people of Kenya to their social oppression and economic exploitation under the neo-colonial policies of the government. The second level reflects the organised, underground resistance that has given an ideological and organisational direction to the resistance of the people. The resistance at the third level was based overseas but which reflected, supported and was part of the resistance within Kenya. These two aspects of resistance - local and foreign - came together as a joint force to oppose the local ruling class and its imperialist backers.

Worker Resistance

Worker resistance throughout the country was in the forefront of direct action against oppressive laws and economic exploitation through strikes and related actions, reminiscent of the practice during the colonial period. Seen as an overall systematic resistance, these strikes and other struggles helped to build a movement against the regime, which has come down heavily against trade unions. It banned strikes and imprisoned leadership of trade unions. And, in the end, the Central Organisation of Trade Unions (COTU) was affiliated into the ruling party, KANU, thus ending its role as a workers' organisation to fight for economic and political rights of working people. But this did not suppress working class militancy as militant activists and shop stewards, isolating the official leadership, took the real leadership. Year after year, thousands of workers broke KANU laws and went on strikes for their rights.

When Moi came to power in 1978, he enforced the blind chanting of the slogan *Nyayo* demanding that people blindly follow in his footsteps without question or debate, as he was following the footsteps of the previous President, Jomo Kenyatta. A particularly significant development, indicating greater readiness to voice open opposition to the regime and to Moi personally, was the resolution passed by over 1,000 shop stewards at a meeting at Solidarity House in Nairobi to make arrangements for the Labour Day celebrations in April, 1989. They resolved that "they will answer njaa, njaa[56] ('hunger', 'hunger') instead of nyayo, nyayo to the *harambee*[57] call in the forthcoming

---

56 Njaa (Kiswahili): hunger, famine; Nyayo (Kiswahili): footsteps, referring to Moi's policy of following Kenyatta's footsteps in ensuring KANU dictatorship and pro-imperialist policies.

57 Harambee (Kiswahili): Pulling or working together. Kenyatta used the slogan to silence opposition to his rule and to extract funds from Kenyans. Most of the "voluntarily" raised funds ended up in the pockets of the elite instead of being used for the intended purpose - development projects.

Labour Day celebrations."[58]

The significance of this lies in the fact that the workers had bypassed the government-controlled COTU in their resistance and instead created their own organisation to continue their struggle. In addition, over a thousand activists organising and coming together was no mean an achievement in a country where a meeting of over five people was illegal if an official licence had not been obtained. Moreover the secret police monitored and suppressed any such democratic activity. The workers overcame all these obstacles to bring to the forefront the most important failure of the government - the economic mismanagement that brought vast fortunes to a select few (including Moi who was reputed to be the 5th richest man in the world) and untold misery to the majority of people.

But it is the daily struggles of the workers that gave true significance to the growing worker movement in Kenya in this period. Not willing to accept the situation, which meant daily erosion of their already very low standard of living, the workers intensified their struggles for a decent living wage and their economic, social and political rights. Mwakenya's (1987b) publication, *Kenya - Register of Resistance, 1986*, breaks down the workers' demands into three categories:

> Economic Demands: for higher wages, land and employment.
>
> Social Demands: safety at places of work, improved working conditions, adequate health facilities, adequate and relevant education.
>
> Political Demands: right to organise, right to assembly, union rights, support other workers, liberation from the entire oppressive system.

It is significant that Kenyan workers, as well as Mwakenya, saw workers' rights in the same way as Mau Mau did: that workers' rights should include social and political as well as economic rights as legitimate demands of the trade union movement. This was the key demand of the trade union movement as set up by Makhan Singh, Fred Kubai, Bildad Kaggia and

---

[58] Daily Nation, 17-04-1989.

others during the colonial period under the East African Trade Union Congress. This aspect is further explored in Durrani (2015b). The colonial administration, as well as the independent Kenyan government, legislated to remove workers' political rights from trade union remit - an aspect that has gravely weakened the trade union movement in Kenya. The same laws are in operation in Britain today with similar results.

Workers' resistance in this period took various forms: strikes, demonstrations, boycotts, work-to-rule, refusal to accept unfair practices. The media have been forced by the regime not to report fully on such militancy or to underplay their revolutionary significance. An examination of some worker resistance in the first few months of 1989, taken from *Upande Mwingine*, shows the extent of such resistance:

- 2000 Mombasa Municipal Council workers went on strike for more wages (January).

- 100 workers of the Gaturi Farmers Co-op Society, in Embu went on strike and demonstrated for their rightful wages (January).

- 150 workers of Nzoia County Council in Trans Nzoia went on strike for wages

- 600 workers in the open-air workshops went on strike and demonstrated when the Thika police tried to evict them from their work area. They attacked the police, many of whom were injured (January).

- 630 Kitale Municipality Workers went on strike for increased wages.

- 300 workers of the Rolmil Kenya Ltd in Kiambu went on a go-slow strike for increased wages, house allowance, leave entitlement and travelling allowance (January).

- 700 workers of the Pan-African Paper Mills, Webuye went on strike and fought police and the paramilitary GSU with stones, pieces of wood and acid (March).

- 200 workers of Lanar Road Construction Co., Bungoma held a demonstration in support for their demands for higher wages and better working conditions (April).

- 100 workers of the Athi River Mining Ltd went on strike for higher wages (May).

- 180 workers of Atta Ltd, Mombasa went on strike for higher wages in spite of being faced by armed police (May).

- 200 workers of Cosmo Plastics Ltd, Nairobi went on strike for better working conditions and right to permanent work after being considered 'casuals' after 8 years' of work (May).

- 250 workers of Afrolite Ltd, Nairobi went on strike for higher wages (June).

- 350 workers of Woodmakers (K) Ltd, Nairobi went on strike for higher wages (June).

These are just a few examples of strikes in the first six months of 1989. The actual number of workers taking strike action had been consistently increasing. Whereas 42,527 workers went on strike in 1986, the figure had jumped to 110,870 in 1988, indicating a higher level of militancy among workers. It should also be noted that as strikes were illegal in Kenya, workers going on strike risked losing their jobs and facing other "punishment". In addition, the Government's response to all strikes was to send in armed police and GSU (General Service Unit)[59] so striking workers, especially their leaders, ran the risk of being beaten up and held in remand or imprisoned where they got tortured as a matter of routine. Yet strikes continued.

---

59 The General Service Unit (GSU) is a paramilitary wing of the Kenyan Military and Kenyan Police, consisting of highly trained police officers and special forces soldiers, transported by seven dedicated Cessnas and three Bell helicopters. Having been in existence since the late 1940s, the GSU has fought in a number of conflicts in and around Kenya, including the 1963 – 1969 Shifta War and the 1982 Kenyan coup. The Kenyan police outlines the objectives of the GSU as follows, "to deal with situations affecting internal security throughout the Republic, to be an operational force that is not intended for use on duties of a permanent static nature, and primarily, to be a reserve force to deal with special operations and civil disorders". Wikipedia. Available at: http://en.wikipedia.org/wiki/General_Service_Unit_(Kenya) [Accessed: 05-04-17].

Over the ten year period since Moi came to power, the situation of workers got increasingly harsh. Not only was there more unemployment (often hidden in official figures), but even those in paid employment who got the official minimum wage (not all workers got this) could not afford to maintain themselves and their families with the ever escalating price rises of basic material needs. As the International Monetary Fund (IMF) and the World Bank increased pressure for anti-worker policies, as the transnationals increased their super-profits, as Moi and those around him corruptly drained away the country's wealth, the burden of these policies fell on the shoulders of working people. The increasing number and intensity of strikes, work stoppages, demonstrations and similar actions remained the main weapons available to the working class in their struggle against a regime that sought to satisfy, not the interests of the majority of people, but those of foreign and local elite who drained national resources. In this situation, there was an increase in worker militancy and strikes became routine.

Mwakenya (1978a) provides a good summary of workers' resistance and links it to peasants' resistance:

Workers have been hit hardest by the repressive colonial dictatorship through slave wages, arbitrary bans on strikes, police violence against striking workers and the co-option of official trade union leadership by the state. Nevertheless workers have been at the forefront in the struggle against the oppressive system. The underground workers organ Upande Mwingine shows that in 1986 alone there were over 75 cases of major strikes involving over 49,000 workers in various factories, commercial premises and other institutions all over the country. This parallels similar actions of defiant demonstrations by peasant and small traders. In the same year there were 35 recorded incidents involving over 15,000 peasants. What is documented for 1986 reflects the pattern of workers/peasants revolts since independence. Taken as a whole, the workers strikes and the peasant revolts and demonstrations between 1963 and the present amount to a mass movement against the neo-colonial economic and social system.

This naturally leads to understanding resistance by peasants.

Peasant Resistance

For hundreds of years, Kenyan people's resistance to foreign armies of occupation and plunder had, at its centre, peasant resistance to the killings, massacres, forced labour, eviction from and confiscation of land, the destruction of livestock and other properties. It was the issue over land that initially gave impetus to the War of Independence against British colonialism. The resistance movement that finally brought independence in 1963 had, significantly, the aim of returning land and freedom to the people. Mau Mau was forged as an alliance between the rural and urban proletariat on the one hand, and the peasants on the other. Thus land and control over natural resources have always been a key factor in Kenyan people's resistance.

Under the KANU regimes of Kenyatta and Moi, issues relating to the return of people's land were not resolved, instead the local and settler elites and transnational corporations consolidated their grip on this basic national resource. They have in fact been further aggravated. Landlessness, the single most significant issue in Kenya before and after independence, continued to increase. People were forced to squat on their own lands and finally forced out of land altogether. Land shortage was particularly acute in Central and Western Kenya and at the Coast. The Coast has had years of land problems as whole townships and vast areas were handed over to foreign multinationals and local speculators aligned to the powerful political elite for quick profit. The most fertile lands in the highlands were easily available to transnational agribusiness (for example, Brooke Bond and Del Monte) who 'own' millions of acres while peasants were crowded over marginal plots. There was also a small, but powerful, class of Kenyan landowners, led by politicians, with an insatiable greed for more and more land.

An additional factor under Moi was his foreign policy, which benefited imperialist powers. He won Western support by handing over strategic areas for U.S defence and military use, particularly in Northern Kenya and at the port in Mombasa. This, together with the finds of oil and other minerals, meant that pastoralists and peasants were being hounded out of their ancestral homes without any provision of alternate means of survival. In fact, the Moi-KANU regime declared war on Kenyan Somali nationality, which he had tried to suppress by massacres, mass arrests, detentions, jailing and torture. Ever faithful to the advice of IMF and World Bank, the neo-colonial regime additionally put peasants under immense economic pressures.

All these factors resulted in the Kenyan peasant and pastoralist reverting to their colonial practices of resistance. No week passed without reports of peasant resistance to the Moi government's policies and attacks on government officials.

The following is a selection, again from *Upande Mwingine* records, of peasant resistance during the first half of 1987:

- 400 angry peasants of Igembe, Meru marched to offices of Kenya Tea Development Authority to protest at lack of transport for their tea (Jan.).

- Busia peasants boycotted deliveries of cotton in protest at not being paid their dues on time (Jan.).

- 1000 Gilgil peasants refused to follow orders of government officials in connection with land ownership (January).

- 21 peasants of Soi, Kakamega beat up a government official (Feb).

- Peasants without land refused to follow government orders to vacate government land at Kerio East, Elgeyo Marakwet. (Feb).

- More than 1000 angry peasants demonstrated against delays in payment for last year's coffee crop, Gachuku, Nyeri. They had to face terror from riot police. (Feb).

- 100 peasants at Three Rivers Farm at Trans-Nzoia defended their rights to their 600 acre farm being claimed by a local politician whose family member was killed during the confrontation (March).

- Peasants growing sugar joined hands with workers of Nzoia Sugar Co, Bungoma and set 700 hectare of land with sugar on fire (March).

- 1000 peasants fought angry battles with armed police in protest at the Leisure Lodge Hotel in Ukunda at the Coast which was claiming their 300 acre farm. The police shot one peasant dead and injured another, while 7 policemen were also injured (March).

- 2,500 peasants defied a government order to leave government land at Mt. Elgon, Bungoma (April).

- 1000 peasants refuse to obey government Chief to leave their 300 acre farm at Diani, Kwale (May).

- 3,000 peasants at Muhoroni, Kisumu refused to follow orders from government officials and KANU politicians to contribute 3/- shillings for every ton of sugar (May).

- 1000 peasants defy government orders to vacate their land within 21 days so that a private company can take it over, Diani, Kwale (May).

- 50 peasants marched from Narok to Nairobi in protest at the interference from a Minister and administrative officials in their farm's elections (May).

- Peasants at Olokurto, Narok, refused to leave government land and defied police who had been sent to force them out.

- 5000 coffee-growing peasants at Murang'a refused to harvest coffee for two months in their struggle against Kagima Coffee Co-operative Society (May).

The above examples give an indication of the geographical breath of peasant resistance. It was present throughout the country. Peasants used varying methods of demanding their rights and often used violence against corrupt government officials and armed police and officials of transnational corporations. At the same time, because of the shortage of land which resulted in high cost, it often became necessary for a large number of peasants to pull their resources to purchase one farm. This came in useful when they faced common problems: thousands of owners found strength in defying government directives, whereas individual plot owners may fear taking direct action. These examples show that peasants as a class joined hands with workers in resisting the policies of the government. Conditions were ripening in the countryside for a more systematic and organised resistance by peasants. Underground resistance movements got much support from the peasants. Indeed the government's use of the army against peasants showed its fear of this resistance building up into a formidable force.

Student Resistance

Together with workers and peasants, students became the third force that actively opposed the neo-colonial Government. Students in Kenya had always voiced the concerns and views of the struggling people. It is the youth who assumed the role of articulating the political and economic consciousness and aspirations of the working people of the country. The youth made up over 50% of the population and derived their political consciousness from the material conditions of their own lives as well as from the experiences of their parents who in the main were workers and peasants.

The government attempted to turn students into docile acceptors of whatever they are taught. School, college and university syllabi have been controlled to remove any progressive ideas, similarly removing the militant ideology and aims of Mau Mau and the War of Independence. Their cultural and social activities were vetted to ensure no mention of any local relevant events which could inspire independent thought took place. In short, the whole educational process was geared to produce unthinking people who aped foreign bourgeois ways and agreed to all *nyayo* ideas.

But students never accepted this. They consistently resisted not only the colonial and imperialist-orientated elements of the education system itself, but also resisted the socio-economic system that blindly followed Western capitalist ideas which encouraged corruption. They instead sought a united student national movement which would ensure free circulation of ideas and links with fellow students from Africa and other progressive students from around the world.

The strength of student resistance was indicated in 1988 when thousands of students throughout the country went on strike. Just as an example, the students from the following schools were on strike over just two months September and October, as recorded by Mwakenya's *Upande Mwingine*:

> Murang'a College of Science and Technology; Kenyatta University (5,000 students); Kenya Science Teachers College (800 students); Kisii Teachers Training College; Moi Teacher Training College, Eldoret (650 students); Nyabola Girls High School, Kasipul, South Nyanza; Nginda Girls High School, Murang'a; thousands of first year students on National Youth Service at Gilgil from Universities of Nairobi, Kenyatta, Egerton and Moi fought running battles with riot police and NYS after many women students had been raped by the servicemen, some students were said to have been shot down. Nyanchwa Teacher Training College, Kisii; Murang'a Teachers College (500 students); Nkuene High School, Imenti, Meru; Itatani Secondary School, Machakos; Mutungulu Girls High School, Kangundo; Ngere High School, Kisumu; Ruaraka High School, Nairobi; Chulaimbo High School, Kisumu, Ringa High School, Kasipul, Nyanza; Malava Girls High School, Kakamega; Agoro Sare High School, South Nyanza; Maragoli High School, Vihiga, Kakamega; Gendia Secondary School, Kendu Bay, South Nyanza; Kenyoro High School Kisii; Ongaro High School, Kisii; Matare High School, Kisii, Manyatta High School, Kisii; Sori High School, Nyakite, Kisii; Agenga High School, Kisii; Mwer High School, Siaya; Sengani Hugh School Machakos; Kirimara High School, Nyeri; Isebania School; Kisumu Technical School; Onjiko High School, Kisumu; Sigomere High School, Siaya; Kambere High School, Gem, Siaya; Miwani High School, Kisumu; Nyabondo High School, Kisumu; Sameta High School; Jomo Kenyatta High School, Nakuru ...

... the list seemed almost endless. This was an indication of the serious opposition faced by the government in the education field. Different issues sparked strikes in different schools but overall the message from students to the government was clear: they were no longer willing to accept mismanagement, corruption, poor educational standards and lack of teachers and books. They were not satisfied with silent protests, but took action to change the situation. Indeed the government managed to overcome the serious crisis in education only by closing the school year early. But the crisis was not by any means over. The following year, 1989, saw more school strikes taking place. It is interesting to note that in many cases teachers and parents joined hands with students. Again, in most cases the presence of armed police did not deter students. Seen in conjunction with worker and peasant resistance, these student activities gave a national perspective to resistance to the Moi Government.

Students were also in the forefront of writing and distributing underground pamphlets setting out their demands. This was especially true of universities. Students at the University of Nairobi, for example, produced a vast amount of such literature, reflecting the militancy of the students there. Indeed a tradition of at least one enforced closure per year was the norm as the government dealt with student protests by closures. New repressive regulations were introduced after every closure, but this did not stop student militancy. Indeed most Student Union leaders ended up being thrown out of the University and being jailed or detained. For example, Mwandawiro Mghanga ended up with a 5-year jail term and Oginga Ogego with 10 years. The student newspaper produced at the School of Journalism of the University of Nairobi reflected socialist tendency among students, as Omanga & Buigutt (2017) show:

> The Anvil was a student newspaper at the University of Nairobi launched in the mid-1970s after its predecessor The Platform was shut down and its editors suspended from the university. Initially designed to be less militant, The Anvil forged a quasi-Marxist identity at a time of both widespread post-colonial disillusionment in Kenya and a largely conformist 'patriotic' press. In this context, the paper shows how 'Marx' became a symbol through which The Anvil, arguably the most fearless publication of its time, summoned a politicized 'student' public by offering alternative imaginaries of the nation. Drawing from literature on nationalism, publics and from media theory, the paper shows how this socialist lens was routinely used to interpret both local and off-shore events as a tool for proximate political agency by drawing on black cosmopolitanisms, anti-colonial sentiment and Cold War politics.

The Anvil started in 1976 as a training newspaper at the School of Journalism, with sponsorship from the Danish Agency for International Aid (DANIDA). It "was mysteriously shut down" (Omanga & Buigutt (2017) in 1992. Meanwhile the Student Union itself published its own newspapers, including *University Platform and Sauti ya Kamukunji* published in the early 1980s by the Student Organisation of University of Nairobi (SONU). They were all calling for radical change in Kenya to settle unsolved issues at the time of independence and so attracted Government ire.

Mwakenya (1987a) summarises student resistance:

> After the banning of K.P.U. , democratic opposition was led by University and Secondary school students. Nairobi and Kenyatta University students unions played a major role in fighting for democracy and human rights, and opposing neo-colonialism and foreign military bases in Kenya. They demonstrated in the streets, wrote leaflets, spoke in public and student gatherings, and in so many ways helped expose the reactionary character of the KANU regime.

The significance of all these student activities is not only in its own time period. They represented a new generation which refuses to accept a corrupt, man-eat-man society. The future of Kenya in reality lay in their hands. And they indicated their rejection of the regime's policies.

Progressive Members of Parliament also joined the growing movement of national resistance. Mwakenya (1987a) provides an overview of national resistance:

> In parliament radical MPs as individuals or as informal caucuses also offered democratic resistance. Resistance also found expression in culture and the Arts, in particular in books and theatre. But there was a price to pay for this democratic resistance. The end of the 1970s saw student movements being crushed and many students and lecturers maimed by police and G.S.U. violence. Others were imprisoned or banished from the university. Members of parliament were murdered and others imprisoned; social welfare organisations were banned and radical cultural centres destroyed. There is no doubt that during this period, the students bore the main burden of

democratic consciousness, often paying for their patriotism with expulsions, imprisonments or deaths.

The students resistance supplemented that of the workers, manifested in the increase in the number of strikes and that of the peasants who showed their resistance by attacking corrupt co-operative officials and at times even uprooting cash crops imposed on them.

The period 1970-80 can rightly be called the decade of struggle for democracy. The prevailing thinking among progressive people was summed up by Willy Mutunga:

Imperialist capital, locked in the hire-purchase business, pervades both aspects (productive forces and means of ownership) of production of our material goods. The roles which modern imperialism has imposed on Kenya find effective expression in our laws. Nobody denies that Kenya is an exploited country where workers and peasants are exploited by imperialist capital of the international bourgeoisie, who are the ruling class in Kenya. The bourgeoisie own the means of production here. They (compradors) will live and die with imperialism.[60]

The whole nation resists...

Workers, peasants, students ... all had their own forms of struggle against the unpopular elite government. But as Mwakenya (1987b) points out in the *Register of Resistance, 1987*, the lower petty bourgeois had also joined the ranks of those resisting and struggling against the government. The significant point about this was the vast numbers involved in this protest. For example, when teachers protested against the government's sudden policy of reducing their housing allowance in September 1988, almost 160,000 members of the Kenya National Union of Teachers planned to go on strike. So serious was this action that the government was forced to withdraw its planned reduction of housing allowance. Similarly over 80,000 drivers, *manambas*, *matatu* owners and other transport workers brought national transport to stand-still when they boycotted work in March 1988. It forced

---

60 Quoted by Mdlongwa, "Kenya Laws are Vehicles of Imperialism" *in* Omanga and Buigutt (2017).

the Government to withdraw the new policies affecting the industry.

The unpopular 1988 'queuing' elections in which Moi won a false mandate, gave rise to massive election boycott and mass demonstrations against the fraudulent elections. Moi had hoped to prove his popularity to his international backers U.S.A. Britain, IMF and World Bank, and to give a democratic veneer to his dictatorial rule. In the event, the resistance of the voters robbed him of his 'victory'. Umoja (1988), in its publication, *The Struggle For Democracy in Kenya; Special Report on the 1988 General Elections in Kenya* documented the resistance of the Kenya people to the elections. Thousands of people marched in protest at the 'cooked' elections results. For example, over 4,000 people including women and young children in Taveta marched over four miles from Daranjani to Taveta in protest against the falsification of election results. They stoned local government officials and forced the closure of all offices and shops. All communication links with the rest of the country were cut. Fierce battles raged between the people and the armed police who had to be reinforced by the para-military GSU (General Service Unit). Over 100 people, including women and children were arrested; 10 people were seriously injured and had to be hospitalised. The police killed at least one man, aged 66.

Similar mass protests were organised throughout the country. They indicate a qualitative difference in the resistance. Mass protests were fast becoming a way of life in Kenya. Such protests brought together people from all classes opposed to the Government.

Similar mass tactics were used by the students of the University of Nairobi between November 13-15, 1988 when the Government arrested the entire student leadership. More than 3,000 students, reported Umoja (1987), "regrouped and a running battle between them and the (armed) police in the streets of Nairobi started".

But the largest and more significant mass demonstration took place in Mombasa where people's grievances with landlessness, unemployment, poor wages, and the presence of the hated U.S military were always just below the surface. The Mombasa mass protest arose as a result of the government suddenly cancelling a rally organised by Muslim youth on

October 30, 1987. Umoja (1987b) sets the scene:

> More than 4000 people formed an orderly procession to seek an audience with the Provincial Commissioner (PC). But instead of the PC holding a dialogue with the people, he unleashed armed police at them.

In self-defence, the people faced the police. With strong involvement of Muslim women and the youth, they boldly attacked the provincial headquarters. They later marched to the Central Police Station and attacked it too. The youth adopted guerrilla hit and run tactics in the narrow streets of the Old Town area. The subsequent hide and seek continued till about 2 o'clock in the morning.

The people's anger at what happened to them on October 30 erupted once again on 4 November during the massive procession to mark the birth of Prophet Mohammed. The youth used the religious procession to once again air their defiance and express their demands for the right to organise and assemble.

There was obviously a strong organisation behind the mass protests. They even issued a record of their side of the struggle in an underground pamphlet entitled *Yaliotokea hapa Mombasa mnamo tarehe 30-1-87*. (Events in Mombasa on 30 January, 1987).

Kenyan people turned to other forms of resistance as well. Many parts of Nairobi, for example, were closed areas to the police, similar to the situation during the Mau Mau period. Any police officer who ventured there ended up being murdered. Increasing cases of death of policemen and government officials at the hands of people occurred. The following are some examples from *Upande Mwingine*:

- Police constable killed at Mathare in Nairobi (Sunday Times, 12-2-89)

- A policeman was shot in the leg at Nakuru after a policeman shot dead a woman (Sunday Times, 12-02-89)

- Senior superintendent of police was hacked to death by people of Lukoye, Mumias (Sunday Times, 12-02-89)

- A sub-locational KANU Vice-Chairman in Kakamega District, Gilbert Okello, was slashed to death by people (03-03-89). This is the second incident this year when a Kanu official in Kakamega was hacked to death.

- A Kanu youthwinger, Samuel Maba, was admitted to hospital with deep cuts on head and neck same incident as above.

- Lawrence Mbare, the acting chief for Shamakhokho location in Hamisi was assaulted with a panga by local people. He was admitted to hospital (03-03-89).

- Constable Salim Limo murdered at Huruma Estate, Nairobi on August 20 1988 (Daily Nation, 02-03-89).

The spirit of resistance was captured by a Kisumu woman who was being evicted by the Kisumu Municipal Council from her home where she had lived for over 15 years. In October 1988, Council askaris went to evict her. But the brave woman was ready for them. She first threw boiling water on them and then fought them off with a panga (machete), injuring them. The people have begun to say 'no' to exploitation and oppression. As *Upande Mwingine* said:

Wakati wo wote

Mahali po pote

Watu wakigandamizwa

Kisasi watalipizwa

Mapambano yatazuka.

(Rough English translation)

Every time

Every place

When people are oppressed

A price will have to be paid
The struggle will blossom everywhere.

That indeed was the situation in Kenya towards the end of 1990s with resistance to government policies.

PART 4: UHURU, 1963: UNDERGROUND ORGANISED RESISTANCE

Underground Organised Resistance

December Twelve Movement

The tradition of organised underground resistance in Kenya goes back to the beginning of the 20th Century and continued throughout the colonial period. But the tradition did not end with the achievement of independence. It continued throughout the period of Kenyatta's regime and intensified under Moi, as the US-backed regime consolidated its neo-colonial grip over the country.

This survey examines only one of the groups that was active in this period - the December Twelve Movement (DTM) which later emerged as Mwakenya. This should not be seen as an indication that there were no other underground groups. It is the one whose publications are most readily available and with whose work the author is most familiar. While Mwakenya was a Kenya-based group, there were others based overseas. *Africa Events* explains the widespread solidarity and human rights groups around the world:

> ... those who went into exile became part of the international solidarity movement with Kenyan political prisoners, a movement that started with the formation of the London-based Committee for the Release of Political Prisoners in Kenya. This later inspired other campaigns in Scandinavian countries, India, Japan and North America...
>
> Some Kenyan exiles who got involved in human rights campaigns, started organising themselves as political activists, resulting in such externally-based groups as UKENYA, formed in London in 1986, and which in October 1987 joined other groups to form Umoja wa Kupigania Demokrasia Kenya (United Movement for Democracy in Kenya), with UMOJA as its Kiswahili acronym. As part of its activities,

this movement has produced some seminal documents on Kenya, in particular Struggle for Democracy in Kenya: Special Report on 1988 General Elections in Kenya (1988) and Moi's Reign of Terror (1989). Still more Kenyan political organisations in exile mushroomed in Africa, West European and North American countries, some of which are the Kenya Patriotic Front (KPF), Me-Katilili Revolutionary Movement (MEKAREMO), Kenya Anti-Imperialist Front (KAIF).

Mwakenya (1987b) provides details on the situation in the country and the formation of the December Twelve Movement:

> ... the most dramatic development, since the ban of K.P.U. [Kenya Peoples' Union] and the suppression of centres of democratic dissent, was the emergence of worker/peasant based underground groups. They began articulating an ideology that fully reflected the workers' struggle. The seventies saw the development of a vigorous underground press best symbolised by Mwanguzi which ran to more than twelve issues. Between 1974 and 1982, the underground groups and newspapers had become the real voice of the Kenyan people. This culminated in the formation of the December Twelve Movement with its mass newspaper Pambana (widely and heavily distributed in May 1982). Pambana placed on the political scene in Kenya a set of demands and vision by which the unfolding political struggles could be seen and be judged. As can be seen from the early issues it linked the Kenya people's struggles to those of the Third World and particularly to the revolutionary traditions of South and Central America, El Salvador, Nicaragua, and Cuba for instance. Pambana struck terror in the ruling circles provoking a national debate in parliament and among the people on the streets. The regime reacted with its usual anti-people instincts.

One of the most important underground publications of the December Twelve Movement (DTM) was issued in 1981. It was *InDependent Kenya*, published by the group Cheche Kenya an earlier name of the December Twelve Movement. *InDependent Kenya* documented from the perspective of the Kenyan working people, the history of Kenyans' struggle for independence, the struggle of militants and conservatives within the Kenya

African National Union (KANU), the corruption that became a way of life within the regime, and the cultural dependency on imperialism. *InDependent Kenya* was cyclostyled and widely distributed through underground channels in Kenya. It was later published in a book form in London by Zed Press in 1982 and was sponsored by the Journal of African Marxists "in solidarity with the authors".

December Twelve Movement's (DTM) activities represented continuation of resistance from pre-independence ones. DTM had a very clear, well-defined ideological position that opposed the capitalist outlook of the ruling class and their party. It was active in articulating its ideological position, policies and outlook, not only among its active members grouped in secret cells, but also in disseminating these to its actual and potential supporters among the masses. It was not a mass movement and recruited into membership only those who showed clear grasp of its ideological stand and were willing to put into practice their commitments. The emergence of the December Twelve Movement marked the end of the attempts by democratic forces to form legal opposition parties. Earlier attempts to regroup within KANU and to make it more democratic and responsive to national needs had failed, reflecting the total surrender of the comprador class to imperialist interests in order to pursue its own economic interests. It became the historical role of the December Twelve Movement and other resistance movements to articulate the new phase in Kenyan politics where it was possible to struggle for national democratic rights only at an underground level.

It was DTM's newspaper *Pambana, the Organ of the December Twelve Movement*, however, which had the widest circulation and the greatest impact in post-independence Kenya. The first issue was published in May 1982. To begin with, it used the language of the Kenyan working people, Kiswahili. It took a strong principled anti-imperialist position and based its arguments on an analysis of neo-colonialism.

December Twelve Movement's programme became in effect an alternative to that of KANU's essentially capitalist one. DTM stood for a national democratic revolution which could unite all national forces opposed to imperialism and the neo-colonial comprador regime. As *Pambana* made clear, the December Twelve Movement supported all genuine Kenyan organisations and individuals, "fighting any aspect of local or imperialist reaction". It set out the tactics of achieving a broad unity of all democratic forces and, in the process; it clearly isolated the comprador class.

The short-lived coup of August 1982 was, at one level, a reflection of the developing democratic forces. The coup's message (Kenya Coup, 1982, Broadcast) reflected the desire of millions for an alternative political system from the KANU one. It was clearly a vindication of DTM's programme, which appears to have influenced the coup leaders:

> Over the past few years, this country has been heading from an open to a closed, inhuman and dictatorial society. The fundamental principles for which many of our people sacrificed their lives during the heroic struggle for independence have been compromised in the interest of a few greedy and irresponsible bandits.
>
> Over the past six months, we have witnessed with disgust the imposition of a de jure one-party system without the people's consent, arbitrary arrest and the detention of innocent citizens, censorship of the press, intimidation of individuals and general violation of fundamental human rights.
>
> This ruthless oppression and repression is reminiscent of the past colonial days which Kenyans thought were buried at independence. A gang of local tyrants has emerged whose only function is to terrorise and intimidate with senseless warnings. Rampant corruption, tribalism and nepotism have made life almost intolerable in our society. The economy of this country is in shambles due to corruption and mismanagement. The cost of living in Kenya today is among the highest in the world. Wananchi can no longer afford to meet the basic requirements of life, due to exorbitant prices of basic necessities such as food, housing, rent, transport.
>
> Kenyans are among the highest taxed people in the world today ... our armed forces have heeded the people's call to liberate our country once again from the forces of oppression and exploitation in order to restore liberty, dignity and social justice to the people.

The aftermath of the coup altered the political scene in Kenya. Realising how little public support it had, the KANU Government increased repression to new heights: it relied even more on the military. Many patriots and democrats who had been active before the coup were brutally murdered or illegally detained. All pretences to democracy were removed. Economically, the Moi regime aligned itself even more firmly to US imperialism, which now acquired military facilities in the country in return for supporting the unpopular regime. At the same time, the coup ended prematurely the developing revolutionary forces from gathering more support and setting up an appropriate organisational and ideological framework to challenge the government on a stronger basis. As it is, the coup gave the Moi government an excuse to undermine every strand of resistance to its rule and arrest, detain and "disappear" those it saw as opposing its rule. This included the growing trade union and student movements and also DTM leadership. With strong support from Britain and USA, it re-established its rule, but with an even more oppressive rule. It is difficult to speculate how the forces of resistance would have developed had Moi not used it to silence all opposition. It is fair to say, however, the resistance movement suffered a setback with Moi's reign of terror unleashed in the wake of the coup.

The December Twelve Movement (DTM) just about survived Moi's attacks on all forces opposed to him but as a much weakened force following the brutal actions to jail, detain or eliminate its members and leaders. It continued the production of *Pambana* and the second issue came out in July 1983. It summed up the experiences following the coup and exposed the attempts of "the ruling clique and their army to instil fear amongst the people." It identified the root causes of the problems facing people and resolutely called for unity to defeat "the enemy", adding:

> We cannot remain silent when our right to good housing, adequate food, decent clothing and education have been denied us by this oppressive regime. Twenty years after independence we have been reduced to the position of beggars ... Even the Parliament has not been able to change anything. It will not be able to change anything. We are still hungry and we know that our children will suffer even greater hunger if we do not now make the necessary effort and sacrifice to change the present conditions.

Pambana drew strength from the revolutionary traditions of the Mau Mau's use of struggle songs to mobilise people. In its issue of July 1983, for example, it ran the following revolutionary song entitled *Kenya Our Country*:

Kenya our county

Our land, our sweat, our blood.
Listen
to the voices of our children,
The voices of workers,
The voices of peasants,
the exploited
the oppressed
those who are tortured for nothing.

Our beloved motherland
In chains of servitude.
Break the chains
Of parasites
Of capitalists
Of neo-colonialism.

For how long shall they continue stealing your wealth?
For how long shall they continue exploiting your children?

It is a matter for tears. It is a matter for sorrow
for us your children.
What can we do to restore you dignity?

We are the ones who work the industries
We are the ones who work the land
We are the ones who build this country.

Look
How our hands are blistered
How our backs are bent
How we now stoop
For shouldering the burden of production.

Mother, look at us now
Look at our lives
It is sad.
But for how long are we going to cry?
For how long are we going to live in pain?

No!
We must unite and struggle
For our rights.

We refuse to live in poverty
We refuse to be treated like foreigners
In our own land.

We refuse to die of hunger
We refuse
To be tortured
To be exploited
To be oppressed.
Here comes the dawn
Let us struggle on to victory.

One of the effects of Moi's attack on DTM was the dispersal and exiling of many activists. Those forced to seek refuge in other countries found new homes in Britain, USA, the Scandinavian countries, in Africa such as in Zimbabwe. These groups remained politically active and joined hands with the Kenya-based activists and together they emerged as Mwakenya in 1987. It is now known as Mwakenya-DTM.

Mwakenya

The history of Kenya shows a strong continuity of resistance against colonialism and imperialism. As the concrete conditions changed and as new contradictions developed, the resistance movements also underwent changes to resolve new contradictions.

These changes in resistance took place at the level of theory as well as in its practice. The strand of resistance that was so strong in Mau Mau never died. It continued in the post-independence period and has had to undergo various qualitative changes in response to the changing contradictions.

The December Twelve Movement continued this tradition in the late 1970s and 1980s. After the coup of 1982, DTM forces regrouped and emerged as Mwakenya – Muungano wa Wazalendo wa Kukomboa Kenya (Union of Patriots for the Liberation of Kenya). Events were to prove that many practices of DTM which had given it strength were not carried on into Mwakenya and that that perhaps led to its decline in the long term. Among these was a relaxation of the strict recruitment policy of DTM and an attempt to become a mass party opening up membership to all. Many people became members without a clear ideological stand and without having proved their commitment in practice. And yet there were important achievements made by Mwakenya in the period after its formation.

However, Mwakenya's achievement was strongest in setting out a clear political and ideological framework in opposition to the KANU government's pro-Western, pro-capitalist programme. It did so with an evidence-based analysis on the conditions of the time and the state of contradictions in the society. Based on such analysis, its two documents became important in guiding its policies and also on raising awareness among people.

The first document was Mwakenya's *Draft Minimum Programme* which set out the history of neo-colonialism in Kenya and also traced the history of resistance in Kenya. It also gave the background to the formation of Mwakenya itself and recorded its publications and Congresses. The most significant part was "the Fundamental Goals and Objectives of Mwakenya". The publication of the *Draft Minimum Programme* marked a new stage in the anti-imperialist struggle in Kenya. Once again, an underground opposition Party challenged the monopoly of KANU as the true spokesperson for the masses of Kenyans. No longer could KANU claim its exclusive right to speak for all the classes in Kenya. It now became obvious that KANU spoke for the comprador class in Kenya while Mwakenya and allied progressive movements represented the interests of the rest of the people. The challenge to KANU was on ideological and organisational fronts as well, as Mwakenya set out the demands of the "oppressed and exploited classes of Kenyan people" and called upon the people to overthrow the entire neo-colonial system, seize political power and establish a peaceful state of democracy and social progress." The silent class struggle since independence was formally brought into broad daylight. Proclaiming its stand that "In struggle lies the Way Ahead", the document quotes from its resistance poem *Ni haki yetu kupigania haki zetu* (It is Our right to fight for our rights).[61]

Ni Haki Kupigania Haki

Ni haki yetu kupigania haki zetu
Ni jukumu letu kupigania haki zetu
Kutopigania haki ni hatia
Hatutahifadhi haki bila kupambana
Ni haki ya wote, ya kila mmoja
Apate chakula cha kutosha
Awe na nguo na nyumba
Hii ni haki, ni msingi wa maisha
Ni haki ya watu kupata mahitaji haya
Kwa njia ya kazi, ya kutoa jasho
Sio kwa njia ya ukarimu au unyonyaji
Ni haki ya wote kuwa na kazi
Wakinyimwa haki hiyo ya kazi
Watu wana jukumu kubadalisha
Mfumo unaokataza haki hiyo
Ni haki yetu kupigania haki zetu

April 1985

English translation

---

[61] The poem was written by Nazmi Durrani, a veteran of DTM days.

Our Right to Fight for Our Rights

It's our right to fight for our rights

it's our duty to fight for our rights.

Not to fight for our rights is a crime

We cannot preserve our rights without struggle

It's the right of each and everyone

To have food

Clothing and shelter

This is a right, the very foundation of life.

It's the right of people to get these necessities

By way of work, by sweating for them

Not through charity or exploitation.

Work is the right of all.

If denied the right to work

People have the duty to change

the system that denies them this right .

it's our right to fight for our rights

Karimi Nduthu, the National Co-ordinator of Mwakenya was "brutally assassinated by agents of the Moi dictatorship on 23 March, 1986" for continued resistance to the brutal KANU-Moi regime. This showed that the regime still feared Mwakenya. Karimi's death was a blow to the organisation, but it began to recover over the years.

Kenya, Register of Resistance, 1986

The second important document published by Mwakenya in 1987 was *Kenya, Register of Resistance, 1986.* This is a detailed record and analysis of the resistance against the government by the working people of Kenya, subdivided into actions by workers (industrial proletariat and agricultural proletariat), peasants, lower petty bourgeoisie and progressive intelligentsia. The Introduction is itself an important analysis of the intensifying class struggle in Kenya, with KANU exposed as the party of comprador bourgeoisie and Mwakenya is shown as the party of the working people. It is worth looking in detail at the Introduction for it is the clearest class analysis of the situation in Kenya, explaining the role played by both KANU and Mwakenya:

> At independence in 1963, the KANU regime opted for capitalism. But it was not an independent capitalism. It was, and still is, an extension of Western imperialism. That means that our economy is foreign owned. The main banking and other financial institutions are owned by Western monopolies. So are our industry and commerce. The symbol of this domination is IMF and the World Bank. These two dictate Kenya's economic and social politics. Today the KANU regime merely supervises the domination of our economy; politics and culture [are controlled] by U.S-led imperialism. Every year more wealth flows out of the country than comes in. This wealth goes into the pockets of these foreign companies and their owners. The little that remains in the country goes to the minority wealthy classes that act as *mbwa kalis* of foreign Western interests. But it is not the foreign companies and their owners and local supervisors who make that wealth. The wealth is made by the workers and peasants of Kenya. Kenya is a class divided society. There is a class struggle in Kenya and it is intensifying day by day.

The *Register* prepared by *Upande Mwingine* (The Other Side), an allied group of Mwakenya, was perhaps the first systematic post-independence record of resistance by workers, peasants, students and other Kenyans. It set a standard on how to investigate and assess the state of resistance. It was the first attempt after the pioneering records of working class history that Makhan Singh published in his two books (Singh 1969, 1980). Although it lacked the lively historical records that Singh provided, it still had the raw material for understanding and interpreting the history of working class in Kenya.

Mpatanishi, an organ of Mwakenya, explains the emergence of the Movement in issue No. 14 (August, 1985). It says that Mwakenya was formed as a result of merger of "local and foreign based liberation organisations fighting to overthrow the present neo-colonial regime in Kenya." The same issue of *Mpatanishi* sets out the strategy of armed struggle as the only way of resolving the major contradiction in Kenya. Events were to show not only that that the organisation was not strong enough to carry out an armed struggle, but that the conditions were not appropriate for such a shift in policy at that time. Perhaps the shift reflected the internal struggle within the organisation with divided opinion as to the correctness of a move to armed struggle at that point in time and whether politics or military should direct policies.

Resistance goes Overseas: the Birth of Umoja

More and more Kenyans have to flee Kenya for expressing their democratic rights and who subsequently face prison, detention, torture or even death. Kenyan organisations have been established wherever Kenyans have settled. On the occasion of thirtieth anniversary of Kimathi's death on 18 February 1987, a new Kenyan organisation was launched in London. This was Umoja wa Kupigania Demokrasia Kenya – Movement for Unity and Democracy in Kenya, Ukenya. It released its Manifesto and an important document, "From Kimathi to Mwakenya; Resistance in Kenya Today" which was delivered by it Spokesperson, Yusuf Hassan at a meeting in London. This was followed by a number of Kenyan organisations overseas coming together to form Umoja. *Africa Events* (1989) explains the background and looks at some publications:

> Some Kenyan exiles who got involved in human rights campaigns, started organising themselves as political activists, resulting in such externally-based groups as UKenya, formed in London in 1986, and which in October 1987 joined other groups (in USA, Scandinavian countries, Australia, and some African countries) to form Umoja wa Kupigania Demokrasia Kenya (United Movement for Democracy in Kenya) - Umoja-Kenya. As part of its activities, this movement has produced some seminal documents on Kenya, in particular "Struggle for Democracy in Kenya: Special Report on 1988 General Elections in Kenya" (1988) and "Moi's Reign of Terror: A Decade of Nyayo Crimes Against the People of Kenya (1989)".

Umoja was formed at the Unity Conference on October 16-19, 1987 in

London when the following organisations came together:

Organisation for Democracy in Kenya (Sweden)
Muungano wa Demokrasia Kenya (USA)
Kenya Democratic Alliance (Norway)
Kamati ya Ukombozi wa Kenya (Africa)
Patriotic Alliance of Kenyans (Africa)
Committee for Democracy in Kenya (Denmark)
UKENYA: Movement for Unity and Democracy in Kenya (Britain).

The Resolution and Final Statement issued on October 20, 1987 (Umoja, 1987e), at the end of the Conference, sets out the reasons for the formation of Umoja. It lists some problems and weaknesses that oversees resistance faced and said that "realising these weaknesses, the delegates of the organisations present [as above] decided to dissolve themselves and form a single democratic organisation of all patriotic, democratic and progressive organisations operating outside Kenya - Umoja wa Kupigania Demokrasia Kenya (United) Movement for Democracy in Kenya" popularly known as Umoja. The Resolution further stated its support for "the resistance being waged inside the country by the underground people's party, Mwakenya... Umoja as a support movement hereby declares its total support for Mwakenya and its political demands set out in its *Draft Minimum Programme*".

Mwakenya (1987a) sums up the contribution of resistance from abroad:

Since independence, there had always been some Kenyans in exile, reflecting the different moods and upheavals in the country. For instance during the war between the KANU regime and the North-based forces of Northern Peoples Progressive Party, many Kenyan refugees were driven into the neighbouring countries of Somalia, Ethiopia, Uganda and Tanzania. The K.P.U. period and the University crisis saw a few more people into exile. But following the post-coup intensified repression Kenyan exiles were scattered all over the world so that soon there were pockets of Kenyan exiles all over the world. Thus the 1982 repression also created conscious and organised resistance abroad. Beginning with the London based Committee for the Release of Political Prisoners in Kenya with its bulletin Kenya News, which was formed in July 1982, Kenyans in exile became part of an international solidarity movement which soon extended to Sweden, Denmark, Norway, U.S.A., Japan, Zimbabwe, Nigeria, Tanzania, Uganda and several other countries. Secondly, Patriotic Kenyans abroad continued trying to organise themselves. This culminated in the formation of progressive organisations such as KAIF (Kenya Anti Imperialist Front); the London based UKENYA (Movement for Unity and Democracy in Kenya); the Sweden based O.D.K. (Organisation for Democracy in Kenya) and others. By 1986/87 the brutal character of the neo-colonial regime had been exposed to the world. The national resistance and the reaction of the regime to it was decisive in this change of perception.

Kenya Committee For the Release of Political Prisoners

Besides the work of overseas Kenyans, a number of support committees were formed overseas in support of the democratic struggle in Kenya. Among them was the Kenya Committee for the Release of Political Prisoners in Kenya in London. The work of such committees should not be underestimated as they helped to raise consciousness in these countries and also gave strength to activists in Kenya that their struggle was seen and heard overseas. A brief look at the London Committee illustrates this point.

The Kenyan people's struggle against neo-colonialism within the country had the support of Kenyans based overseas and progressive people around the world. Among other roles, these external forces played a crucial role in alerting international public opinion, foreign governments and international bodies, about the real situation in Kenya. Such external forces have consisted of solidarity movements as well as organisations of politically active Kenyans who had to flee Kenya for their political activities. Such Kenyans formed political and social organisations that supported the struggle for liberation at home.

An example of a solidarity movement in colonial times was the Kenya Committee, which was active in 1950s. Kenyatta, Ochieng Oneko, and Mbiu Koinange were active in London during the colonial period, with Kenyatta being well known in the Pan African Movement.

Such activities continued in the independence period after 1963 as well. There are solidarity organisations in Britain, Sweden, and Japan, among other places. The London-based Committee for the Release of Political Prisoners in Kenya was formed in 1982 and published *Kenya News* and other documents bringing human rights violations to the notice of the international community. It organised a 'Focus on Kenya' seminar in 1983 and issued a statement on the occasion of the seventh anniversary of its foundation. London was traditionally the centre of Kenyan exile community since independence. Among solidarity groups in London was the The Committee for the Release of Political Prisoners in Kenya which was formed in 1982 and has played a leading role in alerting international community about the true situation in Kenya. Besides publishing *Kenya News*, an irregular newsletter, it published many important documents.

The Committee organised a one-day Conference entitled Focus on Human Rights in Kenya on July 2, 1988. It has also issued numerous statements on the abuse of human rights in Kenya. Each issue of the *Kenya News* focused on an important topic of the day and also carries a well-researched up-to-date list of political prisoners in Kenya. The following list gives the main article carried by each issue of Kenya News:

- No. 1 (July 1983): One Year later; Political Prisoners Still Jailed in Kenya.

- No.2 (Nov. 1983): Democratic Image - Repressive Reality.

- No. 3 (April 1984): Stop This Massacre ("The barbaric attack by the Kenyan security forces on defenceless citizens in the North East Province killed more than 1,000 people").

- No.4 (Oct.1984): Drought is a Big Business.

- No. 5 (May 1985): Sunday Bloody Sunday (The massacre of students at the University of Nairobi, Sunday, Feb. 10, 1985).

- No.6 (June 1985): The Kenyan Woman: A Decade of Oppression.

- No.7 (August 1986): State of Emergency; Help Close Moi's Torture Chamber.

- No.8 (March 1987): Torture in Kenya Intensifies; There is no giving up, Diaries from a Torture Chamber; Routine Methods of Extorting Information.

- No.9 (Feb. 1989): Moi's Police: Licence To Kill; Ten Years of Terror.

It will be seen that while the government in Kenya was keen to ensure that the world was unaware of its oppressive rule, organisations such as the Committee ensured that the world knew about the human rights situation in Kenya.

During 1980s the struggle in Kenya intensified, the government of Moi made increasing use of imprisonment, massacres, murders, looting and a total disregard for the rule of law. Those who raised their voice to challenge the tyranny were jailed, detained, "disappeared" or forced into exile. As the struggle intensified, and the activities and the voice of progressive Kenyans went underground, there was an urgent need for progressive voices around the world to be heard in support of the struggle for democracy in Kenya. Among the first one to do so were progressive people in Britain. They formed the Committee for the Release of Political Parties in Kenya in 1982.

In order to understand the historical context of the contribution that the Committee made to the struggle in Kenya, it is necessary to travel back in time to the 1950s during Kenya's War of Independence led by Mau Mau. British Government's position was to suppress Mau Mau in the most brutal way. Progressive thinkers in Britain at that time also supported Kenya's demand for independence and formed the Kenya Committee for Democratic Rights for Kenya African based at 86 Rochester Row, London, SW1. The Committee provided information about the situation in Kenya to Members of Parliament, the media and those on its mailing list. It published "Press Extracts for the Years of the Emergency, 1952-1960" where it provided on-going records on events in Kenya from press and other sources. At the same time, it established links with Kenyans in Kenya and Britain and came to be trusted by those active in the struggle. This included the Kenya Land and Freedom Army (KLFA, Mau Mau) who maintained links with the Committee from their forest headquarters. This included a letter from KLFA dated 7 April, 1955 which was reproduced in full by the Committee in its Press Extracts. It also reprinted "A letter to the people of Britain on behalf of the Kikuyu people" from the *Daily Worker* of September 7, 1953. Some work of the earlier Committee was examined earlier in the book.

Thus the Kenya Committee in 1980s was part of the on-going support that progressive people in Britain have given to the people of Kenya. Although much had changed from the 1950s to the 1980s, the need for unbiased information and records of what was happening in Kenya was the same. Both the periods saw the same negative attitudes from British Government and the Establishment, the same hostility and misreporting by the biased mainstream media. And so, like in the 1950s, there was a need in the 1980s for the new Kenya Committee to collect and disseminate correct information to the British people.

And the Committee for the Release of Political Prisoners in Kenya fulfilled that need. The Committee was instrumental in alerting international community about the true situation in Kenya. It published an irregular newsletter, the *Kenya News* which ran to nine issues from 1983-89. Each issue of the *Kenya News* focused on an important topic of the day and also carried a well researched up-to-date list of political prisoners in Kenya.

The Committee also issued numerous statements on the abuse of human rights in Kenya and undertook campaigns on behalf of many political prisoners in Kenya. It produced a large amount of other documents, including the first issue dated May 1982 of Pambana, the Organ of the December Twelve Movement which was circulating underground in Kenya. Some other documents include:

- Law as a tool of political repression in Kenya. August 1982.

- Repression intensifies in Kenya since the August 1st coup attempt. January 1983, 20 pp.

- Release the political prisoners in Kenya. July 1982 (reprinted March 1983), 12 pp.

- University destroyed; Moi crowns ten years of Government terror in Kenya. May 1983, 16 pp.

- It organised a 'Focus on Kenya' seminar in 1983 and issued a statement on the occasion of the seventh anniversary of its foundation.

During the 1990s, popular resistance continued to undermine President Moi's attempts to bottle resistance. As in 1982, at the time of the coup, opposition to the government gathered momentum. The cry for political change began to be heard everywhere. *Africa Events* reported that "unfretted corruption in high places, intolerance of dissenting views, and the widening of the gap between the rich and the poor appear to have lent some weight to the proponents of political change" (August/September 1990). It gave a background to the public anger and activism:

> Since January [1990], the calls for pluralism have been expressed in every corner of the country. The impetus of the campaign for democracy gained momentum following the politically motivated murder of the Foreign Minister, Dr. Robert Ouko, in February this year. Protesters took to the streets shouting "Down with Moi" and urging the government to resign. Scores of the demonstrators were shot dead by the police.

Such local and international pressure eventually forced Moi to remove Clause 2A which made Kenya a one-party state. Mwakenya had already warned Kenyans of the dangers of "Moism without Moi" (Mwakenya, 1992) and this was further explained by its Spokesperson, Ngugi wa Thiong'o, in answer to the question, "Since the Kenya government has now allowed opposition parties to be registered, and some changes have taken place, what is MWAKENYA's position?":

> MWAKENYA welcomes any democratic gains by the Kenyan people. But the mere removal of Clause 2A (which made Kenya a one party state) from the Kenya constitution does not mean that anything has changed in Kenya fundamentally. Political repression did not begin in 1982 with the legalisation of the one-party state. Even before 1982, political parties were still not allowed to function although Kenya was legally a multiparty state. Students Organisations, the Academic Staff Union, the Civil Servants Union, the Kamiriithu Community Education and Cultural Centre and social welfare organisations, had been outlawed. Workers' organisations were not allowed to function freely. More than five people could not meet without police licence even if they were meeting for a family tea party or for a funeral. And above all, the Chief's Act and the Preservation of the Public Security Act had stood threateningly over the head of every Kenyan; these two notorious Acts had taken away all the human rights of Kenyans even the ones mentioned in the same flawed constitution.

The Spokesperson goes on to give the reasons for the formation of the underground movement:

It is these conditions that made us go underground in mid-Seventies under the umbrella of the December Twelve Movement. These conditions have not changed at all. We in MWAKENYA have been fighting for the thorough democratisation of the Kenya society and not just for the removal of Clause 2A; and we shall continue to do so until democracy becomes a way of life in our country. The right to organise - and organisation does not just mean political parties - is a human right and not a privilege. So is the right to choose.

Thus at the end of the period covered in this book there has been some progress in that political parties can now be registered and take part in elections. But as Mwakenya's statement above says, the conditions have not changed fundamentally. As events were to show, corruption and violence at the time of elections have become entrenched and inequality has increased even more. And as the conditions for working people get worse, resistance also continues. And the struggle for liberation continues.

Illustrations 4: Underground & Overseas Resistance

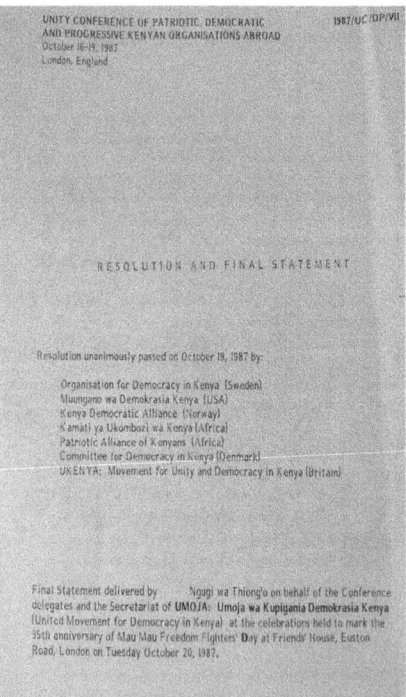

THE ODK DECLARATION

WE OPPOSE THE DESPOTIC MOI-KANU REGIME

Issued by:
THE ORGANISATION FOR DEMOCRACY IN KENYA (Sweden)
24th of May 1986, Stockholm, Sweden

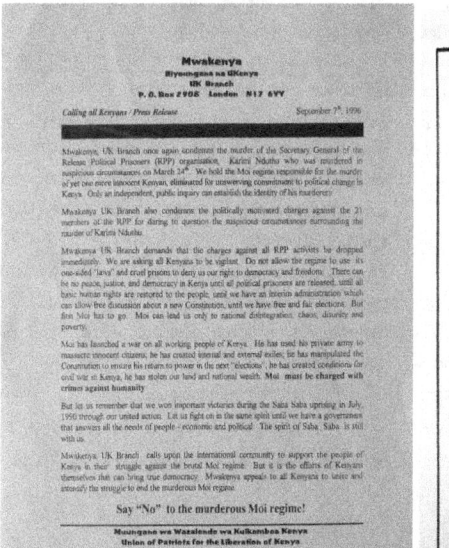

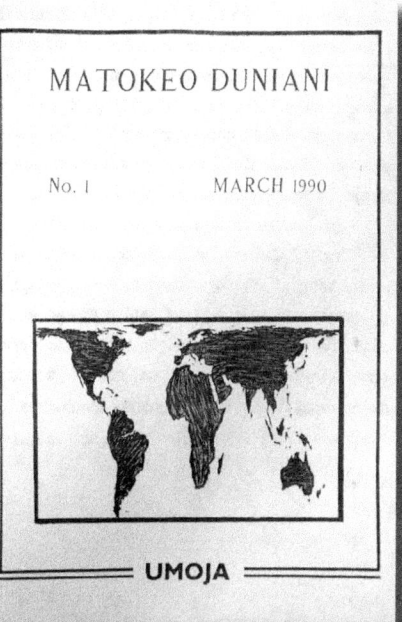

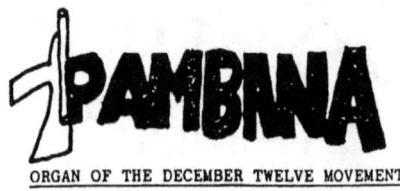

ORGAN OF THE DECEMBER TWELVE MOVEMENT

MEI/MAY 1982   Na./No. 1

MSIMAMO WETU

Wakenya tumehainiwa, na mapinduzi tuliyoyamwagia damu nyingi ili kuikomboa inchi yetu sasa yamepotoshwa na kunajisiwa.

Leo, baada ya miaka 22 tangu chama cha KANU kiundwe, na miaka 20 tangu tudanganywe kwa uhuru uongo, hali ya maisha yetu imezoroteka kabisa kabisa. Hawa viongozi wetu majambazi wamelitupilia mbali jukumu lao la kuyaongoza maisha yetu na wametutendea jinai kubwa hata kuliko ile ya wakoloni: wametunyamazisha kwa nguvu, na wametupokonya haki yetu ya kushiriki katika harakati za taifa letu. Haki zetu za kujieleza, za kusema tunalotaka, za kukutana tunapotaka zote zimetupwa jaani.

KANU na serikali yake wameuchafua uchumi wetu, wameufuja ushirikiano wetu, wameleta mafarakano baina yetu huku wakituibia na kurundika pesa nyingi na miliki ya taifa. Wamewapa wabeberu inchi yetu ili waifanye chombo cha siasa zao za kutudhulumu na kambi ya majeshi yao ya kutunyanyasa. Na hatia hizi zote za jinai zimetendwa eti kwa jina la "maendeleo" na porojo la Nyayo la "mapenzi, amani na umoja".

Huu, ndugu zetu SI uhuru.

Huu ni ubeberu, ukoloni mambo-leo wa hali mbovu kabisa. Wakenya wamepigana vita vingi hapo zamani ili waitoe Kenya katika utumwa wa aina hii. Hawakupigana ili maisha yao yazidi kuzoroteka! Kweli tulifanya makosa, makosa ya kutowang'oa wasaliti kati yetu, makosa makubwa ya kuwaacha vibaraka vya wakoloni kuungana na kutu-

OUR STAND

Kenyans have been massively betrayed. The revolution we launched with blood has been arrested and derailed.

Today, more than 22 years after KANU was formed and almost 20 years after a fake independence was negotiated, the broad masses of Kenya are materially and politically worse off than ever before. The criminally corrupt ruling clique, sanctioned by KANU has isolated itself from the concerns of our daily life and has committed a crime among many others, more brutal than any that British colonialism ever did: they have silenced all opposition and deprived us, forcibly and otherwise, of the very right to participate in Kenya's national affairs. The sacred rights of expression and association have been cast aside.

KANU and its government have disorganized all spheres of economic production, have scattered all communal efforts at organization, have sowed unprincipled discord and enmity among our peoples, and have looted unspeakable sums of money and national wealth. They have finally given our entire country over to U.S. imperialism to use as a political and military base. All these crimes have been wrought in the name of "progress and prosperity" and ina smatterings of "love, peace and unity".

This is NOT independence.

This is neo-colonialism in its worst for Kenyans have fought many battles in order

■ COVER STORY MOMENT OF TRUTH

MWAKENYA'S STAND

In this exclusive interview, Ngugi wa Thiong'o, the Spokesperson for MWAKENYA (Union of Patriots for the Liberation of Kenya) which has been operating underground, since 1970s sets his movement's position on the current political changes in Kenya

Since the Kenya government has now allowed opposition parties to be registered, and some changes have taken place, what is MWAKENYA's position?

MWAKENYA welcomes any democratic gains by the Kenyan people. But the mere removal of Clause 2A (which made Kenya a one-party state) from the Kenya constitution does not mean that anything has changed in Kenya fundamentally. Political repression did not begin in 1982 with the legalisation of the one-party state. Even before 1982, political parties were still not allowed to function although Kenya was legally a multi-party state. Students Organisations, the Academic Staff Union, the Civil Servants Union, the Kamiriithu Community Education and Cultural Centre; and social welfare organisations, had been outlawed. Workers organisations were not allowed to function freely. More than five people could not meet without police licence even if they were meeting for a family tea party or for a funeral. And above all the Chief's Act and the Preservation of the Public Security Act had stood threateningly over the head of every Kenyan; these two notorious Acts had taken away all the human rights of Kenyans even the ones mentioned in the same flawed constitution.

It is these conditions that made us go underground in mid-Seventies under the umbrella of the December Twelve Movement. These conditions have not changed at all. We in MWAKENYA have been fighting for the thorough democratisation of the Kenya society and not just for the removal of Clause 2A; and we shall continue to do so until democracy becomes a way of life in our country. The right to organise - and organisation does not just mean political parties - is a human right and not a privilege. So is the right to choose.

But don't you accept that there is marked change now compared to what has been happening in the past, especially from 1982, when no opposition was entertained by the government?

Of course the situation has changed. The culture of silence and fear under Moi's Reign of Terror has been broken. Kenyan people are now more out-spoken. What used to be voiced underground is being shouted from mountain tops, so to speak. The removal of Clause 2A is an outcome of the Kenya people's rejection of that culture of silence and fear. In that sense, the removal of that Clause and whatever democratic gains are a victory to all those who have been struggling internally and externally over the years.

We in MWAKENYA, and our predecessor, The December Twelve Movement, and with our allied organisations like the Committee for the Release of Political Prionsers in Kenya formed in London on July 2, 1982; and also the externally-based Umoja-Kenya (Umoja wa Kupigania Demokrasia Kenya - The United Movement for Democracy in Kenya) are proud to have been at the forefront of this struggle by the democratic forces to defy and finally break the culture of silence and fear; and to sensitise the International Community to the repressive character of the Moi-Kanu regime.

But despite this we must not let the present euphoria make us forget the fact that Moi and KANU, who have all along been part of the problem, are still controlling the State.

So does it mean that MWAKENYA will not participate in the democratization process, at least legalize itself by seeking registration so that it can operate above ground?

In our statement of January 8, 1992 titled "Moism Without Moi is as Dangerous as Moism With Moi" we have stated that under the prevailing circumstances we are not going to seek registration.

Why not?

There are a number of reasons. When - what we called the fraudulent - queueing elections of 1988 were held, MWAKENYA and its allied organisation, Umoja-Kenya, issued a 10 point declaration rejecting the legitimacy of the outcome. The results of the elections were the same thing as a *coup d'etat* by Moi and his cohorts. We then called for the right to organise, to choose and to have multi-party elections under conditions that would guarantee fairness and freedom. We still stand by that declaration. We believe that Moi and KANU have not the slightest political or moral legitimacy. Kenya is being ruled by an illegal president, an illegal parliament and an illegal political party. So the official position is that MWAKENYA has not the slightest intention of seeking registration under the Moi-KANU re-

Kenyan riot police armed with batons move to clear demonstrators off the streets of Nairobi after President Moi banned a pro-democracy rally *Photograph: Sayyid Azim/AP*

THE LAND & FREEDOM ARMY,
KENYA PARLIAMENT,
NYANDARWA,
KENYA
4th April, 1955

The longer the emergency the poorer the country becomes both Kenya and England and the more the enmity and hatred grows strong, and worse still the British Empire will be blamed by the world for its injustice.

In Kenya there has been an average death rate of a hundred persons daily since the declaration of the emergency. The death has been due to weapons, starvation, & treatment which are organised by the Kenya Government.

Who will pay all this cost? Definitely the British Empire which has appointed and supervised the Kenya Government is responsible for the cost.

There is no other peace or settlement of Kenya troubles except:— WIYATHI, UHURU, FREEDOM, of self-government to the Kenya Africans.

Kenya's War of Independence

PAMBANA

ORGAN OF THE DECEMBER TWELVE MOVEMENT

JULY 1983   No. 2

From the first issue of PAMBANA...

1. Firmly opposes the robbery of our national resources and wealth by imperialist interests be they multinational corporations, banks or foreign governments. Kenya's wealth and labour must benefit Kenyans only.
2. Condemns in the strongest of terms the criminally corrupt and traitorous band of thieves who govern this country and who have allied themselves with US imperialism to keep us perpetually down.
3. Is totally opposed to the presence on Kenyan soil of US and any other military bases.
4. Supports all genuine, democratic and liberation movements fighting for people's self-determination in and outside Kenya.

KENYA: THE STRUGGLE CONTINUES

EDITORIAL

PAMBANA STANDS FOR UNITY

When the first issue of PAMBANA came out in May 1982, the people of Kenya and all freedom-loving people of the world received it with great joy. It filled Kenyans with hope and great expectations. It made them see that it was possible to change the prevailing oppressive conditions and create a better life for all Kenyans. This is what they had always looked forward to—an organ which would unite the poor and the exploited against the Kenyan ruling class and their foreign masters. Such a unity is what PAMBANA stands for.

PAMBANA united the poor and all those who love freedom and democracy; it united the workers and peasants all over Kenya; it united all the patriots in the civil service, the police and the army; it united students, teachers, lawyers, journalists, doctors, nurses, secretaries, mechanics, shop assistants and other workers. They all hailed PAMBANA's call for a relentless struggle against imperialism.

KANU IN THE SERVICE OF EURO-AMERICAN IMPERIALISM

Here in Kenya, the oppression of people is systematically done on behalf of Euro-American imperialists by the KANU-led ruling class. The imperialists milk our country dry while their watchdogs, the KANU-led regime rule over us like gods. These "gods" felt threatened by the unity and consciousness created by PAMBANA. They responded by detentions without trial, imprisonment on trumped-up charges and indiscriminate torture of Kenyans. Anyone who dared to speak for democracy and constitutional rights was thrown into detention. Journalists, teachers, lawyers, workers, students, peasants were harassed mercilessly. They underwent brutal police interrogations. They were put into custody and prison because they dared to demand their democratic rights; they dared oppose a one-party dictatorship; and what is more they dared oppose the granting of military bases to the United States of America.

The Kenyan comprador ruling clique cunningly exploited the attempted coup of August 1, 1982 to kill thousands of innocent people, especially our young patriotic Kenyans, and to cow people into accepting the regime's murderous rule. The regime used the occasion to silence the voices of patriotic youth who sincerely believed in changes that would lead to democracy and socialism.

For three continuous months (August, September and October 1982), the ruling clique and their army used guns to instil fear amongst the people. Moi's soldiers raped our women; robbed Kenyan peasants and workers of their property; snatched clothes, shoes, watches and radios from people travelling in 'matatus'; went into people's homes and took anything they wanted from innocent and unarmed people. They took the little that the workers had saved through sweat and blood. Thus the army clearly showed they were the enemy of the people. They behaved like the U.S. soldiers in Vietnam; the elders said that they behaved like the colonial British 'johnies' during the British-imposed State of Emergency. The army, trained and groomed by the Americans and the British, was mercilessly used against the people. We are totally opposed to these murderous brutes, going under the name of Kenya Armed Forces. We oppose an army which guards the property of foreign capitalists and their comprador agents. But these soldiers are children of peasants and workers, and so when they use force against the people of their own class, it is like raping their own mothers.

There is no difference between the leaders of KANU and the leaders of neo-colonial regimes like Chile, El Salvador, Guatemala, Honduras, Indonesia, Philippines, Pakistan, etc. These countries have military comprador regimes created by US imperialists to perpetuate the exploitation of workers and rob the wealth of these countries. In these countries, the struggle of

The harassment and the torture against us by the Moi-Mulinge regime

peasants and workers to bring about democracy and socialism has reached a high stage. These people will surely defeat the fascist foreign-supported regimes as the peoples of Vietnam, Kampuchea and Nicaragua have done.

On August 1, 1982 the people of Kenya expressed their deep-rooted desire to change their condition of daily oppression by their attitude to the coup attempt. Thousands of people all over the country celebrated the announcement of the coup because it showed that it was possible to become free from oppression by the police, the administration, city council 'askaris', and the whole government machinery administered by corrupt and unpatriotic government officials; that it was possible to free themselves from the oppression of foreign lawyers, and some Kenyan lawyers too, who are the willing tools of the 'mbwa kali' class. For thousands of hungry and unemployed, any change that would modify the prevailing conditions was welcome. This explains their enthusiastic reception of the news of the August 1 attempted coup.

MILITARY-BACKED KANU REGIME INTENSIFIES REPRESSION

The KANU government, with its army, attacked and tortured unarmed people. Thus the government and the comprador-ruling class, exposed their true face as the enemy of the people. The authoritarian regime of Moi must repress all opposition with brutal force. How shall we ever forget the threats, the harassment and the torture against us by the Moi-Mulinge regime in 1982?

The military-backed KANU regime has continued the oppression, this time under the guise of defending and upholding the constitution. Yet most Kenyans know the regime has no respect even for its own laws and constitution as shown by the kangaroo military courts, the students' show trials and many political jailings and detentions. Biased judgements against workers in trade union disputes with foreign-owned companies are the order of the day, while cases of corruption involving directors, managers, and senior civil servants are often dropped. Foreign judges (Europeans, US and British Asian) are highly-paid rubber stamps. Unpatriotic Kenyan (African & Asian)

330   *Kenya's War of Independence*

THE POLITICS OF FOOD

For many years now, in newspapers and radio, we have been fed with government propaganda and that of World Bank or other foreign 'experts' that food shortages are a normal state of affairs in our country. They say that there is not sufficient arable land in Kenya. They tell us that our population is too high and is rapidly increasing and therefore not everyone can be fed. They tell us that we do not have enough Kenyan expertise. They tell us that capitalist agricultural production is the only type of agriculture possible.

These are brazen lies spread by imperialists and their agents so that they can continue exploiting our country. The production process and the distribution of wealth is done in a way which enables the imperialists to make high profits. For a capitalist maximising profits is the overriding concern. The aim is to invest as little as possible and with as little risk for the highest possible returns. A capitalist even makes profits from our misery. When the capitalist is a foreigner as is the case in our country, this means the continuous drainage of our wealth to foreign countries, thus making our country poorer and poorer as theirs become richer and richer.

We must therefore know and understand that there are other systems of agricultural production which would enable us to produce more food, sufficient for everyone and even have a surplus. There is no doubt this is possible. It has happened in other countries which have dared to throw out imperialists and have afterwards adopted a system of agricultural production that puts people's basic food requirements first. Let us have a look at some of these countries.

CHINA

We can learn a lot from China. When China was dominated by imperialists from Britain and the USA, famine was endemic. It is only after 1949, that is after their victorious war against local and foreign domination, that Chinese people were able to make plans related to their own lives. In agriculture, for instance, the peasants were given land to grow food crops for their own consumption instead of cash crops for export. Science and technology were used to solve land problems like soil erosion, flooding or water shortages. Bridges and canals were built in addition to dams for storing water for irrigation during the dry season. Instead of importing expensive gadgets they developed appropriate machinery for the needs of their country and people. Thus within a few years of ousting imperialism China managed to do away with hunger. Today, China is able to feed all its 1,000 million people.

In short, it is only when a country uses all the knowledge available to serve and meet the needs of its people that it is able to satisfy people's basic needs like food. But this is only possible when imperialist foreigners have been driven out of the country.

CUBA

Cuban history is similar to that of China. When Cuba was dominated by US imperialism, starvation among the working people was chronic. Under Batista's puppet regime, Cuba had become a paradise for millionaire playboys from the USA. It was only after the overthrow of the Batista regime in 1959 and the throwing out of US imperialists, that Cuba was able to solve food problems for the working people. For the first time, it became possible for Cuba to use agricultural knowledge to satisfy the people's needs instead of producing for the benefit of markets abroad. For example, before 1959 very few Cubans were able to eat fish although Cuba is a fishing country with over 5,000 km of coastline. Fish was very expensive and only rich Cubans, tourists and other foreign visitors could afford it. This anomalous situation changed after 1959. The lives of fishermen changed for the better. Better fishing methods were developed even as fishing increased. At the same time, fish prices came down and many people were able to afford it. Today, fish is a cheap but nutritious protein-rich food available in ordinary Cuban homes. It is no longer the preserve of the rich. As a result, hunger and food related diseases have been eliminated among the ordinary people in that country.

NICARAGUA

Before the people of Nicaragua, under the leadership of the Frente Sandinista de Liberacion National (FSLN), the Sandinistas, liberated themselves from neo-colonialism and US-imperialism, over 40% of the land was owned by only 2% of the population plus a few rich foreign land owners. The peasants were squeezed on to only 3.5% of cultivable farmland, while the Somoza family and their close associates owned more than 2.5 million acres. Nicaragua was ruled by the US-supported Somoza dynasty, one of the most corrupt and hated dictatorships in Central America. Most workers and peasants lived in hunger.

After 1979 when the Somoza puppet regime was overthrown through the Sandinista led armed struggle, people's democracy was introduced and agricultural production was put on a new footing. Land was confiscated from the corrupt and rich land owners and their foreign associates without compensation and restored to the people or brought under state control. Food production rose and after only a short time, the Nicaraguans became self-sufficient in food; peasants were able to feed themselves properly, and the surplus was sold cheaply to other Nicaraguans and so food consumption rose by 40%. They were even able to export some of the surplus. A healthy well-fed population is the basis for development.

NORTH KOREA

Since North Koreans defeated imperialism and snatched back their independence, agricultural development progressed in leaps and bounds. Before 1959, total grain production was less than 2 million tons yearly. By 1979, it had reached over 9 million tons per annum with an expected increase to 15 million tons within the next few years. In the 70s, agricultural production grew by 30% every year. In 1974, one hectare produced about 6 tons of rice and 5 tons of maize. By 1980, this production had increased to 7.2 tons of rice and 6.3 tons of maize per hectare. This is only possible because in North Korea it is the people themselves who are responsible for their agricultural production (unlike in the US-controlled South Korea, where a few compradors and their US-backers control agricultural production). The food produced in North Korea is used to feed the people (unlike in South Korea where poverty and hunger reign amidst an overfed super-rich US-backed oligarchy).

LESSONS FOR KENYANS

These few examples of a system of agricultural production based on people's needs show clearly that food shortages are not caused by the lack of knowledge, or the size of the population or even indeed the size of arable land. It is caused by the system of land ownership and of capitalist export- and profit-orientated agricultural production pursued by the get-rich-quick comprador class and their foreign backers.

These examples teach us that in order to make agricultural production meet and satisfy the people's needs, we must first snatch back our economic and political independence from the imperialist foreigners.

Only after getting rid of imperialist-backed oppression, shall we be able to take new directions in food production:

1. Productive land must be in the hands of the masses;

2. The people must be responsible for the production and distribution of food;

3. Production of food crops and not cash crops must be given priority;

4. Food should feed Kenyan people first before it is exported. Feeding people is more important than earning foreign exchange for importing BMWs, Volvos, Mercedes Benzs and other luxury items.

China, Cuba, Nicaragua, North Korea and many other socialist countries have banished hunger and starvation by adopting a different path of development. But in Kenya, despite the fact that we have some of the best agricultural land in the world, many poor people still suffer from hunger, malnutrition and as in the case of northern Kenya, from mass starvation. The majority of our people go hungry in a country where the weight-reducing industry (massage-parlours, hormone-injections, weight-reducing clinics, saunas, etc.) for the overfed few is thriving.

In Kenya, imperialist foreigners and a few rich come first, but in Cuba, China, Nicaragua and North Korea, the peasants and working people come first. In these countries, the people had to wage an armed struggle to free themselves from the stranglehold of imperialist-backed oppression before they could be responsible for their own food production. A relentless struggle against the alliance of the comprador mbwa-kali ruling class and Euro-American imperialism is the only way we Kenyans can use the wealth of our country to satisfy our own needs and banish hunger. The defeat of imperialism in its neo-colonial stage is a necessary first-step for our development as a Kenyan people.

> **From the first issue of PAMBANA . . .**
>
> This newspaper supports all genuine Kenyan organisations and individuals, fighting any aspect of local or imperialist reaction and in particular:
> 1. Small farmers and producers against government and 'co-operative' theft and mismanagement;
> 2. Workers against IMF-enforced low wages and anti-strike controls;
> 3. The millions of unemployed in their right to employment;
> 4. Small businessmen against foreign monopolies;
> 5. Indigenous professionals against fake expatriate 'skills';
> 6. Teachers, students and pupils against irrelevant, authoritarian colonial education;
> 7. Committed intellectuals and journalists against official muzzling;
> 8. The poor and the landless in their demands for land reform;
> 9. All poor people against ever-increasing rents, prices and declining real incomes;
> 10. The entire dispossessed population against a corrupt puppet government and its ever-repressive police rule.

> *This is a translation from Kiswahili of the underground newspaper Pambana.*

Enough food for their own consumption is produced by this collective farm in Leon, Nicaragua.

Kenya's War of Independence

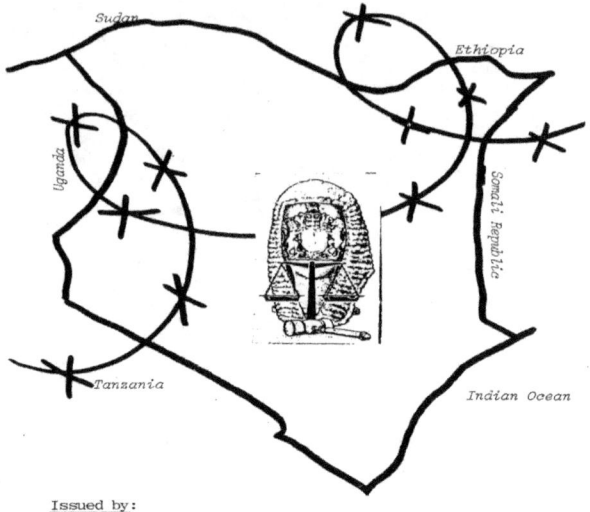

SIX LESSONS FROM THE LIFE OF A PATRIOT

Field Marshal Dedan Kimathi was born in Gatanga sub-location, Tetu Division Nyeri, on October 31, 1920. That was also the year when Kenya was declared a British colony after being ruled as a British protectorate and as a company property from 1888. Colonial rule against the people was imposed through the coercive machinery of the law, the army, and the police. People were forced to leave their land to become serfs and squatters in the big farms stolen from them by foreigners and to become wage slaves in the new capitalist industries and plantations. The people of Kenya united in their opposition to every form of British colonial oppression.

Kimathi grew up under these conditions of brutal colonial aggression on one hand and the resistance of the people against it on the other. He sided with the forces of resistance. His life is a lesson to us today as we struggle against neo-colonialism. Every revolutionary Kenyan must learn from his life.

1. As a student, Kimathi organised night classes in which he passed on to the youth all he himself had learned during the day. In those days, not all young people were able to attend school. Because of teaching others, Kimathi became an example to be followed. He became a selfless agent for the spread of education among workers and peasants.
The life of a revolutionary must be an inspiration to others. A revolutionary must be prepared to educate the people politically and also learn from them.

2. In colonial schools, and even in his brief period in the colonial army, Kimathi courageously organised against brutality and tirelessly tried to raise the people's consciousness about the need for unity against oppression.
Fighting against oppression is the duty and responsibility of every patriotic Kenyan.

3. Even as a clerk and as a teacher, he continued fighting oppression and organising the people. Very often he found himself in trouble with his employers. He was forced to change jobs many times.
Patriotism demands sacrifice even if it means giving up one's job and a comfortable family life. Revolutionary struggle is a life-time commitment.

4. He joined the Kenya African Union (KAU) which was then the democratic organisation of Kenyan people. He spoke out against colonialism. He was not afraid to show his real feelings of hatred of oppression. He knew he was fighting for justice.
A patriot must be imbued with hatred of all forms of oppression.

5. He volunteered to work as a political education teacher for KAU. He was later elected the General Secretary of the Murang'a branch of this organisation. He worked hard day and night. No task was too big or too small.
For a revolutionary no task is too menial or too big. A revolutionary must be prepared to work hard day and night. The revolution is not a tea-party.

6. Kimathi started his revolutionary struggle in his home area before he was given higher responsibility at the national level as a member of the KLFA (Mau Mau) High Command and later as the Commander-in-Chief of the KLFA. All revolutionary work starts at home or wherever one is.
If you cannot struggle against oppression wherever you are you will not gain the necessary experience for participating in and explaining our national revolutionary struggle. A revolution starts with you wherever you are.

KENYA NEWS
BULLETIN OF THE COMMITTEE FOR THE RELEASE OF POLITICAL PRISONERS IN KENYA

STOP THIS MASSACRE

KENYA NEWS
BULLETIN OF THE COMMITTEE FOR THE RELEASE OF POLITICAL PRISONERS IN KENYA

SUNDAY BLOODY SUNDAY

Kenya's War of Independence

The struggle continues: Police dispersing Kenyans who were protesting through hunger strike in Uhuru Park (Freedom Corner) in March 1992 – calling for the release of political prisoners. (Photo: Khamis Ramadhan, Nairobi).

Conclusion: *Uhuru Bado* [62]

> "General, your tank is a powerful vehicle
> It smashes down forests and crushes a hundred men.
> But it has one defect:
> It needs a driver.
>
> General, your bomber is powerful.
> It flies faster than a storm and carries more than an elephant.
> But it has one defect:
> It needs a mechanic.
>
> General, man is very useful.
> He can fly and he can kill.
> But he has one defect:
> He can think."
> — Bertolt Brecht

The history of Kenya parallels trends in many other countries, in Africa and elsewhere. The colonial government passes on power to a class it has created and nurtured and which ultimately rejects the interests of people who had borne the brunt of fighting colonialism. They have been relegated to the margins of the society by the new comprador class. There is a show-democracy underpinned by a number of political parties, but all serving the interest of the ruling classes on whose behalf they manage economic and political power. People are expected to believe that a change of parties at the so-called democratic elections will help their cause. This is a major mistake if followed. The crucial dividing line between the contending forces in Kenya is between those seeking "merely political change" and those who are seeking social transformation, as Furedy (1989) points out:

---

62 Kiswahili: *Uhuru*: Independence; Bado: "Not [achieved] Yet".

The danger of obscuring the conflict of interest between those whose objective is merely political change and those who aspire to social transformation is a theme stressed in the writings of Marx, Engels and Lenin. The experience of Uhuru in Kenya and more broadly in Africa and the calls for a 'Second Independence' from radical quarters confirm the continued relevance of Marx's observations.

The key issues of which class is in power and on whose behalf it rules is obscured by propaganda from the ruling classes. The contradiction between Homeguards and Mau Mau can be seen as the former looking for political change while the latter demanded social transformation. That contradiction has not yet been resolved. If the workers' forces are to continue the legacy of Mau Mau and fight for social transformation today, they will need to free themselves from the ideological and historical blinkers that imperialism has created for them. Liberating their minds from colonial and imperialist thinking entails recognising class struggles as the key reality in Kenya, before and after independence. Quoting Marx and Engels, Furedi (1989), warns of the danger that faces the working classes and people:

Marxist literature, with its emphasis on the primacy of class interests, anticipates the problem of alliances between different social forces fighting for national liberation. Marx and Engels warned about the fragile links that drew together conflicting interests around the struggle for freedom. In their writings they continually emphasized that it is often the propertyless masses that do all the fighting while the rich stand on the sidelines waiting to snatch the fruits of their victory:

> It is self-evident that in the impending bloody conflicts, as in all earlier ones, it is the workers who, in the main will have to win the victory by their courage, determination and self-sacrifice. As previously so also in this struggle, the mass of the petty bourgeois will as long as possible remain hesitant, undecided and inactive, and then, as soon as the issue has been decided, will seize the victory for themselves, will call upon the workers to maintain tranquility and return to their work, will guard against so-called excesses and bar the proletariat from the fruits of victory. [Marx, K. and Engels, F. (1978), 'Address to the Central Authority of the League', in Marx and Engels: Collected Works, vol. 10, 1978].[63]

---

63 Marx and Engles, writing in 1850, have some relevant points to make about the

The danger of obscuring the conflict of interest between those whose objective is merely political change and those who aspire to social transformation is a theme stressed in the writings of Marx, Engels and Lenin. The experience of Uhuru in Kenya and more broadly in Africa and the calls for a 'Second Independence' from radical quarters confirm the continued relevance of Marx's observations.

The elections of 2017 have raised once again the question of what is the main contradiction in Kenya. The power-struggles between political parties broadly representing the interest of ruling classes are creating an illusion that they are fighting for all the people of Kenya. In the process, they are creating more divisions along nationality (the so-called tribes) lines, while obscuring class struggle. This strengthens the hold of capitalism and its corporations over Kenya and marginalises once again working people. Mutunga (2017) sums up the current situation in Kenya:

> The Kenyan elite, like many in Africa, has not identified or supported our national interests. They do not represent us patriotically in national relations with either the West or the East, preferring to build their own personal power bases among foreign interests, national and international cartels (invariably called the licit and illicit economies, and rightly deemed "invisible government" that we NEVER elected.
>
> By keeping us divided the Kenyan elite have been able to stay in power by violating our material needs at every turn. And, the invisible governments keep applauding, putting profits before us, the people.
>
> Competition for political power has become an industry for the elite. Within the national strategic plans and visions lurk personal plans and visions of the elite on how profits will be made, resources raided, wasted, pillaged, and grabbed, so billions are generated so they can buy the next election.
>
> The bottom line is - This status quo MUST GO!

And that is the struggle facing people in Kenya today. The status quo will not disappear on its own. It has too many powerful vested interests, local and foreign. It will need to be pushed out, just as Mau

---

situation in Kenya today. For this reason, a fuller version of the above quote is reproduced in Appendix .

Mau pushed out colonialists.

*

This brief look at resistance activities in and outside Kenya indicates that resistance in Kenya has indeed become a way of life. While this brings this book to a close, the resistance continues in Kenya with many notable victories in changes to the Constitution and the freedom to form political parties. However, Mwakenya's warning about *Moism With Moi* has indeed come true as new political parties and leaders emerge but the system that created the unequal, oppressive capitalist system remains in place, again supported by USA and Britain with additional support from one of imperialism's most oppressive ally, the Israeli apartheid state. But as history shows, resistance is always present where there is oppression and exploitation. The War of Kenya's Independence has achieved its early goal of independence from British colonialism. But its other goal of independence from economic and political bondage to imperialism is an on-going process that still has some way to go.

Kabubi's (2002) assessment of the legacy of Mau Mau provides a path for the future:

> Mau Mau hastened Uhuru. If not for Mau Mau fighters, the colonialists would have stayed longer. There should be full official recognition of Mau Mau fighters after independence. There should be a Mau Mau museum and monuments. How can the younger generation be taught when Mau Mau's legacy is not preserved? The history of Mau Mau should be collected and records should be properly kept and relevant materials should be published. Only then will people appreciate what Mau Mau did for Kenya.

The comprador government and leaders of Kenya are not likely to follow this path, just as they are not prepared to follow Algeria's example in condemning colonialism. It remains for the people themselves to ensure that the voice of Mau Mau guerrillas and leaders, their actions and their vision are never forgotten and that they guide the direction of future government actions. They are the real foundations of Kenya's history and its future.

The history of Kenya, particularly in the independence period, shows the need for resistance parties and movements to come up with a clear ideological stand and have a vision that can inspire working people to stand up and fight for their rights. Mau Mau came up with a clear programme under the call for "land and freedom" which were the burning issues of the time. Equality and fairness were part of the demands of Mau Mau, as symbolised by Kimathi. Pio Gama Pinto articulated Mau Mau demands in the early years of independence. Militant trade unionists like Makhan Singh, Fred Kubai and Bildad Kaggia and others put Mau Mau's vision into practice. Oginga Odinga was victimised for his call for socialism and J. M. Kariuki was murdered for his call to avoid a country with ten millionaires and 10 million beggars. He, among others, advocated a fair land policy.

In the independence period, once Kenya Peoples Union was banned by the comprador regime, it was the underground movements that came out with radical policies and programmes to oppose the conservative ones from KANU, which sought to disguise capitalism under the so-called "African Socialism" agenda as a way of maintaining the status quo. The December Twelve Movement - Mwakenya, among other underground movements, stood for socialism based on Marxist principles, an anti-imperialist outlook and showed a grasp of the nature of the class struggle in the country.

In contrast, the unstated policies of the main political parties in Kenya today are to protect the interest of capitalism and imperialism through an alliance of local elites and their international partners - the multinational corporations, under the watchful "guidance" of the International Monetary Fund (IMF), World Bank and World Trade Organisation (WTO). State power in Kenya - as in other capitalist countries - is used to support this exploitative alliance at the expense of working people. Liberation movements in Kenya and in Africa would do well to base their policies on the three principles that are essential for real liberation from capitalism and imperialism: socialism, anti-imperialism and an alliance with working people in the all important class struggle.

There can be no better way to understand Kenya's past and to prepare for future battles of liberation than to study Pio Gama Pinto's analysis (Pinto, 1963a) at the time of independence, but which is even more relevant today:

Kenya's Uhuru must not be transformed into freedom to exploit, or freedom to be hungry and live in ignorance. Uhuru must be Uhuru for the masses -

uhuru from exploitation, from ignorance, disease and poverty.

The sacrifices of the hundreds of thousands of Kenya's freedom fighters must be honoured by the effective implementation of the policy - a democratic, African, socialist state in which the people have the right to be free from economic exploitation and the right to social equality. Kenya's uhuru must not be transformed into freedom to exploit, or freedom to be hungry and live in ignorance. Uhuru must be uhuru for the masses - uhuru from exploitation, from ignorance, disease and poverty.

Events have shown, however, that the aims of the uhuru that Pinto and others died for have not been met even after 50 years of independence. Barnett's (1972) assessment is even more urgent today:

> The story of "Mau Mau", Kenya's peasant revolt of 1952-56, as well as its aftermath in the years leading up to and following the "granting" of independence to this British colony, should be studied carefully for the lessons that can be learned from such bitter failures. Political independence without genuine decolonization and socialism yields continued misery and oppression for the peasant-worker masses. Karigo's prayer, as with those of other peasants and workers caught up in the web of neo-colonial accommodation after long years of struggle, will not be answered. His and their children will be forced to fight again.

It is hoped that this book can play a small part in enabling "peasant-worker masses", young and old, to learn and understand the lessons from the "bitter failures" that capitalism and imperialism inflicted on working people with the active assistance of their local allies. For them and for Kenya, the future is struggle.

References & Bibliography

Aaronovitch, S. And K. (1947): Crisis in Kenya. London: Lawrence & Wishart.

Abdalla, Abdilatif (1989). Personal communication, London. *Kenya Twendapi? (Where are we heading in Kenya?)*.

Adekson, J. 'Bayo (2007): The Algerian and Mau Mau revolts: A Comparative Study in Revolutionary Warfare. *Comparative Strategy*. Vol. 3 (1) pp. 69-92.

Africa Events (1990a): " Countdown to Freedom" (Cover story). Vol. 6 (8-9) August-September.

Africa Events (1990b): *Roots of the Revolt*. 6 (8-9) August-September..

Aiyar, Sana (2015): Indians in Kenya: the Politics of Diaspora. Cambridge, Mass.: Harvard University Press.

Alam, S.M. Shamsul (2007): Rethinking Mau Mau in Colonial Kenya. New York, Palgrave Macmillan.

Alam, S. M. Shamsul and Gachihi, Margaret (2007): Women and Mau Mau. Chapter in Alam, S.M.S.(2007).

Amnesty International (1988): Kenya: Torture, Political Detention and Unfair Trials. July, 1987 (Update issued in 1988). London: AI.

Anderson, David (2005a): Histories of the Hanged, Britain's Dirty War in Kenya and the End of Empire. London: Weidenfeld & Nicolson, 2005.

Anderson, David M (2005b): Truly inglorious end to Britain's 'dark, gritty and nasty' days of Empire in Kenya. Available at https://www.timeshighereducation.com/features/truly-inglorious-end-to-britains-dark-gritty-and-nasty-days-of-empire-in-kenya/194044.article [Accessed: 08-08-17]

Anderson, David M. (2016): Making the Loyalist Bargain: Surrender, Amnesty and Impunity in Kenya's Decolonization, 1952–63. *The International History Review.* pp. 48-70. Published online: 19 Sep 2016. Available at: http://www.tandfonline.com/doi/full/10.1080/07075332.2016.1230769 [Accessed: 09-06-17].

Angelo, Anaïs (2017): Jomo Kenyatta and the repression of the 'last' Mau Mau leaders, 1961–1965. *Journal of Eastern African Studies.* Vol.11, No. 3, pp.442-459.

Barber, Noel (2004): The War of the Running Dogs: How Malaya Defeated the Communist Guerrillas, 1948-60. London: Cassell.

Barnett, Donald L. and Njama, Karari (1966): Mau Mau from Within: Autobiography and Analysis of Kenya's Peasant Revolt. New York: Monthly Review Press.

Barnett, Donald L. (1972): "Kenya: two paths ahead". Introduction to Muchai (1973).

Barnett, Donald (1973): Introduction to Kabiro (1973).

Barton, Frank. (1979): The Press in Africa: Persecution and Perseverance". New York: Africana Publication Co.

Bolsover, Philip (1953): Kenya: What Are the Facts? London: The Communist Party.

Brecht, Bertolt (1935): Questions From a Worker Who Reads. Available at: https://www.marxists.org/subject/art/literature/brecht/ [Accessed: 01-06-17].

Brockway, Fenner (1953): Why Mau Mau? An Analysis and a Remedy. London: Congress of Peoples Against Imperialism.

Brogan, B. (2005, January 15). It's time to celebrate the Empire, says Brown. *Mailonline*. Available at: www.dailymail.co.uk/news/article-334208/Its-time-celebrate-Empire-says-Brown.html [Accessed:13-11-16].

Bruce-Lockhart, Katherine (2014): "Unsound" minds and broken bodies: the detention of "hardcore" Mau Mau women at Kamiti and Gitamayu Detention Camps in Kenya, 1954–1960Bufacchi, Vittorio (2017): Colonialism, Injustice And Arbitrariness. *Journal of Social Philosophy*. Volume 48 (2) 117–237.

Bufacchi, Vittorio (2017): Colonialism, Injustice and Arbitrariness. *Journal of Eastern African Studies* Vol. 8 (4).

Chandan, Amarjit (2015): What Makhan Singh Means to Me. *In*: Durrani, S. (2015b).

Cheche Kenya (1981): *Cheche Kenya: Independent Kenya* (1981). Cheche Kenya. Reissued by Zed Press, London. 1982. "Sponsored by the *Journal of African Marxist* in solidarity with the authors".

Clayton, Anthony and Donald C. Savage (1974): Government and Labour in Kenya, 1895-1963. London: Routledge. 2016 print.

Cobain, Ian (2012): Mau Mau torture case: Kenyans win ruling against UK. *The Guardian*. 05-10-2012. Available at: http://www.guardian.co.uk/world/2012/oct/05/mau-mau-veterans-win-torture-case [Accessed: 08-01-13].

Cobain, I. (2016). The History Thieves: Secrets, Lies and the Shaping of a Modern Nation. London: Portobello Books.

Conboy, Martin Jairo Lugo-Ocando and Scott Eldridge (2014) Livingstone and the Legacy of Empire in the Journalistic Imagination. *Ecquid Novi: African Journalism Studies*, 35:1, 3-8. Available at: http://www.

tandfonline.com/doi/pdf/10.1080/02560054.2014.887334. [Accessed: 09-06-17].

Corbyn, Jeremy (2012): Preface to Riri (2012?), reproduced in Appendix B.

Corfield, F. D. (1960): Historical Survey of the Origin and Growth of Mau Mau. Cmd. 1030. London: HMSO.

Coup Broadcast. Voice of Kenya, Nairobi. August 1, 1982. Reproduced in Race and Class Vol. 24 (3) 1983 pp. 325—326.

Crimes Britain: the book (2017). London: Crimes of Britain

Cushion, Steve (2016): A Hidden History of the Cuban Revolution: How the Working Class Shaped the Guerrilla Victory. New York: Monthly Review Press.

Davies, Ioan (1966): African Trade Unions. Harmondsworth: Penguin Books.

Davis, Mary (2017): Why Was There A Revolution In Russia In 1917? *Morning Star* 04-11-17. Available at http//morningstaronline.co.uk/a-058c-Why-was-there-a-revolution-in-Russia-in-1919#.Wf8jracZEJ. [Accessed: 05-11-17]

December Twelve Movement: *Pambana, the Organ of the December Twelve Movement.* 2 issues were published in May 1982 and July 1983.

Dowden, Richard (2005): State of Shame. *The Guardian.* 05-02- 2005. Available at: www.guardian.co.uk/books/2005/feb/05/featuresreviews.guardianreview6 [Accessed: 24-04-17].

Drum (1965): Africa Mourns a Brother. May, 1966.

Durrani, Naila (2017): A brief Outline of Kenya Asian Participation in Kenya People's Resistance Against Imperialism, 1884-1963. *In* Durrani, Nazmi, Naila Durrani and Eddie Pereira (2016).

Durrani, Nazmi (2017): Jaswant Singh Bharaj. *In*: Durrani, Nazmi, Naila Durrani and Eddie Pereira (2017).

Durrani, Nazmi (forthcoming) Tunakataa! (We Say No).

Durrani, Nazmi, Naila Durrani and Eddie Pereira (2017): Liberating Minds, Restoring Kenyan History: Anti-imperialist Resistance by Progressive South Asian Kenyans, 1884-1965. Nairobi: Vita Books.

Durrani, Shiraz (1986) : Kimaathi, Mau Mau's First Prime Minister of Kenya. London. Vita Books.

Durrani, Shiraz (2006): Never Be Silent: Publishing and Imperialism in Kenya, 1884-1963. London-Nairobi: Vita Books.

Durrani, Shiraz (1997): The Other Kenya: Underground and Alternative Literature. *Collection Building* (1997). Vol. 16(2) 80-87.

Durrani, Shiraz (2008): Information and Liberation: Writings on the Politics of Information and Librarianship. Duluth, MN,USA: Library Juice Press.

Durrani, Shiraz. (2013). Mau Mau: The Revolutionary Force From Kenya. *Communist Review* Nos. 67-69.

Durrani, Shiraz (2015a) Ed.: Makhan Singh, a Revolutionary Kenyan Trade Unionist. 2015. London: Vita Books.

Durrani, Shiraz (2015b): Reflections on the Revolutionary Legacy of Makhan Singh. *In*: Durrani, Shiraz (2015) Ed.: Makhan Singh.

Durrani, Shiraz (forthcoming): Pio Gama Pinto, the Assassinated Hero of the Anti-Imperialist Struggle in Kenya, 1927-1965. *In:* Durrani, Shiraz (Ed.): Pio Gama Pinto, the Assassinated Hero of the Anti-Imperialist Struggle in Kenya, 1927-1965.

Edgerton, Robert B. (1990): Mau Mau, an African Crucible. London: I.B.Tauris.

Elkins, Caroline (2005): Britain's Gulag: the Brutal End of Empire in Kenya. London: Pimlico.

Every Leader Who Has Stood Up For Africa's Right To Economic Self-determination Has Been Eliminated. *in How Africa*. Available at: http://howafrica.com/every-leaders-who-has-stood-up-for-africas-right-to-economic-self-determination-has-been-eliminated/#page. [Accessed: 08-04-17]

Fabian Colonial Bureau (1944): Kenya: White Man's Country? London: Fabian Publications & Victor Gollancz.

Furedi, Frank (1973): The African Crowd in Nairobi: Popular Movements and Elite Politics. Journal of African History. Vol. 2 (1973), pp. 275-290.

Furedi, Frank (1989): The Mau Mau War in Perspective. London: James Currey.

Gachihi, Margaret Wangui (1986): Role of Kikuyu Women in the Mau Mau (1986). MA Degree thesis. Nairobi: University of Nairobi.

Gatabaki, Njehu. (1983): "20 great years of independence". Nairobi: Productions and Communications.

Githuku, Nicholas K. (2016) Mau Mau Crucible of War: Statehood, National Identity and Politics of Postcolonial Kenya. New York: Laxington Books.

Gott, Richard (2001): White Wash (Book review of Ornamentalism: How the British saw their Empire by David Cannadine. The Guardian, 05-05-2001. Available at: https://www.theguardian.com/books/2001/may/05/historybooks.socialsciences. [Accessed: 21-05-17].

Great Britain. Colonial Office. Parliamentary Delegation to Kenya. Report (1954). Quoted in Barnett, Donald and Njama, Karari (1966): Mau Mau From Within. New York. Monthly Review.

Great Britain. Department of Education (2013): National Curriculum in

England: History Programmes of Study. Statutory Guidance. Available at: https://www.gov.uk/government/publications/national-curriculum-in-england-history-programmes-of-study/national-curriculum-in-england-history-programmes-of-study. [Accessed: 22-03-17].

The Guardian (2017): French election: Macron sparks Algeria row as Fillon hit by fresh blow. 16-02-2017. Available at: https://www.theguardian.com/world/2017/feb/16/france-inquiry-into-presidential-candidate-francois-fillon-to-remain-open?CMP=Share_AndroidApp_Gmail. [Accessed: 18-02-2017].

Gumbihi, H. (2016, October 23). Lost Without a Trace in Police KDF [Kenya Defence Force] Hands. *The Nairobian*.

Gupta, Vijay (1981): Kenya: Politics of (In)Dependence. New Delhi: People's Publishing House.

History of Kenya, 1952-1958. (1976): A guide to the exhibition by Kenyan artists Mule wa Musembi, Kitonyi wa Kyongo, Kitaka wa Mutua and Mutunga wa Musembi held at Cottage Crafts, Nairobi in 1976. Publicity leaflet. Exhibition organised by Sultan Somjee.

Honest Accounts 2017: How the world profits from Africa's wealth. Published by a coalition of UK and African organisations, including Global Justice Now, Health Poverty Action and Jubilee Debt Campaign. Available at: http://www.globaljustice.org.uk/sites/default/files/files/resources/honest_accounts_2017_web_final.pdf?utm_source=Global+Justice+Now+press+release+list&utm_campaign=17a92094cc-EMAIL_CAMPAIGN_2017_05_17&utm_medium=email&utm_term=0_166972fef5-17a92094cc-288067141&mc_cid=17a92094cc&mc_eid=6149d72169 [Accessed: 11-06-17].

Huggler, Justin (2016): Germany to Recognise Herero Genocide and Apologise to Namibia. *The Telegraph*. 14-07-2016. http://www.telegraph.co.uk/news/2016/07/14/germany-to-recognise-herero-genocide-and-apologise-to-namibia/Available at: [Accessed: 18-02-17].

"Hunting the Mau Mau" under the sections British military strategy in Kenya; the RAF in Kenya; British units involved in the Emergency in Kenya. Available at: www.britains-smallwars.com/kenya/index.html [Accessed: 19-01-12].

Itote, Warahiu (1967): Mau Mau General. Nairobi: EAPH.

Jones, Owen (2015): The Establishment and How They Get Away With It. (London?): Penguin.

Josh, Sohan Singh (1977): Hindustan Gadar Party, a Short History. New Delhi: People's Publishing House.

Kabiro, Ngugi (1973): Man in the Middle. Life Histories from the Revolution No. 2. Richmond, B.C., Canada: LSM Information Centre.

Kabubi, Anna Wamuyu (2002): Interview, "A Fight of Her Own: Conversation with Anna Wamuyu Kabubi" [Mau Mau name, Cinda Reri]. "Women and Mau Mau", Interview by S. M. Shamsul and Margaret Gachihi. *in*:Alam (2007).

Kaggia, Bildad (1975): Roots of Freedom 1921–1963: the Autobiography of Bildad Kaggia. Nairobi: East African Publishing House.

Kaggia, Bildad, W. de Leeuw and M. Kaggia (2012): The Struggle for Freedom and Justice: the Life and Times of the Freedom Fighter and Politician Bildad M. Kaggia (1921-2005). Nairobi: Transafrica Press.

Kamau, John (2017): Hassan, the mysterious Somali trader who funded Mau Mau fighters. *Daily Nation* 19-04-2017. Available at: http://www.nation.co.ke/news/Hassan-mysterious-Somali-trader-who-funded-Mau-Mau-fighters/1056-3882956-ev05ha/index.html. [Accessed: 10-04-17]

Kariga, Mzalendo: Kenya Ripe for Revolution. *New Africa News* (Melbourne, Australia) No. 71 Nov. 1983 – Jan. 1989, 4-7.

Kariuki, Josiah Mwangi (1975): Mau Mau Detainee: the Account a Kenyan African of his Experiences in Detention Camps, 1953-1960. Nairobi: Oxford University Press.

Kasrils, Ronnie (2013): How the ANC's Faustian pact sold out South Africa's poorest. *The Guardian*. 24 June 2013. Available at: http://m.guardian.co.uk/commentisfree/2013/jun/24/anc-faustian-pact-mandela-fatal-error [Accessed: 08-04-17]

Kenya Committee for Democratic Rights for Kenya (London). (1952-60): "Kenya Press Extracts". Photocopies of the Extracts available in the Kenya Liberation Library. The Committee was based at 86 Rochester Row, London. SW1

Kenya Coup, 1982, Broadcast. Available at: https://www.youtube.com/watch?v=yscEH2BMPr0. [Accessed: 05-04-17]. Voice of Kenya: August 1.

Kenya Human Rights Commission (n.d.): Redress for Historical Land Injustice in Kenya: A Brief on Proposed Legislation for Historical Land Injustices. Nairobi: Kenya Human Rights Commission.

Kenya News. An irregular publication of the Committee for the Release of Political Prisoners in Kenya.

- No. 1 (July 1983): One Year Later; Political Prisoners Still Jailed in Kenya.

- No. 2 (Nov. 1983): Democratic Image – Repressive Reality.

- No. 3 (April 1984): Stop This Massacre ("the barbaric attack by the Kenyan security forces on defenceless citizens in the North East Province killed more than 1,000 people").

- No. 4 (Oct. 1984): Drought is a Big Business.

- No. 5 (May 1985): Sunday Bloody Sunday (The massacre of students at the University of Nairobi, Sunday Feb. 10, 1985).

- No. 6 (June 1985): The Kenyan Woman: A Decade of Oppression.

- No. 7 (August 1986): State of Emergency. Help Close Moi's Torture Chamber.

- No. 8 (March 1987): Torture in Kenya Intensifies. There is no Giving Up, Diaries from a Torture Chamber Torture, Routine Methods of Extorting Information.

- No. 9 (Feb. 1989): Moi's Police: Licence to Kill, Ten Years of Terror.

Kinyatti, Maina wa (1980): Thunder From the Mountain: Mau Mau Patriotic Songs. London: Zed Press. 1980.

Kinyatti, Maina wa: Kimathi Letters. Nairobi. London. Heinemann: Zed Books. 1986 (1987).

Kinyatti, Maina wa (1977): Mau Mau, The Peak of African Nationalism in Kenya. Special issue of *Kenya Historical Review* 5(2) 1977 287-311: Some Perspectives on the Mau Mau Movement.

Kinyatti, Maina wa (1978): Foreward. Ndegwa, R. N. (Comp.,1977): Mau Mau: A Select Bibliography. Nairobi: Kenyatta University Press.

Kinyatti, Maina wa (1980): Thunder from the Mountains: Mau Mau Patriotic Songs. London. Zed Books.

Kinyatti, Maina wa (2d ed. 2000): Mau Mau: A Revolution Betrayed. Nairobi, London: Mau Mau Research Centre, Vita Books.

Kinyatti, Maina wa (2008): History of Resistance in Kenya, 1884-2002. Nairobi: Mau Mau Research Centre.

Kitching, Gavin (1980): Class and Economic Change in Kenya: the Making of an African Petite Bourgeoisie, 1905-1970. London: Yale University

Press.

Koinange, Mbiyu (1955): The People of Kenya Speak for Themselves. Nairobi. Reprinted in 1979 by Business Forms & Systems, Nairobi, Kenya.

Koinange, Mbiyu and Aching Oneko (1952): Land Hunger in Kenya. London: The Union of Democratic Control. No. 3 in the Series, Africa and the Future.

Kubai, Fred. (1983): The struggle for independence; background to the nationalist movement. Gatabaki, Njehu (1983).

Labour Trade Union of Kenya (LTUK) (1936): Struggle Between Capitalists and Workers Has Started in Earnest. LTUK leaflet issued during the 1936 strike. Makhan Singh Archives, University of Nairobi (translated from Gujarati by the author).

Lessons from Latin America on Fighting Colonialism (2016). teleSUR, 23-04-2016. Available at: http://www.telesurtv.net/english/analysis/Lessons-from-Latin-America-on-Fighting-Colonialism-20160423-0036.html. [Accessed: 24-05-17].

Laski, Frida (1954?): Foreword *in* Pankhurst (1954?).

Leakey, L.S.B. (1954): Defeating Mau Mau. London: Methuen.

Lehulere, Ou pa (2017): The Corruption of a Dream. *Pambazuka News*. April, 06.

Leigh Day (2016): Historical Background. Available at: https://www.leighday.co.uk/International-and-group-claims/Kenya/The-Mau-Mau-claims/Historical-background-to-the-Mau-Mau-claims [Accessed: 14-11-16].

Louati, Yesser (2017): The Colonial Republic. *Red Pepper*, June-July.

Leys, Colin (1975): Underdevelopment in Kenya: the Political Economy of Neo-Colonialism, 1964-1971. Nairobi: Heinemann Educational Books.

MacDonald, Malcolm (1976a): MacDonald Papers, University of Durham. Correspondence re Kenya 1969-1981. 76/7/44.

MacDonald, Malcolm (1976b): Interview given on April 24, 1976 by the Rt. Hon. Malcolm MacDonald to Arnold Raphael and Celia Curtis. MacDonald Papers, University of Durham. Correspondence re Kenya 1969-1981. 76/7/44.

McGhie, John. (2002): "British brutality in Mau Mau conflict". The Guardian. (London). November 9, 2002.

Maina, Kenneth [Ken] (2016): Revealed: Kenya's Biggest Landowners. Nairobiwire, 08 July, 2016 http://nairobiwire.com/2016/07/revealed-kenyas-biggest-landowners.html [Accessed: 26-09-17)

Maina, Paul (1977): Six Mau Mau Generals. Nairobi: Gazelle Books.

Maloba, Wunyabari O. (1998): Mau Mau and Kenya: An Analysis of a Peasant Revolt. Oxford: James Currey.

Maloba, W.O. (2017): The Anatomy of Neo-Colonialism in Kenya: British Imperialism and Kenyatta, 1963–1978. London: Palgrave MacMillan. Histories and Modernities Series.

Mamon, Saleh (2014): Kenya Resistance, Repression and Revolt: A Timeline. London: Kenya Land and Freedom Depository. Details about the Depository are available at http://www.popsamiti.org/kenyalandfreedom.html [Accessed: 19-08-17]. The Timeline is reproduced in Appendix C.

Mathu, Mohamed (1974): The Urban Guerrilla. Life Histories from the Revolution No. 3. Richmond, B.C., Canada: LSM Information Centre.

Maxon, Robert & Ofcanksy, Thomas (2000) Historical Dictionary of Kenya. 2d ed. Lanham, Md & London: The Scarecrow Press.

Millner, Ralph (1954?): The Right to Live. London: The Kenya Committee.

Mirii, Ngugi wa (1979): On Literacy Content. Institute for Development Studies, University of Nairobi. Discussion Paper No. 340.

Mkhatshwa, Jabulani: Kenya, From the Wananchi Declaration to MWAKENYA. The *African Communist* No. 116 (1989) 65-72.

Mohsin, Moni (2016): Empire Shaped the World: There is an abyss at the heart of dishonest history textbooks. *The Guardian*. 30-10-16. available at: https://www.theguardian.com/commentisfree/2016/oct/30/empire-shaped-world-abyss-heart-dishonest-history-textbooks [Accessed: 11-04-17].

Moi, Daniel arap Moi (1986): Kenya African Nationalism: Nyayo Philosophy and Principles. The original article refers to the title of the book as "A History of Kenya's African Nationalism".

Monbiot, George (2012: Dark Hearts. The *Guardian*. 24-04-2012. Available at: http://www.monbiot.com/2012/04/23/dark-hearts/. [Accessed: 20-05-17].

Mpatanishi. "The official central journal of Mwakenya to co-ordinate only the disciplined cadres". Issue no. 14 (Aug. 1985) was a Special Issue with the lead article, "Liberation Organizations Merge and formalize MWAKENYA."

Muchai, Karigo (1973): The Hardcore. Life Histories from the Revolution No. 1. Richmond, B.C., Canada: LSM Information Centre.

Field Marshal Muthoni (2007): Conversations with A Freedom Fighter. Interview. Available at: http://wherehermadnessresides.blogspot.com/2005/09/conversations-with-freedom-fighter.html. [Accessed: 19-04-2007].

Mutunga, Willy (2017): Will the Kenyan elite ever grow up? *The Star* (Nairobi) . 16-09-17. Available at: https://www.the-star.co.ke/

news/2017/09/16/will-the-kenyan-elite-ever-grow-up_c1636126. [Accessed: 16-09-17]

Mwakenya (1985-89): *Upande Mwingine*. Unpublished underground "monthly and annual documentation of the resistance deeds and actions of workers, peasants and students etc in industry, commerce, plantations, schools and colleges, carried out by Upande Mwingine [the Other Side], the underground workers' Organ". Mwakenys (1987b). Copies to be available at the Kenya Liberation Library being set up in Nairobi.

Mwakenya (1987a): Draft Minimum Programme.

Mwakenya (1987b): Kenya; Register of Resistance, 1986.

Mwakenya (1992): Moism Without Moi is as Dangerous as Moism With Moi. Press Statement. January 8.

Mzalendo MWAKENYA, The mass newspaper of MWAKENYA. Many issues published, e.g. The Moi-Kanu Clique Continue to Crush Democracy in Kenya (March, 1988).

Ndegwa, R. N. (Comp.1977): Mau Mau: A Select Bibliography. Nairobi: Kenyatta University Press.

News from Africa Watch No. 1, December, 6. 1989 (London). [Later named: *Human Rights Watch Africa*].

Newsinger, J. (2006): The Blood Never Dried: A People's History of the British Empire. London: Bookmarks.

Ng'otho, Kamau (2008): Secret land deal that made Kenyatta first president. *Daily Nation*. 20-09-2008. Available at: http://www.nation.co.ke/news/-/1056/473158/-/5gb13cz/-/index.html [Accessed: 29-01-2017].

Ngugi, Patrick. (1987): The nerve centre of struggle for uhuru. Daily Nation (Nairobi). November 3.

Nkrumah, Kwame (1965): Neo-Colonialism, the Last Stage of imperialism. Available at: https://www.marxists.org/subject/africa/nkrumah/neo-colonialism/introduction.htm. [Accessed: 19-09-17)

Odinga, Oginga (1968): Not Yet Uhuru. London. Heinemann.

Omanga, Duncan & Kipkosgei Arap Buigutt (2017): Marx in Campus: Print Cultures, Nationalism and Student Activism in the Late 1970s Kenya. *Journal of Eastern African Studies.* Vol. 11 (4). DOI: 10.1080/17531055.2017.1380763.

Oneko, Ramogi Achieng (1966): Detention days. *in Pio Gama Pinto, Independent Kenya's First Martyr - Socialist Freedom Fighter* (1966).

Osborne, Myles (2010): The Kamba and Mau Mau: Ethnicity, Development, and Chiefship, 1952-1960. *International Journal of African Historical Studies* Vol. 43, No. 1 (2010). https://www.jstor.org/stable/25741397?seq=1#page_scan_tab_contents [Accessed: 28-4-17].

Pambana, Organ of the December Twelve Movement. Mwakenya.

Pankhurst, Richard K. P. (1954?): Kenya: the History of Two Nations. London: Independent Publishing Co.

Panfilova, Vera (2017): Russia Revolution: Ten propaganda posters from 1917. BBC News (online). 05-11-17. Available at www.bbc.co.uk/news/world-europe-41833406 [Accessed: 12-11-17]

Patel, Ambu H. (Comp.) 1963: Struggle for Release Jomo and His Colleagues. Nairobi: New Kenya Publishers.

Patel, Zarina. (1997): Challenge to colonialism; the struggle of Alibhai Mulla Jeevanjee for equal rights in Kenya. Nairobi: Zand Graphics.

Patel, Zarina. (2006): Unquiet, the Life and Times of Makhan Singh. Nairobi: Zand Graphics.

Pereira, Benegal (2016): Life and Times of Eddie H. Pereira (1915-1995) *in* Durrani, Nazmi (2016): Liberating Minds, Restoring Kenyan History: Anti-Imperialist Resistance by Progressive South Asian Kenyans, 1984-1965. Nairobi: Vita Books.

Petras, James and Henry Veltmeyer (2018): The Class Struggle in Latin America. London: Routledge.

Pinto, Pio Gama (1963a): Glimpses of Kenya's Nationalist Struggle. *Pan Africa. Also published as a monograph*: Nowrojee, Viloo and Edward Miller (Editors, 2014): Glimpses of Kenya's Nationalist Struggle by Pio Gama Pinto. Nairobi: Asian African Heritage Trust.

Pinto, Pio Gama (1963b): A Detainee's Life Story. *in*: Patel, Ambu H. (comb) pp. 155 - 157.

Pio Gama Pinto, Independent Kenya's First Martyr - Socialist Freedom Fighter (1966). Nairobi: Pan African Press Ltd.

Quinn, Kate (2015): Foreword to Cushion, S. (2016).

Rawcliffe, D. H. The Struggle for Kenya. London: Gollancz.

Riri, Dan Thea wa (2012?): Justice for Freedom Fighters. London: Mau Mau Justice Network.

Roseberg, Carl G. and John Nottingham (1966, reprinted 1985): The Myth of "Mau Mau": Nationalism in Kenya. Nairobi: Transafrica Press.

Seidenberg, Dana April (1983): Uhuru and the Kenya Indians: the Role of a Minority Community in Kenya Politics, 1939-1963.

Singh, Makhan (1963): Comrade Makhan Singh (Autobiography). *in* Patel, Ambu (Comp.). Reproduced in Durrani, S. (Ed. 1015).

Singh, Makhan (1969): History of Kenya's Trade Union Movement to 1952. Nairobi: East African Publishing House.

Singh, Makhan (1980): Kenya's Trade Unions: Crucial Years, 1952-56. Nairobi: Uzima Press.

Slaughter, Barbara (1999): "How Britain crushed the 'Mau Mau rebellion' – Channel Four TV's Secret History – Mau Mau". A report on the programme is available from: <http://www.hartford-hwp.com/archives/36/026.html> [Accessed: 2201-2017].

South African History Online (1965). Search under Mau Mau and Kenya. Available at: http://www.sahistory.org.za. [Accessed: 04-08-17].

Spencer, John (1983): James Beauttah: Freedom Fighter. Nairobi: Stellascope.

The Struggle For Kenya's Future. The document was written as "part of a collective effort by several Kenyans and myself [Don Barnett]...It was mimeographed and distributed at the Kenya African National Union (KANU) conference held in Nairobi, Kenya in December 1961" - Don Barnett in Muchai, K. (1973): 5-9.

Tamaduni Players, Nairobi. (1978). Publicity material.

Tandon, Yash (2017): Kenya Elections from a theoretical and global perspective. *Pambazuka* News. August 04.Telesur (2017): Algeria Demands France Recognize 'Colonial Era' Crimes. Available at: http://www.telesurtv.net/english/news/Algeria-Demands-France-Recognize-Colonial-Era-Crimes--20170705-0049.html [Accessed: 06-07-17].

Tandon,Yash (2017c): Reflections on South Africa: whose capital, whose state? 01-09-2017. Available at: yashtandon.com/reflections-on-south-africa-whose-capital-whose-state. Accessed: 31-12-17).

Tharoor, Shashi (2016): An Era of Darkness: The British Empire in India. New Delhi: Aleph.

Tharoor, Shashi (2016b):Theresa May should 'beg forgiveness' for Britain's colonial 'sins' – Indian MP. 5 Nov, 2016. RT Question More. Available at:

https://www.rt.com/uk/365249-may-india-apology-tharoor/. [Accessed: 09-06-17].

Tharoor, Shashi (2016c): Does Britain Owe Reparations to India and Other Former Colonies? *South China Morning Post*. 4-12-16. Available at: http://www.scmp.com/week-asia/opinion/article/2050394/does-britain-owe-reparations-india-and-other-former-colonies [accessed: 30-06-17].

Thomsen, Lars Ulrika (2017): The Anniversary of Lenin's *Imperialism*. The *Communist Review*. No. 82. Winter 2016-2017.

Truth Justice and Reconciliation Commission of Kenya (2013) [TJRC]: Final Report. Available at http://digitalcommons.law.seattleu.edu/tjrc/ [Accessed: 08-04-17]. Vol.IIA.

Tweedsmuir, Lord (1946). Quoted in Aaronovitch, S. and K. (1947).

Umoja: (1987a). Legacy of Resistance in the Kenya Coast. Background Paper presented at the Unity Conference of Patriotic, Democratic and Progressive Kenyan Organisations Abroad No. 1987/UC/BP/11.2 (1). London, 16-19 October 1987. Unpublished "draft for discussion".

Umoja (1987b): Mombasa People Champion Resistance Against the Kanu's Undemocratic Rule (Press Statement, 24-11-87).

Umoja: (1987c). Resistance in Northern Kenya, 1890-1963. Background Paper presented at the Unity Conference of Patriotic, Democratic and Progressive Kenyan Organisations Abroad No. 1987/UC/BP/11.2 (2). London, 16-19 October 1987. Unpublished "draft copy for discussion".

Umoja (1987d): Women in Kenyan People's Resistance to Imperialism, 1884-1963. Background Paper presented at the Unity Conference of Patriotic, Democratic and Progressive Kenyan Organisations Abroad. Background Paper No. 1987/UC/BP/11.3. London, 16-19 October 1987. Unpublished "draft copy for discussion".

Umoja (1987e): Resolution and Final Statement. Unity Conference of

Patriotic, Democratic and Progressive Kenyan Organisations Abroad, October 16-19, 1987. London, England.

Umoja: (1988): Struggle For Democracy in Kenya; Special Report on the 1988 General Elections in Kenya. (1 June, 1988) Background Paper No. 1).

Umoja: (1989): Moi's Reign of Terror; A Decade of Nyayo Crimes Against the People of Kenya. London: Umoja. Background Document No. 2.

Umoja Co-ordinator (1987): Progressive Forces Must Unite For a New Kenya. Statement from the Co-ordinator at the Unity Conference of Patriotic, Democratic and Progressive Kenyan Organisations Abroad. London, October 16-19.

Venys, Ladislav (1970): A History of the Mau Mau Movement in Kenya. Department of Asian and African Studies, Faculty of Philosophy. Prague: Charles University.

Vltchek, Andre (2016): Western "Culture" is wrecking Entire Continents. Information Clearing House. Available at: http://www.informationclearinghouse.info/article45787.htm [Accessed: 07-11-16].

Wasserman, Gary (1976): Politics of Decolonization: Kenya Europeans and the Land Issue, 1960–1965. Cambridge: Cambridge University Press.

Woolf, Leonard (1944): Preface to Fabian Colonial Bureau (1944).

World Federation of Trade Unions (WFTU, 1952): Terror in Kenya: the Facts Behind the Present Crisis. London: WFTU.

Yaliotokea Hapa Mombasa Mnamo Tarehe 30-1-87. (What happened in Mombasa on 30 January, 1987). Underground leaflet, Mombasa.

APPENDICES

A: Jeremy Corbyn: The Fight for Justice Continues

Corbyn, Jeremy (2012): Preface to Riri (2012?), riri, Dan Thea wa (2012?): Justice for Freedom Fighters. London: Mau Mau Justice Network

Only a century ago at the height of Empire, Europe controlled two-thirds of the world's land. The Empires were for mercantile demands, rivalry with others and for enormous wealth for a few. Currently there is a rave of modern historical interpretation of the supposed advantages of Empire, the cultural domination associated with it and our debt to it. The interpretation is essentially naive at best, dishonest in reality and dangerous as a story in its dishonesty.

The European Empires came because of greed and the preparedness of European countries to inflict brutality and cruelty on peoples who they subjugated. The slave trade brought wealth and cruelty and death by the tens of thousands, yet in a massive self-delusion Britain's role in abolishing the trade and then the practice is somehow seen as heroic.

History and Empire are presented as being fundamentally good to the world; the Imperial trappings and Colonial life style always presented in film images of liberal thinking white Europeans are presented as ensuring order and production amidst restless natives who were ultimately grateful for the intervention.

Few countries and experiences have had more films made about this than Kenya. Controlled by Britain as part of the Scramble for Africa in the latter part of the nineteenth century it was always earmarked as a colony for European settlement and development as an England in East Africa, unlike neighbouring Uganda which was exploited rather than settled.

The end of Empires started in Versailles in 1919 as the European powers fought each other to a standstill. The "victors", Britain and France, exacted retribution on Germany and united to oppose the new Soviet Union. They also divided up the spoils of the Ottoman, Austro-Hungarian and German Empires among themselves through the dubious mandates under the auspices of the League of Nations. Economically unsustainable as the Empires were the indebted Europeans imagined it would go on forever.

Settlement in Kenya continued and the 'White Highlands' resulted from the land rush and greed of the Europeans. Occupying land and developing a farming system that made them personally wealthy was part of the process, but also a social system that was arrogant separate from the huge African majority around them. Sustained by arms and arrogance they thought these privileges would last forever.

The death knell of Empire was the Second World Imperialist War; the massive losses and defeat of fascism served to expose the hypocrisy of the rhetoric of anti-racism in Europe and colonial subjugation elsewhere. India and Pakistan gained independence in 1947 at a terrible price and cost of millions of lives. The rest of the European Empires would have two or three decades of wars ahead. The Colonial administrators, all trained in the superiority of Empire, believed Africa was "not yet ready" and that only self-government or 'dominion' status was appropriate.

In Kenya self-government meant a system that guaranteed the interests of the white farming group that controlled the reins of power, and gave a legal veneer to land grabbing and occupation.

The ideas of Pan-Africanism were given root in the Manchester Conference of 1945 that laid a pathway for African unity and independence.

These ideas and leadership were the bedrock and foundations of all independence struggles in Africa; and of course met with violent European opposition.

The wars in Algeria and Vietnam waged by the French were particularly sharp examples of this violence, but they were ultimately futile.

In Kenya the British poured more and more troops into a struggle that was as ultimately hopeless as it was vicious and cruel. The British Army used methods borrowed from the Nazi concentration camps, cruelty and humiliation as bad as anywhere by any colonial power. The jailing, torture and killing of African people went on behind a cloak of secrecy and a media campaign of presenting the European Settlers as victims at the hands of brutal African savages. As ever this violence of occupation was accompanied by the dishonesty of compliant newspapers in Britain. But, it changed, eventually. Independence was won and Kenya was born as a nation.

Kenyatta opposed re-opening the whole issue of justice for the Mau Mau victims of Britain. This policy suited his political approach, and suited the ex-colonial rulers who shipped to Britain tens of thousands of pieces of crucial incriminating evidence of torture and abuse, fuelled by racist beliefs. The records were then hidden in obscure Foreign and Commonwealth Office stores.

The victims who survived never gave up the struggle and with unbelievable determination fought on, initially in a hostile environment in Kenya, but nevertheless fought on.

When they finally made it to the Royal Courts of Justice in the Strand, London, it was a victory in itself. The firmly held British view was that the whole thing was a matter for the Government of independent Kenya; while at the same time the same Foreign and Commonwealth Office was deliberately hiding the evidence it held.

Just seeing the aged victims in Court was an extraordinary feeling of sympathy and admiration for them and their legal team.

Justice in this case can never be entirely done; compensation for what happened may be paid, an apology may be given but lives lost, the villages burnt, the reign of terror the British troops imposed in a colonial era that was rapidly approaching the sunset, will never be forgotten.

We are in an era of historical re-writing of the whole role of Empire and its alleged civilising qualities. Empires are set up for military power, for financial gain; the brutality of the exploitation, the theft of land and the imposition of unfair laws is the price paid by the victims. To achieve this exploitation, the colonising Empire needs an ideology of racist superiority to justify it to its own population, and to enable its agents to carry out this process.

The history of struggle for justice by these Kenyans is one of total determination, and is an example to many others who also suffered in other colonies.

Liberation, which I chair, was founded as the Movement for Colonial Freedom, and it fought many campaigns, including one to expose the brutality of the British rule in Kenya. It published the book "The Truth about Kenya" in 1955, written by Eileen Fletcher, a former rehabilitation officer of the colonial administration of Kenya. She resigned in disgust at what she saw and knew and wrote about it in five devastating chapters on Concentration Camps, White Supremacy, Starvation of Children, Torture and general misadministration generously allowed the Colonial administration to make a reply which she firmly dealt with on the last page of the booklet. This issue of repression was raised repeatedly in the British Parliament particularly by one of the founders of the Movement for Colonial Freedom, Tony Benn and fellow founders Fenner Brockway, Barbara Castle and Leslie Hale.

Liberation continues the work of the Movement for Colonial Freedom, since, of course, independence did not always bring justice, peace and truth in the former colonies. As everywhere else in the world, the fight for justice continues in these countries.

Jeremy Corbyn MP
Chair, Liberation
September 2012

B: Selected Documents

The Struggle For Kenya's Future (1972)

Reproduced from:
Barnett, Donald (1972): Kenya: Two Paths Ahead. Reproduced from
    Muchai, Karigo (1973): The Hardcore. Richmond, BC, Canada:
    LSM Information Centre.

As part of a collective effort by several Kenyans and myself [Donald Barnett], the following article was written, mimeographed and distributed at the Kenya African National Union (KANU Conference held in Nairobi, Kenya in December 1961.

*

The struggle for Kenya's future is being waged today on three distinct though interrelated levels -political, racial and economic. It seems to us that we Africans are being allowed to "win" in the first two spheres as long as we don't contest the battle being waged on the third, all-important economic level.

Since the end of the Second World War, Great Britain, knowing it could not contain the wave of nationalist revolutions spreading throughout the colonial world, has embarked on a course of "guiding" these nationalist movement down a path most conducive to the perpetuation of British and multinational capitalist economic domination. The old colonialism involving direct political control is fast dying and a quick transition to the new colonialism for which the United States had framed such an admirable model in Central and South America is felt necessary to avert a *genuine* social revolution, which would result in economic as well as political independence and thus stop the flow of Kenya's surplus capital into the banks of the western capitalist world. The British Master Plan is thus quite simple in outline: "Carefully relinquish political control to a properly indoctrinated group of the "right kind" of Africans, i.e., those whose interests are similar to and compatible with our own, so that we retain economic control." In short, the British Government wants to leave in political *form* so that its capitalist "sponsors" might remain in economic *content*. Put into slogan form, this plan would be: LEAVE IN ORDER TO STAY.

What are the techniques being employed by the British to facilitate our transition from colonial to neo-colonial status, Though they are many, we shall here mention two of the most important. First is a technique which might be called *Racial Harmony: A Disguise for the Recruitment of African Stooges and frontmen.*

Realizing that their old set of economic policies and privilege for European Settlers and non-African businessmen had resulted in the almost complete absence of Africans within the middle class, the British Government undertook hurried plans to recruit Africans to economic positions which would allow them to become the spokesmen for this class. It was necessary, in brief, to sufficiently break down the colour barriers so as to allow the formation of a "multiracial" economic front whose Spokesmen would have black faces even while its planners and largest profit makers remained European and Asian. They proceeded to allow us freehold titles to our land and the right to grow certain cash crops, such as Arabica coffee, so that an African landholding group might emerge which, employing cheap African labour just as their European counterparts, would find its interests identified with the capitalists of the dominant economic group. Today, in addition to the resettlement scheme, we are bombarded with talk of mergers between the Kenya National Farmers' Union (KNFU) and the African Farmers and Traders Association; between the African, Asian and European Chambers of Commerce, and even between African and European Medical Associations. These intended mergers are clear evidence of a calculated plan (revealed most boldly by Blundell and Delamere during a recent meeting of the KNFU) on the part of the economic elite to partially dissolve racial barriers in order to consolidate its position along class lines and to use Africans as frontmen and spokesmen for its interests.

"Africanization" is the term used for the process by which selected Africans are being recruited to executive or bureaucratic posts and thus acquiring a vested interest in the status quo - an interest it shares with a growing number of businessmen, professionals and prosperous farmers and which manifests itself in a desire for "economic stability" and the rule of "law and order". All these moves parade themselves, of course, as signs of the coming racial harmony, as humanitarian gestures reflecting a genuine change of heart among the avowed European racists.

Interestingly enough, we hear our African colleagues shouting that they want to "stabilize" an economy of poverty and wage-slavery for the masses and to perpetuate a body of "law and order"which acts as the moral and militant protector of those who currently control this economy. Aren't they aware that this economy they wish to "stabilize" is at the root of Kenya's present backward economic condition, shipping abroad or spending on lavish consumption the surplus capital generated yearly by our labour? Don't they know that in times of crisis, when their economic interests are threatened by the imminence of sweeping social changes, the reactionary elements of countries throughout history have taken refuge and attempted to consolidate their forces under the banners of "law and order" and the need for "stability"? Don't they know from their own experiences in Kenya's recent revolutionary effort and the British repression that some of the gravest crimes of man against man are committed under the banner of "law and order"?

Let us investigate this body of law and decide whether we want the system of economic inequality which it protects through the maintenance of order. At present we are merely echoing the slogans put forward by those who stand to lose by our gains, who are now profiting by a system which exploits us; who, in fact, drafted and imposed that very body of law which our people are daily forced to follow in unbearable degradation and humiliating poverty. Let us instead struggle against a "stability" which is in fact stagnation; let us struggle to liberate that vast reservoir of creative ability which now lies dormant amongst our people; let us, in short, create a new society which allows to each man the right to eat, the right to the products of his labour, the right to clothe, house and educate his children, the right, in short, to live in dignity amongst equals. It is a socialist society we should be struggling to build, a system which, unlike capitalism, concerns itself with the welfare of the masses rather than with the profits and privileges of a few.

A second technique being utilized so that our rulers might "leave in order to stay" can be called *Nationalism: A Colonialist Substitute for Ideology*. Nationalism is essentially a negative philosophy based on strong popular feelings, demanding freedom from foreign political domination. It is no substitute for a positive ideology. The British, along with many other colonial powers, have attempted to utilize this negative political slogan (which, by the way, they themselves have popularized) to forestall or hinder the emergence of a revolutionary ideology, which they feared might mean the end of their economic domination. A set of ideas, carefully articulating the Kenya peoples' present condition and needs and putting forward in bold terms a rational program for Kenya's future economic development, could not but frighten Kenya's present and potential capitalist investors. This is so because planning and rationality regarding the economic and social development of a people are not the virtues of an exploitative capitalist system. We see this wherever we find an economically backward country fathered by western capitalism. Whether we look at Kenya, British Honduras or economic dependencies of the United States such as Liberia or Chile, we see the same thing: mass poverty and illiteracy combined with highly profitable foreign-owned extractive industries in agriculture or minerals.

Nevertheless, our political leaders and other spokesmen plead for more foreign investment, promising to honour existing Contracts, protect land rights and maintain the stability we've talked of earlier. They seem willing, in fact, to do almost anything so long as their nationalist's dream of "political" independence is given them. They seem willing to sell everything so that we might inherit a political power stripped of the ability to make far-reaching economic decisions. Political power is essentially a means, an instrument in the hands of a people which entitles them to make decisions regarding their future development. If we are to inherit a Government unable to make the vital decisions necessary for our economic development, then political independence will be a shallow victory indeed; the victory of a man who, spotting a great feast ahead, is satisfied with a dry bone thrown by the wayside. Our political leaders who shout nothing but "Uhuru sasa" will be proud and arrogant in their fine clothes and cars on the day our cherished independence arrives; but those who have thrown us this bone will chuckle to themselves, knowing that the real victory was theirs, while our people will face perhaps another decade or more of poverty and deprivation.

Without an ideology for vast social and economic change our politicians are easy game, regardless of their high motives and intentions, for the international corporations. It is difficult to fight something you do not see clearly, and the eyes of our leaders appear blurred by the din and wail of press and radio concerning the coming *Uhuru*, by the unquestioning enthusiasm displayed at the utterance of wilting slogans by the throngs of poor peasants which comprise their following, and by their growing international "status "and the continued invitations by "important" people to cocktails at the New Stanley Hotel. Their lack of sound ideology based on firmly held principles of human worth and dignity will make them easy prey for the foreign industrialist and financier, always ready with an envelope of money in return for political favours. In this kind of atmosphere opportunism rules the day: every man for himself and each with a price, willing to sell his political influence to the highest bidder.

The unity which can be achieved by nationalism alone is weak and thinly covers the many severe antagonisms in our society. Thus in Kenya today, with the goal of Uhuru seen clearly on the road ahead, individuals, tribes and vested interest groups are starting to vie for positions of strength and privilege; with the coming of independence the veneer of unity is smashed and all the latent antagonisms come to the fore. Real unity, you see, cannot be based on a slogan or on an illustrious personality; it can only be achieved by an ideology which unifies people in a common struggle and program. Let us then fashion an ideology which will unify the vast majority of our people by articulating their needs and by advancing a program of socialist development in agriculture and industry which promises to eradicate poverty, disease and illiteracy, a program which will draw out the creative talents and energies of our people, giving them that personal dignity and pride which comes from socially constructive and productive activity. Let us, in short, provide our people with the ideological and organizational tools necessary for the achievement of genuine independence and development. Let us not sell them cheaply down the glittering path of neo-colonialism and social, economic and cultural stagnation.

***

Unfortunately, since the above was written, Kenya has unmistakably entered the path of neo-colonial accommodation. The Kenyatta regime, even before the flag-waving independence ceremony of 12 December 1963, had embarked on a course of self-aggrandizing opportunism and blatant disregard for the peasant and worker masses of Kenya. Virtually every warning contained in this article, every "pitfall of national consciousness' Fanon cautioned against in his *Wretched of the Earth*, has been succumbed to in a Kenya which today is the very antithesis of that creative and developing socialist nation hoped for by radical Kenyans in 1961. Leaders of integrity and dedicated to serving the interests of the masses, men such as Pio Gama Pinto, Bildad Kaggia and Oginga Odinga, have been assassinated, deported, imprisoned or harassed and intimidated into silence and accommodation. Kenya is today a police state run by a mafia-like clique of self-serving politicians-cum-businessmen. Jomo Kenyatta, two-time betrayer of the Kenya masses (in 1953-4 at Kapenguria and l962-3), largest African landowner in Kenya, leader of the new Black bourgeoisie and of the corrupt bureaucratic bourgeoisie which comprises the government, was described to me in l962 by Pio Pinto - then editor of *Sauti ya Mwafrica* and a top Kenyatta advisor - as simply an "amoral man". Pinto was assassinated by the regime on 24 February l965 and Kenya has yet to replace him.

Toward those like Karigo Muchai, whose life history you are about to read, and the thousands of others who fought in the forests, reserves and towns during Kenya's unsuccessful "Mau Mau" revolt, the Kenyatta regime has shown nothing but scorn and contempt. This became clear in a Speech by Kenyatta shortly after his release in 1962. At Githunguri, an African run Teacher Training School turned into a butchery during the revolt, where over one thousand Kikuyu were hung by the British forces of law and order, Kenyatta referred to Mau Mau as "...a disease which has been eradicated and must never be remembered again" . For those who remembered the promises of the revolution, to which the detained "leaders" paid lip service on the eve of "independence", the repression was swift and severe.

Karari Njama, co-author of *Mau Mau from Within* , described the situation to me in a letter dated 12 July l965.

The Kenya revolution is now a mere history covered by a sweeping statement that everyone fought for freedom until we grabbed it from the Colonial Imperialists - and that no forest fighter should call himself a freedom fighter. This being strongly advocated by the Government shows that the forest fighters' past service is not appreciated. I am filled with great regret on realization of the fact that the forest fighters' survivors, the widows and orphans of those who volunteered to sacrifice their lives in order to liberate the Kenya nation from colonial rule, have no place to enjoy the fruits of their fallen parents' and husbands' labour. Indeed, many of them are still jobless, landless and as hungry as before. And worse, they are covered by shame because of their participation in our unrecognized fight for freedom. The realization that nobody now admits to having promised them that they could occupy the stolen land if they could get rid of the white settler is a shocking one. The Government has ruled that there is no "free land" and that anyone who wants to occupy land would have either to buy it direct from the settler or from the Government - which will buy it from the Settlers and then sell it to peasant farmers. The peasant who succeeds in getting land would then get a loan from the Government to develop his farm.

Please note that last year a number of Mount Kenya forest fighters, who had remained in their hideouts for the last eleven years before independence, returned to the forest and stated that they wouldn't come out again until they were given free land which they were promised and which they had fought for eleven years. The Government sent its forces to Mount Kenya with authority to shoot them as "enemies of peace". Their leader and three others were shot dead; the rest surrendered. Government threatened all the other forest fighters, warning them that if they wanted anything free they had better go back to the forests and be prepared to fight against the Government - which was quite strong enough to combat them. One Member of Parliament criticised the Government for this and he was dismissed from his position as Parliamentary Secretary to the Ministry of Education. He was rebuked as being anti-Party, anti-Government, anti-President and an advocate of imported Communism.

Karigo Muchai was trying desperately to scratch out a living for himself and his family when I met him in Nairobi in February 1962. Without land, without a job, he was making charcoal in the forest and selling it as a mini-trader on the streets of the city. His life history was taped in Kikuyu then translated into English by Ngugi Solomon Kabiro, another Kenyan whose life history you will read in this series. I am responsible for editing the final draft of this English version.

The story of Karigo Muchai reveals in simple unreflective terms the experiences, struggles and sacrifices of a Kikuyu peasant, son of a squatter on a white settler farm, who joins the peasant-based revolt for Land and Freedom, fights for these objectives until captured, and then spends six cruel years as a *hardcore* in over a dozen detention (i.e. concentration) camps. It is the unrecognized and unrewarded sacrifices of men like Karigo which Karari Njama refers to above. In 1962 Karigo could still hope for "...a decent job or a piece of land to cultivate" in order to provide for his family after independence. "These are the things we Kikuyu fought and died for," he said. "I only pray that after independence our children will not be forced to fight again."

The story of "Mau Mau", Kenya's peasant revolt of 1952-56, as well as its aftermath in the years leading up to and following the "granting" of independence to this British colony, should be studied carefully for the lessons that can be learned from such bitter failures. Political independence without genuine decolonization and socialism yields continued misery and oppression for the peasant-worker masses. Karigo's prayer, as with those of other peasants and workers caught up in the web of neo-colonial accommodation after long years of struggle, will not be answered. His and their children *will* be forced to fight again.

Don Barnett
Vancouver, B. C.
11 September 1972

Kimathi's Truce Offer (1953, An extract)

Extracts from Dedan Kimathi's truce offer, August 20 1953.

"...there is no such thing as Mau Mau. . . . . . the poor are the Mau Mau. Poverty, could be stopped, but not by bombs or other weapons . . . . . The policy of the Kenya Government of driving people away without good grounds, and of confining them to their reserves, has resulted in a thousand-fold increase in Man Mau in the forests. Young men and women, and even old persons, are in the forests because they are afraid of being killed, or badly beaten, or confined as they are by the policy of the Kenya Government ...... if colour prejudice is to remain in Kenya, who will stop subversive action, for the African has eyes, ears and brains."

Kimathi's terms for a truce were that the Security Forces should leave the Kikuyu reserves.

Source:

Kenya Committee for Democratic Rights for Kenya (London). (1952-60): "Kenya Press Extracts". Photocopies of the extracts available in the Kenya Liberation Library. p.36. 20-08-53

The Kenya Terror (1953)

A letter written to the people of Britain on behalf of the Kikuyu people

This letter is to greet you and to give you news from here.

Things here have grown terribly bad and I am sure that you don't get the whole truth of how things are here, because it is only the papers you read, which are written by the white Mau Mau in Kenya.

The Homeguards you hear about are the greatest enemy of the country because of what these people have done together with the white Settlers, things which no one will forget for many hundreds of years to come.

Those among the Homeguards who had previously had disputes about land or cash crops or of any kind, took advantage of the emergency to eliminate their adversaries.

If you happen to be well off and a certain Homeguard happens to be jealous of you, this is the time when they get rid of you.

PAYING OFF

They find this is a good time to exterminate these people. The Homeguards are given permission to do whatever they like, to kill anybody without reference to any higher authority.

Such things are happening more in places where people are less educated like Githunguri, Kiamwangi and Gatundu.

In their meetings the Homeguards, jot down lists of names of those whom they want to kill, take it to show the district officer who gives them a motor car at night, and then they fetch every man from his home, put them in the car and then shoot them, some in the car, others at cross-roads, leaving the bodies there, and others they take to the forests and shoot them there.

Some of the bodies they take to Kiambu and in the morning they are said to be terrorists.

This sort of thing has been going on for a long time and those who are doing that work are both Homeguards and White Mau Mau the Kenya Police Reserve.

MANY KILLED

I cannot tell you the names of all the people who have been killed, but I can mention of a few like Njoroge wa Kago (Simeoni) and Stefano, the father of Thiani: those are from Waidake school and were taken from their houses by the Kenya Police Reserve on denunciation from the Homeguards. From Githunguri side the people who were also killed on April 1 are: Naftali Boro, a popular doctor, Kageche wa Gacagwi, Muiruri wa Gacagwi, Gathua wa Wagagiki, Kinyanjui wa Mwathi, Gathita wa Kinganga, Ngumba wa Gatuku, Wainaina wa Njogu, Karugari, Ndaba wa Kanugu, Githare wa Njiri, Njuguna wa Karu, Mbatia wa Kierere, Mbogu wa Rungatho, Kamau wa Wakierere, Kimani wa Waikanga, Makena wa Njuki, Muya and many others.

All those were killed by Homeguard and White Mau Mau, the Police Reserve, and they were taken from their homes at night on Wednesday. Gikuni wa Wang'ang'a was killed the same night and many others

MEN CASTRATED

On Limuru side Wakiru, Mbuthia wa Mukoma, Muika wa Maye, Kirubi wa Kungu, Muiru wa Gikanga, Gathitu, Wakari, Kihugu wa Njuguna, Njoroge wa Githu and many others. The people I am telling you about were all fetched from their houses and killed though innocent.

Because of these killings of innocent people whenever those concerned feel like it, many young people feel compelled to go away from home for fear of death. Even the older men are no longer at home. The houses of those who go away from home for fear of death or castration are being burnt and many men have been castrated by the White Mau Mau. Many of their homes have been burnt and many of their children were burnt inside them. No goods or property are allowed to be taken out of the burning huts, not even cash, it has all got to be burnt.

HOMES BURNT

None of the houses are burnt during the day, they are always burnt at night, and even the houses of people who were arrested in the past are now being burnt. The house of Kungu Karumba has been burnt and that of Dedani Mugo has been demolished. Waira Kamau's house has also been demolished and many other homes.

What is happening here is terrible - even we are not living at home. The Reverend Bwana Gatungu and Charles Karao were arrested in May and were sent to Kajiado. In the past they have been carrying out cleansing ceremonies. Whether you know anything or not, you must say that you took the Mau Mau oath, because if you refuse to do so, your home and that of the locust will be the same, or you will be given to the white Settlers, who will certainly shoot you without mercy

WOMEN BEATEN

Another terrible thing now happens at certain locations for example at Gathage water mills. There the women of that side are compelled to go to the mill, where they are shut in and all their clothes taken off. From 5 p.m. to 6.30 they are forced to go into the water behind the dam with their hands raised above their heads; they are up to their necks in water and stay there for 25 to 50 minutes. Then they are taken out, still naked, and they are beaten and beaten, being at the same time told to say that Kenyatta administered the Mau Mau oath to them at his home, which is not for away.

A great number of women are continually in this trouble. The women of Majugu's location are in a great trouble. They are being arrested and all their clothes taken off them. When a woman says she does not know about the Mau Mau oath, boiling water is kept nearby, and is poured on her breasts until her skin comes off there and then and she is just left there. If she is dead, she is dead. If not, that is her own business.

EXTERMINATED

What I could tell you is that nobody is allowed to move from one village to the other without pass, even Indians are not allowed to enter Kikuyu country. The reason is that they should not disclose what is happening here. There are some villages in which the population has been completely exterminated. Even to gather information which I have given you in this letter is not easy.

There is another new thing. It is to arrest anybody without discrimination, children as well as women. People are being arrested in hundreds and thousands without being given any reason why. Some are beaten, others detained, and then given three, five, six or seven years imprisonment. They are said to be Mau Mau. They are lined up, then dived into sections and then told: section one, one year; section two, two years, and so on and you are not to ask why".

Source:

Kenya Committee for Democratic Rights for Kenya (London). (1952-60): "Kenya Press Extracts". Photocopies of the extracts available in the Kenya Liberation Library.

pp. 39-40. Reprinted from the *Daily Worker.* 7-Sept. 1953.

The Land & Freedom Army Letter (4-4-1955)

THE LAND AND FREEDOM ARMY,
KENYA PARLIAMENT,
NYANDARUA,
KENYA.

4th April 1955.

The President
The Kenya Committee,
86, Rochester Row,
London, S. W. L.

Dear Sir,

In reference to our letters dated 18/3/55 and 25/3/55 both signed by the Prime Minister, Sir Dedan Kimathi, I would hereby submit the following on behalf of the Kenya Parliament.

The two and a half years of emergency past in Kenya means genocide, destruction of Kenya Africans, Kenya beings and Kenya wealth. Truly these are unfriendly actions but certainly war actions in revenge to the enemies.

I wonder whether Kenya is a British subject, and if so does it mean that British administrators are foolish men and women, who cannot by any means cure the Kenya disease, or does it mean that they enjoy the suppression of the Kenya Africans?

The longer the emergency the poorer the country becomes, both Kenya and England, and the more the enmity and hatred grows strong; and worse still the British Empire will be blamed by the world for its injustice.

In Kenya there has been an average death rate of a hundred persons daily since the declaration of the emergency. The deaths have been due to weapons, starvation, and mistreatment which are organised by the Kenya Government.

This calculation would mean about ninety thousand persons (90 000) have died and in addition to that one million pounds per month is being used in order to carry on the genocide; while the country's wealth (personal) is used twice as much.

Who will pay all this cost? Definitely the British Empire which has appointed and supervised the Kenya Government is responsible for the cost.

I therefore accuse the Governor of Kenya, Sir Evelyn Baring, and General Sir George Erskine, Commander in Chief of East Africa, in the London Parliament, House at Commons, for what 1 have written and for the following reasons:

1. The whole length one the whole cost of the emergency is due to them.

2. The whole blame of the British Empire injustices by the world, is due to them.

3. None of them has ever stated the truth of Kenya in the London Parliament or answered correctly what is asked of Kenya. (We have noted this from the newspapers).

4. They are untrusted persons, none of them wishes to find out the source of Kenya troubles and hence get the cure, but all they are after is surrender offer.

5. Both have signed three deceiving promises (Treaty) for surrender offer of which none of them is fulfilled. The first was signed on the 24th August 1953, and the second on the 18th January 1955, stating that "No one will be prosecuted for any offence connected with the Emergency which he may have committed prior to 13th January 1955" printed by the Government Printer, Nairobi, for the Department of Information, Kenya - no reference. There are more than eighty thousand (80,000) African detainees in camps who are having no trials at all. Why haven't they released these Africans as they signed on the 18th January 1955? What was the use then of these papers with their initials?

6. Last month the Secretariat Nairobi, and the Military Chief of Staff communicated with our soldiers of the low ranks with the help of Mr. Henderson of the Police C. I.D. and here again both signed a letter saying that they would like to have some delegates from the Land and Freedom Army for peace discussions.

We noted this to be a big trick, for none of them would write to the Prime Minister Sir Dedan Kimathi, neither to the Chief Secretary of the State for the Kenya Parliament. Neither would they let this be known by the Kenya Legislative Members or Settlers or Africans. What peace or promises could be done by two persons who are fighting in the darkness where no person sees or hears what they are doing?

7. The same kind of trick was done by the Governor and General Sir Erskine in March 1954, referring to General China's case.

8. Both have divided the Kenya Africans into many parts and always are creating hatred between the parties and forcing the parties to fight each other and supply the groups with weapons - firearms and ammunitions.

Our delegates are always ready to state the truth of Kenya in public hearing but will not agree with any secret movement led and signed by the Governor of Kenya and Gen. Sir George Erskine with their hypocrisy and their injustices.

I hereby enclose the 18th January 1955 "Promise" signed by the Governor and Gen. Sir George Erskine which has not yet been fulfilled by them.

Yours faithfully
Chief Secretary of the State,
General Sir Karari Njama
4.4.55

P.S.   N.B. There is no other peace or settlement of Kenya troubles except; - WIYATHI, UHURU, FREEDOM of self-government to the Kenya Africans.

Source:

Kenya Committee for Democratic Rights for Kenya (London). (1952-60): "Kenya Press Extracts". Photocopies of the extracts available in the Kenya Liberation Library.

pp.133 b & c.

C: Research Aid

Saleh Mamon (2014): Kenya Resistance, Repression & Revolt: A Timeline

The Timeline was compiled by Saleh Mamon for the "Kenya Land and Freedom Depository" London exhibition in November 2014 curated by Tajender Sagoo & Saleh Mamon. Details of the exhibition are available at: http://www.popsamiti.org/kenyalandfreedom.html [Accessed: 19-08-2017]. The author and Vita Books are grateful to Saleh Mamon and Tajender Sagoo for permission to reproduce the Timeline in this book.

1888: BRITISH COLONISATION BEGINS

1880S: RESISTANCE BY COASTAL PEOPLES

Indigenous forces led specifically by Mbaruk Rashid, Simba Ahmed Fumoluti, Fumo Bakari and Fumo Omari resist British invasion. Mbaruk led partisan forces as a guerrilla commander in a decisive battle from 1895-1896. These forces attacked and overran seven British fortresses along the coast. The battle united the coastal nationalities and their Arab allies. Tide turned against the resistance when the British brought military forces from Sudan, Egypt and India and deployed African mercenaries which drove the resistance fighters across the border to Tanganyika where they were forced to surrender by the German invading army. This defeat led to the occupation of Mombasa as the political and military headquarter of the British. (Kinyatti, p.1-2).

1890S: THE TAITA MOUNT STIFF RESISTANCE

Further inland (west of Mombasa), the Taita-Taveta people put up stiff resistance over eight years to British invasion. Initially it was led by Commander Mwangeka, the leader of the Taita military forces in the Mragua region. In 1898, two great battles were fought in the Magangi and Irisi region. (Kinyatti, p2- 3)

1888: WAIYAKI'S AND THE GIKUYU RESISTANCE IN THE CENTRAL REGION

Waiyaki (Waiyaki wa Hinga) led a strong local Gikuyu resistance against takeover of rich agricultural land. Although he signed a treaty with the British, he led a force that burned down the Fort Lugard. He was abducted and killed in 1892. Following Waiyaki's death, the Gikuyu continued their resistance until 1902 throughout the central region and faced savage repression. (Kinyatti, p9-16)

1895 (ONWARDS): THE AKAMABA PEOPLE RESIST COLONISATION

In November 1895, Akamba forces led by commander Mwana wa Muka attacked and overran the military base at Mukuyuni in the Iveti region. The war spread widely across the region. The British used divide and rule strategy and set up chiefs who collaborated with them. They launched a savage offensive against the partisan forces with slaughter of unarmed population and indiscriminate destruction of property. The Akamba's finally surrendered their sovereignty. (Kinyatti, p7-9)

1895: BATTLES IN WESTERN KENYA

Fierce battles were fought in western Kenya against British invasion in the Abukusu lands. These took place at Lumboka near the present-day Bungoma and another at Chitambe's fort near the current Webuye town. The British suffered enormous losses but were able to defeat the resistance using a large army and superior weapons. (Kinyatti, p21-25)

1896: CONSTRUCTION OF THE UGANDAN RAILWAY BEGAN AT MOMBASA.

1896: VAGRANCY ORDINANCE LAW PASSED 1898: THE SOMALI MILITARY CAMPAIGN IN NORTH EAST

In Northeastern Province, the Somali forces led by Mohammed Abdille Hassan waged courageous military campaigns against British invaders until 1920. (Kinyatti, p25)

1900 (ONWARDS): KOITALEL LEADS THE NANDI RESISTANCE IN THE RIFT VALLEY

Koitalel becomes the supreme commander of the Nandi resistance in the Rift Valley region after land seizures for railways. He attacked British bases and the British seized the Nandi livestock, burnt their home and granaries and murdered women and children. In 1905 Koitalel was murdered in cold blood at a meeting to agree a truce. The Nandi put up strong resistance well into 1911. (Kinyatti, p17-19)

1900: AFRICAN PASSES ORDINANCE 1901: RAILWAY LINE REACHED

KISUMU

1902: FIRST WHITE SETTLERS ARRIVE TO TAKE UP LAND IN KENYA'S CENTRAL HIGHLANDS.

1902: NATIVE HUT AND POLL TAX

The colonial state enacted several measures to impose taxes and to ensure forced labour supply. These included hut and poll taxes and the Native porters and Laborers Ordinance.

1904: MASTERS AND SERVANTS LAW

This law is heavily biased towards employers and designed to discipline employees. It also banned trade unions.

1905: THE ABAGUSSI ENGAGE THE BRITISH AROUND KISII

A major battle took place between the Abagussi and the British invaders. The Abagussi armed with pikes, spears and arrows faced shotguns, rifles and machine guns. They resorted to guerrilla war. The British established a base at Getembe (now Kisii town). The leader behind the resistance was a woman, Morra Ngiti. In 1908, Otyeno, another leader, speared the British commander Northcote who survived. This led to a destructive British revenge of extermination and destruction. Otyeno was arrested and killed. (Kinyatti p23-25)

1906: THE ELGIN PLEDGE RESERVES HIGHLANDS FOR EUROPEANS

The European Settlers who controlled the Land Board recommended that the colonial government reserve the highlands for exclusive European settlement. In 1906, Lord Elgin, the British Secretary of State for Colonies, pledged that the Kenya highlands should not be granted to Asians or Africans. Africans living in the highlands were dispossessed and moved to reserves. (Maxon & Ofcanky, p91)

1907: THE BRITISH COLONIAL ADMINISTRATION MOVES FROM MOMBASA TO NAIROBI

1910: THE MASTER AND SERVANTS ORDINANCE

This set out parameters of exploiting Kenyan African labour on a casual basis from the African reserves. Men on the other hand cooked for European Settlers, tended European livestock, milked and took milk to the market for sale on behalf of their employer. It defined short-term or casual labour as adult labour engaged on daily or monthly basis, a 30 day ticket or 90 day contracts. Casual labour made it possible to combine wage labour with African agricultural work. Women as well as juveniles were engaged as daily paid casual labourers in the settler farms. (Kinyatti, p29-35)

1911-14: ME KATILILI LEADS THE GIRIAMA RESISTANCE

North of Mombasa around Lamu, the Giriama people resisted colonisation. Mekatilili, a woman led the Giriama people in a rebellion against British administration and policies. She was captured and exiled but returned home to continue her opposition. (Kinyatti, p3-7)

1914: KENYAN AFRICANS RECRUITED IN THE BRITISH ARMY DURING WWI

The British and Germans engaged in a war of attrition across the Kenya/Tanganyika border and across Tanganyika and the Malawi border. 200,000 Africans were recruited into the British army and one fourth of them lost their lives. The war devastated an area five times the size of Germany and the civilian suffering was on a scale unimaginable in Europe.

(Plaice)

1915: THE CROWN LAND (S) ORDINANCE

This ordinance sealed the fate of Asian and African land ownership in the Kenya highlands. Under the ordinance, the Government of the British East Africa Protectorate was empowered to veto any land transaction involving people from non-European racial backgrounds. The Crown Lands Ordinances transferred millions of acres of African land to the ownership of Europeans. Accordingly, land not owned by Europeans eventually became "Crown Land" and Africans owned no land according to the law (Kinyatti, p30-31)

1915 ONWARDS: LAND GRABS ON A MASSIVE SCALE

The land seized from indigenous people was handed over to white Settlers, speculators, military personnel, merchants, bankers and big capitalist companies. Some examples are: East African Syndicate got 320,000 acres; Uplands of East African Syndicate got 350,000 acres; Grogan Forest Concessions 200,000 acres; Delamere family got 100,000 acres; Colonel Lord Frances Scott (uncle of Duchess of Gloucester) appropriated more than 350,000 acres. (Kinyatti, p31)

1915: THE NATIVE REGISTRATION ORDINANCE

This forced all African adult males to carry identification whenever leaving the reserves.

1915-16: GHADAR PARTY MEMBERS HANGINGS AND DEPORTATION

Indians belonging to the Ghadar(Revolution) Party were detained, deported or hanged for possessing and distributing their party newspaper. Bishan Singh of Jalander, Ganesh Das & Yog Raj Bali of Rawalpindi were sentenced to death. Eight people were imprisoned for terms ranging from six months to 14 years. Three other were shot and two were hanged. In December 1915, Keshvlal Dwivedi, Chief Clerk in the High Court was sentenced to death for possessing a letter from Sitaram Acharia, the leader of the Ghadar movement in East Africa and a collection of "seditious" newspaper clippings. L.M. Savle, another active organizer was sentenced to death for the same offence. (Durrani, p43)

1918 (MAY ONWARDS): THE TURKANA REVOLT

The Turkana army under the leadership of Ebei and Lowalel defeated an invading British force of over 1,500 soldiers at the Battle of Kangalia. It took the British forces, despite their modern weapons, three years to conquer the Turkana land. (Kinyatti, p20-21)

1918: THE RESIDENT NATIVE LABOUR ORDINANCE (RNLO)

This defined both the legal status and the labour obligations of the squatters who had been dispossessed of their land.

1919: THE NATIVE AUTHORITY ORDINANCE

This racist law was a fatal blow to African traditional and culture. It turned virtually all African functionaries into "slave" raiders of their own people and forced the majority of Kenyans into a state of estranged enslavement in their own country. African heritage and culture- religion, gods, arts, music, dance, dress, food, educational system, history, languages, circumcision systems, philosophy, names etc., were condemned as primitive, evil and barbaric. (Kinyatti, p33)

1919: SOLDIER SETTLER SCHEME

2,000,000 acres of land were seized from the Nandi reserve without compensation and allotted on 999-year leasehold as a reward to British veterans of World War I – leading to a large scale displacement of Kenyan Africans. (Durrani, p29)

1920: THE NATIVE REGISTRATION AMENDMENT ORDINANCE

This made it compulsory for African males above the age of 15 to carry a *kipande* around their neck at all times. The *kipande* was an identity document which featured basic personal details, fingerprints, and an employment history. The main intent of the policy was to impose a forced labour policy. *Kipande* caused much resentment. Africans were deprived of all basic human rights. They were forbidden to travel in certain areas, to sleep in certain areas, even to accept employment in certain areas or to bring their families from the rural areas to urban centres without colonial authorization. (Kinyatti, p30)

1921: KENYA BECOMES BRITISH CROWN COLONY

A British governor administered the colony. The European settler population reached 10,000.

1921(JUNE): YOUNG KIKUYU ASSOCIATION FOUNDED

YKA is the first genuine anti-imperialist movement formed in June in Pangani, Nairobi under the leadership of Harry Thuku. It organized mass rallies against the *kipande* system, forced labour policies, sexual assaults on African women by white Settlers, racial segregation, expropriation of land and the system of taxation. It demanded the establishment of a democratic system and the equal distribution of the nation's wealth. Within a very short time a large force of the African working class in all the main towns in the country was mobilized. The asociation formed an alliance with progressive Indian political organisations, groups and individuals whose contributions enriched and deepened the anti-imperialist movement. (Kinyatti, p37)

1921(JULY): EAST AFRICAN ASSOCIATION FORMED

YKA dissolved and a nationwide and regional nationalist anti-colonial movement, the East African Association (EAA) was formed. Harry Thuku was elected as its chairman. Harry Thuku was dismissed from his job in the colonial civil service. EAA built international links with W.E.B. Du Bois's National Association of Colored People (NAACP) and Garvey's the Universal Negro Improvement Association (UNIA). A.M. Jeevanjee and Varma represented the EAA at the second Pan African Congress in London in 1021. EAA adopted a political manifesto with 14 demands. (Kinyatti, p39)

1922 (MARCH 14): HARRY THUKU ARRESTED AND 250 PROTESTORS KILLED

The colonial authorities arrested the leaders of EAA, Harry Thuku, Waiganjo wa

Ndotono and George Mugekenyi. Mass protest erupted in Nairobi. Protestors marched to the police headquarters from Pangani. Police opened fire on unarmed protestors. Fleeing protestors were also fired upon by white Settlers and game hunters at the nearby Norfolk Hotel. 250 protestors were shot dead and hundreds were seriously injured. Muthoni wa Nyanjiru and Macaria wa Kiboi, two leaders of the demonstrations were martyred. Mass arrests and imprisonment followed to terrorize the people. Arrested leaders were imprisoned without trial. Thuku was exiled to Kismayu in Somalia for several years and returned to Marsabit prison until his release in 1930. EAA as banned. (Kinyatti p41-43, Durrani p48-49)

1922 (MARCH): THE FIRST GENERAL STRIKE IN NAIROBI

This was triggered by the arrest of Harry Thuku and the massacre of protestors. The workers' demands included the wide nationalist demand articulated by the EAA. These were the abolition of the *kipande* system and forced labour, the improvement of wages and working conditions, the reduction of taxes, the return of African lands, improvement in education and the election of Africans to the Legislative Council. (Durrani,p51)

1923: DEVONSHIRE PAPER AND CONSOLIDATION OF WHITE LAND OWNERSHIP

The paper clearly stated that Kenya is an African territory and for that matter African interests should be paramount. This was a shift from the official policy of the primacy of European interests. But the declaration did not change African plight. The Paper further consolidated the dual policy of Europeans in exclusive areas and Africans in reserves. (Durrani, p 51-52. Kinyatti, p49. Elkins, map p6))

1924/25: KIKUYU CENTRAL ASSOCIATION FOUNDED

The Kikuyu Central Association (KCA) was formed under the leadership of James Beauttah and Joseph Kang'ethe and other KCA militants. The new party adopted the EAA's anti-imperialist stance and political programme and campaigns for the release of Harry Thuku and other detained leaders. In 1926, James Beaturah was transferred to Uganda. This deprived the KCA movement of his leadership. (Kinyatti, p48)

1927: JOMO KENYATTA BECOMES GENERAL SECRETARY OF KCA

Jomo Kenyatta took up the full time job as KCA General Secretary and Editor-in-Chief of the party organ, *Muigwithani*. Kenyatta, Joseph Kang'ethe and Jesse Kariuki travelled across the country to explain the party's program, recruited new party members and established new party branches. (Kinyatti, p 52)

1928: KCA MEMORANDUM TO HILTON YOUNG COMMISSION

KCA submits a memorandum to the Hilton Young Commission demanding the end to land dispossession, the release of detained EAA leaders, the abolition of the *kipande* system, the repeal of restrictions on planting coffee and other crops, the exemption of hut and poll tax for women, improvement to education and technical training for Kenyan Africans etc. (Kinyatti, p53)

1929: KENYATTA SUBMITS PETITION IN LONDON Kenyatta submits a KCA petition to British authorities in London making democratic demands. (Kinyatti, p55)

1930S: EMERGENCE OF CULTURAL RESISTANCE

Cultural resistance against imperialism emerged in this period e.g. *Miti ya Kenya* movement and Kariang'a Educational Movement. This was a reaction to the attack on indigenous culture, customs, traditions and religion by the Church, politicians and educationalists (Kinyatti p 57-60)

1930 (SEPTEMBER): THUKU RELEASED, KENYATTA BECOMES KEY FIGURE

Kenyatta returned home as hero. Thuku was released from detention and expelled from the KCA. Kenyatta emerged as the central figure in the anti-colonial movement. (Kinyatti, p61-63)

1934 (MAY): KENYA LAND COMMISSION NULLIFIES KIKUYU LAND CLAIMS

The Report of Kenya Land Commission denied and nullified virtually all Kikuyu land claims against European expropriation.

1935: PRO-BRITISH AFRICAN GROUPS EMERGE

The British begin to create a loyalist class to divide the Kenyans. Thuku and his supporters form a pro-British party-the Kikuyu Provincial Association (KPA). The pro-British Kikuyu Association was renamed as Kikuyu Loyal Patriots (KLP) (Kinyatti, p62)

1938: NATIVE LANDS TRUST AND THE CROWN LANDS (AMENDMENT) ORDINANCES

These sanctioned the further takeover of the best and most fertile lands in the highland region. Peasant landowners were evicted forcefully after relentless resistance. They were forcibly collected and dumped at Olenguruone in the Rift Valley to start their lives from scratch where disease and hunger killed many of them. The discovery of gold in Kakamega led to clashes and further evictions. (Kinyatti, p63-64,86)

1938: FOUNDING OF THE KENYA TEACHER'S COLLEGE (KTC) AT GITHUNGURI

Mbiyu wa Koinange founded the college which was to become the centre of radical education.

1938 (JANUARY): THE AKAMBA ANTI-DESTOCKING RESISTANCE

The colonial regime used armed police and military forces to seize cattle from the Akamba to provide meat to a Leiberg's canning factory at Athi river by auctioning the cattle. The Ukamba Members Association (UMA) coordinated the anti-stocking resistance through petitions and demonstrations nationwide. Their leader Muindi wa Mbingu arrested and deported to Lamu Island. Facing mounting resistance, the authorities suspended the de-stocking policy. (Kinyatti, p65-68)

1938: ALLIANCE BETWEEN KCA AND LABOUR TRADE UNIONS

The KCA leadership formed an alliance with the Labour Trade Union of East Africa (LTUEA) under the leadership of Makhan Singh.(Kinyatti, p69)

1939: THE TAITA HILLS ASSOCIATION FORMED

Taita Hills Association (THA) was formed as a protest against land alienation and cultural encroachments in the Taita country.(Kinyatti, p68-69)

1939 (AUGUST): STRIKE PARALYSES MOMBASA

A Strike paralysed Mombasa especially the Kilindini harbour. Over 6,000 workers went on strike demanding equal pay for all workers and better treatment of African labour. Labour unions were becoming stronger in the colony. Paramilitary police reinforcements were sent to break the strike. Many workers were killed and many more seriously wounded but the workers stood firm. This demonstrated the worker's courage and a landmark development in the history of the working class in Kenya. (Kinyatti, p70)

1940 (MAY): MAKHAN SINGH ARRESTED IN INDIA

Colonial authorities arrested Makhan Singh in India for his trade union and political activities. He was imprisoned for five years without trial. (Kinyatti p.92)

1940 (MAY): COLONIAL GOVERNMENT BANS KIKUYU CENTRAL ASSOCIATION (KCA), UKAMBA MEMBERS ASSOCIATION (UMA) AND TAITA HILLS ASSOCIATION (THA)

At the outbreak of WWII, the offices of the three organizations were closed and their publications banned. Twenty three nationalist leaders were imprisoned without trial and not released until 1944. The KCA went underground as Kiama Kia Ndemwa Ithatu (KKNI- the party of three letters) (Kinyatti, p70-71)

1944: Kenya African Union (KAU) founded

The KAU was formed as a national united front against colonialism in the context of deepening misery and suffering among the masses. Racist laws restricted all freedoms for Africans and segregation prevailed in all walks of life. KKNI leaders began to draw a strategy for protracted struggle against colonialism. This was spurred by the return of the Second World War veterans. More than 100,000 Kenyan Africans served in the British Armed forces. Half of them died in the battlefield, thousands never returned, many thousands returned damaged for life. They returned to the home villages to die in poverty. Many such as Stanley Mathenge, Paul Ngei, Bildad Kaggia, General China and General Kago were radicalised by the war experience and exposure to revolutionary and anti-imperialist ideas. (Kinyatti,p75-83)

1945 (FEB): KENYATTA AT INTERNATIONAL CONFERENCES

Kenyatta represents the Kenyan trade unions at World Federation of Trade Unions (WFTU). He represents Kenya at the 5th Pan-African Congress held in Manchester in October.

1945 (APRIL 28): LEADER OF *DINI YA MSAMBWA* IMPRISONED

Elijah Masinde the leader of *Dini ya Msambwa* (DYM) a powerful anti- imperialist politico-religious movement in the country arrested and incarcerated in a mental hospital as a 'schizophrenic'. (Kinyatti, p87)

1947 (JUNE): JOMO KENYATTA BECOMES LEADER OF KAU

KKNI leadership met with Governor Mitchell. Mitchell rejected any suggestion of Kenyatta joining the Legislative Council and asked him to run for a Local Native

Council. Kenyatta rejected this offer. (Kinyatti, p78)

1947 (JANUARY): FORTY YOUTH MOVEMENT FOUNDED

The Forty Youth Movement (FYM) organized and held its first public meeting at Kariokor Market, Nairobi. It had a radical political leadership which wanted to organize people to expel the British from Kenya. In rural areas it opposed forced cattle inoculation and forced labour terracing work in the Highlands. In the urban centres, it fought to stop exploitation, corporal punishment, the *kipande* system, the segregation laws etc. (Kinyatti, pp.83-85, Durrani, p.99)

1947 (JANUARY 13): GENERAL STRIKE IN MOMBASA

The General Strike was organized by newly formed African Worker's Federation (AWF) under Cege wa Kibacia's leadership. 15,000 workers participated. 400 were arrested. It was repressed brutally with some strikers killed and many seriously injured. They won concessions. On August 22, Cege is arrested, secretly tried and banished to Kabarnet in the Rift Valley. The AWF was banned. (Durrani, p83, Kinyatti, p920)

1947 (FEBRUARY ONWARDS): THE OLENGURUONE RESISTANCE

The Kikuyu peasants of the Rift Valley province of Olenguruone were given notice of eviction from their land. They used anti-colonial oath to resist eviction and they courageously resisted the eviction for two years. (Kinyatti, p86)

1947 - 48: DYM WAGES GUERRILLA WAR

Masinde was discharged in May 1947. He denounced British occupation, condemned Christianity as a religion of the oppressor and the white missionaries as tools of colonialism. He organized a rally at Chitambe to commemorate the 1985 Abukusu uprising. The DYM waged a guerrilla war against the British. (Kinyatti, p87)

1948 (FEBRUARY): MALKISI MASSACRE

About 2500 followers of DYM demonstrated against the establishment of a missionary station in Kitosh. Police used live fire to kill eleven protestors and injured many more to suppress the protest. Masinde was captured on 16 February 1948. He was deported to Lamu Island and was not released until 1962 (Kinyatti, p 89)

1948 (ONWARDS): KENYATTA JOINS KTC

Kenyatta joined KTC as a teacher and administrator. He brought Afrocentric approaches to the curriculum and made the college a base of radical politics and cultural nationalism. He toured the country mobilizing people for independence. (Kinyatti, p81)

1949 (MAY DAY) EAST AFRICAN TRADE UNION CONGRESS FOUNDED

The labour movements joined together to form East African Trade Union Congress (EATUC) under the leadership of Fred Kubai and Makhan Singh. The colonial regime refuse to register it on the grounds that it was a 'communist' front. The union mobilized the working class across the country. (Kinyatti, p.94-95)

1949 (NOVEMBER) FORCIBLE EVICTION OF KIKUYU FROM OLENGURUONE

The peasants in Olenguruone were forcibly evicted. The colonial forces carries out beatings, rape, burning of homes and granaries, destruction of crops and confiscation of livestock. (Kinyatti,p86)

1950: A POLITICAL SPLIT EMERGES WITHIN NATIONALIST FORCES

A Political split began to develop between the leadership of KAU and KAU militants, trade union leaders and radical youth. The split was between constitutionalists and radicals. A coalition of political anti-imperialist social forces came into being under the leadership of underground KKNI especially in central Kenya: the Agikuyu Age-Group Association; the Independent School and Church movement, the Olenguruone Resistance Movement, the central Kenya KAU militants, the Gikuyu Land Board Association, the militant leadership of KTC, Mumbi Central Association, the African Women League, the FYM, trade union leaders and progressive petty-bourgeoisie. (Kinyatti,p102)

1950 (FEB 20): KKNI INSTITUTES ANTI- IMPERIALIST OATH

The KKNI underground movement instituted an anti-imperialist oath, *Muuma wa Tiiri* for its members to develop national leadership and to heighten national consciousness. Secrecy, discipline and loyalty were demanded. (Kinyatti, p103)

1950 MARCH 4: EATUC LAUNCHES A BOYCOTT

EATUC launched a successful boycott of the visit of the Duke of Gloucester who was to present a charter giving Nairobi official city status on March 30. This was denounced by the white settler regime as 'communist agitation'. Kenyatta and EAU executive denounced the boycott. (Kinyatti, p95-97)

1950 (MAY 1): GENERAL STRIKE, MAKHAN SINGH AND OTHERS JAILED

Colonial authorities banned the May Day procession in Nairobi organized by EATUC. Its leaders were arrested. On May 16th, a nationwide general strike was declared and it spread from Nairobi to all major towns in the country. The colonial authorities declared the strike illegal. The EATUC was banned. Mwangi wa Macaria and Makhan Singh were held in prison until 1961. (Kinyatti, p98-99)

1950 (MAY 12): THE TERM MAU MAU NAME ENTERS THE POLITICAL LEXICON

Thirty nine Kenyan farm workers were arrested in Naivasha. They were tortured by the police and accused of belonging to an unlawful society They were jailed for seven years each with hard labour. The colonial press seized the name 'Mau Mau' as the name of the movement. The name entered the political dictionary. It was estimated that 90 percent of the 1.5 million Kikuyu had taken the oath for land and freedom. (Kinyatti, p105-106, Elkins, p54)

1950 (AUGUST, 12): MAU MAU PROSCRIBED

British authorities proscribed the Mau Mau movement. Suspected leaders were arrested, tortured and imprisoned. (Kinyatti,p107)

1950 (NOVEMBER): KAU DELEGATION TO LONDON FOR PEACEFUL TRANSITION

KAU sent a delegation of two people with a petition for ensuring a peaceful transition to African self-government, more African representation, end to racism, abolition of *kipande* system, more land for Africans, and better education, wages and housing. The Colonial Secretary refused to receive the memorandum. KAU also met with white liberal group Kenya Citizens' Association to discuss the transition. The European Settlers opposed any constitutional engagement and sought greater control of the country and seek permanent reservation of highlands for Europeans.

(Kinyatti,p118)

1951 (FEBRUARY): KAU HOLDS ANTI- MAU MAU RALLIES

KAU organized a series of anti- Mau Mau meetings addressed by Kenyatta and others. KAU decided to expel any official with any political connection with Mau Mau and KKNI and hand them over to the colonial authorities. In response, radicals mobilized to win elections for the key posts of Nairobi KAU Branch. (Kinyatti p120-125)

1951(MID): THE MAU MAU CENTRAL COMMITTEE SET UP

The Mau Mau Central Committee (MMCC) consisted of 12 members. It invented a new powerful anti-imperialist weapon, the Oath of Unity (*Muuma wa Uiguano*). Higher level of oaths included, the Oath of war, and the Oath of leadership. The MMCC called for a boycott of business, city buses and foreign-made beer. It called for an end to prostitution or socialization with the Occupiers. (Kinyatti, p111-113)

1951(NOVEMBER): KAU CONGRESS SPLITS ALONG IDEOLOGICAL LINES

The KAU Party Congress split into three ideological groups- the right pro- British, the liberal anti-colonialist nationalists and the revolutionary left. (Kinyatti, p109-110)

1951: MMCC FORMS GROUP OF THIRTY

The MMCC formed a new body the Group of Thirty to organize financial resources, build underground cells across the country and to organize an armed wing for the movement. The armed wing, under the leadership of Stanley Mathenge, became the Kenya Land and Freedom Army (KLFA). The main task of the KLFA was to (1) safeguard the security of the movement (2) disseminate its political information and programme among the masses (3) to recruit cadres (4) to collect intelligence (5) to collect weapons and ammunition (6) to administer anti-imperialist oath (7) to eliminate enemies of the movement (8) to garner financial resources. The guerrilla army entered the Nyandarwa (Aberdares) and Kirinyaga (Mount Kenya) forests. In Nairobi, military training was accelerated and discipline and secrecy reinforced. (Kinyatti, p117)

1952: KAU DENOUNCES MAU MAU

KAU leadership including Kenyatta organized rallies to denounce the activities of the underground movement and the Mau Mau. Some collaborated with the Colonial authorities and betrayed the names of some of the leaders. The MMCC leadership summoned Kenyatta and after a heated argument made an agreement that the anti-Mau Mau meetings scheduled by the authorities for him would be cancelled and that he should remain neutral. (Kinyatti p119-126)

1952 (APRIL 4): COLLECTIVE PUNISHMENTS ORDINANCE

This gave the authorities the power to impose fines on whole villages and was used with growing regularity as the Emergency deepened. (Anderson p46)

1952 (JUNE): MMCC FORCES PREPARE FOR MILITARY OFFENSIVE

The MMCC instructed General Mathenge, the Mau Mau army commander-in-chief to prepare for a military offensive. (Kinyatti, p127)

1952 (AUGUST 8): SETTLERS PUSH FOR EMERGENCY

Settlers leaders held an emergency meeting and passed resolutions demanding emergency powers, elimination of Mau Mau leaders and the arrest of KAU leaders. (Kinyatti, p128)

1952 (7 OCTOBER): CHIEF WARUHUI ASSASSINATED

Senior Chief Waruhui, the government's 'tower of strength' is assassinated in Kenya. He had recently spoken out against the Mau Mau. The authorities use this to mount a massive propaganda campaign against the Mau Mau (Kinyatti, p128)

1952(OCT 20): BRITISH GOVERNMENT DECLARES A STATE OF EMERGENCY

Governor Baring declares an Emergency. The British government sends troops to Kenya. Lancashire Fusiliers is the first battalion to arrive. Six battalions of King's African Rifles are based in Kenya. Two further battalions follow in 1953 bringing the total to nine military battalions in all. (Anderson, p390,391)

1952 (OCT 21):ONE HUNDRED NATIONALIST LEADERS ARRESTED

The security services launched Operation Jock Stock. 180 alleged nationalist leaders including Jomo Kenyatta were arrested. They were chained and sent to a concentration camp in Kajiado where they were tortured. Administrators of Karing'a independent schools and churches, teachers, pastors, and students were arrested and imprisoned without trial. (Elkins p35, Kinyatti, p128)

1952 (OCTOBER): AFRICAN POLITICS, PRESS AND CULTURAL INSTITUTIONS SHUT DOWN

All political activity in urban centres is suppressed and anti-imperialist press was banned.

1952 (OCT 21): 'WE WILL FIGHT TO THE LAST MAN' LEAFLET

The MMCC distributed a leaflet in Nairobi entitled *'We will fight to the Last Man'*. The development of a radical anti-imperialist movement shocked the foundation of the colonial state. (Kinyatti, p132)

1952 (OCT 23): KENYA WAR COUNCIL FORMED

To prepare for an armed struggle, the Mau Mau leaders transformed the Central Committee into the War Council (Kenya War Council). (Kinyatti, p138)

1953 (OCTOBER 23): MAU MAU STATEMENT *"THIS IS THE VOICE ON NEW AFRICA"*

Noting the developments towards fascist policies, the MMCC issued a second underground statement titled *"This is the Voice of New Africa"* (Kinyatti, p133-134)

1952 ONWARD TO 1963: MASSIVE PSYOPS PROGRAMME LAUNCHED BY THE BRITISH

Massive PSYOPS programme was launched by the colonial authorities to justify a genocidal war against the entire population in the Highlands. The Mau Mau are defined as an "abnormality", "a satanic and tribalist movement" and descendants from "savage ancestors of jungle environment". All means were deployed to disseminate racist misinformation – local and international newspapers, radio, mobile cinemas, schools and churches, pamphlets and colonial information service departments. Anti Mau Mau books, films, magazines and pamphlets were produced by prominent Settlers, writers, missionaries and journalists. (Kinyatti, p134-135, Anderson, p279-284)

1952 (14 NOVEMBER): SCHOOL CLOSURES

Thirty-four schools in Kikuyu tribal areas were closed in the continuing clamp down on the civilian population. 250,000 students were left without schools. (Kinyatti p128)

1952 (18 NOVEMBER): KENYATTA CHARGED

Jomo Kenyatta, president of the Kenya African Union and the country's leading nationalist leader was charged with managing the Mau Mau terrorist society in Kenya. He was flown to a remote district station, Kapenguria, which reportedly had no telephone or rail communications with the rest of Kenya, and was held there incommunicado.

1952 (NOVEMBER): MASS ROUNDUPS OF KIKUYUS IN THE RIFT VALLEY

Forced removals of the civilian population began across Kenya. All suspicious Kikuyu outside the reserves particularly those who were living as squatters on European farms were deported to the reserves. Thousands of Kikuyus in the Rift Valley were packed into railcars and lorries and shipped back to the already crowded reserves.

1952 (NOVEMBER): KLFA'S FIRST OFFENSIVE

The KLFA launched their first offensive. This lasted till March 1953. (Kinyatti p105)

1952 (NOVEMBER 23): THE KIRUARA MASSACRE

White and black members of the British security forces massacred as many as a hundred people in the market place of the small village of Kiruara in the heart of Fort Hall District. There were countless such episodes of similar behaviour across Kenya by security services and none of the perpetrators were brought to justice. (Elkins, p51-52)

1953 (JANUARY TO APRIL): THE EMERGENCY REGULATIONS

Governor Baring empowered his government with extreme and wide-ranging laws, called Emergency Regulations. These included provisions for communal punishment, curfews, the control of individual and mass movements of people, the confiscation of property and land, the imposition of special taxes, the censorship and banning of publications, the issuance of special documentation and passes, the control and disposition of labour, the suspension of due process, detention without trial and the imposition of the death penalty. Emergency regulations extend to the control of African markets, shops, hotels, and all transport- including buses, taxis and bicycles. Powers for the creation of concentrated villages in the African reserves, barbed-wire cordons in African towns and in Nairobi, and mini detention camps on settler farms are put in place. (Elkins p35, Kiniyatti p132-133)

1953 (JANUARY 26): PANIC AMONGST THE SETTLERS

Panic spread through Europeans in Kenya after the slaying of a white settler farmer and his family. Settler groups, displeased with the government's response to the increasing Mau Mau threat created their own Commando Units to deal with the threat. Sir Evelyn Baring, the Governor-general of Kenya ordered a new offensive against the Mau Mau under the command of Major-general William Hinde.

1953: THE BRITISH COUNTER-OFFENSIVE

The British deployed thousands of troops and police with armoured cars, warplanes and police dogs. White reinforcements were brought from South Africa, Northern and Southern Rhodesia, Australia, New Zealand. Special forces such as M.I.5 Security Force and Special Air Service Regiment were flown in. A special settler regiment, the Kenya Regiment was set up. The colonial government recruited indigenous anti-Mau Mau forces. These were (1) the Homeguards (*humungaati*) (2) Regular police force (3) Tribal police (4) Paramilitary police force (5) Urban militia (know as *Tai Tai*) (6) the *Tukonia* Unit for screening (7) the *Thaka* unit of informers (7) the Murder Squad Unit for eliminating Mau Mau suspects (8) the Pseudo-Guerrilla Unit. (Kinyatti, p173-74, Elkins, p53)

1953 (MARCH 26): MAU MAU ATTACK THE LOYALIST LARI VILLAGE

The Mau Mau stormed the Lari area to take revenge against the loyalist community's senior statesman, Luka Wakahangara. There were 70 dead and many injured with the razing of 15 homesteads. All the victims were families of local chiefs, ex-chiefs, headmen, councillors and prominent Homeguard. The male heads were leading members of the Lari loyalist community. This was used intensively for government propaganda to shift public opinion against the Mau Mau and divide the Kikuyu community. (Kinyatti, p151, Anderson, p125-127)

1953 (MARCH 26 OVER TWO WEEKS): RETALIATION AFTER LARI

The Homeguards and other elements of security services took revenge after Lari on any person in the area who they could lay their hands on whom they suspected as a Mau Mau sympathiser. There were beatings, torture, shootings and cold-blooded killings. 600 people were killed, 300 homes and 200 granaries were burned down, livestock destroyed and confiscated. (Anderson, p130-132)

1953 (MARCH 30): KLFA'S FIRST CONGRESS

The KLFA held its first Congress at Githugi guerrilla camp in Nyandarwa to coordinate the war effort and to celebrate the KLFA victory at the Battle of Naivasha. Two hundred and fifty guerrilla leaders attended. The congress resolved to establish a twelve member Supreme War Council (SWC). Stanley Mathenge was appointed the Supreme Commander of the KLFA forces and Kimathi became the Secretary General. (Kinyatti, p154)

1953 (APRIL): SPECIAL EMERGENCY ASSIZE COURT

The hanging judges began to hear Mau Mau cases. Over the course of emergency, 1090 Kikuyu went to the gallows, (Anderson, p291) 1953 (APRIL 8):

KENYATTA AND FIVE OTHER LEADERS IMPRISONED

Jomo Kenyatta is sentenced to seven years hard labour along with other leaders Bildad Kaggia, Fred Kubai, Achieng O'neko, Kung'u wa Karumba and Paul Ngei. (Anderson, p67)

1953 (APRIL): KLFA LAUNCHES ITS SECOND OFFENSIVE

The KLFA launched is Second Offensive. It lasts until September 1953. (Kinyatti, p159-172)

1953 (29 MAY): KIKUYU LANDS CORDONED OFF

Kikuyu tribal lands are to be cordoned off from the rest of Kenya to restrict movement of potential Mau Mau suspects.

1953 (JUNE 7): GENERAL ERSKINE TAKES CONTROL

General Erskine arrived in Kenya to end the violence and restore order. He oversaw the deployment of the British battalions, four battalions of King's African Rifles, the Kenya Regiment, an artillery battery, and an armoured car squadron and a Royal Air Force Squadron of Vampire jets and heavy bombers. Their mission was to defeat a Mau Mau force of some 20,000 men and women armed with homemade weapons. (Elkins,p53)

1953 (AUGUST 16): KLFA HOLDS A FOLLOW UP CONGRESS

KLFA held a follow up four day Congress. Mathenge boycotted the Congress. It was attended by more than 5,000 fighters, twelve members of the SWC. The

Congress received reports of the developments on the ground and the impact of the British counterinsurgency on the population. It agreed the tasks of the movement were to consolidate the organizational structure, material structure, communication lines, supply routes, recruitment, propaganda etc. It disbanded the SWC and set up a new political and military body, the Kenya Defence Council (KDC). Kimathi was elected the KDC President and the Field Marshal of all the KLFA forces. The Congress identified eight armies with their commanders and areas of operation. (p185-197)

1953 (OCTOBER ONWARDS): THE PIPELINE SYSTEM SET UP

The system of detention and rehabilitation for Mau Mau suspects was set up. The process would begin at the transit camps and the suspects would be screened and classified. Those classified "white" would be repatriated to the African reserves. Those classified "grey" or "black" would be sent to holding camps. Screening would continue. Those still considered "grey" would be moved to work camps where the detainees would confess their oath voluntarily. Those classified "black" would be sent to special to the special detention camps. Governor Baring places all the detainees in the custody of the Prison Department with very little rehabilitation. (Elkins, p109)

1953 (NOVEMBER): KLFA LAUNCHES ITS THIRD OFFENSIVE

The KLFA launched its Third Offensive in November. This lasted until December 1953. (Kinyatti, p203-209)

1953 (DECEMBER 22): KLFA GENERAL MATENJAGWO KILLED

General Matenjagwe was killed after a surprise attack near Thika (Kinyatti, p203)

1954 (JANUARY - JUNE 1954): KLFA LAUNCHES ITS FOURTH OFFENSIVE

The KLFA intensified its operations on five fronts across Kenya. General Kago led the Murang'a Front and won battles giving KLFA control over the large territory and captured arms and ammunitions from the enemy. General Karia led the campaign in the Nyiri Front. General Ruku commanded the Embu and Meru front. Kiambu front remained the strategic region for KLFA supplies, reinforcements and information before they were sent to guerrillas in the forests. The district was a bridge between Nairobi and Nyandarwa. Nairobi was the headquarters of the national movement and principle source of KLFA supplies and recruitment. (Kinyatti, p241-269)

1954 (15 JANUARY): GENERAL CHINA CAPTURED AND BETRAYS KLFA

General China, the overall commander of the KLFA forces on the Kirinyaga Front, was shot and captured. His death sentence was commuted to life imprisonment after he agreed to help the British to fight and destroy the KLFA. This was a significant victory for the British authorities and a blow to KLFA. He was pardoned after he revealed all the details about the KLFA organization, its connection with the reserves and its supply lines. (Anderson, p232-235, Kinyatti, p232-233)

1954 (FEBRUARY 5): KLFA'S SECOND CONGRESS

The KLFA held its Second Congress at Karathi in Nyandarwa. It was attended by more than a1000 guerrillas, a large peasant delegation and the KWC representatives. The Congress agreed to setting up of Kenya Parliament (KP) composed of twelve members elected through secret ballots.(Kinyatti, p229-231)

1954 (FEBRUARY 15): KLFA ASKED TO SURRENDER

General China worked with the British to hatch a plan for the surrender of the KLFA leadership. He wrote to Kimathi suggesting that nothing further can be gained from the conflict and that they should surrender themselves to British troops waiting in the Aberdare foothills. The KLFA categorically reject the deal and made it clear that there would be no peace talks unless the British agree to unconditional withdrawal of its forces from the country, release all political prisoners and disarm the African auxiliaries. The letter stressed that genuine peace talks must be based on the KLFA Charter. (Kinyatti, p234-235)

1954 (MARCH 31): KLFA'S GENERAL KAGO BURNT ALIVE

General Kago was shot and captured. He refused to cut a surrender deal with the British and then was burnt alive by the colonial forces. (Kinyatti, p251-252)

1954 (MARCH 6): GENERAL TANGANYIKA CAPTURED AND ESCAPES

General Tanganyika, overall field commander of the Kirinyaga KLFA forces was captured through the information China had given to the enemy. KP leaders appointed General Kariba. A delegation of 5 guerrilla envoys met British representatives in Nyeri under the pretext of discussing terms of ending the conflict. China and General Tanganyika were present. General Tanganyika is released to the envoys to take the negotiations forward within seven days. He resumes KLFA leadership. (Kinyatti, p236-239)

1954 (APRIL – DEC): BATTLES ACROSS ALL FRONTS

Fierce battles take place across all the fronts in Kenya – Murang'a, Nyeri, Kirinyaga, Kiambu, Narok and Nairobi.

1954 (24 APRIL): OPERATION ANVIL LAUNCHED IN NAIROBI

Operation Anvil was launched by the British military in Nairobi and its surroundings. The city was sealed for almost a month until 21 May 1945. No Africans were allowed to come or leave the city. Africans were stopped, searched and their homes. 50,000 Africans were screened and 24,100 Kikuyu males (half the total number of Kikuyu in Nairobi) were imprisoned without trial. They were put on special war trains to concentration camps in Langata, Manyani and Mackinnon Road where they experienced untold brutality. Most of the KWC and KLFA leaders and many middle cadres were arrested during Operation Anvil offensive and imprisoned without trial. Pio Gama Pinto, editor-in chief of the pro-Mau Mau paper 'The High Command', was arrested and imprisoned without trial. (Anderson, p200- 205)

1954 (MID MAY): KENYA PARLIAMENT'S THIRD CONGRESS

KP held its Third Congress. In the wake of General China's betrayal, the capture of General Tanganyika, Operation Anvil in Nairobi and Operation Sickle in central Kenya. They decided to stand firm. KP resolved to send guerrilla missions to mobilize Kenya nationals and for support from sympathizers in Uganda. They discussed how to resolve differences between Mathenge and Kimathi. (Kinyatti, p291-294)

1954 (JUNE ONWARDS): FORCED REMOVAL OF CIVILIAN POPULATION IN EMERGENCY VILLAGES

The colonial government launched a war against the Kikuyu civilian population. Between June 1954 and October 1955, in a period of 15 months, 1,077,500 Kikuyu were forcibly moved and resettled in 845 barbed wire villages most of which were little more than concentration camps. This was three quarters of the Kikuyu population estimated to be around 1.4 million. Forced starvation prevailed in these villages. The overcrowded huts were incubators for diseases leading to death. (Anderson p294, Elkins p260- 264)

1954 (JULY- NOVEMBER): RUTHAGATHI- KENYA'S BELSEN EXPOSED

The local community was subjected to a 'reign of terror" at the Ruthagathi Homeguard post. It was an interrogation centre to which suspects were routinely taken for 'screening' from a wide surrounding area. Beatings and torture were allegedly part of the routine. It was also a systematic policy to fine local people. This was typical of the Emergency villages. (Anderson, 301- 307)

1954 (NOVEMBER 22 TO 26): KLFA'S THIRD CONGRESS

KLFA held its Third Congress at Mihuro, Nyandarwa. The main tasks included (1) determine new tactics and strategies (2) settle political disputes (3) discuss China's capitulation and consequences (4) update on political developments and the KLFA stance on negotiations. The Congress received reports from all the fronts. The deaths of Generals Kago, Ole Kisio, Ole Mendet, Mwangi Toto, Kariba and Brig. Gathitu were confirmed. The capture and surrender of General Omeera was confirmed. (Kinyatti, p302- 308)

1954 (DECEMBER): PIPELINE SYSTEM WITH CAMPS IN PLACE

The pipeline system with a complement of camps and prisons was fully in place. There were over one hundred in all, not including the scores of camps run by loyalist chiefs and other run by the private Settlers. There were 21 main detention camps for detainees who were considered hardcore. Poor health conditions, forced labour, starvation, sexual violence and murder prevailed in the camps. One in eight Kikuyu adult males were held in British prison and camp out of the estimated population of 1.4 million. (Anderson, p313, Elkins, p149-153)

1954 (DECEMBER): BRITISH LAUNCH OPERATION HAMMER

The British launched the largest offensive since the start of the war, "Operation Hammer" to destroy the KLFA guerrilla army in Nyandarwa. An armed force of 50,000 troops with armoured cars, tanks, artillery and warplanes were deployed. This lasted four weeks but it failed to destroy KLFA activities. (Kinyatti, p311)

1955 (JANUARY): BRITISH LAUNCH OPERATION BROOM

The British launched a second offensive "Operation Broom". It succeeded in scattering some guerrilla unites and over-running the Mihuro KLFA base where the guerrilla hospital and administrative centre was burnt down. (Kinyatti, p312)

1955 (JANUARY 18): BRITISH OFFER GENERAL AMNESTY

The British offered a general amnesty aimed at bringing the wholesale surrender of the KLFA forces. (Kinyatti, p312)

1955-56: THE BATTLE FRONT

The guerrilla army fought fierce battles against the British on all fronts. (Kinyatti, p323-327)

1955 (MARCH 6-9): KLFA'S FOURTH CONGRESS

The KLFA held its 4th Congress at Chieni, Nyandarwa. The delegates totally rejected the British surrender offer. The Congress set up an all African Revolutionary Government. Kimathi is elected as the Prime Minister. Macaria wa Kimeemia is promoted to Field Marshall and commander of the KLFA forces. The PM set off for a tour of the KLFA major bases in Nyandarwa. (Kinyatti, p312-315)

1955 (MARCH 13-16): MATHENGE'S KRG NEGOTIATES SURRENDER

Mathenge's newly set up Kenya Riggi (KRG) in opposition to Kenya Parliament entered into surrender negotiations with the British first in Nyandarwa and then in Nairobi. (Kinyatti, p316)

1955 (MARCH 30): KLFA ARRESTS KRG LEADERS WHO LATER ESCAPE

KLFA arrested all 27 leaders of the KRG and put them to trial. On the fifth night of the trial 26 of the captives make a dramatic escape. The KP court sentenced the 26 to death in absentia. Some KRG leaders and followers surrendered and gave sufficient information to the British about the infrastructure of the guerrilla army. Some joined the British counterinsurgency. The secretary general of KLFA, Karari Njama deserted and joined Mathenge and later surrendered to the British. (Kinyatti, p317- 319)

1955 (MARCH 26): KLFA HOLDS FIFTH CONGRESS

KLFA held its Fifth Congress at Karuri Ngumane, Nyandarwa. The attendance was roughly about 1700 delegates including peasant representatives. It resolved that there would be no surrender to the British and no negotiations before withdrawal of British forces. It recognized that because of internal splits in the movement and the betrayals of the struggle, the liberation army was on the defensive and had suffered heavy losses on all fronts. (Kinyatti, p322-323)

1955 (MAY 26): MATHENGE KILLED BY BRITISH FORCES

A day after the breakdown of the surrender conference when Mathenge made it clear that he would fight on until Kenya was free and independent, Mathenge and his twelve bodyguards were ambushed in the Munyange forest and all were killed.

(Kinyatti, p 319)

1956: THE BRITISH SET UP A MULTIRACIAL GOVERNMENT

The British set up a multiracial government comprised of the colonial governor, three white Settlers, two Asians and one African. The new government remove racial segregation in public places. It appoints some Africans to high government posts and gives pro-British trade unions a political platform.

1956: BRITISH LAUNCH A MASSIVE OFFENSIVE

The British launched a massive offensive. Around 60,000 British soldiers are deployed against the Mau Mau with tanks, aircraft and artillery. The British consolidated their political and war strategies to wipe out the KLFA. With the help of pro-British KRG, General China and other KLFA turncoats, they penetrated deeper into the liberated areas, destroying guerrilla infrastructure, infiltrating guerrilla units, eliminating their leaders and poisoning water sources and food supplies.

1956 (MID JANUARY): BRITISH OPERATIONS AROUND MOUNT KENYA

The British launched two military offensives the Hannibal and Schemozzle Operations in the south-western and eastern region of Kirinyaga. Heavy bombings set the forest on fire. The major KLFA base at Kirima Kia Nchugi is overrun and burned down. (Kinyatti, p326-327)

1956 (APRIL 10): GENERAL TANGANYIKA CAPTURED

General Tanganyika's force was ambushed near Embu border. The battle raged for two days. The casualties on both sides were heavy. Five guerrillas including General Tanganyika were captured. He is subjected to savage interrogation and torture to coerce him to renounce the armed struggle. On June 8, he was sentenced to death. On July 6 he was executed in Nairobi Maximum Security Prison and buried in handcuffs in an unmarked grave at Kamiti Maximum Security Prison. (Kinyatti p 327-329)

1956 (MAY): EILEEN FLETCHER PUBLISHES 'TRUTH ABOUT KENYA'

Her three-part series "Kenya's Concentration Camps-An Eyewitness Account" was published in the Quaker periodical Peace News. It reveals the torture, brutalities and breaches of the law in the camps. (Elkins p286-289)

1956 (OCTOBER 20): Kimathi BETRAYED, SHOT AND CAPTURED

Kimathi was betrayed by a member of KP. He was shot and captured by an enemy patrol. A day after his capture, the British judge Kenneth O'Connor organized a court around his bed and charged him with organizing and leading an armed resistance against British interests in Kenya. Kimathi refused to reply to the charge. No defence lawyer was present. (Kinyatti p331-332)

1956 (NOVEMBER 26): Kimathi FOUND GUILTY

Kimathi was found guilty and was sentenced to death. He did not ask for mercy from the court but told the judge that if the court allowed he was willing to negotiate the departure of the British from Kenya. (Kinyatti p333)

1957 (FEBRUARY 18): Kimathi GARROTTED

Dedan Kimathi was garrotted in the Nairobi Maximum Security Prison. His body was transported in chains to Kamiti Maximum Security Prison and buried with chains in an unmarked grave. (Kinyatti p334-335)

1959 (MARCH 3): HOLA MASSACRE

At Hola concentration camp, 11 of the detainees were clubbed to death by guards. 77 other surviving detainees sustained serious permanent injuries. Hola exposed the detention, violence, murder, deceit and abuse of power across Kenya during the Emergency. Hola became a major political issue in Britain and the colonial Kenyan government got no backing from the House of Commons. (Elkins p344-353)

1959: KENYATTA TRANSFERRED TO HOUSE ARREST

Kenyatta is transferred from jail to house arrest. The formation of political parties was allowed and African politicians were invited for negotiations in London.

1960: NEGOTIATIONS FOR INDEPENDENCE BEGIN 1961: KENYATTA LEADS KANU

Kenyatta was admitted to the legislative council and led the Kenya African National Union (KANU)

1963 (DECEMBER 12) KENYA BECOMES INDEPENDENT

Sources

Anderson, David (2005) Histories of the hanged: the dirty war in Kenya and the end of Empire.

Durrani, Shiraz (2006) Never be Silent: Publishing & Imperialism in Kenya 1884-1963. London: Vita Books.

Elkins, Caroline (2010) Britain's Gulag: The brutal end of Empire in Kenya

Kinyatti, Maina wa. (2010) History of Resistance in Kenya 1884-2002.

Maxon, Robert & Ofcanksy, Thomas (2000) Historical Dictionary of Kenya accessed Google books (p 91)

Paice Edward Tip & Run (2007)

- Saleh Mamon, October 2014

Ladislav Venys (1970): Mau Mau, A Chronological Outline – A Selection

MAU MAU, A CHRONOLOGICAL OUTLINE OF THE OPERATIONAL PHASE OF THE EMERGENCY WITH CURRENT AND FINAL STATISTICS

October 1952

20th

- The proclamation of a state of emergency signed by the Governor at 5 pm.
- Three more battalions of the K.A.R. added to the three that made up the normal garrison in Kenya.
- At 7:30 pm first of twelve R.A.F. Hastings troop-carriers landed at Eastleigh Airport, Nairobi; the other eleven arrived during the night. They brought with them from the Suez Canal Zone the Headquarters and a company of the 1st Battalion, the Lancashire Fusiliers.
- Before midnight the police started a round-up of Mau Mau suspects. (Majdalany, 119-123)

21st

- By dawn, ninety-nine Mau Mau suspects including Jomo Kenyatta arrested in operation Jack Scott.
- A state of emergency declared in a broadcast by Sir Evelyn Baring, Kenya's - Governor. (Ibid.; Corfield, 159-61)

22nd

- Senior Chief Nderi and two of his policemen slashed to death at a farm near Nyeri while trying to stop a Mau Mau meeting. (Keesing, 12569; Majdalany, 124)

24th

- Fifty newssheets and publications regarded as subversive proscribed. (Corfield, 316)

...

The Year of 1955

- Operation 'Hammer' carried out in the Aberdares with the aim to rout the partisan groups. It lasted one month (January 11 - February 12), ninety per cent of total military forces were employed, but the result was meagre; 99 partisans killed, 32 captured, and 30 surrendered. (Keesing, 14247;

    Majdalany, 233; Kruglov, 66)

- Estimated that in January there were still some 7,000 guerrillas at large, the main centres being the Aberdares, Mt. Kenya and Kiambu forests. (Report on Kenya for 1955, 1; Kitson, 149)

- General Erskine announced that by January 28, altogether 7,811 Mau Mau partisans had been killed, 844 wounded, 349 captured and 828 surrendered: the security forces had lost 470 Africans, 38 Europeans, and 2 Asians killed; in addition, 1,365 African, 30 European, and 19 Asian civilians had been murdered by Mau Mau. At that date, there were about 60,000 detainees in the detention camps and over 17,000 Africans were serving long periods of imprisonment. (Evans, 285)

- A new series of negotiations between the Mau Mau rebels and the Government started in mid-February and continued until May. (Majalany, 235)

- By mid-February, 278,560 Africans had been arrested since the beginning of the Emergency, of whom 111,032 had been tried and about 800 executed. (Kruglov, 68)

- At the end of February, operation First Flute was launched by the security forces and continued for nearly two months (until early April). It took place on the slopes of Mt. Kenya and was expected to destroy the Mau Mau forces in the area. The result: 277 Mau Mau rebels killed, captured or surrendered. (Keesing, 14247; Kruglov, 67} Majdalany, 233)

- Two European schoolboys, C. Twoney, 13, and G. Danby, 15, stabbed to death near Nairobi on April 21st. (Keesing, 14247} Evans, 217)

- By the end of April, altogether 1,106 partisans had surrendered. (Khazanov, 143)

- Mr. W.J. Weaver, a farmer, murdered on his farm on May 1. (Keesing, 14247)

- In mid-May, five special teams formed by the security forces to hunt remaining partisans in the forests. Each team was supplied with ten ex-Mau Mau guerrillas who were to locate the hide-outs of their former colleagues. (Majdalany, 238)

- The Kenya Government delivered an ultimatum to Mau Mau to surrender by May 18. (Baldwin, 234)

- The ultimatum was extended by two additional days. When the negotiations broke down completely on May 20, operation 'Gimlet' was put into effect and went on for two months. The operation was supervised by General Sir Gerald Lathbury who had taken over from General Erskine the command of all military forces in Kenya after the break-down of the truce talks. Six military battalions together with units of police and Homeguard participated in the operation which was taking place in the closed area above the South Nyeri district. The result was meagre: 18 partisans captured, 24 surrendered. (Keesing, 14247; Baldwin, 234-5; Kruglov, 67-8)

- By June, Mau Mau influence had declined a great deal and the Mau Mau rebellion was spoken of as merely a nuisance. Relaxation of the total prohibition of African political association announced by the Government; Africans allowed to form political organizations on a local basis. (Keesing, 14621; Bennett, 138)

- Up to June, over 850 Africans had been hanged since the start of the Emergency. (Evans, 83)

...

The Year of 1956

- Statistics published in Nairobi on January 1st: 10,173 partisans had been killed, 2,274 captured, and 2,124 surrendered; the security forces had lost 512 Africans, 57 Europeans and 3 Asians; altogether 1,600 African, 32 European, and 24 Asian civilians killed; about 20 prominent Mau Mau leaders still at large. (Keesing, 14621)

- A major operation of the security forces carried out near Lake Naivasha in the first three weeks of the year. (Keesing, 14859)

...

- By the end of March, all European and Asian personnel of the K.P.R. (about 10,000 men) had been released to civil life. Only twenty-five volunteers retained in essential posts. (Report on Kenya for 1956, 93)

- In April, one of the principal Mau Mau leaders, General Tanganyika, captured and subsequently sentenced to death. (Kruglov, 69)

- In the course of April and May, the 26th K.A.R. unit returned to Tanganyika; two British battalions, the 1st Gloucesters and the 1st Rifle Brigade, also left Kenya. (Report on Kenya for 1956, 2)

- During the first half of the year Mau Mau activity continued to decline. Mau Mau attacks were limited to about five a month. The number of partisans killed or captured totalled about 200 per month. (Keesing, 14859)

- It was possible to say by the middle of the year that the Mau Mau military forces had been broken. There existed only small and widely dispersed groups of Mau Mau guerrillas. (Report on Kenya for 1956, 2)

- The Commander-in-Chief of the remaining partisans, Dedan Kimathi, wounded on October 17, captured on October 21, brought to trial on November 19, and sentenced to death on November 27th. (He was hanged in Nairobi on February 18, 1957.) (Keesing, 15633; Majdalany, 240-1; Kruglov, 69)

FINAL STATISTICS

Mau Mau Casualties:

11,503 killed, 2,585 captured, 2,714 surrendered (Corfield)

10,527 killed, 2,633 captured (Majdalany)

11,000 killed (Kruglov)

11,500 killed, 5,000 captured (Khazanov)

10,000 killed (Keesing)

Security Forces Casualties:

101 Africans, 63 Europeans, 3 Asians - killed (C)

1,469 Africans, 101 Europeans, 12 Asians - wounded (C)

534 Africans, 63 Europeans, 3 Asians - killed (U)

465 Africans, 102 Europeans, 12 Asians - wounded (U)

524 Africans, 63 Europeans - killed (Wood)

1,167 army and police personnel killed or wounded (Keesing)

Civilian Casualties:

1,819 Africans, 32 Europeans, 26 Asians - killed (Corfield)

916 Africans, 26 Europeans, 36 Asians - wounded (Corfield)

1,826 Africans, 32 Europeans, 26 Asians - killed (Majdalany)

918 Africans, 265 Europeans, 36 Asians - wounded (Majdalany)

1,832 Africans, 32 Europeans - killed (Wood)

1,800 Africans, 32 Europeans, 26 Asians - killed (Keesing)

Detention and Arrests:

(By the end of 1956)

26,625 arrested (Corfield)

38,449 detained (Majdalany)

62,000 arrested and detained (Kruglov)

31,532 detained (Report on Kenya, 1956)

(By January 12, 1960)

1,000 detained (Keesing)

Executed Mau Mau Rebels: 1,068   (Keesing)

Cost of the Emergency: 55,585,424 pounds of sterling (Corfield)

(The comparison of final statistics draws on the following sources:

F.D. Corfield, op.cit., p. 316;

L.U Kruglov, op.cit., p. 70;

F- Majdalany, op.cit., pp. 238, t 241, and 252;

S. Wood, op.cit,, p. 33;

A.M. Khazanov, op.cit., p. 147;

Keesing's Contemporary Archives, op.cit., pp. 17193 and 17145, Report on Kenya for 1956, op.cit., p. 96.)

Shiraz Durrani (1997): The Other Kenya: Underground and Alternative Literature

Collection Building Vol. 16 (2) · 1997 · pp. 80–87 © MCB University Press · ISSN 0160-4953

The other Kenya: underground and alternative literature

Shiraz Durrani

The author

Shiraz Durrani, in exile from Kenya, works as Area Librarian for the London Borough of Hackney at Stoke Newington Library, Stoke Newington, Church Street, London N16 0JS. He has written many articles on the politics of social communication.

Abstract

Most literature available about Kenya today has been written from the point of view of imperialism or of the ruling class. Very little material representing the working people's interests is available. There is also a scarcity of information about material on Kenya (and Africa generally) from the point of view of the working people. This is a reflection of the lack of control over the process of communication and mass media by the working class. Records, literature of the other side – the people's point of view. Lists some important publications from the Kenyan underground which has been systematically issuing major documents and commentary on the ongoing struggle of the people for social justice and economic liberation. Counters the claim by some that there is no progressive material coming out of Africa. Indeed this literature is indispensable for historical research and in the struggle for true democracy. Without this material, the ideology of the ruling class remains unchallenged. It also includes other progressive material. The survey is partisan and no attempt is made to have a "balanced" view, as the ruling class point of view has adequate resources to propagate itself. Makes some recommendations for information workers.

Introduction

It is necessary to have access to the vast amount of underground and alternative literature about Kenya in order to understand the current political, social and economic state the country is in. This alternative literature can provide the real picture of the situation in the country today from the viewpoint of the majority. It provides a barometer of the state of class struggle in Kenya.

While the ruling classes deny the very existence of classes and class struggle, the alternative material listed here provides an entirely different picture. So fearful have the current "leaders" become of the people's victory over oppression, that they systematically distort records of Kenya's past and have even banned open discussion of Mau Mau. In view of this, it is becoming increasingly necessary to interpret and document the history of the struggle for independence from the working class point of view. The lessons of past victories are applicable to today's problems. This has been done by the underground movements and progressive activists and historians – hence the attempt to silence their voice. Some of this "silenced" material is included in this survey.

The importance of underground movements and their publications is recorded by the underground itself:

> The most dramatic development ... was the emergence of worker/ peasant based underground groups. They began articulating an ideology that fully reflected the workers' struggle. The seventies saw the development of a vigorous underground press. Between 1974 and 1982, the underground groups and newspapers had become the real voice of the Kenyan people (Mwakenya (1987), *Draft Minimum Programme*, p. 13).

This survey provides a broad picture of the alternative material – it does not aim to be a complete record of such material. But sufficient material is included to show the wide range of material that is available. It is not possible to list every document published underground as much of it is lost and no organization in Kenya dare openly collect it. It is not certain if any outside institution, with the possible exception of the CIA, has collected such material.

Nonetheless, much material has been collected by Mwakenya, both inside and outside the country. Copies of some of it are available from their overseas branches, including the ones in the USA and in Britain.

Some underground publications

Kenyan-organized underground resistance movement has had an "unbroken continuity – though not always along a straight path – from the 1970s, and in different guises and forms," as the article, "Roots of the revolt" in *Africa Events* points out. This movement draws its inspiration from, and in a sense is a continuation of, the line taken by Mau Mau, especially in the years just before independence. In the early 1980s, it was the December Twelve Movement with the publications *Cheche Kenya* and *Pambana* which carried on the tradition of resistance and of underground press. The name "December Twelve Movement" was later changed to "Mwakenya," a Kiswahili acronym for Muungano wa Wazalendo wa Kuikomboa Kenya (Union of Patriots for the Liberation of Kenya).

Early underground periodicals

- *Mwanguzi* – an underground publication in the 1970s that ran to more than 12 issues.

- *Kenya Twendapi?* (Where are we Heading in Kenya?) – a series of pamphlets (about nine were issued) in 1969. The author, Abdilaif Abdalla, was jailed for writing and distributing it. He was held in solidarity confinement for three years at Kamiti Maximum Security Prison.

- *Cheche Kenya* (Independent Kenya) – published as an underground document in 1981. Reissued by Zed Press, London, 1982 (reprinted 1989).

- *Coup Broadcast.* Voice of Kenya, Nairobi, August 1, 1982. Reproduced in *Race and Class,* Vol. 24 No. 3, 1983, pp. 325-6.

- *Upande Mwingine* (The Other Side) – "the very brilliant, meticulous monthly and annual documentation of the resistance actions of workers, peasants, and students etc. in industry, commerce, plantations, schools and colleges, carried out by *Upande Mwingine*, the underground workers' organ. *Upande Mwingine* has systematically compiled this Kiswahili register of strikes and demonstrations by the working people over a number of years" (Mwakenya (1987), *Kenya; Register of* Resistance, p. 7).

- *Article 5* – a sister publication of *Upande Mwingine*, it kept a record of incidents of deaths, beatings, jailings, and mass punishments carried on by the regime, as opposed to resistance which was recorded by *Upande Mwingine*. The title, *Article 5*, refers to Article 5 of the Declaration of Human Rights, on the freedom of information. Prepared for use by the underground in the mid-1980s.

- *Kauli Raia* (People's Opinion) – *Tunakataa* (We Say No) underground resistance poetry from Kenya. Written by the group Upande Mwingine during the mid-1980s. To be published by Vita Books/Mau Mau Research Center.

- *Pambana, Organ of the December Twelve Movement* – No. 1 (May 1982) was reproduced in *Law as a Tool of Political Repression in Kenya,* August, 1982 (in English and Kiswahili), published in London by the Committee for the Release of Political Prisoners in Kenya. No. 2 came out in July 1983.

- *People's Weekly* – publication of Harakati ya Kupigania Demokrasia (HDK), late 1980s.

Mwakenya's underground publications: a short guide
Mwakenya (Muungano wa Wazalendo wa Kuikomboa Kenya; Union of Patriots for the Liberation of Kenya) has published

various documents, press statements, and leaflets which are widely distributed in Kenya. Some of these are listed below. Mwakenya and its predecessor, December Twelve Movement, have been active since the late 1970s. Mwakenya's existence became known to the government in 1985. "The mention of our name in the local press (*The Standard*, February 13, 1985) alerted the regime to the existence of a new organization under the name Mwakenya" (*Mwakenya Draft Minimum Programme*, p. 17).

Basic documents

- *Kenya: Register of Resistance, 1986.* Nairobi, 1987, 27 pp. Cover in two colours.

- *Mwakenya: Draft Minimum Programme.* Nairobi, September 1987. A5, 35 pp. Type-set, printed, two-colour cover, illustrated. Includes: Towards a national democratic revolution; The immediate political tasks of Mwakenya; The fundamental goals and objectives of Mwakenya; The immediate political demands of Mwakenya; Mwakenya's relationship with other organizations; Mwakenya's appeals to Kenyan people.

- Mwakenya's statement on the current crisis in Kenya, July 11, 1990.

- Mwakenya's Plank 1990 for the Second Republic. Later issued as Kenya Democracy Plank (1991).

- Kenya; Mpango wa Demokrasia, 1991 (in Kiswahili).

- The Mwakenya Stand, 1992.

- Msimamo wa Mwakenya, 1992 (in Kiswahili).
Periodicals

- *Mpatanishi*–underground newspaper, "the official central journal of Mwakenya." No. 7 "appeared with our first proposed draft programme" according to the Draft Mini- mum Programme. No. 14 (August 1985) was a Special Issue entitled "Liberation organizations merge and formalize Mwakenya." Vol. 5 No. 3 (December 1995) contains: Charter for Democracy in Kenya; Moism: State terrorism in Kenya; Remembering Saba Saba; The question of nationalities in Kenya.

- *Mzalendo Mwakenya* – the mass newspaper of the party. "A special issue of our mass newspaper *Mzalendo Mwakenya* was released on February 6, 1985 supporting the then protesting students of the University of Nairobi and condemning the neo-colonial regime for its continued repression of university students and lecturers" (*Draft Minimum Programme*, p. 17).

Some issues:

1. April 1986: It is now guerrilla warfare in Kenya.

2. March 1988: The Moi-KANU clique continue to crush democracy in Kenya.

3. July 1988: Kenya in political crisis!

4. May 1990: The Moi-KANU regime is under siege.

5. October 1991: Mwakenya purges factional clique and renounces "Mkombozi - Mwakenya."

6. November 1991: Moi na Kanu lazima wajiuzulu!

7. November 1991: The Moi-Kanu government must resign!

May 1994: Komesha mauaji na mugawanyiko Kenya; angamiza U-Moi na U-Kanu!
May 1994: Stop genocide and disintegration; away with Moism and Kanuism.

Press releases and general statements

Some examples:

- Moi-USA New "drugs agreements" threaten Kenyan lives (September 21, 1987).

- Moi declares unwarranted war against Uganda (December 16, 1987).

- Moi-KANU regime has no legitimacy to rule Kenya (March 29, 1988).

- Moi unleashes a state of terror on the Kenyan Somalis (November 15, 1989).

- Statement on the current political situation in Kenya (May 25, 1990).

- Letter to all patriotic, democratic, and progressive Kenyans (July 1, 1990).

- Mwakenya calls for a week of prayers ... and a general strike (August 16, 1990).

- Mwakenya yatoa mwito kuwe na wiki moja ya maombolezi ... na mgomo (August 16, 1990).

- Interview with Ngugi wa Thiong'o, spokesperson for Mwakenya. (*Ufahamu; Journal of the African Activist Association,* Vol. XVIII No. 11, 1990, pp. 41-6).

- Hata Bila Moi, Umoi tunapinga! Msimamo rasmi wa Mwakenya kuhusu hali ya mambo nchini (January 1992).

- Stop Moi's reign of terrorism. The statement of Mwakenya at the 7th Pan African Congress, Kampala, Uganda (April 1994).

- Mwakenya-UKenya merger (March 1996).

- Calling all Kenyans (September 1996).

Overseas "underground" publications

Here we shall consider briefly a particular manifestation of publishing which arose as a result of the various waves of repression seen in Kenya over the years, but which have become more intense over the last ten years or so. More and more Kenyans have to flee Kenya for expressing their democratic rights and who subsequently face prison, detention, torture or even death. Kenyan organisations have been established wherever Kenyans have settled. Africa Events explains the background and looks at some publications:

Some Kenyan exiles who got involved in human rights campaigns started organizing themselves as political activists, resulting in such externally-based groups as UKenya, formed in London in 1986, and which in October 1987 joined other groups (in USA, Scandinavian countries, Australia, and some African countries) to form Umoja wa Kupigania Demokrasia Kenya (United Move- ment for Democracy in Kenya) – Umoja-Kenya. As part of its activities, this movement has produced some seminal documents on Kenya, in particular, *Struggle for Democracy in Kenya: Special Report on 1988 General Elections in Kenya* (1988) and *Moi's Reign of Terror: A Decade of Nyayo Crimes Against the People of Kenya* (1989) ("Roots of revolt," *Africa Events,* 1990, Vol 6 Nos 8/9, p. 28).

• Organisation for Democracy in Kenya (Sweden), The ODK Declaration, May 1986, Stockholm.

Some Umoja/UKenya/Mwakenya publications
Documents, statements, reports

- *Katiba ya Umoja wa Kupigania Demokrasia Kenya, Ukenya,* February 1987.

- *Manifesto of UKenya* (*Movement for Unity and Democracy in Kenya*), February 1987.

- *From Kimathi to Mwakenya; Resistance in Kenya Today,* 1987.

- *Kutoka Kimathi hadi Mwakenya; Upinzani Kenya leo,* 1987.

- *Struggle For Democracy in Kenya; Special Report on the 1988 General Elections in Kenya,* June 1,1988, Background Paper No. 1.

- *Moi's Reign of Terror; A Decade of Nyayo Crimes Against the People of Kenya,* January 1989 (reprinted June 1989), Background Document No. 2.

- *Kenya Exiles Support Mwakenya's Call for a Second Republic,* August 1990. Periodicals

- Habari za Umoja; Gazeti la Wanachama wa Umoja, No.1, 1989.

- Matukio Duniani, No. 1, 1990. *Press and other statements issued by Umoja/UKenya*

- Mombasa people champion resistance against Kanu's undemocratic rule. Novem- ber 25, 1987.

- The truth behind the Moi-Kanu regime's

- Statement concerning Margaret Thatcher's endorsement of the repressive and corrupt Moi-Kanu Regime in Kenya. January 21, 1988.

- Umoja rejects the fraudulent general elections of March 21, 1988 in Kenya. April 10, 1988.

- Oppose repressive Constitutional Amendment in Kenya. August 2, 1988.

- Moi; destroyer of Kenya's natural and human environment. March 1, 1989.

- Moi fails in his bid to cover up Nyayo crimes. August 22, 1989.

- Mau Mau Freedom Fighters' Day. October 20, 1989.

- Kenya exiles support the November 16, 1991 pro-democracy rally to be held at Kamukunji, Nairobi. November 13, 1991.

- People's struggle heralds a new age in Kenya. December 12, 1991.
- UKenya's statement at 7th Pan African Congress, Kampala, April 1994.

Unity Conference papers

The following background papers were prepared by delegates attending the Unity Conference of Patriotic, Democratic and Progressive Kenyan Organizations Abroad, October 16-19, 1987, London. The conference was sponsored by Mwakenya and was attended by delegates from seven externally-based Kenyan organizations. The delegates voted to dissolve their individual organizations and all became part of a united movement, Umoja – United Movement for Democracy in Kenya. The former independent organizations became branches of Umoja with a Central Secretariat based in London.

- The heritage of armed struggle: resistance in the Northern Kenya, 1890-1963.
- Kenya Asian participation in Kenya people's resistance against imperialism during the period 1884-1963.
- Pambana: legacy of resistance.
- Resistance in Central and Rift Valley.
- Resistance to imperialism by the people of Nyanza and Western Provinces of Kenya.
- Legacy of resistance in the coast.
- Unity in resistance.
- Women in Kenyan people's resistance to aggression on Uganda. December 22, 1987. imperialism 1884-1963.

Committee for the Release of Political Prisoners in Kenya

The Committee was formed in 1982 and has played a leading role in alerting the international community about the true situation in Kenya. Besides publishing *Kenya News,* an irregular newsletter, it has published many important documents. The Committee organized a one- day conference entitled Focus on Human Rights in Kenya on July 2, 1988. It has also issued numerous statements on the abuse of human rights in Kenya.

- Law as a tool of political repression in Kenya. August 1982.

- Repression intensifies in Kenya since the August lst coup attempt. January 1983, 20 pp.

- Release the political prisoners in Kenya. July 1982 (reprinted March 1983), 12 pp.

- University destroyed; Moi crowns ten years of Government terror in Kenya. May 1983, 16 pp.

Kenya News
An irregular publication of the Committee for the Release of Political Prisoners in Kenya. Each issue focuses on an important topic and also carries a well researched up-to-date list of political prisoners in Kenya. The following list gives the main article carried by each issue of *Kenya News*:

- No. 1 (July 1983): "One year later; political prisoners still jailed in Kenya."

- No. 2 (November 1983): "Democratic image – repressive reality."

- No. 3 (April 1984): "Stop this massacre." (The barbaric attack by the Kenyan security forces on defenceless citizens in the North East Province killed more than 1,000 people).

- No. 4 (October 1984): "Drought is a big business."

- No. 5 (May 1985): "Sunday bloody- Sunday." (The massacre of students at the University of Nairobi, Sunday, February 10, 1985).

- No. 6 (June 1985): "The Kenyan woman: a decade of oppression."

- No. 7 (August 1986): "State of emergency; help close Moi's torture chamber."

- No. 8 (March 1987): "Torture in Kenya intensifies; there is no giving up, diaries from a torture chamber; routine methods of extorting information."

- No. 9 (February 1989): "Moi's police: licence to kill; ten years of terror."

- "Free the political prisoners in Kenya" (publicity material). Leeds-Kenya Support Group, a branch of the Committee for the Release Of Political Prisoners in Kenya, Leeds.

Some relevant material

This is by no means a full list of recommended alternative material on Kenya. Taken as a whole, the following material gives the alternative picture of recent Kenyan history and a background to its current situation.

General

- Alak Malak, especially the series: "Biographies of patriotic Asians" (in Gujarati); "Waesia mashujaa - wazalendo wa Kenya" by Nazmi Ramji (Durrani). e.g. Part 3: Introducing Patriotic Kenyan Asians: Journalists, Editors, Publishers, printers (in Gujarati).

- "Countdown to freedom" (cover story); Roots of revolt, *Africa Events* (London), Vol. 6 Nos 8/9, 1990.

- Durrani, S. (1986a) "Pambana – The legacy of resistance in Kenya, 1963-68," talk given at the Review of African Political Economy Conference, Liverpool, published in *Liberation Struggles in Africa.*

A Collection of Papers from ROAPE Conference, 1986.

- Durrani, S. (1991), "Voices of resistance; underground publishing in Kenya after independence, 1963-90," 29 pp., internal document of UKenya, London.

- Karega, M., "Mwakenya and Kenya's future," *New Africa News* (Melbourne, Aus- tralia), No. 67, 1988 pp. 7-10.

- Karega, M., "Kenya ripe for revolution," *New Africa News* (Melbourne, Australia), No. 71, 1988-89, pp. 4-7.

- Mkhatshwa, J., "Kenya: from the Wananchi Declaration to Mwakenya," *The African Communist*, No. 116, 1989, pp. 65-72.

- "Moi fights off Mwakenya," *African Concord*, March 1987.

- "Mwakenya will not be registered now – Ngugi," *The Standard on Sunday* (Nairobi), January 12, 1992, p. 5.

- "Mwakenya's stand" (interview with Ngugi wa Thiong'o, the Spokesperson for Mwakenya), *Africa Events* (London), Vol. 8 No. 2, February 1992, pp.30-1 (also includes cover story: "Kenya; moment of truth").

- "Ngugi speaks for Mwakenya," *Daily Nation* (Nairobi), January 11, 1992, p. 28.
  Historical material by some Mau Mau writers
  A large amount of progressive material on Mau Mau is now available. The following are listed as examples of the best that is available. They show the advanced ideological and organizational level reached by advanced cadres. The books by Ngugi Kabiro, Mohamed Mathu, and Karigo Muchai are now out of print and the publisher no longer exists. However the London-based Vita Books and the Mau Mau Research Center in the USA are planning to reprint them.

- Durrani, S. (1986), *Kimathi, Mau Mau's First Prime Minister of Kenya,* Vita Books, Middlesex, 52 pp.

- Kabiro, N. (1973), *The Man in the Middle; The Story of Ngugi Kabiro*, LSM Information Center, Richmond, BC, Canada.

- Maina wa Kinyatti (1987), *Kimathi Letters,* Heinemann: Zed Books, Nairobi, London.

- Maina wa Kinyatti (1991), *Mau Mau: A Revolution Betrayed,* Mau Mau Research Centre/Vita Books, New York/London.

- Maina wa Kinyatti (1980), *Thunder from the Mountains: Mau Mau Patriotic Songs*, Zed Books, London.

- Makhan, S. (1969), *History of Kenya's Trade Union Movement to 1952*, East African Pub- lishing House, Nairobi.

- Mathu, M. (1974), *The Urban Guerrilla,* LSM Information Center, Richmond, BC, Canada.

- Muchai, K. (1973), *The Hardcore*, LSM Information Center, Richmond, BC, Canada.

Documenting state terrorism

This section lists some important publications which have documented the reality of state terrorism that is Kenya today. An increasing number of Kenyan publications have begun to record acts of state terrorism. This is supplemented by the very supportive work of various international human rights organizations. Thus this section counters the official image of Kenya as a peaceful country. It suits the regime and its international backers to pretend so. The reality for the people is quite the opposite, as recorded in the following documents.

Kenyan

Reports

- *The Cursed Arrow: A Report on Organised Violence Against Democracy in Kenya*, National Christian Council of Kenya (NCCK), Nairobi, Vol.1, April 1992. The NCCK contemporary report on the politicized land clashes in Rift Valley, Nyanza and Western Provinces. (includes "Chronology of events: October 29, 1991 to 12 April, 1992).

- *Courting Disaster: A Report on the Continuing Terror, Violence and Destruction in the Rift Valley, Nyanza and Western Provinces of Kenya*, report by National Election Monitoring Unit (NEMU) (Council of Elders), April 29, 1993.

- "Deception, dispersal and abandonment; a narrative account on the displacement of Kenyans from Enoosupukia and Maela based on witness, Church/NGO and media accounts," a narrative account not for publication prepared for the Ethnic Clashes Network, under the auspices of The Kenya National Council of NGOs, January 16, 1995.

- *Inter Parties Symposium. Task Force. Report on the Clashes*, NCCK; political parties, except KANU; the International Commission of Jurists (Kenya Section); the Law Society of Kenya; University of Nairobi; the Women's Lobby Group; the symposium took place in May 1992.

- *No Longer Silent; Silent Evictions in Mau Division, Narok District, Kenya*, The National Council of NGOs in Kenya, July 1995.

- *Report of the Parliamentary Select Committee to Investigate Ethnic Clashes in Western and other Parts of Kenya*, Kiliku Report, Nairobi, Sep-tember 1991.

- *Report on Present Situation in Clashes-Affected Areas in Molo and Olenguruone, April to September 1993*, by E.K. Murimi, Executive Secretary, Justice and Peace Commission, Catholic Diocese of Nakuru. Nakuru, *Catholic Diocese of Nakuru (gives names of* 1029 families displaced).

- *State of Human Rights in Kenya. A Year of Political Harassment*, Kenya Human Rights Commission, Nairobi, 1993.

Periodicals

- *Sauti ya Kamukunji, Students* Union, University of Nairobi, early 1980s.

- *The Clashes Update; The Bulletin that Keeps You Ever Updated,* National Council of Churches of Kenya (NCCK) – Christian Outreach Rural Development Services (CORDS), PO Box 45009, Nairobi. Tel: 761948; fax: 212230.

- *The Economic Review; An Authoritative Weekly Newsmagazine,* No. 48, "The Killing Fields," September 1993; PO Box 44271, Nairobi, Kenya. Tel: 219603/4; 219492.

- *Quarterly Repression Report,* Kenya Human Rights Commission, PO Box 55235, Nairobi, Kenya. Tel: 254 2 749233/ 749238; fax: 254 2 749248.
  Overseas
  Reports
  Arrangement is by date of publication.

- *Kenya and "Mwakenya" – More Arrests,* Index on Censorship, Briefing Paper, April 25, 1986.

- *Kenya; Torture, Political Detention and Unfair Trials,* Amnesty International, London, 1987 (update issued in 1988).

- *Kenya: Forcible Return of Somali Refugees; Government Repression of Kenyan Somalis,* World Watch/Africa, London, 1989.

- *Kenya: Harassment of Ethnic Somalis,* World Watch/Africa, London, 1989.

- *Kenya: Suppression of Press Freedom; Banning of Critical Papers and Intolerance of Dissent,* World Watch/Africa, London, 1989.

- *News from Africa Watch,* December 6, 1989.

- *Kenya; Once Again, A Critical Magazine Faces*

Threat of a Banning Order, World Watch/Africa, London, 1990.

- *Kenya; Political Crackdown Intensifies,* World Watch/Africa, London, 1990.

- *Kenya; Screening of Ethnic Somalis; The Cruel Consequences of Kenya's Passbook System,* World Watch/Africa, London, 1990.

- *Kenya; Silencing Opposition to One-party Rule,* Amnesty International, London, 1990.

- *Kenya: Taking Liberties,* World Watch/Africa, London, 1991.

- *Kenya: Briefing for Members of Parliament,* Article 19, London, 1992.

- *Kenya: Recent Threats to Freedom of Expression,* Article 19, London, 1992.

- *Country Report on Human Rights Practices in Kenya 1993,* US State Department, Washing- ton, DC, 1993.

- *Divide and Rule, State-Sponsored Violence in Kenya,* Human Rights Watch Africa, Lon- don, 1993.

- *Failing the Democratic Challenge: Freedom of Expression in Multi-Party Kenya,* Robert F. Kennedy Memorial Center, 1993.

- *Kenya: Divide and Rule, State Sponsored Ethnic Violence,* World Watch/Africa, Lon- don, 1993.

- *Kenya: Shooting the Messenger,* Article 19, London, 1993.

- *Report on Kenya,* State Department, 1993, pp. 128-42.

- *From Relief to Rehabilitation, Reconstruction and Reconciliation: Developments and Prospects for Internally Displaced Populations in Western and Rift Valley Provinces,* UNDP, September 1994.

- *Kenya: Multipartyism Betrayed in Kenya; Continuing Rural Violence and Restrictions on Freedom of Speech and Assembly,*

World Watch/Africa, London, 1994.

- *Kenya; Report for Labour Party,* by Tony Worthington, MP, Westminster Foundation for Democracy, 1994.

- *Kenya: Seeking Refuge, Finding Terror: The Widespread Rape of Somali Women.*

- *Refugees in North Eastern Kenya,* World Watch/Africa, London, 1994.

- *Censorship in Kenya: Government Critics Face the Death Sentence,* Article 19, London, 1995.

- *Displaced Less Visible, Still Suffering; Orchestrated Ethnic Violence in Kenya,* MSF Report on Ethnic Violence in Kenya, Medecins sans Frontieres, Paris, July 18, 1995.

- *Old Habits Die Hard; Rights Abuses Follow Renewed Foreign Aid Commitments,* Human Rights Watch/Africa, Vol. 7 No. 6, July 1995.

- *Playing the Communal Card; Communal Violence and Human Rights,* Human Rights Watch Africa, London, April 1995.

- *Women in Kenya; Repression and Resistance* Amnesty International, London, 1995.

Periodicals
• *Pambana; Kenyan News and Social Justice*

Journal, published by Asian Development Foundation, 130 Little Collins Street, Melbourne 3000, Australia (editors: Ndungi wa Mungai and Richard F. Wootton).

Conclusion

This brief survey shows that much work needs to be done in documenting and making available relevant material on the real situation in countries such as Kenya. African countries are facing increasing marginalization in all fields as a result of the new scramble for their resources in the 1990s. This is particularly evident in the field of information where the development of new technologies is used, not to develop Africa's resources, but to further impoverish its people.

Yet the situation is not hopeless. The present survey shows that there is a vibrant underground working class movement which has the ideas and theories to solve their problems. Progressive people are risking their lives to ensure free flow of information. In the long run, they will find their own solution to the information and other problems they face.

In this context, what role can progressive people around the world, especially in the information field, play? The first demand of the people in Africa is to be left alone by the Western countries to find their own solutions. Progressive people everywhere demand this from their governments. In addition, support for the information activities of the underground and people's movements would obviously be helpful. Very little, if any, such support is forthcoming.

Documenting, collecting and making available alternative material would play an important role in supporting the information struggle of the African people. Collecting only the output from African government sources and from African-based multinational publishers will merely help to reinforce the message of the ruling classes. It is the alternative literature which will redress the information balance, and in the long run help to reinterpret African history from the people's point of view. It is only from this that real progress and development can follow. The availability of such material in British and American universities and public libraries can help to change people's attitudes in these countries.

It is hoped that by making alternative material widely available, libraries in Kenya as well as around the world will enable a better understanding of the struggle waged by the people of Kenya. The real proof of freedom of information is whether libraries dare collect and disseminate this alternative material.

The lesson for library and information workers is that they need to make a conscious effort to collect and make available such alternative material. Without this effort, they are failing in their professional duty. It remains to be seen if the profession is ready for this challenge.

Maina wa Kinyatti (1978): Foreword, Ndegwa's Mau Mau Bibliography

Maina wa Kinyatti (1978): Foreward. Ndegwa, R. N. (Comp.,1977): Mau Mau: A Select Bibliography. Nairobi: Kenyatta University Press.

Besides the British Imperialists and their Christian agents, who have, for the past few years, been remarkably successful in equating Mau Mau with savagery, atavism, terrorism and barbarism there has now emerged a rearguard clique of Kenyan intellectuals, especially from the University of Nairobi, who have joined hands with the imperialists in their attempt to distort the fundamental aims and character of Mau Mau, and, particularly to deny the heroic and catalytic role the movement so decisively played in our national independence struggle.

This anti-Mau Mau clique of intellectuals has used lines of argument similar to those of imperialists. Some dismiss this now-proven pan-Kenyan national liberation movement as a mere tribal or even tribalist movement. This backsliding line they have taken stems from the fact that they have failed to grasp the theory of class struggle as the key link in the study of our history. Equally, they have failed to see the contradictions of the present situation in our country as an expression, albeit in a new setting, of various contradictions of Kenya's anti-Imperialist struggle.

While the Mau Mau movement continues to be treated with contempt and shame, its former leaders, particularly those who, until now, have refused to recant (so-called "hard-cores") continue to be regarded as "terrorists" and are being sometimes considered dangerous to national stability. One rarely, if ever, finds history texts for primary schools, high schools and university that eulogize the heroism of Mau Mau. Apparently it is also discouraged to praise this patriotic movement in public gatherings; further and more telling, Dedan Kimathi, the leader of Mau Mau, has been denied the national recognition he deserves. This is clear-cut debasing of this heroic struggle of our people against British Imperialism.

In essence, those of our people who heroically participated in the struggle, those who sacrificed everything including their own lives for the liberation of this country from foreign occupiers, remember Mau Mau with pride and patriotism. However, the homeguard gun "carrier corps" and others who collaborated with the British during the heat of the struggle remember Mau Mau with guilt, shame and fear. Since some of these individuals are now in positions of power and wealth, they have made it their main job to suppress, alter or destroy much genuine information on the movement; even to mercilessly silence any Kenyan patriot who speaks or writes about this heroic struggle.

In spite of all this, it should clearly be understood that no force on earth will ever destroy Mau Mau heroism for it has become a living memory among the great masses of our people. For them Mau Mau is one of the most glorious and heroic national movements in Kenyan history. It is a movement which reflects, with a strong popular character, our people's steel-will to fight for their freedom and country.

In this background R. N. Ndegwa's excellent bibliography is, to my knowledge, the first serious attempt by a Kenyan to compile many diverse written materials on the Mau Man movement. It should be understood, however, that this bibliography in no way exhausts the sources of information; for there is more information, some of it oral, which still exists for the collecting. For instance, there are people still alive with useful information which is in stark opposition to some current reactionary and pro-imperialist hypotheses. In addition to that, Dedan Kimathi's *Thirty Volumes* on the movement is still hidden under the 30-year Kenya Government secrecy clause. The Kenya National Archives has made no secret of this.

To sum up, R. N. Ndegwa's excellent work is but the beginning of what necessarily must be a long, serious search for this important chapter in our country's history.

Maina wa Kinyatti

Lecturer, Department of History

Kenyatta University College

Nairobi

February 20, 1978.

South African History Online – Towards a People's History
Available at: http://www.sahistory.org.za

Mau Mau

Rethinking Mau Mau in Colonial Kenya
File Format: PDF/Adobe Acrobat
The present work is neither a history of the Mau Mau revolt nor an attempt to review all works ever written on it. No attempt has been made to put the movement ...
www.sahistory.org.za/.../s.m._shamsul_alam_rethinking_the_mau_mau_in_ colobook4you.org_.pdf

The Mau Mau Uprising | South African History Online
The Mau Mau uprising began in 1952 as a reaction to inequalities and injustices in British-controlled Kenya. The response of the colonial administration was a ...
www.sahistory.org.za/article/mau-mau-uprising

Organisers of Mau Mau oath to receive death penalty | South African ...
Jan 18, 2017 ... During the height of the Mau Mau rebellion, Sir Evelyn Baring, governor of Kenya, introduced the death penalty for anyone who organised the ...
www.sahistory.org.za/.../organisers-mau-mau-oath-receive-death-penalty

Mau Mau political prisoners escape from Mageta Island, Lake Victoria
On 5 February 1956, 11 Mau Mau prisoners, serving life sentences escaped from Mageta Island, Lake Victoria in a canoe. This was after the prisoners hacked to ...
www.sahistory.org.za/.../mau-mau-political-prisoners-escape-mageta-island- lake-victoria

Scores of people including a Chief are killed in Lari, Kenya following ...
On 26 March 1953, close to 100 people were killed and scores of others injured at Lari in Kiambu region, Kenya when Mau Mau freedom fighters attacked the ...
www.sahistory.org.za/.../scores-people-including-chief-are-killed-lari-kenya- following-attack-mau-mau-freedom-f-0

Over 400 Kikuyu suspected to be part of the Mau Mau movement are ...
Kenya was administered as a British territory under the East African Protectorate from 1895 onwards. Most land that was appropriated by the colonial ...
www.sahistory.org.za/.../over-400-kikuyu-suspected-be-part-mau-mau- movement-are-arrested-kenya

Over 400 Kikuyu suspected to be part of the Mau Mau movement are ...
Mali was once part of the Great Songhay Empire, but came under French rule in 1892. After almost seventy years of colonial rule, Mali was renamed the ...
www.sahistory.org.za/.../over-400-kikuyu-suspected-be-part-mau-mau- movement-are-arrested-kenya-0

Marx, Karl and Frederich Engels (1850): Address to the Central Committee

Marx, Karl and Frederich Engels (1850): Address to the Central Committee. To the Communist League. From the Appendices to Frederick Engels, Revolution and Counter-Revolution in Germany Foreign Language Press, Peking. 1977 First Edition 1977 pp. 149-64. Available at: http://www.marx2mao.com/M&E/ACL50. html [Accessed: 19-10-17].

In the case of a struggle against a common adversary no special alliance is required. As soon as such an adversary has to be fought directly, the interests of both parties will coincide for the moment, and, as previously, so also in the future, this connection, calculated to last only for the moment, will arise of itself. It is self-evident that in the impending bloody conflicts, as in all earlier ones, it is mainly the workers who will have to win the victory by their courage, determination and self-sacrifice. As previously, so also in this struggle, the mass of the petty bourgeois will as long as possible remain hesitant, undecided and inactive, and then, as soon as the issue has been decided, they will seize the victory for themselves and will call upon the workers to calm down, to return to their work and to guard against so-called excesses, and they will bar the proletariat from the fruits of victory. It does not lie within the power of the workers to prevent the petty-bourgeois democrats from doing this, but it does lie within their power to make it difficult for them to prevail against the armed proletariat, and to dictate such conditions to them that the rule of the bourgeois democrats will from the outset bear within it the seeds of its own destruction, and that its subsequent displacement by the rule of the proletariat will be considerably facilitated. Above all things, during the conflict and immediately after the struggle, the workers must counteract, as much as is at all possible, the bourgeois endeavours at pacification, and compel the democrats to carry out their present terrorist phrases. They must work to ensure that the direct revolutionary excitement is not suppressed again immediately after the victory. On the contrary, they must keep it alive as long as possible. Far from opposing so-called excesses, they must not only tolerate instances of popular revenge against hated individuals or public buildings that are associated only with hateful recollections, but must take upon themselves the leadership of these actions. During the struggle and after the struggle, the workers must, at every opportunity, put forward their own demands alongside the demands of the bourgeois democrats. They must demand guarantees for the workers as soon as the democratic bourgeois set about taking over the government.

The Kenya Land & Freedom Depository

Ideas, Material Culture and the Mau Mau Liberation Struggle

June 2013

We are inviting artists, activists, journalists, thinkers and citizens to contribute to a depository of experiences, reflecting on life in the British colony of Kenya, especially during the Emergency 1950 – 1960 and the Mau Mau liberation struggle.

The Land & Freedom Depositions project seeks to explore the silences present in the ongoing British narrative of Kenya via the construction of a new visual dialogue. We aim to create a space for untold stories. The deposition project will become part of an exhibition to be held in London.

All types of *physical or non- physical items and ideas can be deposited in the project. It can be text based, oral or a photograph of an object or a copy of a Kipande (pass card) or a Loyalty certificate. Or you may want to present a talk or event that can be recorded for the depository.*(please do not submit original material).

Deposits submitted to the project will undergo a system of classification where they will be divided into a white, grey or black group, (in reference to the classification system used in the internment camps).

For the full brief go to www.popsamiti.org or contact Tajender Sagoo or Saleh Mamon.

Background

In October 1952 the British declared a state of emergency in Kenya to suppress a growing independence movement commonly known as the Mau Mau war of liberation. (Mau Mau was also referred to as the Kenya Land and Freedom Army).

There are many people living today who were in Kenya during the Emergency period, in which the British administration operated a colour bar system, racially segregating the African, South Asian and European communities.

Recently, in a case spanning 10 years, three Kenyans Jane Muthoni Mara, 73, Paulo Muoka Nzili, 85 and Wambugu wa Nyingi, 84 took legal action against the UK Government for the torture they suffered at the hands of British officials during the Mau Mau uprising between 1952 and 1960.

In June 2013, the British government announced an out of court settlement with the torture victims.

About

Born in Kenya, Tajender Sagoo is an artist/weaver and curator of the Pop Samiti project based in London. Saleh Mamon is co- curator of the Kenya Land & Freedom Depository project.

Born in Kenya he is currently a Visiting Research Fellow at the Goldsmith Centre of Culture Studies.

This is an independent project, it is not funded by any organisation or institution.

Contact

Tajender Sagoo at popsamiti@gmail.com

Saleh Mamon at salehmamon@yahoo.co.uk

Limehouse Town Hall, 646 Commercial Road, London E14 7HA Mob:075 3047 2483

Index

A

African Government of Kenya 133
African Workers Federation 102, 120
African Workers Union 120
Algeria 24
Algerian War of Independence 79
Anake a 40 118
Anti-colonialism 138
Anti-imperialism 138

B

Belgium 78
Britain 339
British Empire 42, 59
British military establishment 50
Burma 72
Bus Boycott 120

C

Capitalism 49, 85
Central Organisation of Trade Unions (COTU) 286
Cheche Kenya 304
Christian churches 97
Class divisions 95
Class struggle 273
Committee for the Release of Political Parties 319
Comprador class 84
Congo 78
Coup, August 1982 306
Cuban Revolution 45, 83

D

Daily Worker (London) 70
December Twelve Movement (DTM) 310, 303
Democratic political and military authority 130
Divide and Rule 56, 83
Divisive tactics 97

Draft Minimum Programme 310, 315

E

East African Trade Union Congress (EATUC) 109, 288
Emergency 95, 128
Ethiopia 72

F

France 23
Freedom 47

G

Germany 22, 78
Ghadar 47, 96
Gikuyu Iregi Army 129
Gikuyu na Mumbi Trinity Army 129
Giriama 63
Governance 137

H

Harambee 287
Hassan, Yusuf 314
Homeguard 37, 70, 283

I

Independent churches 97
InDependent Kenya 304
India 47, 95
Israel 339
Ituma Ndemi Army 129

K

Kamiriithu Educational and Cultural Centre 285
KAU 97
Kenya 121
Kenya African National Union 305
Kenya African Union 69
Kenya Committee for the Release of Political Parties in Kenya 317
Kenya Defence Council 128, 130, 133, 138
Kenya Inoro Army 129
Kenya Land and Freedom Army 47

Kenya Levellation Army 130
Kenya National Union of Teachers 299
Kenya News 317
Kenya our county 308
Kenya Parliament 138
Kenya Parliament, 1954 133
Kenya, Register of Resistance, 1986 288, 312
Kenya Terror 70
Kenyatta, Jomo 251
Kenya Twendapi 285
Kibachia, Chege 101
Kikuyu 36
Kimathi 138
Kimathi Charter 130
Kimathi, elected as Prime Minister 133
Kimathi, President of KDC 129
Kimemia, Macharia 129, 134
Kisumu 302

L

Labour Trade Union of Kenya 99
Land 47, 56
Liberated territories 122

M

MacDonald, Sir Malcolm 251
Malaysia 20
Mau Mau 45, 46, 63, 68, 84
   Class Stand 138
   Communication System 96
   Ideological Stand 138
Mboya, Tom 283
Mburu Ngebo Army 129
Mei Mathathi Army 129
Me Katilili 63
Military Facilities 307
Military force, Mau Mau 129
Military preparation 119
Misinformation 49
Moi, Daniel arap 57
Moism With Moi 339
Mombasa 300
Mount Kenya 123

Mpatanish 313
Murumbi, Joseph 251
Mwakenya 310
Mwanguzi 284,
Mwathe Conference, 1953 128

N

Nairobi 123
Namibia 78
Nationalities 97
Nduthu, Karimi 312
Neo-colonialism 277, 310, 317
Ni haki yetu kupigania haki zetu 311
Northern Kenya 65
Nyandarwa 123
Nyayo 287

P

Pambana, the Organ of the December Twelve Movement 305, 320
Peasant Resistance 291
Peasants 97, 110, 138
People's forces 46
Petty bourgeois 299
Pinto, Pio Gama 107
Political and military aspects 133
Political education 119
Proletarian world outlook 138

Q

Queuing elections, 1988 299

R

Radical national political movement 110
Resistance 96

S

Second Imperialist World War 47
Second World Imperialist War 115
Semi-liberated rural areas 123
Settler 85
Settlers 69

Kenya's War of Independence

Singh, Makhan 102
Somali 63
Somalia 68
Somali nationality 64
Somali Youth League 66
South Asian Kenyan workers 95
South Asians communities 87
Squatters 87
State of Emergency 120
Struggle For Democracy in Kenya\; Special Report on the 1988 General Elections in Kenya 299
Struggle for Kenya's Future 285
Student Resistance 294

T

Tanganyika 78, 125
Terrorists 76
The Struggle for Kenya's Future 251
Thiong'o, Ngugi wa 285
Three Pillars of Resistance 46, 282
Thuku, Harry 97
Townwatch Battalions 129
Trade union movement 46, 88
Trade unions 83, 95
Trade Unions, Africa 109
Trade unions, International 107
Tribalism 49
TUC 109

U

Ukenya 314
Umoja 315
Umoja wa Kupigania Demokrasia Kenya 314
Unity Conference, 1987 315
Universal Declaration of Human Rights (1948) 59
Upande Mwingine 288, 313
Urembo 125
USA 339
USA imperialism 68, 247, 307
USSR 96

W

War of Economic Independence, 19
War of Independence 17, 45, 76, 96, 110
War of Independence, Strands 88
War of Kenya's Independence 339
Worker Resistance 286
Workers 95, 138
Working class 84, 96, 110
Working class struggles 138

Y

Yaliotokea hapa Mombasa mnamo tarehe 30-1-87 301

Z

Zanzibar 125

Vita Books

Vita Books Kenya
P.O Box 62501-00200
Nairobi . Kenya
info.vitabkske@gmail.com
http://vitabooks.co.uk

Liberating Minds, Restoring Kenyan History
Anti-Imperialist Resistance by Progressive South Asian Kenyans 1884-1965
by. Nazmi Durrani

"It is my duty to take the message of revolt to other[s]. This is the only way to liberate the victims of suffering and slavery", Nazmi Durrani quotes W.L. Sohan in this book. Resistance to imperialism in pre-independence Kenya by progressive South Asian Kenyans propelled the Kenyan liberation struggle to new heights. They were active in almost every field, from publishing progressive newspapers to supplying arms and material to Mau Mau. Liberating Minds consists of biographies of progressive South Asian Kenyans written by Nazmi Durrani. Originally published in Gujarati in the 1980s, they are available here in English for the first time, together with the original Gujarati. Also included is Naila Durrani's 1987 conference paper, "Kenya Asian Participation in People's Resistance", while Benegal Pereira introduces Eddie H. Pereira (1915-1995) and his resistance letters to the Colonial Times Newspaper.

ISBN. 9789966097415
Pages: 202
Dimensions: 229 x 152mm
Illustrations: B/W Illustrations
Published: 2017
Format: Paperback

Makhan Singh. A Revolutionary Kenyan Trade Unionist
by Shiraz Durrani

This book examines the life and work of a remarkable trade unionist and revolutionary. Makhan Singh laid the foundation for radical trade unionism and influenced the liberation struggle in Kenya. He actively participated in the struggles of the working classes in India. For this, the colonial authorities in India and Kenya detained him for over 15 years.

This collection, marking 101 years of Makhan Singh's birth, explores different aspects of his life as a father, a trade unionist, a political activist, a poet and a communist committed to social, political and economic liberation from colonialism and imperialism. His vision, his action and his courage are as relevant today as they were in his time.

ISBN: 9781869886226
Pages: 194
Dimensions: 234 x 156mm
Published: 2016
Format: Paperback

Never Be Silent: Publishing and Imperialism 1884-1963
by Shiraz Durrani

"We will never be silent until we get land to cultivate and freedom in this country of ours"
…so sang Mau Mau activists. The struggle for independence in Kenya was waged at many levels. Never be Silent explores how this struggle was reflected in the communications field. It looks at publishing activities of the main contending forces and explores internal contradictions within each community. It documents the major part played by the communications activities of the organised working class and Mau Mau in the achievement of independence in Kenya.
The book contributes to a reinterpretation of colonial history in Kenya from a working class point of view and also provides a new perspective on how communications can be a weapon for social justice in the hands of liberation forces.

ISBN: 9781869886059
Pages: 280
Published: 2006
Format: Hardback

....

Progressive Librarianship
Perspectives from Kenya and Britain, 1979-2010
by Shiraz Durrani

Public spending is under threat and public libraries are suffering. At a time when libraries can play a critical role in supporting people facing difficult economic and social situations, the dominant conservative model of librarianship has nothing meaningful to say about the role and relevance of libraries. It offers more of the same, but no qualitative change so necessary today. It continues to maintain the myth that there is no alternative to its own policies and practices. There is thus an urgent need to alternative ideas and practices to address people's needs. The progressive librarianship movement is taking up this challenge. It has also been active in Kenya and Britain but its work is not widely know. The Kenyan movement differed from the others in that it grew within the underground political movement in the 1980s - the December Twelve Movement/Mwakenya. Using original documents, this book records this hidden history. In the process, it examines key concepts such as the role of libraries and the relevance of service. Linking library work with the wider social and political concerns, the book explores issues such as politics of information, the role of activism and "neutrality" in library work. It offers an alternative approach to librarianship, to the training of librarians and to organisational change to make libraries more relevant to people's lives.

ISBN: 9781869886202
Pages: 446
Dimensions: 234 x 156mm
Published: 2014
Format: Paperback

Information and Liberation
Writings on the Politics of Information and Librarianship
by Shiraz Durrani

Information and Liberation is a retrospective collection of Shiraz Durrani's articles and conference papers on the politics of information. The book documents the struggle for progressive and relevant information policies and practices over a period of 25 years in Kenya, Britain, and other countries. The book records also the vision, struggles and achievements of many progressive librarians and activists to develop a system and a society which can meet the information, social and cultural needs of all, particularly those marginalised by forces of capitalism and imperialism.

ISBN: 9789966189073
Pages: 384
Dimensions: 254 x 178mm
Published: 2008
Format: Paperback

Vita Books are available from:
African Books Collective
orders@africanbookscollective.com
http://www.africanbookscollective.com/search-results?form.keywords=vita+books

www.ingramcontent.com/pod-product-compliance
Lightning Source LLC
Chambersburg PA
CBHW070804300426
44111CB00014B/2421